Afrindian Fictions

Diaspora, Race, and National Desire
in South Africa

Pallavi Rastogi

THE OHIO STATE UNIVERSITY PRESS
COLUMBUS

Copyright © 2008 by The Ohio State University.
All rights reserved.
Library of Congress Cataloging-in-Publication Data

Rastogi, Pallavi.
  Afrindian fictions : diaspora, race, and national desire in South Africa / Pallavi Rastogi.
     p. cm.
  Includes bibliographical references and index.
  ISBN-13: 978-0-8142-0319-4
  ISBN-10: 0-8142-0319-1
  1. South African fiction (English)—21st century—History and criticism. 2. South African fiction (English)—20th century—History and criticism. 3. South African fiction (English)—East Indian authors—History and criticism. 4. East Indians—Foreign countries—Intellectual life. 5. East Indian diaspora in literature. 6. Identity (Psychology) in literature. 7. Group identity in literature. I. Title.
  PR9358.2.I54R37 2008
  823'.91409352991411—dc22
                                                        2008006183

This book is available in the following editions:
Cloth (ISBN 978–08142–0319–4)
CD-ROM (ISBN 978–08142–9099–6)
Paper (ISBN: 978-0-8142-5747-0)
Cover design by Laurence J. Nozik
Typeset in Adobe Fairfield by Juliet Williams

Contents

Acknowledgments		v
Introduction	Are Indians Africans Too, or: When Does a Subcontinental Become a Citizen?	1
Chapter 1	Indians in Short: Collectivity versus Specificity in the Apartheid Story	23
Chapter 2	Essop's Fables: Strategic Indianness, Political Occasion, and the Grand Old Man of South African Indian Literature	47
Chapter 3	National Longing, Natural Belonging: Flux and Rootedness in Achmat Dangor's *Kafka's Curse*	70
Chapter 4	The Point of Return: Backward Glances in Farida Karodia's *Other Secrets*	92
Chapter 5	Lost in Transplantation: Recovering the History of Indian Arrival in South Africa	114
Chapter 6	Citizen Other: The Implosion of Racial Harmony in Postapartheid South Africa	138
Conclusion	New Directions or Same Old? Afrindian Identity and Fiction Today	161

Interviews
        Deena Padayachee   168
        Ahmed Essop   181
        Farida Karodia   190
        Praba Moodley   202
        Aziz Hassim   212
        Ronnie Govender   222

Notes   235
Bibliography   270
Index   281

Acknowledgments

Scholarly acknowledgments usually follow an established narrative arc. Carefully noting our appreciation for everyone who made the publication possible, we advance to the end, to the most vital thank you of all. Instead of saving the best for last, I want to acknowledge my greatest debt of thanks first. I do not have the words to express my gratitude to Areendam Chanda, beloved spouse, best friend, and favorite economist. For accompanying me to South Africa, helping me comb through archives and transcribe interviews, sitting up at night with a bawling baby as I raced to finalize the book, and holding my hand for the last ten years, I offer him these inadequate words of thanks and love.

I owe a great intellectual debt to my writing groups at Louisiana State University. To Elsie Michie, Daniel Novak, and Sharon Weltman go my deepest thanks for reading multiple drafts of this book and for putting up with my "postcolonial" eruptions in a "Victorianist" cohort. Their patience, intellectual rigor, and generosity are truly peerless. Other colleagues who have read the manuscript in its entirety and for whose critical acuity I am grateful include Susan Weinstein, Gail Sutherland, and Shane Graham of Utah State University. I remain in awe of Shane's encyclopedic knowledge of South African literature and culture. This book is much better for having been read by him. Brannon Costello, Solimar Otero, Angeletta Gourdine, Jacob Berman, and Jocelyn Stitt of Minnesota State University all read portions of the manuscript. I am grateful to them for their instructive suggestions. I would also like to thank my former colleagues at Utah State University for reading very early versions of the book, especially Anne Shifrer and Andrea Tinnemeyer for critical wisdom and unflagging cheerleading.

My department chair, Anna Nardo, deserves a big thank you for all her encouragement and help. Students at LSU who provided excellent research assistance for this project include Thomas Halloran, Tanja Stampfl, and Amber Bourgeois. I would also like to thank my students and colleagues in postcolonial studies and in our beloved, long-running Postcolonial Studies Group—Suparno Banerjee, Erin Breaux, Myriam Chancy, Alison Graham-Bertolini, Sukanya Gupta, Thomas Halloran, Mustapha Marrouchi, Michelle Masse, Patrick McGee, Saiward Pharr, and Tanja Stampfl—for many stimulating conversations, all of which have directly or indirectly shaped this book. Laura Mullen is not in the field, but she has sustained me with wit, friendship, and funky clothing. I could have never acquired the books I needed without the assistance of the Inter-library Loan staff at LSU. Thank you for your patience with me, especially when I returned books late, which sadly became the norm with me.

Although this book was not born from a dissertation, I owe whatever literary skills I can claim to some wonderful professors at Tufts University where I finished my doctoral degree. Two very fine scholars mentored me through the dissertation process. I thank Joseph Litvak for teaching me how to read closely and carefully. I hope that some of his attention to literary nuance has rubbed onto these pages. I am also grateful to Joe for his kindness and generosity as well as his ability to give the severest critique in the nicest possible way. To Modhumita Roy goes my appreciation for sharpening my sensitivity to material politics and history. This book's investment in political occasion is a direct consequence of my many conversations with her on the role of history and material culture in shaping everyday life. Also, thanks to Sheila Emerson and Kalpana Seshadri-Crooks of Boston College for all their kindness through the dissertation years. I am particularly grateful to Kalpana for agreeing to be on my committee, reading my work closely and carefully, and for supporting me even after I left graduate school. The postcolonial/diaspora group at Tufts further honed my ability to think about diasporic issues. I thank Nicole Aljoe, Aimee Alcarez, Anupama Arora, Soledad Caballero, Ide Corley, Robin DeRosa, Prachi Deshpande, Manju Kurian, Carl Martin, and Madhavi Menon for friendship and support. To Madhavi and Prachi, extra thanks for years of good comradeship, inspiring scholarship, and stalwart critique.

Acknowledgments

My travel to South Africa was made possible by support from Louisiana State University, including the College of Research Summer Stipend, the Faculty Research Grant, and the Manship Grant. In South Africa, I thank Ahmed Essop, Farida Karodia, Praba Moodley, Deena Padayachee, Aziz Hassim, and Ronnie Govender for meeting with me. Deena in particular needs a resounding round of applause for organizing the seminar discussed in the conclusion and for taking me for a tour of the Natal countryside that he writes about with such warmth. I would also like to thank Ashwin Singh for making Durban so much fun and Betty Govinden for readily sharing her remarkable work on South African Indian women's writing.

At The Ohio State University Press, Sandy Crooms saw potential in this manuscript and hurrahed me at every step. She was in all respects the perfect editor. To the great folks at editorial—Eugene O'Connor and Meg French—thank you for your patience with a first-time author and for your superb editing. I am grateful to the two reviewers of the manuscript, R. Neville Choonoo and Pamela Cooper, for considering the monograph worthy of publication and for their sensitive critique. The book is much richer for their comments.

Portions of my essay, "From South Asia to South Africa: Locating Other Postcolonial Diasporas," published in *Modern Fiction Studies* 51.3 (Fall 2005): 536–60, appear in significantly revised form in various places in the book. A version of the last chapter on Ahmed Essop, "Citizen Other: Islamic Indianness and the Implosion of Racial Harmony in Postapartheid South Africa," appeared in *Research in African Literatures* 39.1 (Spring 2008): 107–24. I thank these journals for allowing me to reprint the essays in book form.

My family reminds me constantly of a sensible everyday existence outside the realm of academics. Ma and Baba, Bhaiya, Juhi, Naina, Chhottu, Sonali, and Auro have always provided me with good cheer, opening my mind to other worlds, other opinions, and other ways of being. I would like to conclude by thanking my parents, Radha and Aditya Rastogi, whose love, support, and courage in the face of adversity have anchored me all my life. None of this would have ever been possible without them. And Keya, my little flower, this book is for you. Thank you for appearing ten days after it was sent out for review and not four weeks before as you were threatening to do.

Introduction

Are Indians Africans Too, or

When Does a Subcontinental Become a Citizen?

In January 2003, the Indian government sponsored a convention of expatriates from the Indian diaspora. Sixty-three countries were represented. Participants included heads of state from Mauritius and Fiji, Nobel laureates V. S. Naipaul and Amartya Sen, as well as diasporics of Indian origin from Malaysia, the United Kingdom, the United States, the Caribbean, and South Africa. At the conference, antiapartheid activist and writer Fatima Meer rejected the designate of Indian diaspora, arguing that South Africans of Indian origin had fought for acceptance too long and too hard to so easily abandon the South African as the primary signifier of cultural identity (quoted in Waldman).[1] For Meer, identifying as diasporic Indian would necessarily privilege the Indian aspect of South African identity and consequently erase this community's struggle for recognition in South Africa. Meer identified a problem—that of national longing and belonging—that surfaces with regularity in the global South Asian diaspora but resonates with particular force in the polarized racial climate of South Africa.[2]

Afrindian Fictions: Diaspora, Race, and National Desire in South Africa argues that Indians desire South African citizenship in the fullest sense of the word, a need for national anchorage that is a consequence of their erasure in both the apartheid and postapartheid consciousness.[3] This longing for belonging is asserted through an "Afrindian" identity.[4]

The term suggests both an Africanization of Indian selfhood and an Indianization of South Africa. The former is achieved by an affiliation with the indigenous population and an attachment to the African land, while the latter is demonstrated through tracing the changes wrought in South Africa by the Indian presence. Changing oneself as well as being an agent of change in order to claim a South African national identity is the central dialectic underpinning Indian fiction in South Africa.

Yet my analysis of South African Indian fiction does not merely analyze the themes, preoccupations, and generic shifts in a neglected body of work. *Afrindian Fictions* also challenges some of the normative assumptions of postcolonial/diaspora criticism. Although diasporic literary studies have traditionally celebrated cultural fusion, the field has become increasingly codified in terms of the attention it has given to a particular "contact zone": migration from the third world (Africa, the Caribbean, South Asia) to the first (the UK, the United States, Canada) is often commemorated as the exemplary type of intercultural mingling.[5] Postcolonial scholarship, including trends in both South Asian and South African studies, also inclines to be preoccupied with the relationship between the white colonizers and the nonwhite colonized, thus unintentionally reifying the dominance of the West and of whiteness.

Afrindian Fictions unsettles that paradigm of racial interaction and focuses instead on how different *nonwhite* constituencies interact *with each other* in non-Western geographies.[6] It asks, in other words, what happens when migration occurs over an East-South axis rather than an East-West/North-South one. If postcolonial literature has traditionally challenged the hegemony of colonialist metanarratives, South African Indian writing challenges the tendency in postcolonial criticism to create metanarratives of its own.[7] In subverting the dominance of the East-West migratory story in diaspora studies as well as the black-white dyad of South African scholarship, South African Indian fiction counters the internal canons formed within postcolonial literature.[8]

Afrindian Fictions helps develop a new framework of racial contact and diasporic exchange based on the movement of Indians to South Africa in the nineteenth and twentieth centuries; their impact on the collective psyche of a land torn asunder by the repressive machinery of apartheid; and, in turn, the influence of the South African political landscape on the construction of an identity that occupies another place in the black-and-white map of South African race relations. Through an analysis of fiction from the 1970s onward, I trace the specificity of the Indian presence in South Africa and also construct an interpretive lens with which to view the intersection of diaspora, postcoloniality, Indianness, and apartheid.

My attentiveness to political occasion, particularly to the rapidly changing scenario in South Africa in which Indian fiction is composed, underscores the overtly political nature of South African Indian writing itself.

The aesthetic richness of South African Indian writing is also nourished by developments in postcolonial literature in general and by South African and South Asian diasporic literature in particular. Indian fiction reveals many of the concerns of mainstream South African literary discourse articulated by writers such as J. M. Coetzee, Nadine Gordimer, Alex La Guma, and Zakes Mda among others. These include "certain dynamics of South African society, such as tensions between the generations, class divisions and aspirations, political alliances, clashing accounts of tradition, and so on" (Attwell 180) as well as the themes of oppression under apartheid, racial solidarity, and anxieties about the new nation. South African Indian writing further reflects South Asian diasporic issues expressed by "canonical" writers such as Salman Rushdie, Bharati Mukherjee, and Hanif Kureishi. Transnational identities, generational conflicts, and return to roots are dominant concerns here. Because South African Indian fiction is intimately shaped and conditioned by postcolonial literature, it is an exciting new field within that body of writing; yet its difference from the postcolonial norm enables us to look at two important subfields in postcolonial studies—South African literature and South Asian diasporic literature—through an alternative hermeneutic lens.

My intervention also fills the gap in critical studies on South African Indian fiction in particular and South African Indian literature in general. There is very little literary scholarship available on Indians in South Africa. This may be because there has been a surge in fiction published by South African Indians only in the last two decades following the imminent and actual demise of apartheid. However, it must be remembered that literary publication often has little to do with literary proliferation. South African Indians have been narrating their stories since the time they were transported from India as indentured labor in the middle of the nineteenth century, yet their voices are only being heard now.[9]

The reasons for the paucity of scholarship on Indians in South Africa have much to do with Indians occupying a middle place in a dichotomous racial model that had no room for shades of gray, both in its oppressive and oppositional modes.[10] The Indian presence in South Africa disturbed what Loren Kruger describes as "the binary black/white opposition that has structured *anti*apartheid, as well as apartheid, discourse" ("Black" 115). This rupture has been barely recognized as many, if not most, studies of apartheid and its legacy in postcolonial South Africa still conceive of South African race relations as unfolding across a black-white axis.

Rosemary Jolly similarly argues that "as critics, teachers, and students, we need to forge a language beyond apartheid that refuses to hypostatize South Africa as the model in which the colonized black and the settler white eternally confront each other in the 'ultimate racism'" (371). The Indian presence complicates the binary of settler and indigene by introducing a third state of national being: that of postcolonial diasporic.[11] Yet the antiapartheid movement could not encourage such subtleties for fear of diminishing the effectiveness of a unified onslaught against segregation. The specificity of Indian identity was often erased from the grand narrative of the freedom struggle that sought to incorporate all nonwhite people under a singular "black" identity forged by the commonality of white oppression.

Jolly further warns us that "there are . . . marked differences within the black community of South Africa, which includes the Xhosa, the Sotho, the Zulu, immigrants of Indian heritage, and the Cape 'coloreds' of Malay heritage, to name but a few. The differences among these groups are elided, and the hegemony of apartheid maintained, when the groups' literatures are consigned to the monolithic category 'Black South African literature'" (372). *Afrindian Fictions* takes up Jolly's challenge to extend our responses to South African culture beyond the dichotomy of African victim and European oppressor, explode the homogenizing impulses of a unitary black identity, and explore the diversity within "black" literary expression.

One must not be quick to ascribe the sin of omission solely to South African historiography and literary criticism. Students of the phenomenon known as the Great Indian Diaspora are just as likely to erase South African Indians from the diasporic imagination. As Vijay Mishra points out, "the homogenization of all Indian diasporas in terms of the politics of disarticulation/rearticulation with reference to Britain, America or Canada has led to the fetishization of the new diaspora and an amnesiac disavowal of the old . . . what is striking is the relative absence of critical cultural histories of this diaspora" ("Diasporic Imaginary" 427). Similarly, Makarand Paranjape asserts:

> While the writings of the old diaspora are utterly marginalized, they find a new currency when they re-enter the world of discourse via the new diaspora. . . . The subordinate culture of the old diaspora can only be recognized if it reinvents itself in the image of the dominant culture of the metropolis. (10)

The issues that we typically associate with diaspora are those pertaining to

Indian diasporas in the West, including unsettling the power of whiteness, challenging the perception of one's alleged cultural and religious backwardness in the economically developed regions where the migrant has relocated, maintaining emotional and financial ties with the home country, and fearing assimilation into "corrupt" Western culture. Only when the old diaspora reveals those issues—usually when migration *reoccurs* from South to North—do we give this diaspora some critical valence.[12]

Since the South African Indian diaspora also manifests diasporic anxieties that are altered or complicated by apartheid, we often fail to recognize those issues as diasporic, a critical blindness exacerbated by an already narrow definition of migratory exchange in literary scholarship. South African Indians—though displaying what Emmanuel Nelson defines as a "shared diasporic sensibility . . . issues of identity, problems of history, confrontation with racism, intergenerational conflicts, difficulties in building new supportive communities" (xv)—are also actively engaged in the life of the nation, consciously identifying as South Africans first and Indians next despite their relative anonymity in the national spectrum. If South African Indians themselves resist being cast in the role of Indian diasporics, Meer's emphatic declaration quoted in the opening sentences of the introduction being a testimony to this rejection, then it is easier to explain why South Asian diaspora studies have long disregarded a presence that sees Indianness as a secondary allegiance.

South African Indian fiction is only now being recognized as a distinct literary entity. Thus postcolonial scholarship still has enormous holes to fill in its knowledge of this oeuvre. Scholars such as Loren Kruger and Betty Govinden have commented on the erasure of South African Indian literature in South African and South Asian "literary bibliography" (Kruger, "Black" 137, n11; Govinden, "Learning Myself Anew"). A new effort at redressing this absence usually means a *token incorporation* of this body of writing in both fields of critical study.[13] While books on white South African writers such as Nadine Gordimer and J. M. Coetzee have been published from the 1980s onward, there has been an interest in black South African writing only recently.[14] Despite the proliferation of texts studying South African literature in more inclusive ways, the works of South African Indian writers remain neglected.[15]

For example, Christopher Heywood's recently published survey of South African fiction, entitled *A History of South African Literature* (2004), claims that South Africa has five distinct literary groups: "Khoisan, Nguni-Sotho, Afrikaans, English, and Indian." Yet Indian writing is not analyzed in much detail here. As Kruger points out, even Michael Chapman's magisterial examination of South African writing, entitled *Southern African*

Literatures (1996), ignores "the important work of writers whose oblique position vis-à-vis this [black and white] conflict should not exclude them from South African literary history. No South Africans of Indian descent appear in his list of authors" ("Black" 137, n13).

The numerous books, anthologies and journals commemorating the "new" South Africa either erase the Indian presence or incline toward nominal recognition. *Modern Fiction Studies* produced a magisterial special issue entitled "South African Fiction after Apartheid" in 2000; no article on Indian writing appeared here.[16] Derek Attridge and Rosemary Jolly's *Writing South Africa: Literature, Apartheid and Democracy, 1970–1995* (1998) does not include an essay on Indian writing, even though the collection as a whole reflects at length on the nature, tone, and composition of contemporary South African writing.[17] Nahem Yousaf's *Apartheid Narratives* (2001), again, has only one essay on Indian "apartheid narratives." Theodore Sheckels's *The Lion and the Freeway: A Thematic Analysis of South African Literature* (1996) mentions only one South African Indian writer, Ahmed Essop.[18]

The news from South Asian diaspora studies is only a little more heartening. Scholarship, including books and essays, on Western-based writers such as Bharati Mukherjee, Amitav Ghosh, V. S. Naipaul, Salman Rushdie, and Hanif Kureishi abounds.[19] Books studying literary production in these diasporas have also been recently published.[20] Yet no book-length studies of the South African Indian diaspora—either of individual writers or of the literature in its totality—exist. Additionally, many anthologies and collections on the South Asian diaspora only recognize non-Western diasporas as well as the South African Indian community in cursory, rather than comprehensive, ways.[21]

However, in the last few years, some scholars have begun to craft alternative trajectories of diasporic exchange. Much of this scholarship centers on Indo-Caribbean writers; perhaps the singular success of V. S. Naipaul drew attention to this presence. For example, Brinda Mehta's *Diasporic (Dis)Locations: Indian Women Negotiate the Kala Pani* (2004) is a groundbreaking book that uses the "discourse of kala pani," or crossing the "black waters," to think about the gendered specificity of the Indian experience in the Caribbean. Marina Carter and Khal Torabully's *Coolitude: An Anthology of the Labour Diaspora* (2002) offers the idea of a "coolie memory" that unites Indians of indentured origin all over the world, but mentions South African Indians only in passing (215). Both texts, however, offer extremely useful techniques for thinking about Indian-black relations in non-Western regions.

Closer to my project geographically is Loren Kruger's (2001) essay on Achmat Dangor, where she emphasizes the need to craft South-South models of diaspora through the South African Indian presence.[22] While I am deeply indebted to scholars such as Mehta, Carter, Torabully, and Kruger, I push their ideas further in order to construct a model of diasporic encounters based on an East-South paradigm in South Africa. I deliberately use the phrase "East-South" rather than the more common "South-South." The phrase "South-South" highlights the similarity of economic "underdevelopment" but elides the heterogeneity of different geographies. "East-South" is more attentive to the cultural specificity of and the internal diversity within economically "undeveloped" regions of the world.

I also build on some of the critical essays that reflect on the "older diasporas," Vijay Mishra's term for what he calls the diasporas of "classic capitalism" that came into being through the British Empire (421). These include Mishra's seminal essay "The Diasporic Imaginary" and Makarand Paranjape's expansion of Mishra's work. While this scholarship is extremely useful, it has two limitations for my project: Like *Coolitude*, it claims that all indentured immigrants share a common consciousness. The South African Indian population, with its admixture of slaves, laborers, and traders, disrupts the formulation of a homogenous "coolie" selfhood. Mishra and Paranjape also do not really take into account the role of political circumstance in reconceptualizing some of the common anxieties of indentured migrants all over the world.[23]

My extensive comparative focus on South African Indian fiction that foregrounds its ever-shifting shape will enable further scrutiny of the textual representation of nonnormative diasporic interactions as they have played out in South Africa and in Indian diasporas in other neglected geographies. It will also engender a literary interest in other peripheral groups in South Africa that fall outside of the dominant black-white pattern, such as the writings of the Cape Malay/Coloured community. Given the importance of South Africa and the South Asian diaspora in postcolonial studies, the excavation of a body of writing that bestows wholeness and complexity on these very important fields as well as introduces the world to an emergent, exciting, and aesthetically dense body of literature becomes a compelling necessity.

Retheorizing the South Asian Diaspora and Race in South Africa

The impact of South African Indian literature on postcolonial studies can be further explained by outlining the broad issues underpinning this fiction. Analyzing these literary themes reveals the dialectic of sameness and difference from South Asian and South African literary discourses that gives South African Indian fiction its distinctive texture. First and foremost, Indians rupture the polarized arrangement of race on which apartheid was predicated and which postapartheid South Africa has maintained. The Indian presence in South Africa invites us to address the question of what it means to be Indian African in a land divided into an unyielding binary of indigenous African versus settler African.

The South African Indian diaspora is rendered distinctive by the racial tensions engendered by apartheid and preserved even after the end of segregation. Despite its simplistic structure, apartheid created an intricate racial situation: Indians were inserted in a geographic location controlled by a powerful European minority settled in the midst of dispossessed Africans. Indians have had to contend with the forces of whiteness even as they struggled to forge community with the Africans. The triangulated relationship between European settler, African indigene, and Indian diasporic is unique to certain parts of Africa, and involves a reworking of the more common formula for racial interaction in South Africa provided by the authors of the influential *The Empire Writes Back*: that of white settler and black native locked in an unending combat.[24]

Despite this tripartite configuration of races, the Indian relationship with blacks—in all its energy, joy, frustration, and mutual distrust—dominates South African Indian fiction. While whites are present, especially in apartheid-era fiction, as a structuring and mediating presence, South African Indian fiction is equally—perhaps even more—concerned with describing Indian relationships with black Africans, tracing racial solidarity in the apartheid period, and mourning its rupture in the postapartheid period. Khal Torabully's reflections on "Coolitude" in other labor diaspora societies are apposite here:

> Coolitude also seeks to emphasize the community of visions between the slave and the indentured labourer, shared by their descendants, despite the fact that these two groups were placed in a situation of competition and conflict. As such coolitude may be seen as an attempt to bring the past and present of these groups into contact and to go beyond past conflicts and misrepresentations. (quoted in Carter 150)

Despite recognizing the need for harmony between Indians and blacks, "coolitude" serves as a limited model for Indian-African interaction in South Africa as apartheid, and its residue in our postcolonial lives and times, permanently conditions human relationships. Indian-African relationships are also complicated by the fact that in Africa, unlike other parts of the world, blacks are not descendants of slaves—that is, forced migrant labor—like most Indians, but *indigenes*. Two dispossessed groups grappling with each other's presence in a land that historically belongs to one community but also has the other community forcefully staking ownership of that common space creates a situation distinctive to Indian-black relationships in Africa. Indians claiming ownership of land tilled by their indentured ancestors may mimic the violent appropriation of apartheid and colonialism or it may be a politically subversive move that gives subcontinentals, a group traditionally denied national belonging, claims to composite citizenship. This illegibility of political effect reflects the complicated history that Indians and Africans share.

The Indian presence in South Africa not only disrupts the binary of black indigene and white settler, but also extends migratory interaction beyond the dominant paradigm in South Asian diaspora studies: that of white native and nonwhite immigrant negotiating a shared (Western) space.[25] The questions of diaspora, especially those of national identity, minority belonging, cultural selfhood, and multiple allegiances, are refracted through an East-South prism in South Africa as well as complicated by the presence of apartheid. How does the rhetoric of colonialism, with its insistently hierarchical racial schema, determine the relationship between Indians and black Africans? How does the institutionalization of apartheid in 1948 bring Indians and blacks together even as it forces them apart? Is assimilation, engendered by Indians claiming a black identity during apartheid, less problematic than it is in the United States or the UK, where assimilation implies integration into white culture? What happens to solidarity when white oppression, the only force binding two dispossessed groups, ceases to be a factor in race relationships?

Indian fiction thus reflects on the specifically South African problems of diasporic identity such as establishing links with the black population while preserving Indianness, locating oneself within a binary racial formulation, and coming to terms with a legacy of migration based on indenture and slavery as well as trade.[26] Indian writers also tend to be extraordinarily aware of political circumstance, a consequence of the machinery of apartheid that invaded the consciousness of all it compassed in totalizing ways. In other words, *there is a direct and determinate relationship between politics and identity in South African Indian writing*. The atrocities of apartheid ensured that Indians always had material with which, and against which, they could create a literary sense of self.

Muthal Naidoo has further observed a dual focus to the articulation of Indian ethnicity in South Africa: "On the one hand, the consolidation and assertion of an Indian identity and culture, and, on the other, the desire to cut across ethnic boundaries and form alliances with other population groups" (30). Despite their puncturing of racial categories, Indian authors often strategically mobilize an alternative identity, particularly during the apartheid period, in order to be absorbed within a greater community—be it black, Coloured, or in some cases even white—through which they can then seek political franchise. Relatedly, if there is a restrictive articulation of selfhood in this writing, it is usually as South African and not as Indian.[27]

Indian racial and cultural identity, what one might call "Indianness," is therefore slippery.[28] In South Africa, Indianness is altered beyond purity, complicated by the desire to find a political voice only enabled through identification with a larger, non-Indian, community. Yet the contradictory pull of being Indian and the concomitant reluctance to sacrifice Indianness at the altar of a greater communal identity result in a multifarious designation of the Indian self. Consequently, what it means to be South African is also problematized. If Indians can absorb themselves into a black/Coloured/white identity, the lines drawn across communities on the basis of race, religion, and culture become increasingly blurred. The hazy contours of Indian identity in South Africa invite a deconstruction of the rigid apartheid *and* postapartheid categories of black, white, mixed race, and Indian. However, Indian fiction is not just preoccupied with asserting Africanization through racial affiliation. It also actively seeks to Indianize South Africa by interrogating the systemic erasure of Indians in public discourse, inserting Indian cultural practices into national life, and infusing literary conversation with Indian linguistic and cultural codes. Many writers, for example, refuse to italicize certain Indian words, indicating the naturalization of Indian languages in the national psyche.

Indian writing thus asserts a South African identity that never erases the particularity of Indianness even as it claims a *primary* affiliation with South Africa. The theme of longing for belonging is particularly germane in this diaspora as "India" occupies an inaccessible space.[29] Paranjape argues that the old diaspora recognized that "physical return was virtually impossible [therefore] an emotional or spiritual renewal was an ongoing necessity" (9). In the case of South African Indian fiction, even though the "Mother Country" is an icon charged with mythic resonances, there is rarely a desire to return even in a "spiritual" sense. India, then, exists as an empty symbol. The proclamation of a South African national identity, as well as the articulation of a permanent bond with an everyday South Africa rather than with an imagined India, dominates the thematic concerns of South African Indian fiction. The critical genealogy of Indian writing traced in this book asserts, above all, the Indian allegiance to South Africa.

Historicizing South African Indian Identity, Politics, and Identity Politics

The Indian commitment to South African life arises from anxieties about national belonging as well as from the community's extended stay in the country. Any literary narrative of Indian identity, therefore, must be contextualized against the history of subcontinental arrival in South Africa, their dispossession under colonialism and apartheid, and the political struggles they face in the democratic present. On November 16, 1860, the SS *Truro* arrived in South Africa, bringing 340 Indian laborers to work in the sugar fields in the British province of Natal. In her summary of the history of Indians in Africa, Arlene Elder explains that the earliest indentured Indians transported to South Africa were largely of the Hindu faith. Many of these laborers elected to remain in South Africa after the period of indenture had lapsed and acquired land, becoming "artisans of various sorts, moneylenders, small shopkeepers and traders" (116).

Loren Kruger adds that in addition to arriving as slaves well before indenture, many Indians chose to migrate to the African continent, where they could set up lucrative trading practices, making a vital distinction, therefore, between "indentured Indians" and "passenger Indians," all of whom would be codified as a single entity under the taxonomy of apartheid (Black 112).[30] Elder describes the passenger Indians as "mostly Muslims," who migrated to South Africa to establish what they thought would be profitable business enterprises. This community flourished commercially and spread its population to the Transvaal and Cape Colony (116–17). The white settlers, apprehensive of Indian financial prosperity, consequently promulgated divisive laws disempowering Indians.[31]

The distinction between indentured Indian and passenger Indian also has important repercussions on the so-called collective consciousness of the South African Indian community. South African Indian identities are always configured by multiple determinants such as indenture, migration for commercial purposes, language, religion, gender, and class. As a vastly heterogeneous community, speaking in tongues as varied as Gujarati, Tamil, Hindi, and Urdu, and also belonging to different religious faiths, South African Indians are marked more by difference than by similarity. All this makes it difficult to characterize the lives of Indians with a prescriptive label such as "the South African Indian Experience."

One cannot talk about the history of Indians in South Africa without mentioning *the* most famous South African Indian: Mohandas Karamchand Gandhi. Gandhi arrived in South Africa in 1893 as a young lawyer. He returned to India after twenty-one years, leaving behind one son and his family in South Africa. Gandhi has often been criticized for failing to forge links with black Africans.[32] Whatever his deficiencies, it is indisputable that Gandhi radicalized the South African Indian community by creating the Natal Indian Congress (NIC) in 1894 and the newspaper the *Indian Opinion* in 1903. Both entities served as forums of protest against the treatment of Indians in South Africa.

Historian Surendra Bhana also credits the NIC, and by extension Gandhi, with gestating *Indianness* as a sensibility:

> [T]he Natal Indian Congress (NIC) sought to weld together the diverse cultural and religious immigrants from the Indian subcontinent into a single, coherent, and secular organization. In the process of the NIC's creation, "Indianness" came into being and subsequently became firmly embedded in South Africa's politics. In the early years of the NIC's existence, "Indianness," in its restricted sense, was central to the organization's efforts to win rights for the immigrants. ("Indianness Reconfigured" 100)

In addition to unifying the Indian population through the idea of a shared Indianness (that was, as Bhana points out, problematically dominated by a certain class), Gandhi also agitated against indenture and to have Indian marriages recognized by the law.

The impact of Gandhi on South African Indians, particularly in their response to political oppression, should not be underestimated. Later events in India, especially his humiliation of the British Empire through simple acts of defiance, also rendered Gandhi a symbol of hope, of what nonviolent resistance could achieve. The South African Gandhi opened up a space for political awareness among the Indian community, a social consciousness that underpins every text discussed in this book. Christopher Heywood says that "part of the Indian literary heritage in South Africa entails adopting, negotiating, and escaping the *Satyagraha* [Gandhi's strategy of nonviolent resistance] tradition" (231). In the fiction I examine, not only do we encounter the concept of *Satyagraha*, but Gandhi himself appears repeatedly as a mobilizing trope, a motif that distinguishes South African Indian fiction from its global counterparts, as no other Indian diaspora can claim Gandhi the way the South African one can.[33]

Elder reports that "according to the 1980 census, there are 795,000 Indians in South Africa, more than on the rest of the African continent" (117). The 2001 census states that Indians in South Africa now number 1.1 million, or 2.5 percent of the entire population ("South Africa

Grows"). An overwhelming majority of South African Indians claim South African nationality by birth and not by legal change of citizenship. Yet, as social anthropologist Rehana Ebr.-Vally notes, until 1961, subcontinentals in South Africa were considered to be Indian "citizens" who were merely living in South Africa. In 1961, tired of India's complaints about the treatment of Indians under apartheid, the National Party conferred citizenship upon South African Indians. Indians now came exclusively under white South African jurisdiction and the Indian government had no *locus standi* to protest the mistreatment of "its" citizens. Not until 101 years after the SS *Truro* brought into Natal the first wave of indentured labor were Indians seen as South Africans under the law (Ebr.-Vally 84).

Indians, and all other nonwhite people, continued to be steadily disenfranchised following the institutionalization of apartheid in 1948. Various legislation marginalizing Indians included the Pegging Act (1943), which barred Indians from owning land in white areas. Although Indians were also subject to the vagaries of the Immorality Act (1950) prohibiting sexual relations between the different races, they were hit hardest by the Group Areas Act (1950), which appropriated Indian property in prime locations and relocated Indians to arid areas.[34] Indians may have been dispossessed by the apartheid regime, but a certain group of business-minded Indians managed to acquire vast amounts of wealth during the segregation years.[35] These rich traders and merchants exemplified the stereotype of the rapacious Indian that then became the stereotype for Indians in general. The perception of Indians as white stooges was further aggravated by the segregationist government deciding to grant privileges to a chosen few by amending the constitution in 1983 to include "separate and subordinate houses" for the Coloured and Indian populations. As Anne McClintock and Rob Nixon point out, "if the Coloureds and Indians were to be persuaded that they were entitled to white privileges, they could not be lumped together with the disenfranchised blacks under the category 'nonwhites'" (346). However, the Indian community overwhelmingly opposed the government's effort to fracture the will to power of nonwhite insurgency.

In that vein of resistance, many intrepid Indians, such as Fatima and Ismail Meer, Yusuf Dadoo, Monty Naicker, Indres Naidoo, and Ahmed Kathrada, actively participated in the antiapartheid movement.[36] Thousands of other anonymous Indians engaged in antigovernment uprisings throughout the apartheid years, including the Soweto demonstrations in the late 1970s.[37] Kogila Moodley says "Indians [also participated] in philanthropic activities outside the group, especially on behalf of Africans. These include Indian doctors offering lower cost medical attention to

African patients, businessmen raising bursaries for African university students, building a school in Kwazulu and Indian manufacturers helping to set up factories to be run by Africans" (454). As even this brief recapitulation reveals, Indians have a long history of political activism *and* fraternity with black Africans.[38]

Despite active solidarity during the apartheid period, the relationship between Africans and Indians has been historically fraught, especially in the province of KwaZulu Natal, where approximately 80 percent of the Indian population resides. As Ashwin Desai states, "by the end of the 1940s there were numerous potential points of conflict between African and Indian. At the level of the labour markets, Indians and Africans competed for jobs and joined racially exclusive unions to defend their interests. At the level of trade, Indian monopoly in the 1930s was challenged by an increasing number of aspirant African traders" (9). The tension between Indians and Africans was enhanced by the "in-between" position of Indians in the apartheid schema. Smitha Radhakrishnan points out that even though "Indians were denied citizenship rights . . . the hierarchical system of apartheid also offered Indians certain privileges over Africans due to their status as the buffer group. These privileges included a higher standard of education than Africans', relatively better housing and health care, and the earmarking of middle management and clerical jobs" ("Time" 267).[39]

Mutual hostility between Indians and blacks reached its peak in 1949 with the Cato Manor riots, where "50 Indians and 87 Africans had been killed. Thousands of Indian stores and dwellings were destroyed or damaged" (Desai 12). In another explosion of festering relations between Indians and Africans, Phoenix Ashram, a commune built by Gandhi, was plundered and looted by Africans in 1985. The relationship between Indians and Africans was further vitiated by the elections of 1994, which saw an embarrassing number of Indians vote for the National Party, the political organization that instituted apartheid in 1948. Scholars interpret the 1994 Indian vote as fractured across class and reflecting deep anxieties about economic and political opportunities under a black government (Dhupelia-Mesthrie, Desai and Maharaj). The election of 1999 saw some Indians abandon the National Party and vote for the Democratic Party instead (Dhupelia-Mesthrie 27).

Indians are now actively participating in South African political life as never before. Historian Uma Dhupelia-Mesthrie points out:

> Under the new government, led by the ANC since 1994, several Indians occupy high-profile positions in cabinet, provincial and local gov-

ernment. President Mandela's cabinet had no fewer than five Indian cabinet members, a couple of Indian deputy ministers, and his personal adviser was an Indian . . . Thabo Mbeki's cabinet of 1999 has four full cabinet ministers who are Indian . . . the Speaker of Parliament is an Indian. The Chief Justice of the country is an Indian. (27)

Even though Indians have made rapid advances in postapartheid South Africa, certain trends, however, suggest that the new nation is not necessarily as multicultural and egalitarian as it imagined itself to be.

According to Dhupelia-Mesthrie, Indian insecurity in democratic South Africa stems from apprehension over "declining welfare grants, an increase in crime rates and a perceived decline in education as resources are shifted within the province [KwaZulu Natal]" (28). Thomas Hansen claims that the postapartheid period saw "a restructuring of the labour and employment laws in order to strengthen and empower the African majority. These measures resulted in massive job losses and the economic marginalization of the Indian community that for years had inhabited a relatively cushioned position in South Africa's economy" ("Melancholia" 297). Affirmative action, in particular, is an area of great contention: "A common refrain of Indians is that 'for years apartheid discriminated against us as we were too black, now we are not black enough to gain from affirmative action'" (Dhupelia-Mesthrie 28).

Race, then, is still a major determinant of government-granted privilege as well as a marker of Self-Sameness and Otherness. As Desai somberly reflects, "the emergence of the 'Rainbow Nation' signaled for many the beginning of new things. However, under the rubric of the rainbow it became apparent that the past was imposing itself on the present. For those who envisaged the loosening of their ethnic clothing they soon found it sticking more closely to their bodies as the political settlement unfolded" (108). Though the end of apartheid heralded a better world that had profound consequences for cultural production, among other things, for South African Indians, in many important ways, the more things changed, the more they remained the same.

South African Indian Identity and Fiction Today

As the brief history narrated above reveals, Indians have been systematically erased in the national consciousness by the apartheid regime that operated primarily on a black versus white register. This binary thinking that froze people into uncrossable identities continued in the postapartheid period even as the new South Africa claimed to welcome, indeed celebrate, difference. As Radhakrishnan claims, "South African Indians gained citizenship but lost certain material privileges . . . [they are now] caught between the historical power of a white minority and the contemporary power of the African majority" ("Time" 263) and that the "postapartheid state took care to not alienate white citizens, but according to the majority of South African Indians I interacted with . . . there was no similar explicit effort to include Indians" (268).[40]

The spillage of apartheid ontologies into the postapartheid present is not surprising. In violently hierarchical and racialized societies, where "core universal values of equality, citizenship and justice were denied [to dispossessed groups,] . . . the granting of minimalist citizenship does not mean that these distinctions can now simply be erased" (Ahluwalia 510). Indians, therefore, have a profound unease about their place in South Africa, an apprehension exacerbated by their religious, linguistic, and cultural difference.[41] Correspondingly, *Afrindian Fictions* rests on a simple argument: Indians desire South African citizenship in the most complete meaning of the term. I use citizenry not only in the juridical sense but also as implying national belonging and commitment to the nation-state. National belonging does not extend in one direction; rather, composite citizenry suggests that the citizen owns the nation just as the nation owns its citizens.

Here I echo C. L. R. James's notion of "participatory" citizenship and "the good life [which is] that community between the individual and the state" (quoted in Mehta 131). According to Kent Worcester, James also:

> [A]scribed the exceptional character of social life in ancient Greece to two main factors: mass participation in the institutions of the city-state and the dense emotional and political bonds harmonizing the individual with the wider community. Since . . . citizens . . . had an authentic voice in the polity, they felt an intense attachment to the city-state. (166)[42]

South African Indian fiction exposes the thick "emotional and political bonds" that Indians share with "the wider community" in order to argue for national belonging. Pal Ahluwalia's comments on citizenry in an Australian context are also apposite here. Calling for the necessity of creating "a single concept of post-colonial citizenship," Ahluwalia argues that "this is not a process that can be decreed formally by legislation but is one that is tied integrally to the imagination. It is a process that has to recognise that becoming an Australian is not about conquering but about belonging to a political community of equal and consenting citizens" (504).

If citizenry is a "process," facilitated by acts of the "imagination" rather than solely by law, literature then assumes a central role in acquiring national selfhood. In wholeheartedly embracing South African citizenry, Indian writers subordinate the transnational cosmopolitanism that has often characterized East-West diasporas by anchoring themselves firmly to the nation-state. *Afrindian Fictions* reinscribes the primacy of the nation in diaspora studies, a field that has increasingly normalized global migrancy and a worldly nationless sensibility as the predominant form of diasporic culture.[43] While diasporas can be nationalistic in their aspirations, the diasporic's patriotic zeal is often directed toward the maintenance of the home country.[44] The South African Indian presence reveals an intense nationalism that is tied to the host country. Indians in South Africa also demonstrate how transnationalism (roots in multiple locations) and nationalism (the proud proclamation of a national identity in the "host" country) are not two mutually exclusive states of being.

The first half of the book studies Indian fiction during the apartheid period, while the second half studies Indian fiction following the dissolution of apartheid. Emphasizing the symbiotic relationship between genre and theme, I argue that Indian writers tended to use short fiction, including story collections and novellas, to assert national belonging during apartheid.[45] Material and ideological exigencies determined the provenance of form, as writing short fiction made economic sense because of the limited opportunities to publish under apartheid; the diversity of the short story collection also encapsulated the oppositional impulses of racial solidarity and ethnic specificity that Indians characteristically negotiated during the high point of segregation. The changing social scenario following the official end of apartheid in 1994 made the novel a more attractive form in democratic South Africa.

Less subject to the pressures of political solidarity, Indian writing becomes highly experimental in the postapartheid era, constantly bursting the boundaries of South African fictional convention by using historical, epic, romance, comic, and mystery novels to discuss themes of belonging, citizenry, racial identification, and the preoccupations of the new nation. While these tropes were also present in apartheid-era writing, the shift in political circumstance yields significant changes not only in genre but also in theme and ideology. Indian fiction during the apartheid period unhesitatingly identifies with black Africans in order to challenge the segregationist imperative and to accrue the voice and power of mass movements. The fictional representation of this interracial harmony comes undone following the end of apartheid.[46]

Many Indian writers recognize their culpability in maintaining racial division even as they critique black Africans for an ethnocentrism of their own. Although such a conceptualization suggests a pessimistic vision of race relations in contemporary South Africa, Indian fiction becomes more subtle—generically, thematically, and ideologically—in the postapartheid period. This variety necessarily engenders a more nuanced vision of race relations than was allowed by the dictates of the antiapartheid imperative that insisted on a common black identity to combat white oppression. Moreover, Indian criticism of the new South Africa emerges from emancipatory citizenship earned in the old South Africa. In their systemic oppression as well as in their participation in resistance politics, Indians acquired the right to call themselves South African during apartheid and, therefore, the right to critique the nation-state in the postapartheid period. Holding the postcolonial nation accountable for the failure of its promises, then, makes Indians more South African, not less.

I highlight the theme of national belonging through the idea of an "Afrindian" identity. As the term suggests, Indianness exists in South Africa in an *Africanized* state. In the apartheid period, Indians proclaim their African identity through *race*. In addition to affiliating with black Africans to attain political voice, some Indian writers foreground South Africa's history of racial cross-fertilization to underscore the biological Africanization of Indian identity. In the transition and postapartheid periods (1990 onward), racial affiliation incorporates a spatial affiliation, particularly asserted through *place*. Many Indian writers highlight their bond with the land, thereby asserting their rootedness and belonging in the African soil. Yet another way of claiming citizenry emerges from appealing to the effects of the extended periodicity of the Indian presence in the African continent, something only East-South diasporas, which emerged from colonial economies, can do. Postapartheid fiction also asserts the Indianness of South Africa by revealing the hybridization of the national consciousness and by infusing the cultural imaginary with Indian themes, allusions, and cultural referents. Fiction composed in the democratic present thus signals to a movement from a tentative articulation of selfhood to a rambunctious celebration of the Indian presence in South Africa. All these literary gestures have the same agenda: to procure full and complete national belonging for Indians.[47]

Chapter 1, "Indians in Short: Collectivity versus Specificity in the Apartheid Story," studies the proliferation of the short story in apartheid-era Indian fiction. I situate three short story collections—Jayapraga Reddy's *On the Fringe of Dreamtime* (1987), Agnes Sam's *Jesus Is Indian* (1989) and Deena Padayachee's *What's Love Got to Do with It?* (1992)—against literary developments within black writing in general. The apartheid story is marked by the necessity to challenge the segregationist prescriptive. For

Indians, however, subscribing to the antiapartheid imperative was complicated by the existence of contradictory high anxieties: the neuroses engendered by their erasure from the public imagination and the alienation bred by racial, religious, cultural, and linguistic difference. Indians, therefore, felt the need to assert their South Africanness by proclaiming a shared blackness. However, a unitary black identity also risked effacing the Indianness already made fragile by migration and public invisibility. The variety provided by the short story collection offers an excellent opportunity for conveying these contradictory impulses of collectivity versus specificity.

I continue to study short fiction under apartheid in chapter 2, "Essop's Fables: Strategic Indianness, Political Occasion, and the 'Grand Old Man' of South African Indian Literature." The relationship between political occasion and ethnic identity reflects not only the investment of Indians in South African public life but also the instability of ethnicity during moments of political change. The changing Indianness encountered in Ahmed Essop's work enables us to examine key issues in diaspora studies such as assimilation, citizenry, and national belonging, and how these everyday concerns of migratory communities are altered by the unique context of apartheid. Essop's novella *The Emperor* (1984) cautions Indians against retreating into ethnic enclaves. The *Hajji Musa* collection (1978, 1988) reveals the interplay of different nonwhite cultures in the supposedly "Indian" area of Fordsburg. In *Noorjehan and Other Stories* (1990), published in the year that saw the beginning of the end of apartheid, Indians actively seek to absorb the white oppressor into the "new" multiracial South Africa, thereby earning their own place as participatory *citizens* rather than as *diasporics*.

A preoccupation with the role of Indians in the new nation also characterizes transition-era (1990–1994) fiction. Chapter 3, "National Longing, Natural Belonging: Flux and Rootedness in Achmat Dangor's *Kafka's Curse*," focuses on South Africa's evolution to a multicultural democracy. *Kafka's Curse* can be read as a short story cycle and as a novel. Its compositional structure encapsulates the shift in South African Indian fiction, particularly the move from realistic short fiction in the apartheid period to longer, more inventive narratives in the postapartheid period. The novel is dominated by the motifs of racial metamorphosis, transgression, and boundary crossing. In its relentless documentation of the possibility of movement, *Kafka's Curse* reveals the untenable natures of taxonomies that depend on strict boundaries and argues that all South Africans are in the state of flux typically associated with migratory populations. Yet the South African version of hybridity that emerges from centuries of covert racial fertilization is characterized by neurosis and anxiety and is radically different from the intercultural fusion celebrated by diaspora theorists such as Homi Bhabha and Salman Rushdie.[48]

The book then moves to the postapartheid period. Each chapter examines a different shift in Indian fiction in the democratic present, always situating literary turns against larger cultural and political changes. Chapter 4, "The Point of Return: Backward Glances in Farida Karodia's *Other Secrets*," contextualizes Karodia's writing against two important literary movements in postapartheid South Africa: returning to the apartheid past in order to understand the postapartheid present and participating in a new culture of introspection and psychological meditation. A literary sense of return orchestrates Karodia's rewriting of her own fictional narrative, *Daughters of the Twilight* (1986), in order to absorb the changing scenario of the present into her articulation of Afrindian identity in *Other Secrets* (2000). Literary return enables Karodia to thematize issues relevant to Indianness in postapartheid South Africa and also functions as a metaphor for the changes taking place in Indian identity *and* Indian writing from the apartheid to the postapartheid periods. The historical sense suggests a return to the past in order to plug the holes in national memory. By schematizing the psychic, cultural, and social lives of Indians under apartheid, Karodia's critical vigilance reveals how Indianness has altered itself to a South African context. The literal sense of return celebrates the exile's arrival in South Africa, a coming home that allows her to reconfigure the various facets of her identity enabling the emergence of a diverse Afrindian self.

While Karodia's fiction returns to the apartheid past, the parameters of historical recovery are pushed back even further by the two novels studied in chapter 5. "Lost in Transplantation: Recovering the History of Indian Arrival in South Africa" examines the migratory journey of Indians as indentured labor and as traders through two historical novels: Praba Moodley's *The Heart Knows No Colour* (2003) and Imraan Coovadia's *The Wedding* (2001). A preoccupation with narrating the act of migration has characterized *all* South Asian diasporas. The South African Indian recuperation of the migratory past demonstrates how the unique circumstances of Indian arrival in South Africa alter our understanding of diasporic paradigms. Descendants of indentured and passenger Indians *differently* articulate *shared* concerns such as egalitarian citizenship, memory, hidden histories, relationships to the British Empire, the Indian contribution to South African life, their oppression preceding apartheid, affiliation with black Africans, and the emergence of Afrindian identities. Yet, like other South African historical novels, Moodley's and Coovadia's writings also have a presentist agenda: to garner these themes to affirm the South Africanness of Indians *and* the Indianness of South Africa in the here and now.

The last two chapters celebrate the literary inventiveness made possible in the postapartheid period. The final chapter, however, takes a very different turn in showcasing yet another important moment in democratic South Africa: the rupture of race relations. Chapter 6, "Citizen Other: The Implosion of Racial Harmony in Postapartheid South Africa," examines the postapartheid fiction of Ahmed Essop through the lens of Afrocentrism. As power changes hands from black to white, those inhabiting in-between states are assailed for being alien and foreign. *The King of Hearts* (1997) reflects on the fraught relationship between Indians and the other races during the postapartheid era, while *The Third Prophecy* (2004) problematizes the accommodation of the Indo-Islamic community within the contours of a secular nation. Like his apartheid-era writing, Essop's postapartheid fiction also comes back to the instability of ethnic identity in the time of rapid political change, even as it foregrounds the theme of unbelonging, alienation, and dispossession to expose the falsity of a nation's sense of self. The failure of postcoloniality reveals a disillusionment with the new nation-state that characterizes not only postapartheid South African writing but also most other postcolonial literatures.

The breakdown of racial solidarity and of postcoloniality itself is also reflected in a brief conclusion based on a study I conducted in Durban, South Africa, in December 2005. "New Directions or Same Old? Afrindian Identity and Fiction Today," reflects on subcontinental identity through a critical analysis of a seminar with the South African Indian literary community. The writers attending this meeting discussed issues consistently raised in this book: rage at an inward-looking Afrocentrism, a sense of unbelonging in the rainbow nation, despair at the insularity of South African Indians, and frustration over disavowal of the Indian past. "Every Indian has a story to tell," claimed a participant, "but no one is interested in listening to us." Since I want this book above all to have *listened* to the unheard stories that Indians have always had to tell,[49] *Afrindian Fiction* closes with interviews I conducted with important South African Indian authors, letting the writers tell the story of their stories in their own voice.

1

Indians in Short

Collectivity versus Specificity in the Apartheid Story

It is appropriate that the opening chapter of a book whose argument rests partly on the relationship between genre and political occasion begins with a scrutiny of form. This chapter discusses three South African Indian writers—Jayapraga Reddy, Agnes Sam, and Deena Padayachee—whose skillful deployment of the short story is vital to understanding the dialectical impulses underpinning apartheid-era fiction. The chapter interrogates the relationship between form, the antiapartheid imperative, and the Africanization of Indian identity. It also examines the articulation of dissent through the vehicle of short fiction, focusing on how the tightness of the short story allows or restricts the expression of a loose concept such as Afrindian selfhood. Finally, it connects the effacement and revelation of ethnic identity to the East-South model of diaspora and the disruption of South African racial binaries that the project as a whole foregrounds.

Literary critics generally concur that the short story dominated fictional production in apartheid-era South Africa, especially among dispossessed nonwhite communities.[1] Few scholars explain the reasons for the ascendancy of the short story as comprehensively as writer/critic Zoe Wicomb. However, Wicomb marshals her assertions without accommodating the differences among the various "black" constituencies. Although Wicomb's work underpins this chapter's theoretical framework, I modify her general formulations on South African short fiction to absorb the particularity of the Indian experience.

Wicomb charts the initial development of apartheid-era black writing in magazines such as *Drum*, one of the few outlets, along with other periodicals, available to black writers until the Congress of South African Writers (COSAW) was established to promote black writing in the 1980s. While useful in producing black unity as well as creating a forum for black voices in the 1950s, *Drum* did not always serve as a literary advocate for the specificity of the Indian experience.[2] Yet *Drum*'s indirect impact on South African Indian writing cannot be discounted.[3] In the rigidly censored climate of apartheid, *Drum* ensured the circulation of black oppositional writing through an elaborate network of dissemination. *Drum* also encouraged stylistic innovation by publishing articles that combined factual reportage with the narrative strategies of fiction.[4]

Staffrider, a literary magazine claiming to represent the "entire spectrum of the South African population," was founded in 1978 (Oliphant, *Ten Years* ix). Indian writers such as Ahmed Essop, Achmat Dangor, and Jayapraga Reddy were published here. Like *Drum*, *Staffrider* "exerted pressure on the institutionalized notions of writing as well as the rigid demarcations between genres and modes . . . [and] . . . stimulated debate around questions of the relationship between fiction and documentary reportage" (*Ten Years* ix). Periodicals such as *Drum* and *Staffrider* helped create a dominant literary sensibility among *all* nonwhite South Africans who preferred the short story over the novel and fused styles and themes to create "docustories." Magazine publishing thus demanded a certain generic sensibility—tight, short, and self-contained pieces—that created a natural selection for the short story.[5] Because apartheid silenced all black voices, organizations such as COSAW expended their resources on showcasing the diversity of South African writing by circulating as wide a range of authors as possible. "Collections and anthologies" facilitated this agenda better than novels (Wicomb, "South African Short Fiction" 162).

Wicomb further elaborates on other economic circumstances that had consequences for the profusion of short story writing during the apartheid years:

> English, for instance, not being the first language for most who write in it, makes the shorter form a more manageable choice. Lack of means, lack of privacy in overcrowded housing conditions, geographical instability (for many writers were also activists whose safety depended on being constantly on the move)—all these militated against attempting . . . the novel. ("South African Short Fiction" 162)

These linguistic and fiscal exigencies were probably also true of South African Indian writers, as subcontinentals may have used Indian languages not only to assert their distinctiveness but also to maintain links with India. Indian facility with formal English could also have been weakened by the common interruption of education by incarceration, dislocation, and poverty. While the brevity of the short story allowed those less familiar with the language to deploy the genre, the English medium of the texts also circulated them among different races and linguistic groups.

Indian writing was further influenced by the other economic and political determinants Wicomb credits for the rise of the short story. Since Indian families tended to be large, the issue of having the privacy to compose extended pieces of prose forcefully determined the importance of the short story in South African Indian fiction. Indians were also subjected to the ruthless dispersal facilitated by the Group Areas Act, which extirpated better-off Indians from large homes and relocated them in small, warren-like residences. Like black Africans writers, many Indian writers were activists of some sort. This meant that they were subject to government harassment and did not have the mental or physical space in which to write longer works such as the novel.

The reasons for Indians using short fiction as their dominant expressive medium become particularly compelling because of the "teacherly" possibilities embedded in the short story. Wicomb claims that the "brevity [of the short story] has a pedagogical advantage that is widely exploited in schools for teaching about other cultures" ("South African Short Fiction" 163). In its ability to reach a wider audience because of its length and variety, the short story collection brought the Other into the purview of different communities and challenged the segregationist prescriptive that isolated each group in its own enclave. Indians were among the few nonwhite South Africans subject to the anxieties of diaspora, particularly those centered on recuperating the Indian culture lost in the act of migration. Indians, therefore, felt a dual narrative responsibility. They needed not only to preserve their Indianness, but also to familiarize other races with their culture in order to counter the "taint" of their foreignness. The "pedagogical advantage" of the short story collection was particularly useful for recording and showcasing Indian identity.

Infusing the short story collection with insurgent promise, Wicomb argues next that the genre naturally lends itself to apartheid-era resistance politics:

> [T]he wide use of the form [was] an effective medium for challenging received views and for offering new self-definitions—not least because

of its relatively rapid production and circulation. [S]tories, as opposed to a single novel, can represent a number of different situations or plots in which human behaviour can be staged. ("South African Short Fiction" 164)

Wicomb credits the short story collection with opening itself to a wealth of representational possibilities that register an oppositional politics *quickly*.[6] The need to exhibit a unified black identity in order to combat the divisiveness of apartheid—what can be called the antiapartheid imperative—was also related to the "didactic agenda" of the short story. The years between 1975 and 1990 saw a rise in Indian literary production in general and in the Indian short story in particular. That time period was characterized by brutal governmental oppression, yet antiapartheid resistance also reached its apex in the last fifteen years of segregation.

Annemarie Van Niekerk points out that "the late 1970s and 1980 witnessed a resurgence of popular resistance and of the national liberation movement . . . the period is inscribed by a vociferous conflict of the most salient historical forces at work in contemporary South African society" ("Aspects" 36).[7] The 1970s and 1980s present a unique moment in South Africa, one in which the counterpoints of repression and resistance are locked in a deadly battle. Black literature emerging from this period necessarily invokes a politics of resistance through solidarity and the forging of alliances between different ethnicities in defiance of apartheid strictures.[8]

For Indians, however, subscribing to the antiapartheid imperative was complicated by the existence of contradictory high anxieties: the neuroses engendered by their erasure from the public imagination and the alienation bred by racial, religious, cultural, and linguistic difference. Indians, therefore, felt the need to assert their South Africanness more than most other groups.[9] Those gestures of belonging were made by forging links with the black population in order to Africanize Indianness and to register the revolutionary potential of mass movements. However, a unitary black identity also risked effacing the Indianness already made fragile by migration and public invisibility. The short story collection offered an excellent opportunity for conveying the contradictory impulses—of collectivity versus specificity—without compromising the text's revolutionary possibilities.[10] Andries Oliphant, former editor of *Staffrider*, points out that "the fractured and discontinuous articulations which a body of short stories produces over a particular period further provide . . . a field of multiple perspectives in the divergent perspectives and experiences" ("Fictions").

"Multiple perspectives" allow the short story collection to inscribe the impulses toward collectivity and specificity as a complex dialectic rather than as a simple opposition.

A gloss on the terms "collectivity" and "specificity" is necessary here. The former operates at two levels in South African Indian short fiction: first, collectivity is invoked through the articulation of a common "black" identity rather than an Indian identity. Deploying "black" as a designation for Africans, Indians, and Coloureds replaces apartheid taxonomy with an alternative nomenclature based on a common history of oppression. The term "black" allows dispossessed groups agency in the ascriptive process, giving them the voice and power of large-scale resistance. Collectivity also functions at a second level in South African Indian literature. Many South African Indians use the voice of other nonwhite South Africans in their writing. Once again this is a rejection of the "no" of apartheid. If segregation mandated that races must be separated because they were different, an Indian writing in the voice of a Coloured or black African suggests that the Self-Same can enter the consciousness of the Other—indeed, become the Other—thus obscuring the "shadow lines" of alterity.[11] In seeking affiliation with indigenous Africans, both manifestations of collectivity engender the emergence of an Afrindian identity and South African citizenship. If a celebration of collectivity risks reinscribing the essentialism of the binary frame of race relations that this project challenges, the politics of specificity function as a corrective to the reductiveness of collectivity.

Specificity, then, implies an expression of particularity. For example, references to Indian mythology, language, food, clothing, and other cultural habits often infiltrate these texts. The term also foregrounds the articulation of Indian anxieties and concerns such as the relevance of arranged marriage in a changing social scenario, the role of women outside the domestic realm, and the desire to maintain Hindu and Muslim religious practices in diaspora. Specificity allows Indian writers to teach other South Africans about subcontinental culture and so render Indians familiar and recognizable.

The theme of specificity is further complicated by what Sue Marais defines as a "sense of personal culpability." According to Marais, the apartheid-era "short fiction cycle" is subject to a dual imperative: "The first of these comprises a defiant attempt to assert the bonds of affinity . . . while the second denotes the opposite by emphasising the divisions between, and within communities and the concomitant sense of personal culpability, of dislocation, and of psychic fragmentation in individual consciousness" ("Getting Lost" 31). All three writers discussed in this chapter are aware that many Indians often naturalize the grand design of apartheid by retreating into ethnic cocoons. Consequently the "sense of personal culpability" exists as a warning to abandon apartheid hierarchies and instead follow the politics of collectivity. Specificity, in other words, should not be isolationist. The racial tensions percolating below Indian writing reveals that the division between apartheid and postapartheid fiction is not as absolute as it may seem to be. Even as the latter suggests a dramatic shift in genre, theme, and ideology, many of the anxieties coming to the fore in the postapartheid period are merely *pre-expressed* as the dangers of specificity rather than absent in apartheid-era fiction.

The tension between collectivity and specificity also has consequences for the alternative model of diaspora that this book foregrounds. The unique scaffolding of apartheid created diasporic identities that were radically different from those engendered in other states of migratory being. The classic diasporic dialectic oscillates between carving new identities while retaining identification with the "old" country.[12] In South Africa, the elaborate negotiation between past and present, homeland and "hostland," migrant and indigene, unfolds differently. Indians were unable to maintain the usual ties with the home country in segregationist South Africa for fear of jeopardizing their already tenuous claims to South African national identity and because of South Africa's isolation during the apartheid years. Thus, the empowering alterity of diaspora—its power to effect social and cultural change—is seemingly deferred by the amalgamation of nonwhite South Africans under the unitary insignia of black resistance. However, the emancipatory potential of diasporic dynamism still emerges: *not* by evoking a mythologized pure India, but by using a strategic specificity to create an Indianized South Africa, one that has all the room in the world for South Africanized Indians.

A Refusal to Be on the Fringes of South African Life

Jayapraga Reddy's short fiction subscribes to the antiapartheid imperative in its fable-like essence. Insurrectionary prose is often meant to be straightforward and simple in order to reach a vast majority of people rather than just the educated elite. Correspondingly, many stories in Reddy's collection *On the Fringe of Dreamtime* (1987) intertwine morality tale with political allegory. However, Reddy's literary strategies are often subtle despite their structural determinacy. According to Annemarie Van

Niekerk, "many of [Reddy's] stories were written in the course of the seventies and eighties," a period that we have already marked as the apex of apartheid *and* of antiapartheid resistance ("Aspects" 35). As with other nonwhite South African writers, Reddy's work was initially acknowledged overseas; she was first published in South Africa in *Staffrider* magazine ("Aspects" 36). For Reddy, the circumstances of magazine publishing partially explain her preference for the short story.[13]

While Reddy rarely invokes what Loren Kruger calls "a broader black identity" ("Black" 113), she inscribes the politics of collectivity into her fiction by writing in different voices: Coloured, black, *and* Indian. Although risking the charge of appropriating the Other, this key strategy of antiapartheid resistance often destabilizes the boundaries of alterity. Reddy has claimed in an interview with Rajendra Chetty that she "has also tried to show that one doesn't have to be white to write about whites, or black to write about black people. The writer must be versatile and reflect life as it's lived" (*South African Indian Writings* 369). In communicating her empathy with other nonwhite South Africans, Reddy defies the divisions of apartheid that segregated each community into physical, geographic, and even literary groups.[14]

Even as Reddy writes in non-Indian idiom, the variety embedded in the short story collection allows her to evoke the specificity of Indian life and culture under apartheid. "The Spirit of Two Worlds" uses gender emancipation as a motif for racial solidarity. The conflict in the story centers on Sharda, a new daughter-in-law, who "by bringing in her new ideas and an alien lifestyle . . . had upset the smooth running of her home" (10). Sharda represents the world outside: the South African context that impinges on the private lives of Indians in order to politicize them into action. In the end, the old matriarch, who had fiercely resisted the forces of change, embraces the two worlds by embracing Sharda's child. In offering to care for the child while Sharda goes out to work, the matriarch fuses two disparate ways of being: "The spirit of two worlds had emerged in a new beginning" (16). While the most obvious references to the two worlds are the two generations of Indian women, the fact that one symbolizes private, insular Indianness and the other the presumably more racially diverse public sphere suggests that Indian identity must make gestures of inclusivity rather than of exclusivity.

In mobilizing the figure of the child to articulate her social agenda, Reddy deploys a popular allegory in postcolonial fiction: one in which the child becomes the symbol of the nation as well as an encapsulation of its anxieties. Salman Rushdie's *Midnight's Children* (India), Bapsi Sidhwa's

Cracking India (Pakistan), Tsitsi Dangarembga's *Nervous Conditions* (Zimbabwe), Ben Okri's *The Famished Road* (Nigeria), Jamaica Kincaid's *Annie John* (Antigua), and Merle Hodge's *Crick Crack Monkey* (Trinidad) are all manifestations of this allegory. Miki Flockemann, however, sees the child, particularly the girl child, as a dominant motif in South African fiction that "reflects a common trope, namely the child's gendered rite of passage into a given South African race/class hierarchy" ("Asian Diasporas" 75).

In South African *Indian* fiction, the repeated deployment of the child as trope encapsulates and extends both representational modalities. The child functions not only as a metaphor for the nation and of racialized hierarchies but also as a symbol for the Indian community. Compared to most other South Africans, Indians in South Africa are a relatively recent presence who only discovered literary voice in the later half of the twentieth century. The genre of South African Indian fiction is therefore a young one. The child in fiction by South African Indians allegorizes the youthfulness of the genre as well as the youthfulness of the history of the Indian presence in the national consciousness. But like a strident child clamoring for attention, this is a presence that refuses to be effaced. In "The Spirit of Two Worlds," the fusion of two worlds, inscribed on the body of the child, makes it the symbol of hope and revival as well as of Indian integration into South African life.

Indian identity thus yields to the pressures of the world outside even as it seeks to separate itself. "Market Days," set in what is most likely an Indian bazaar in Durban, describes the Africanization of Indians and the Indianization of South Africa:

> A White woman sailed out followed by her *African* maid bearing heavily laden baskets. *African* women with baskets balanced on their heads, moved with an enviable ease. . . . [A] group of Hindu swamis stood in their saffron robes, holding brass trays containing ash and flowers which they handed out at random. . . . *African* vendors trundled their ice-cream carts along the road. . . . A market reflects the life of its people and this was just part of the life that flowed through it daily. (40–41; emphasis added)

Notice the repeated mention of the African presence in the Indian marketplace. Instead of expanding Indian identity outward, Reddy demonstrates that Indians can bring Africans into their purview, thus showing us the other aspect of Afrindian identity: its ability to not just change itself but also to effect change. If South African Indian fiction is characterized by a split between an Africanized Indian identity during the apartheid era and an Indianized South Africa in the postapartheid period, Reddy's marketplace suggests that the Indianization of South Africa was always already taking place in the apartheid period, only subsumed under more pressing political exigencies. Reddy emphasizes the interactions between races and the effects of Indians *as Indians* on the national psyche.

The title story, "On the Fringe of Dreamtime," addresses the Group Areas Act. An Indian man visits his old home, which is now inhabited by white people. Startled out of his reverie by a white woman, the old man thinks "her whiteness was another alien intrusion into his dream" (62–63). The connotation of whiteness as alien and intrusive suggests that Indians, rather than whites, can claim the South African land because of their history of suffering and political radicalization. This is another staple strategy of inversion encountered in apartheid-era Indian fiction, where Otherness and unbelonging are imposed onto the whites while Indians assert an enduring connection to the land and its people. The East-South axis of diaspora underlines national belonging through an appeal to the extended periodicity of the Indian presence that goes back centuries. Diaspora, with all its negative associations of alienation and instability, is projected onto the settler Europeans, while Indians assume the status of rooted indigene.

Later the old man stops by an old Hindu temple: "The blackened ruin conjured up the fragrant smoke of incense and fruit offerings. . . . At such times the spirit of sharing and oneness was strengthened" (66). While the "old" Hindu temple suggests the longevity of the Indian presence in South Africa, the temple in ruins is also an important metaphor for the destruction of Hindu Indian identity. Reddy's language here is suffused with racial imagery.[15] The phrase "blackened ruin" suggests that apartheid has ruined a pure Indianness (the temple has been destroyed under the Group Areas Act, after all) which now must Africanize (or blacken) itself in order to survive. The "blackened ruin" also signals the persistence of memory. The images that follow the phrase "blackened ruin" are those of Hindu religious practice but with positive associations: "*fragrant* smoke of incense and fruit offerings." In other words, it is the blackness of the ruin, rather than the ruin itself, which highlights, foregrounds, indeed enables, Indianness. The Africanized Indianness that emerges with force here is represented as a *blackened ruin*, thus suggesting that Indian identity can only exist as an African shard, never in its pure form. Reddy encapsulates collectivity and specificity not as two contending forces but as symbiotic corollaries. She brings together the binary forces of diaspora—of integration and particularity—in a model based on empathy and alliance with blacks and not whites.

The rhetoric of affiliation used here is similar to the discourse of Black British solidarity. Forged in the 1970s, Black British alliances deployed "black" as an umbrella term for all nonwhite Britons. Yet the rhetoric of a common blackness is staged differently in South Africa. Blacks are not only the majority in South Africa but also the indigenes, unlike in England, where blacks constitute an even smaller ethnic group than Asians. Citing Kobena Mercer, Avtar Brah points out that in Britain, "the sign 'black' was mobilised also as a displacement for the categories 'immigrant' and 'ethnic minority' which, throughout the 1960s and 1970s, had come to denote racialized re-definitions of belonging and subjecthood" (98). In Britain, nonwhites used the term "black" to claim British status defiantly, but because of the recentness of the immigrant experience could not claim indigenous status there.

In South Africa, renaming Indians as black—and thus striking an alliance with the indigenes—doesn't merely suggest "a displacement for the categories immigrant and ethnic minority" but also a strident assertion of indigenity by association. Claiming indigenous status is different from claiming citizenry. Citizenry suggests that since Indians have been in South Africa for centuries and have suffered and contributed to the country, they are citizens *now*. Indigenity suggests that Indians were *always* South African and therefore don't need to justify their presence.[16]

Reddy's writing also articulates the tentative and fragile nature of this alliance between Indians and black Africans. "Friends" examines the dynamics between an Indian and her African maid. The relationship between "maid and madam" is an important theme in South African culture that is repeatedly depicted in genres as diverse as Anne Landsman's novel *The Devil's Chimney* (1999), the documentary *Maids and Madams*, and the popular cartoon strip *Madam and Eve*. What happens, asks Reddy, when Indian women become madams and acquire the social power that comes with wealth?

In "Friends," Sadhana's black servant, Bessie, wants to buy her daughter Phumza a dress like the one Sadhana's daughter Asha has. Sadhana tells Bessie that the dress shouldn't be like the one she bought for *her* daughter. While the story unfurls across the axes of class and gender, it also takes on racial implications. That Sadhana doesn't want the servant's daughter to wear clothes like her own child's suggests that rich Indians are reproducing the structures of apartheid by enacting black-white power dynamics. As Van Niekerk points out, "Friends" is a "fictional illustration of the practical operation of overlapping and interacting power hierarchies by demonstrating how oppressed people are often coresponsible for keeping the chain of oppression intact by co-operating, instead of breaking the chain" ("Introduction" to *Raising the Blinds* 25). The description of Sadhana as white madam also brings to mind "Marketplace," with the "[w]hite woman [sailing] out followed by her *African* maid bearing heavily laden baskets" (40). If the earlier story suggests that black people carry the burden of whiteness, "Friends" claims that black people also carry the burden of Indianness. Often, Indianness is enabled at the expense of blackness and not *through* blackness, as suggested by the blackened ruin in the title story.

The tension between Bessie and Sadhana seeps into the relationship between their children and comes to a head through the girls' battle for ownership of a doll that brings to Phumza's mind a "large lifelike doll with a blue dress and golden hair" that she has seen in a store (109). Asha breaks the doll in a petulant fit. The broken doll is then rescued by Phumza. Seeing her friend with the discarded doll, Asha seizes the doll back. The doll serves as a symbol of whiteness, echoing other texts of racial desire, such as Toni Morrison's *The Bluest Eye* (1970). That Asha mutilates the doll suggests her anger at the whiteness that she wants so much, enacting what Flockemann calls "a complex hegemony of desire" ("Asian Diasporas" 75). That Phumza can only claim the doll in its mutilated/discarded form suggests that Indians have greater access to a pure whiteness, thanks to their relative wealth, than the black Africans, who can only claim a mutilated/discarded whiteness. The mutilated doll also recalls the blackened ruin, suggesting that to be nonwhite in apartheid South Africa is to be mutilated and ruined.

Reddy's stories thus reveal how other determinants, especially those of class, influence Afrindian identity. Middle-class Indians such as Asha desire whiteness. Working-class Indians, such as the old man in the story about the blackened ruin, desire blackness. In deftly uncovering the various strands of Afrindian identity emergent in South Africa, Reddy foregrounds the East-South model of diaspora as well as complicates our understanding of South African race relations. The unique system of apartheid created various kinds of racial affiliations, including those based on altruism and those based on expediency. In aligning with blacks, Indians situate themselves as rooted indigene. In aligning with Europeans, Indians become the intrusive alien, always in a state of diaspora.

Reddy's fiction uses the multiple thematic possibilities afforded by the short story collection to their fullest extent. Among the different impulses she deploys in her search for South African citizenry are the ideas of collectivity inscribed in her using other nonwhite voices as well as gender to think about issues of race. She also reflects on the excess of specificity by showing us how Indians subscribe to apartheid categories and compromise the resistance movement that called for unity amid the different South African communities. For Reddy, Indians, because of their relative privilege, are more to blame for the persistence of segregationist discourse than the black Africans, a value system that characterizes apartheid-era fiction in general. Unless it is to expose the negative effects of specificity, Reddy's articulation of Indian particularity is never just in isolation but always infiltrated and hybridized by the African world outside, even as Indianness hybridizes the African world itself.

Inserting Indians into South African Life

Agnes Sam's collection of short stories entitled *Jesus Is Indian* was published in 1989.[17] *Jesus Is Indian* achieves a clearly articulated political agenda: to absorb Indians into the fabric of the nation by highlighting the South Africanness of their daily lives, their voluntary collectivity with black Africans, and to uncover the specificity of Indian cultural identity in South Africa. The title too is significant in this context: "Jesus Is Indian" we are told in bold type, followed in smaller print by the subtitle "and Other South African Stories." The suggestion of Indian as "Other South African" is significant. The Indians are Other in a land divided into an unaccommodating racial binary. But by describing the collection as South African and yoking it to the lead story ("Jesus Is Indian") with the words "and other," the text brings the matter of Jesus being Indian into the ambit of what is South African. In other words, the title suggests that Indian themes are very much a part of South African life.

The agenda mentioned above is motored through genre. On the one hand, Sam spins politically charged tales exhibiting the unifying sentiments of the "Black Consciousness" movement. On the other hand, story after story lovingly depicts the particularity of South African Indian life. In any other form, the twin emphases, and the rapid movement from one theme to another, might seem dizzying and unconvincing. But because a story that invokes black identity does not necessarily leak into a story dealing with the specificity of Indian identity, we consider each story as a discrete whole even as we configure the collection *as collection* in order to understand the dialectical nature of Indian writing in apartheid-era South Africa.

The story "High Heels," for example, examines how South African Indians carve out a relentlessly Christian identity—the narrator's name is Ruthie and her brothers are called Matthew, Thomas, Mark, and Paul—yet they still cannot give up prior claims to Hindu Indianness. The narrator's mother maintains a shrine where she probably worships a Hindu god. The carefully hidden shrine is symbolic of Indian culture in South Africa and reveals the concealment of ethnic identity in the face of the pressures of assimilation.[18] It also recovers the history of many indentured Indians who were forced to convert to Christianity upon arrival in South Africa so that their marriages would have sanction in the eyes of South African law and their children's claim to inheritance would be recognized (Sam 10, 131). Miki Flockemann suggests that "the 'meaning' of the secret Hindu prayer room . . . emerges as a trope running through the collection as a whole, and . . . establishes a dialogue between the present and the past" ("Asian Diasporas" 76). If the "meaning" of the hidden shrine is symbolic of South Africa's discovery of its Indian population, it also suggests that the subcontinental constituency is one whose Indianness may be harbored under layers of an—often voluntary—integration, but which refuses to be eradicated.

When her grandfather finally shows her the secret shrine, Ruthie's response is significant:

> On the box is a little oil lamp with a red chimney and little trays and vases made of brass and gold and silver. Tata lifts the red glass chimney from the lamp. He strikes a match. A yellow flame leaves up. He lights the lamp. Then he touches an orange stone. It has two hollows. Tata takes a handful of grey powder from one hollow and places it in the other. Then he strikes another match. Again a yellow flame leaps up. He puts the flame to powder. Blue smoke curls up into the room.
>
> Tata says '*Saamberani*.' . . .
>
> He joins his hands and begins to sing softly. I can't understand what he says. . . . But I like his singing. It's not like the singing in church. (22)

The staccato writing reveals the fragmented consciousness of the child as she encounters an overwhelming world that is radically different from the one she in which she typically dwells. Ruthie likes her grandfather's singing, especially reveling in its difference from singing in church.

Sangeeta Ray says that Ruthie "has become one of the initiates whose daily participation in the rituals of the Catholic church is subverted by the knowledge of the existence of the other prayer room in 'Christian' Indian houses" (7). The name Ruthie, and its biblical echoes of gendered migration, also situate the narrator as "Ruth the model émigré" (the phrase is Bonnie Honig's) who confronts the bifurcated heritages that she now knows she has to inhabit.[19]

Unlike some of her other contemporaries who interject Indian words into the narrative in a matter-of-fact way, Sam italicizes the Indian word *Saamberani* and also provides detailed notes of explanation in a glossary. The intonation *Saamberani,* according to the notes, means "an Indian word, for the incense burnt when praying or when someone dies to keep the newly deceased spirit at rest" (133). The italicization of Saamberani suggests that Indian linguistic practices and religious habit do not belong in South Africa. This also ties into the secondary meaning of Saamberani, which is to "keep the newly deceased spirit at rest." Indianness may be the "newly deceased spirit" that must be put to rest through the invocation of Saamberani, yet that the grandfather chants Saamberani in a carefully maintained Hindu shrine suggests that the spirit is not dead, but rather only hidden. Moreover, the notes section explaining the presence of "unfamiliar" words glosses not just Indian words but also Afrikaans, Xhosa, and Zulu words. This may be because Sam published her work in England and therefore catered to an English audience. Yet the tripartite index of European, Asian, and African words suggests that Sam reconfigures South African race relations across an axis that refuses to sustain the binary of black and white and instead triangulates itself to accommodate the Indian presence. This triangulation metonymically represents the larger project of the East-South praxis of diaspora: its rupturing of the black-white dichotomy that has characterized places such as South Africa.

Jesus Is Indian thus reveals an Indianness that is always already Africanized even as it showcases cultural particularity. In the title story, the child narrator, Angelina, keeps getting into trouble at school because she uses Indian words in her essays (such as "Hama" instead of "Mother"), earning her the ire of her teacher, the aptly named Sister Bonaventura. When the sister tells Angelina to take out the non-English words "because I don't know them," Angelina replies, "I can teach you sister. Is easy" (28). This reflects the pedagogical aspirations of the book. Like her narrator, Sam will also teach us what Indian words and Indian culture mean in the framework of her South African collection.

Later, Sister Bonaventura asks for Angelina's mother's *Christian* name and Angelina replies that it is Kamatchee. "Little Cabbage," asks the sister. "Your mother's name is Little Cabbage?" (31). The narrator continues to claim that her mother's Christian name is indeed Kamatchee, to which Sister Bonaventura continues to reply that Kamatchee is no *Christian* name. Angelina then goes home and asks her mother why she doesn't have a Christian name:

> Hama laugh. Hama holds her head up high and makes it wobble about. She say, "*What* that sister know? Hey? Don't Jesus wear a dhoti like Gandhi? Don't Hama talk to Jesus in our language? Don't Jesus answer all Hama's prayers? Don't Honey get a rich husband? You so clever, what you think that means? Hey? You electric light children and you don't know? Jesus is Indian. You go to school and tell that Sister." (33; emphasis in original)

Flockemann points out that Hama "effectively turns the tables on Sister Bonaventura by appropriating Christianity, but on Indian terms" ("Asian Diasporas" 79). While Hama's speech divests Jesus from the domain of white Western Christianity, the comparison with Gandhi is also significant. Although Indians in South Africa now number more than a million, for most people the juxtaposition of Indian and South Africa brings Gandhi to mind. It was in South Africa that Gandhi learned about discrimination. It was in South Africa that Gandhi first put forward his principles of satyagraha (or nonviolent resistance) in a cohesive way. It was in South Africa that Gandhi found out what it meant to be a racialized Indian.[20]

Both Gandhi and Jesus suggest self-realization as well as resistance to oppressive political structures and function as symbols of what the South African Indian community can become. The resistance of South African Indians may not have the world-changing consequences of a Gandhi or a Jesus. Even though their opposition to cultural hegemony operates in small, encoded ways—such as wearing a dhoti and speaking in an Indian language—South African Indians are resisting all the same. Angelina summarizes Hama's speech in school, adding, "I tell Sister I never going to call Hama 'mother.' Even when I am writing English in my book" (33). Angelina expects chastisement from her teacher, who instead says to her, "[A]ll right Angelina." Following this endorsement from authority, Angelina walks home "swinging my page boy haircut and pulling in my stomach and pushing out my chest" (33).

That a child whose identity is relentlessly figured as South African in the public sphere of school and as Indian in the private sphere of home is able to melt these binaries of public/South African and private/Indian shows us how Sam, like Reddy, uses the discourse of childhood to not only metaphorize the youthfulness of the Indian presence but also to carve out a place for South African Indians—both as South Africans *and* as Indians—within the wider political landscape. Flockemann supports this assertion by stating that Sam deploys "representations of 'Asianness' to destabilize dominant discourses of identity in ways that have implications for the process of democratization" ("Asian Diasporas" 72).[21] Thus, Sam looks forward to a more democratic South Africa that accommodates the Indian community as not just an extension of black South Africans but also as Africanized Indians.[22]

Sam's collection also explores how Indian identity is shaped by black culture in the midst of the strictures of apartheid that isolated each community geographically and emotionally. If apartheid demanded that Indians—already apart because of race, religion, culture and language—be segregated even further, then Sam's fiction situates itself against that directive by claiming that Indians are South Africans—black South Africans—too. Sam thus blurs the ethnic differentiation she elaborates in the stories discussed above. Many stories emphasize Indian interaction with other South African ethnicities, especially black South Africans. In "The Well Loved Woman," Chantal's older sister Kamilla returns from England, where she proceeds to disregard Indian custom with reckless abandon. When Chantal, the main character, speaks to an African man, her community is shocked that an Indian girl is talking to a black man. Chantal asks, in "all innocence," why "can't an African marry an Indian?" following which she is slapped by her mother and beaten by her brothers (51).

While Chantal's family's response highlights Sam's criticism of gendered separatism, Sam also challenges the notion of Indians as isolationist:

> He [the African man mentioned above] was standing watching the door as they entered. Kamilla simply walked up to him and they stood for several minutes looking at each other. Neither touched nor spoke. Then Kamilla put out her hand to touch his face. Turning to the child, then to the man, she said, "Maqhmoud, this is my son, Maqhmoud." (52)

Kamilla might just be making friendly overtures to a stranger; yet there is also a sense of romantic intrigue between Indian and African. Earlier Chantal had asked Kamilla how she would know that she is in love. Kamilla tells her "'when you feel you want to put out your hand and touch a man'" (50).

Jaspal Singh reads Kamilla's interaction with the African man as an instance when taboos are reconstituted: "[W]hile Kamilla hopes for new choices for the newly educated generation, the Indian way of life, which has stood unchanged for decades, persists and dictates what it means to be an Indian woman in diaspora, particularly in third world spaces" (213). While this is certainly true, the fact that both Indian girls are attracted to the African man suggests how much Indians want to violate the taboos instituted by apartheid *and* by Indian insularity. This desire for Africanization is particularly true of Chantal and Kamilla who are many generations removed from the subcontinent and therefore cannot subscribe to the proscriptions of an imagined, mythic India. As Sam warns us against the ethnocentrism that results from the inward glance, she also constantly challenges the idea that Indians are ethnocentric. The Africanization of Indian identity in this instance emerges from an emotional, but still politically powerful, "hunger for connectedness" with the Other.[23]

Stories such as "The Storyteller" and "And They Christened It Indenture" evoke the Africanization of Indians by tracing the extended presence of subcontinentals in South Africa. Sam reminds us that the Indian presence has been grafted onto South Africa through a long process of loss and pain. "The Storyteller" claims that the illiterate indentured laborers who came to South Africa could rely only on telling tales in order to maintain memories of the narratives erased by the violently hierarchical nature of indenture and apartheid record keeping. "And They Christened It Indenture" has a sequential relationship with "The Storyteller." The second story examines the horrors of indenture—or the aftermath of the voyage described in "The Storyteller"—constantly deploying a wry irony that characterizes much of Sam's fiction. In these stories, Sam recuperates the forgotten history of indenture, especially the lack of legal rights accorded to Indians. Thus she inserts the trauma of the Indians into the national collectivity by memorializing the past.[24]

It is significant, however, that these two stories come at the very end of the collection, right after the other stories that assert the solidarity of Indians with other disenfranchised South African populations in various ways. Sam suggests that Indians are Indians only in the final analysis. Only after they have claimed their South African citizenry through articulating collectivity with the black population can they then assert the specificity of indenture, an experience that is uniquely Indian. Genre once again enters the narrative in significant ways. Through the form of the short story collection, Sam can negotiate themes such as universalism, specificity, and the tension between collectivity and particularity by creating different characters and settings around whom these issues can coalesce. Ray's thoughts on Indian identity in *Jesus Is Indian* are particularly apposite here: "Sam's fictional characters occupy multiple spaces which . . . reveal heterogeneous, multiple identities which are complementary and contradictory, but which because of their very pluralization reveal the moment of emancipation from static configurations of meaning" (12). Sam may rescue her characters from absolute binaries such as South African and Indian, but she refuses to assign them the obviously in-between place that diaspora studies have traditionally celebrated.[25] Instead she suggests that though Indians may be Indians at some moments, they are always already South Africans first.[26]

Doctoring Hope and Fear

In 1991, Deena Padayachee, a South African Indian doctor, won the first Nadine Gordimer short story competition.[27] Written mostly during the apartheid years but published in 1992, during the transition period, Padayachee's short fiction reflects the same public aspirations as Reddy's and Sam's, including those of "teaching" other South Africans about Indian culture, asserting Indian claims to South African citizenry, tracing the Africanization of Indian identity and emphasizing collectivity by asserting racial solidarity as well as by writing in black and Coloured voices. Padayachee also expresses an ominous disquiet about Indian internalization of apartheid-era racial hierarchies. J. U. Jacobs's comments on Nadine Gordimer's short story collection *Jump* (1991)—whose publication date is close to that of *What's Love Got to Do with It?*—aptly describe the mood of Padayachee's collection: "The stories are set in the late 1980s where many of the apartheid laws had been abolished but not yet the state that created them. South Africans were intensely aware of living on the threshold of a future into which they projected their hopes or fears" (198).

Hope and fear provide a steady counterpoint in Padayachee's fiction. While his stories celebrate racial solidarity, they inject a tone of foreboding, more consistently than either Sam or Reddy, in noting the persistence of racial boundaries despite external gestures of community and commonality. Yet the collection's title, evoking Tina Turner's famous song (like Reddy's echo of the film *Imitation of Life* in the story "Friends") links itself not only to black African culture but also to international black culture. This gesture of racial affiliation takes on a global dimension of solidarity rather than a merely local one. It also demonstrates that South

African Indian writing is not produced in a literary vacuum; instead, it is intimately conditioned not only by postcolonial discourse but also by developments in other minority cultures. Paying homage to a worldwide black culture further functions as a distancing device that separates the authors from the prejudicial views of their characters.

The opening story, "The Visitor," reflects the collection's structuring theme of ethnic (dis)harmony. Padayachee explores the consciousness of a black man raiding the Indian section of a township that includes Phoenix Ashram, a commune built by Gandhi during his twenty-one-year stay in South Africa. Overhearing the mention of the Mahatma, the narrator says, "Of course we had not learned about him [Gandhi] in school. I knew very little about him at that time" (14). The vertiginous impulses of apartheid traced here neglected to inform black Africans not only of their own history, but also of the other communities that constitute South Africa. The narrator then encounters the ghost of Gandhi: an old man with "horn-rimmed spectacles, skinny body and bald pate" (15). Before he leaves, "Gandhi" tells the narrator to take care of the debris plundered from the ashram: "'Look after these things,' he said in his gentle, squeaky voice, 'they are of Africa'" (17; emphasis added).

South African Indian fiction constantly calls upon Gandhi for inspiration in a way that no other Indian diaspora can. Writer after writer evokes Gandhi and Gandhi's contribution to South Africa, not only to claim citizenry but also to emphasize the abiding relationship between India and South Africa through the prismatic figure of the Mahatma. Among the items in the wreckage is Gandhi's autobiography. That this canonical work in the Gandhi oeuvre is also said to be "of Africa" suggests that Gandhi himself is of Africa. By making the "Father of the Indian nation"—the man who symbolizes India—South African, Padayachee asserts the South Africanness of *all* Indians. The memorialization of Gandhi against the pillaging of Phoenix Ashram also resurrects his forgotten message of nonviolence. The didactic agenda that characterizes South African Indian short fiction in general is established from the very first story itself.

If African-Indian relationships are depicted through images of plunder and looting in "The Visitor," the story entitled "A Different Kind of Standard Four" asserts the interracial harmony that characterizes much of apartheid-era fiction. After having built a school for the Indian community, the narrator's father claims, "[I]f we had not been able to work with the African people, there would have been little that we could've done" (23). The father then asks his son: "'I've heard you speaking of the Great Trek and the Greeks and the Romans, but have you learned anything about the

African peoples? Of the Zulu Culture and the history of Mozambique?'" (26). Only after interrogating his son's knowledge of African history does the father question his son's awareness of India. "'I took the trouble to learn a little about *our* ancient culture and something of *our* intellectual heritage'" (27; emphasis added), claims the father. The articulation of an expansive "our" as well as its double repetition loops back to the antiapartheid imperative. By placing African culture first in the list of educational imperatives, the father suggests that Indians are Africans first and Indians only in the last analysis. This brings to mind Sam's strategic placement of the two stories that deal exclusively with Indian identity at the very end of her collection and only after she has repeatedly highlighted the Africanization of Indianness. Padayachee thus participates in a larger rhetoric of apartheid-era identification where Indianness occupies a prominent place, but one that is always subservient to Africanization. The relegation of Indianness to secondary status is a key difference from other diasporas where identity construction usually involves the negotiation and fusion of two competing states of being into a hybrid, harmonious whole.[28]

If the antiapartheid imperative dictated that literature needed to be propagandist, and therefore clearly articulated, writers like Padayachee often found a way to circumvent that restrictive agenda by putting literary form into play. Andries Oliphant characterizes Padayachee's writing as "conventional realist . . . [that] . . . rearticulate well-worn sociopolitical themes in thinly fictionalized narratives of life under apartheid" ("Fictions"). However, Padayachee uses the spaciousness of the short story collection to explore its inventive possibilities to the fullest extent. Ostensibly about subterranean vermin seeking to sow discontent amongst the various above-the-ground communities and so initiate a takeover, "A Pestilence in the Land" also focuses on the professional struggles of Dr. Pillay. Padayachee neatly splits his story into two: In the part about the vermin occupation, he plays with metaphor and symbolism in a lighthearted but allegorical way. When the story moves to discussing the "real world," the narrative is shadowed by a grimness that mirrors the political circumstances of South Africa. In bifurcating his aesthetic approach, Padayachee expands the antiapartheid imperative to include generic innovation without necessarily subverting its revolutionary potential.[29]

"The Guests" similarly bursts the boundaries of grimly realist fictional convention by deploying the ghost story genre to highlight political issues such as the Group Areas Act and the forceful relocation of Indians under its auspices. Darrell, a white boy, has recently moved into a house from which an Indian family has been rehabilitated. The story revolves around his relationship with the ghost of Vimla, an Indian girl, who meets him every night and narrates the hidden history of the house. South African Indian fiction often uses metaphors of burial, hiding, and ghostly presences. The ruined temple in Reddy's "On the Fringe of Dreamtime," the secret Indian shrine in Sam's story "High Heels," and the spirit of Gandhi in Padayachee's "The Visitor" suggest that Indians are a ghostly, secret, hidden presence that needs to acquire actualization in the eyes of the majority population.

Significantly, the house is full of shadows, whispers, and the sounds of Indians crying. The haunted house serves as a powerful metaphor for the erasure of Indians in South Africa and their refusal to allow their presence to be negated. Homi Bhabha's comments on being homeless versus being unhomed are appropriate here: the latter is "'taking the measure of your dwelling in a state of incredulous terror" (quoted in Jacobs 200). Even though Indians are homeless, as the restless wandering embodied by the spirit of Vimla suggests, they refuse to be unhomed. In their work on "Ghosts and Shadows" in the Eritrean diaspora in Canada, Atsuko Matsuoka and John Sorenson state that the "concept of 'ghosts and shadows' . . . show(s) how the past is not forgotten, but is vitally alive in the present and shapes the experience of exiles today and in the future. The ghostly and shadowy past haunts the present of those in the diaspora as they create new identities on the basis of imagined homelands and play a role in shaping them" (153). In diaspora, ghosts become a symbol of home and the homeland that exercise a powerful hold on the migratory consciousness. While asserting the same nostalgia for place and rootedness, Padayachee uses the ghost to configure home as *house*, a literal dwelling place not situated in a mythic India but in the reality of South Africa.

In extending the "hidden histories" motif, Indian recipes are found in a secret compartment. While highlighting the pedagogical method (recipes, after all, direct, guide, and teach), recipes also suggest the systematic following of instructions in order to arrive at something complete. The appearance of recipes suggests that the Indian presence is a viable, albeit hidden, aspect of South African life. The raw materials are there. They just need to be methodically brought together so that the Indian presence can realize its fullness and complexity and cease to be a ghostly, shadowy presence. The images of recipes, ghosts, secret shrines, blackened ruins, and the recurring presence of the child suggest that South African Indian identity is simultaneously fetal, shadowy, incomplete, and unrealized.

Padayachee's fiction also thematizes the trope of "personal culpability," a motif recurring in Reddy and Sam's work. "The Finishing Touch," for example, reflects the anxiety that Indians will participate in the structures of apartheid rather than dismantle them. The protagonist, an Indian man named Muthusamy Coopoosamy, wants to change his name to a European one: Michael Cooper. Padayachee refuses to invest this gesture with any kind of serious meaning, suggesting that the transformation from Muthusamy Coopoosamy renders Michael Cooper into a figure of fun: "It was becoming the vogue for Indians to have shortened English names like 'Pat' for Pathmanandan or 'Terence' for Thenageran" (34). Bringing to mind Reddy's story "Friends," this story warns us that Indians' affiliating with the white population—the infiltrators and the colonizers—will only detract from Indian claims to South African nationality and defuse the potency of the antiapartheid imperative. "The Finishing Touch" ends with the transformed Michael Cooper giving "his friend a benign look of self-assured superiority much like that he had so often seen the whites give the nonwhites" (43). Nomenclature is not accidental here. Rather it shows us how Indians resist their Africanization by Europeanizing themselves, an identity change that also results in an attitude change from sympathy to superiority.

Unlike some of the later writers who hold black Africans as culpable as Indians for deteriorating race relationships, Padayachee, like Reddy, places the blames mostly on Indians, although occasional ruptures in the narrative suggest that black Africans themselves are also responsible for maintaining racial boundaries. The title story in this collection, "What's Love Got to Do with It?" is set in "the only black medical school in the country" and depicts a plural educational structure where people of different races, religions, and creeds not only interact with each other but are also intimate with each other (153). Almost. Ostensibly about the love affair between two Muslim Indians, Shenaz and Riaz, who are from different sects, the story confronts the racialism of supposedly open-minded Indians who are ready to befriend Africans but not allow them to enter their lives in any sort of personal way.

In the usual blurring of the private and the public that characterizes South African fiction, the inter-sect romance is set against a highly charged political background: The government arbitrarily decrees that the Africans be removed to a separate medical college.[30] "The response of the coloured, African, and Indian students was immediate and predictable—they went on 'indefinite' boycott and wrote to every medical body in the land, to UNESCO, and the World Medical Association" (165). The fraternity between Indians, blacks, and Coloured South Africans is emphasized here. The story ends with the government giving in and allowing the university to remain one of the few multiracial campuses in the country. In a move that deftly allegorizes the political, Shenaz and Riaz marry without the parental opposition they previously feared.

Teboho, a black African who is secretly in love with Shenaz, says: "'If a goddam Memon [Muslim] from a community different from Shenaz's could have married her, I shouldn't have been put off by these coolie clowns!'" (170). The comradeship articulated above is instantly undermined. Teboho is incensed that Shenaz can defy cultural prescriptions only so much. The idea of marrying a black man never enters her mind, even though she joins the boycott against separate education for blacks and Indians. Padayachee demonstrates how a confederation unable to invade one's intimate relationships and based solely on political oppression will only live as long as the oppression itself. But in having a black African describe Indians in racist terms ("coolie clowns"), Padayachee demonstrates also how blacks contributed to racial disharmony, a rupture of solidarity that South African Indian writers emphasize in the postapartheid period.

Thus Padayachee documents the limits of Afrindian identities; indeed, of their superficiality that precludes any intimate contact. His celebration of the Africanization of Indian identity is always aware, painfully aware, of the limits of its own ability to transgress. Even as apartheid-era writing reflects racial solidarity, it also reveals the tenuous nature of Afrindian identity, poised to withdraw into itself after the removal of the external structures of apartheid. *What's Love Got To Do with It?* foregrounds the imminence of racial antagonism that characterizes the postapartheid period. While Sam and Reddy focus more on the need for political comity, Padayachee, writing close to the end of apartheid, offers an anticipatory vision that reflects a different tension: the fear that the end of political oppression means the end of political collectivity. The end of collectivity means the dominance of specificity. Ethnic particularity existing without the corrective of collectivity implies the resurrection of the segregationist rhetoric of the apartheid past.

Gathering the tropes of collectivity and specificity in South African Indian short story collections enables us to examine the unique concerns and anxieties of Indians in South Africa. If collectivity runs the risk of reestablishing reductive binaries of us versus them, black versus white, the interjection of specificity infuses collectivity with a necessary internal diversity, reminding us that South Africa is composed not only of blacks and whites but also of Indians. Collectivity allows Indians to seek citizenship by participating in resistance politics and by affiliating with black

Africans. Specificity, however, expands the definition of citizenship to include Indians not only as blacks but also as Indians. But specificity has its own share of hazards that often end up consolidating the boundaries of apartheid. The recollection of collectivity, then, defuses the segregationist impact of specificity. Genre thus forcefully determines the prevalence of theme. The multiple consciousnesses underpinning these texts is reflected through the medium of the short story collection, which enables the authors to, as the word suggests, *collect* their various perspectives in one forum without being accused of being contradictory.

The tropes of collectivity and specificity also permit a reconsideration of diasporic discourse. The assertion of collectivity—with its strident claims to blackness—is a rejection of the unbelonging associated with diaspora. Instead, the articulation of a common blackness bestows not only citizenry but also indigenity on Indians. Yet the recurring representation of Indians in terms of incompleteness—as ghosts, children, recipes, hidden shrines, and the keepers of secrets—suggests that the Indian presence in South Africa is still a shadowy, insubstantial one, but will accrue the substantiality of indigenity and citizenry through its affiliation with black Africans. Reddy, Sam, and Padayachee also anticipate the shift in South African Indian writing in the postapartheid period, where belonging is affirmed by foregrounding the Indianization of South Africa rather than emphasizing the South Africanness of Indians. Yet Indians are only allowed to be Indian in the postapartheid period because they have demonstrated their South Africanness in the apartheid era. Lest the staging of Afrindian identity in this fiction seem too celebratory, it is important to underline that it is hardly uncritical. Afrindian identity is often determined by class, with upwardly mobile Indians aligning themselves with whites. Indian identity is also limited in terms of the *extent* of its Africanization, where racial attachment may mean public solidarity but not private intimacy. All three writers reveal the plural ways in which Africanization occurs, a multiplicity that can be appropriately recorded through the possibilities of the short story collection.

2

Essop's Fables

Strategic Indianness, Political Occasion, and the Grand Old Man of South African Indian Literature

In an interview with Rajendra Chetty, Ahmed Essop claims that his fictional oeuvre is marked by a focus on the diversity of the human condition rather than an obsessive rumination on political repression: "I felt that in my writings I should present a comprehensive whole, rather than selecting one aspect, the apartheid aspect, the aspect of oppression" (*South African Indian Writings* 352).[1] From this assertion, one might think that the Grand Old Man of South African Indian fiction relegates apartheid to just another part of Asian life in Africa. Such an assumption would be erroneous. As the carefulness of his rhetoric indicates, Essop stages a gesture of rebellion rather than one of dismissal: "That [apartheid] was one aspect of our lives. *It was not to constitute our entire life*" (352–53; emphasis added). Essop depicts the amplitude of daily life in the South African Indian community in rich, evocative, and humorous detail to make a political statement: He refuses to allow apartheid to colonize his consciousness and take from him the fullness of life. Despite this disavowal of the centrality of segregation, apartheid and its aftermath still determine the shape of Essop's fiction.

The smattering of literary criticism that has engaged with Essop's work in some detailed way also does not view politics as the thrust of Essop's writing.[2] South African novelist Christopher Hope claims that an all-encompassing satire drives Essop's fiction:

> What Essop does ... is to gently satirise all the major ethnic groups. ... He is, if you like, as disenchanted with his own community as with others, black, white, mixed-race, and others. Over all of them a kind of gentle ruefulness plays, and that is so rare in South African writing and so singular that I really can't think of anybody else who does it in quite this way. (Hope and English 103)

Although astute in his estimation of the expansiveness of Essop's satire, Hope does not link satire to political intent. Moreover, his assessment of Essop's writing as "bleak" and "gentle" misses the palpable political anger that fuels Essop's prose. Similarly, even though Robyn English concedes that Essop "makes a very effective mockery of the bizarre divisions of South African society" (99), she argues that Essop is "a writer who has turned his face against the overtly political style of many of his contemporary novelists" (99). These readings are symptomatic of other interpretations of Essop's work which claim that an "overtly political" consciousness does not govern his fiction in the way that it influences other South African writers. The refusal to centralize politics amid the plethora of other issues that Essop raises—marriage, women's rights, Islam, and sexuality—is an effort to recognize the internal diversity in South African writing during segregation. Important though that endeavor is, South African writers cannot but be influenced by apartheid. Essop may be far too subtle a writer to engage with politics in a crudely explicit way. However, the architecture of apartheid casts a giant shadow against which his work unfolds.³

In order to uncover the political texture of Essop's fiction, this chapter examines the connection between Indian identity and social upheaval in Essop's apartheid-era writing.⁴ Essop's novella *The Emperor* (1984) cautions Indians against retreating into ethnic enclaves. The *Hajji Musa* collection (1978, 1988) reveals the interplay of different nonwhite cultures in the supposedly Indian inner-city suburb of Fordsburg. If Essop seeks an articulation of solidarity based on white oppression in the first two texts, he rewrites his own rejection of white people in *Noorjehan and Other Stories* (1990), published in the watershed year that saw the beginning of the end of apartheid. Essop's Indians in this collection actively seek to absorb white people into the "new" South Africa, thereby earning their own place as citizens rather than as diasporics.

Essop's work thus stands as a defiant testimonial against the closed exclusivity with which Indian diasporas in non-Western geographies have sometimes been characterized. In an essay comparing the "old" or "exclusive" Indian diasporas in Fiji, the Caribbean, and Africa to the "new" or "border" diasporas in Canada, the United States, and the United Kingdom, Vijay Mishra claims that the former "were diasporas of exclusivism because they created relatively self-contained 'little Indias' in the colonies" ("Diasporic Imaginary" 422). Even though Mishra laments the lack of scholarly attention paid to the "old" diasporas, he still privileges new migration by suggesting that Indian diasporas in the West are marked by movement, flux, and change, unlike the old diasporas that are suspended in a state of eternal stasis.[5] In showing how Indian identity changes according to South African political circumstance, Essop reveals the possibilities for fluidity and exchange embedded in *all* diasporic domains, old and new. The changing Indianness encountered in Essop's work also speaks to the instability of Indian identity, indeed to the instability of self-knowledge, even during the period of antiapartheid resistance that demanded the presentation of a unified front. Essop reveals that Indianness is contingent on political circumstances and cannot be pinned down. His writing thus counters conceptions of Indianness as a static monolith, bent on maintaining a purist sense of self.

The relationship between politics and migratory identities also demonstrates the uniquely South African characteristics of the Indian diaspora as well as the impact of the Indian presence on South African conceptions of race. Segregation afflicted every aspect of South African life. Thus, the "usual" issues that characterize diasporic communities in other geographies—assimilation, a minority's will to power, maintaining "old world" cultural paradigms, and affiliations with other disaffected communities—take on a different hue. The debate around assimilation, for example, resonates differently in South Africa. The term has usually evoked nonwhite adaptation to the norms of the white majority in Western geographies. In South Africa, assimilation often involves a calculated integration with the disenfranchised black population and does not carry the derogatory connotations that integrating with white populations may elsewhere.[6] South African Indians acquire political power and national belonging through a strategic assimilation via the politics of identification.[7] Moreover, the diasporic desire to retain the old culture is subsidiary to the antiapartheid imperative. Indianness cannot help extending itself outward to embrace its African Other despite—or perhaps because of—the paradoxical presence of segregation.

Hybridity, a term that postcolonial studies initially normalized as the fusion of white and nonwhite, also takes on a different tone in South Africa.[8] The defiant mixing of blacks and Asians and their relegation of whites to intruders and invaders asks us to subordinate whiteness in our formulation of cultural hybridity in South Africa. The migratory selfhood ineradicably altered by apartheid not only reflects an East-South model of diasporic encounters but also foregrounds a South African manifestation of Indianness that disturbs the polarized racial categories of apartheid. Yet Indian identity in South Africa is not simply driven by apartheid. Essop's early fiction—spanning little more than a decade—also reveals how *quickly* Indian identity adapts to a political scenario that changes from the certainty of apartheid to the uncertainty of transition.

The Afrindian identity Essop adopts shows the extent to which Indianness has Africanized itself as well as how this Africanized Indianness is not constant but always *emergent*. AbdouMaliq Simone's thoughts on the mutability of Coloured identity are pertinent to understanding the changes in Indian identity that Essop's fiction traces: "Rather than thinking about ethnicity as some immutable essence, it is more accurately conceptualized as the locus of relations among differences whose content and boundaries are incessantly shifting—what Amselle describes as a 'fluid space of composition, decomposition, and recomposition'" (161). This chapter demonstrates how Indianness composes, decomposes, and recomposes according to political circumstances, exposing the extreme fluidity of diasporic identity in highly charged, rapidly changing political scenarios. If diasporics eventually "settle down" in the host country, Essop's transitional Indianness reveals that rootedness in South Africa does not evoke the stability implied by the terms "settle" and "rooted."[9] Instead, Indians make themselves more South African by marking their presence with the flux involved in adapting communal selfhood to the political moment.

Essop's changing Indianness always goes back to the desire for a citizenry denied to all nonwhites, but especially to Indians because of their "foreign" origins. Whether it is decrying Indian insularity in *The Emperor*, revealing the dialectic nature of Indian-African interactions in *The Hajji Musa* collection, or helping fulfill Mandela's dream of an egalitarian South Africa that welcomes even the white oppressor in *Noorjehan*, Essop's fiction depicts Indians as active agents of national change. But this ability to effect change alters Indians as much as they alter South Africa. Essop prepares Indians for democratic belonging by asserting their South Africanness through acts of political solidarity *and* by redefining the term "South African" to include a changing Indianness. The emancipatory citizenship acquired by Indians through their resistance to apartheid and by their participation in nation-making in the transition period allows Essop's later fiction to challenge the direction taken by the postapartheid state and hold it accountable for the failure of its promises.[10]

Isolationism versus Interaction in *The Emperor*

Essop's slim novella *The Emperor* was published in 1984 at a time when the antiapartheid movement was acquiring a momentum that foreshadowed the eventual demise of segregation.[11] *The Emperor* is also an allegory of ancient Indian history, particularly in its retelling of the story of the Indian king Ashoka (286–231? BCE), who famously turned to a life of Buddhist pacifism after confronting the human costs of empire building. In Essop's novella, Dharma Ashoka entertains similar megalomaniacal aspirations. The newly appointed principal of an Indian school in Lenasia, he proceeds to rule the institution with an iron fist. Multiple acts of rebellion erupt as a consequence of his autocracy, including the disappearance of Mr. Ashoka's son Deva. The novel ends with Mr. Ashoka surveying the spoils of his imperial plunder, but, unlike the character's historical predecessor, the fictional Ashoka is not given a second chance. Essop's emperor hangs himself, a suicide described in very stark terms in the closing sentences of the novel.

The novel thus deviates significantly from historical analogy even as it uses history to structure its narrative concerns. Essop's rejection of historical veracity can be seen as not just an abjuration of archival truth but also as the relegation of Indian history to secondary status in South Africa. The Indian past—here the historical narrative of Ashoka—can be transplanted to South Africa, but that past can never perfectly allegorize its African surroundings. Instead, stories from India must adapt to the South African circumstances in which they are recomposed. Essop uses Indian history as an allegorical meditation on Indians in South Africa, but Africanizes that history by changing Ashoka's story to reflect the segregationist scenario.

The Emperor is first and foremost a critique of Indian isolationism. Essop encourages Indians to discard the isolationist stance encouraged by apartheid and instead celebrate a politics of inclusion and interaction. To that end, Mr. Ashoka functions as an emblem of separatist Indian doctrine, whereas Zenobia, the English teacher, functions as an emblem of Indian interaction with the other races. In elaborating on Mr. Ashoka's isolationism, Essop criticizes the structuring principles of Hinduism that can be pressed into the service of apartheid, an analogy that justifies the exclusion of the Indian community from other disenfranchised groups on the basis of maintaining a distinctiveness of culture. The novella reminds Indians that they are South Africans first and Indians next. In order to fully participate in South African life, Indians need to expunge aspects of their Indianness that prevent the articulation of a broader political identity. Like Jayapraga Reddy, Agnes Sam, and Deena Padayachee, Essop warns us about the perils of an excessive exhibition of ethnic identity.

The Emperor also posits a parallelism between repressive Indian social customs and the repressive machinery of apartheid South Africa. Mr. Ashoka is the principal of the *Aryan* High School, although he later changes its name to Ashoka High School. The term Aryan brings to mind the philosophy of racial purity on which much of apartheid was predicated, as well as reminds us that the Aryans came to ancient India as *conquerors* and settled into north Indian culture.[12] In decrying Indian absorption with racial purity—who else but ethnic absolutists would commemorate the "Aryanness" of Indians by naming an Indian high school Aryan High School—Essop situates Indian preoccupation with caste and color as startlingly similar to apartheid's obsession with racial codification.[13]

The link between apartheid and Hindu social morphology in *The Emperor* is reiterated through an article written by Mr. Ashoka and Dr. Whitecross, the superintendent of schools, entitled "Differential Educational Criteria for the Twentieth Century." At the heart of the article is the assertion that "It should be evident to all clear-thinking teachers that the official policy of Differential Education as practised in South Africa follows closely the unique system evolved in India by its sages" (177). The fact that the Aryans supposedly established the caste system endows the structure with greater legitimacy in the eyes of the Europeans, who also claimed to descend from the Aryans. The ancient history of differentiation gives the rhetoric credence as "noble truth." Finally, the language of differentiation is couched in the language of civic reform: It stands for law and order. Multiculturalism would yield nothing but lawlessness.

The analogy between segregation and subcontinental social stricture is also important in terms of blurring the boundaries between ideologies in the apartheid and postapartheid period.[14] As I have shown in chapter 1, the disruption of racial harmony that characterizes the postapartheid period can also be located in the apartheid period, where it is subsumed by more pressing issues, such as the need for racial solidarity. In the postapartheid period, many black Africans foreground this charge of Indian ethnocentrism and insularity. In writing a text that is a scathing critique of Indian insularity, Essop almost seems to be warding off such criticism by highlighting how he *himself* does not support ethnic insularity. This anticipatory gesture further legitimizes his critique of *black ethnocentrism* in the postapartheid period.

Essop seeks to mobilize Indians into political action by showing how they participate in the very system that oppresses them. To become South

African, Indians need to eradicate hierarchical aspects of Indianness. Essop thus unequivocally condemns what has often been considered the heart of diasporic identity: the desire to maintain the distinctiveness of originary cultural paradigms.[15] Instead, *The Emperor* claims that the unique social scenario in South Africa overpowers the usual diasporic impulses, especially the desire to retain the premigratory culture. Rowland Smith suggests that Indian characters such as Ashoka

> reveal themselves—like many of their community—to be essentially guests, eager to adapt to the ethos of their hosts who hold power. To share genuine power in the host state outside their self-contained communities is neither conceivable nor desirable. This trait distinguishes Essop's fiction from that of black South African writers. The world they create may reflect the wonderland-absurdity of apartheid law but its centrality to South African life is never at issue. (69)

This reading is part of a theorizing of migratory possibilities that boxes Indians settled in non-Western regions into sealed ethnic enclaves and thus denies them agency and authority. Smith endorses the perception that Indians themselves do not want to be considered South Africans as they remain in a state of suspended animation, eternally poised to return to a mythic India.

Essop's writing, however, challenges this stereotype. Indians have been present in South Africa for centuries. Their memories of an India to which they can easily return have been irretrievably lost. The oppressive structure of apartheid also radicalized Indians into political action and therefore to an enduring commitment to South African life. In claiming that Indians "are eager to adapt to the ethos of their hosts who hold power," Smith suggests that Indians are also eager to assimilate into white culture. Certain characters may hold segregationist views, but they are invariably the objects of satire, which even Smith concedes. Instead of marshaling a cast of characters who cannot imagine what it is like to command "genuine power" outside of the hermetic confines of the Indian community, Essop seeks to activate Indians into political solidarity so they can earn their place in the annals of the nation as fully empowered citizens.

Nowhere is this critique of Indian isolationism more clearly articulated than in the allegorized figure of Dharma Ashoka. Mr. Ashoka is a purist, racially as well as educationally and culturally:

> During his inaugural presidential address he made this policy statement: . . . What happens in the outside world of politics and economics

is of no concern to us. If we drag the world into the classroom and get embroiled with its concerns the purity of education will be lost. (5)

Mr. Ashoka argues that bringing politics and economics into the purview of education will result in a jeopardizing of its *purity*, always a loaded word in apartheid South Africa. After he takes over the position of principal, Mr. Ashoka continues to impose a discriminatory structure onto the schooling system: Boys need to socialize apart from girls, and teachers are prohibited from teaching outside a rigorously structured curriculum.

If Ashoka represents the exclusionary aspects of South African Indian culture, then Zenobia, the English teacher, partakes of multicultural proclivities and refuses to categorize according to rigid taxonomies. As a teacher, she "made her range beyond the prescribed play, poem or novel to other literatures and cultures, from ancient Greece, to Persia, to India, to China" (40). Essop uses education as a metaphor for the isolation versus interaction debate set up in the novella and, through Zenobia, stages a rebellion against the separateness of apartheid. In refusing to succumb to the pedagogical dictates of Mr. Ashoka, Zenobia makes the world—ancient Greece, Persia, India, and China—into her classroom. Zenobia is set up as a viable alternative to the doctrinaire isolationism of the Indian community: what the Indian community should become as opposed to Mr. Ashoka's representation of what the Indian community should discard. Once again the uniqueness of diasporic exchange in the South African scheme of racial oppression comes into play here. While nonwhite communities have had to rally against white racism all over the world, the imperative to align with black Africans is unique to segregationist South Africa. Not only are blacks the largest ethnic group here, but South Africa is their land historically. By affiliating themselves with the indigenous inhabitants of South Africa, Indians can validate their own sense of belonging.

Essop seemingly disturbs his binary formulation of protagonists (Ashoka/Zenobia = Isolation/Interaction) by introducing a third Indian character, the hedonistic Prince Yusuf: "He was the most handsome man Mr. Ashoka had ever seen in his life. He was enclosed in fashion's best: there was an expensive, hand-tailored, dark brown check suit; a beige shirt and matching tie decorated with rust-coloured proteas" (86). Proteas may ring alarm bells, as it was the national flower of apartheid-era South Africa. Prince Yusuf represents another type of Indian, who is urbane, sophisticated, and ready to use his Indianness as a gateway to white life. He opens a fragrance store in downtown Johannesburg that caters to every imperial fantasy of Eastern stereotype:

> The façade and arched doorways [were] ornamented with gold Islamic calligraphy and foliate patterns in multi-coloured mosaic. . . . The interior of the salon radiated a soft aura of beauty and mystery, contrasting strongly with the carnival vulgarity of the other shops in the street. (97)

The store is a riot of color with ornate Islamic calligraphy. The inside suggests quietude and mystery, again tropes associated with the Islamic Orient. The contrast with the "carnival vulgarity" of the other stores that populate the street is significant. Essop's use of the word "carnival" is highly suggestive, revealing, as it does, a moment when social borders and taboos may be subverted.[16] Prince Yusuf refuses to partake of the carnival potential of his surroundings and remains, like Mr. Ashoka, a symbol of Indian isolation as well as a fetish of simplistic racial stereotypes.

When Prince Yusuf challenges the separation of races, he does so by establishing predictable relationships with white people. Mr. Ashoka's friendship with Prince Yusuf opens new vistas for him. In following Yusuf to social gatherings in white women's homes, Mr. Ashoka observes how bored European women approach the East as if it embodies the exoticism denied to them in their own lives. One of them tells him: "All my life I have been dying to meet a learned Indian gentleman. You belong to a cultured race of such ancient lineage that I can only tremble in your presence" (107). Despite the possibilities that the mere fact of interracial interaction in the highly regulated environment of apartheid suggest, Eleanor reduces Mr. Ashoka and Yusuf to symbols of a culture that is at once alien and exotic rather than an everyday part of South African life. This is asserted again a few pages later when Eleanor claims that "'Persians, Indians, you are all the same, coming from the divine Orient'" (111). The taxonomy of apartheid that relegates all Asians to an undifferentiated mass that somehow doesn't belong in South Africa is reiterated here. The word "divine"—evocative of a realm different from the earthly, the daily, the South African—confirms that even after a century in the African continent, the common perception of Indians is that they belong to the "divine Orient" and not to South Africa.

Eleanor then professes that she will be Mr. Ashoka's disciple, learning "truth at your feet" (112). Another woman is equally enthusiastic: "'How wonderful to be in a harem,' Anne-Marie yearned biting a toasted buttered roll, laden with grilled shrimp, 'to be bathed in perfumed water by jeweled black eunuchs and have poets read their poetry to you. I wish I lived in Arabia'" (113). If the excesses of Arabia attract Anne-Marie, Essop is quick to point out the excesses of her world, comprised of "toasted buttered roll, *laden* with grilled shrimp." Anne-Marie sighs for a harem where she will be waited on by black eunuchs. Of course, the irony is that she *is* being waited upon by black eunuchs: Yusuf and Mr. Ashoka. In allowing white women to reduce them to Oriental stereotypes, "black" men, Essop suggests, have been castrated. Mr. Ashoka's interaction with Eleanor and Anne-Marie may defy the segregationist imperative, yet such contact tends to be hierarchical and stereotypical, with the Indians catering to the Orientalist expectations of their white audience.

The racial interaction articulated above can also be theorized in context of the debate around assimilation that characterizes all migrant societies. Assimilation has traditionally suggested integration into the norms and paradigms of the dominant group. In South Africa, assimilation is a more complicated issue. Assimilating into black culture is politically liberating, even though it means an erasure of particularity; assimilating into white culture in South Africa, unlike Indian diasporas in the West, means assimilating into a minority culture. In Western diasporas, Indians cannot shun alliances—however strategic—with whiteness. Living in the West necessarily means a daily negotiation with white people. In South Africa, even though whites are a gateway to power, as they are in the West, diasporics can abjure contact with white people, as they are not the majority.

Thus, if Indians were seen as middlemen—interpreters between white and black—Essop argues that Indians should *climb down* the ladder of racial hierarchy and join hands with the disenfranchised. This is, again, a common rhetorical trope that we encounter in South African Indian fiction (Reddy's story "Friends" and Padayachee's "The Finishing Touch" come to mind here): Indian writers are extremely clear that aligning themselves with whites will compromise their claims to egalitarian citizenship. This rhetoric of identification also distinguishes the Indian diaspora in South Africa from its other global cognates. There are few places in the world where Indians allied with other nonwhite groups the way they have in South Africa, allied to such an extent that they undo the specificity of nomenclature by calling themselves black.[17] We see the emergence of not just an East-South model of diasporic exchange but a uniquely South African one.

The Prince Yusuf encounter, however, is more cautionary than diversionary. Stridently critical of Indian racial isolation, Essop nevertheless reminds us that there is a wrong kind of racial interaction and a right kind of racial interaction. The former never repudiates the gradations of apartheid, but instead actively participates in their conservation through cultural pandering and exclusivity—the only black people we encounter in the Prince Yusuf section are servants in the white women's homes. The latter is diffuse, egalitarian, and takes from many worlds, as Zenobia's global pedagogy reveals. Again, this allows for an alternative mode of racial interaction: one that pushes Europeans into the background rather than attempting to negotiate with whiteness.

After warning us against the dangers of the wrong kind of racial interaction, Essop returns to the dominant theme of this novel. Through the allegorized figures of Ashoka and Zenobia, Essop not only represents the warring factions of isolationism and interaction, but also injects this debate into contemporary arguments on Indian education. An article on the theme of education in the *Teacher's Chronicle*, presumably authored by Zenobia or her cohort, claims that education is diverse not divisive:

> By education is meant . . . the development of the capacity for abstract thought; the maturing of the range of human sensibilities, sensuous and sensual, intellectual, aesthetic, emotional, intuitive; the refinement of the perception of life values; the animation of the creative faculty where fusion of the imagination and the intellect gives birth to new structures and forms. (179)

Essop's characters often assert political collaboration and resistance through essays, manifestos, and newspaper reports. As we have already noted in chapter 1, the blurring of documentary and fiction is an important literary technique in apartheid-era writing. The more usual strategy is to combine factual occurrences into fictional genres. Fact thus masquerades as fiction. Essop, however, inverts that literary strategy: He inserts interjections that *appear* to be nonfiction into fiction. Fiction thus masquerades as fact. The slippage of fiction into fact not only gives Essop's writing more credibility by allowing parts of it to appear "real," but also shows us how apartheid-era fiction can be structurally complex without compromising the political efficacy of revolutionary writing.

If Mr. Ashoka's view of education, as articulated in his manifesto with Whitecross, is that education should be sealed from the tawdry world of politics, Zenobia's side claims a symbiotic relationship between education and political contingency. The "new structures and forms" borne out of the humane education they demand can be seen as an allegory for the Afrindian identity that South African Indians have to carve for themselves by interacting with the world outside, educationally, professionally, and socially. Although Zenobia loses the disciplinary hearing that Mr. Ashoka has manufactured against her for protesting his authoritarian policies, the court still recognizes her right to dissent. The popular support surrounding Zenobia, moreover, leads Mr. Ashoka to realize that his totalitarian tactics have failed.

Unlike the historical Ashoka, who finds redemption through his conversion to Buddhism, Essop's Ashoka is damned. When Deva vanishes toward the end of the novel, Mr. Ashoka blames himself for his son's disappearance: "Or—the thought came to him with the certainty of an apocalyptic illumination—had the god taken his son away from him because he was tainted, irredeemably tainted, in this incarnation? Yes, his beloved Deva would never return home while he existed. He would only return once his father's bad aura was no longer a presence" (188). Mr. Ashoka then hangs himself. The novel ends on the imminence of that action with the words, "he entered the strong-room and pushed the heavy steel door until it closed on the light" (189). Depressing though the last words of the novel may be, the ending is not hopeless if we continue to think of Mr. Ashoka as a figure of isolation.

Essop claims that South African Indians should abjure—indeed, kill brutally—all feelings of separatism, authoritarianism, and purity in order to seek political empowerment with other disenfranchised constituencies. That Mr. Ashoka's death is a suicide and not a murder suggests that the repudiation of oppressive discourses has to result from an internal self-change rather than through an external stimulus. Mr. Ashoka's use of the rope from the flag of the apartheid regime as a noose underlines the fact that it is his untenable desire for racial purity that kills him. Although the metaphor of flag as noose might be heavy-handed, its prior history in the novel makes it an apposite vehicle for Mr. Ashoka's death. As a dutiful servant of the apartheid regime, Mr. Ashoka had flown the flag on all important occasions, despite the outrage from students and teachers alike.

In having the Indian dictator kill himself using the fetish of white dictatorship, Essop brings together Indian and apartheid absolutism once again. He also asserts that dictatorship itself—both Indian and white *Herrenvolk*—must not only die a violent death in order to be eradicated, but that this revolution should be achieved through a process of active self-realization.[18] *The Emperor* holds Indians, and Indians alone, culpable for reinforcing apartheid-era boundaries, even as it reveals how many Indians refused to participate in racial divisiveness. In his next collection Essop shows us the vibrant racial exchange and political resistance that are possible when Indians and black Africans actually cross racial boundaries and engage in mutual symbiotic interactions.

Effacement and Revelation in *Hajji Musa and the Hindu Fire-walker*

Even though most of Essop's other work does not engage with politics in the allegorical way of *The Emperor*, apartheid still underpins his fiction. Discussing the stories in *Hajji Musa and the Hindu Fire-walker* (1978, expanded and republished 1988), Rowland Smith affirms the above assertion: "Essop's distinctive trait in these early stories is his ability to create both the minutiae of Johannesburg's exuberant Indian community and to suggest the continued menace of the larger outside world before which that self-protecting oriental enclave is humiliated and powerless" (65).[19] While Smith emphasizes the omnipresence of apartheid in this collection, the phrase "self-protecting" once again foregrounds the Indians-as-guests mentality that Essop constantly repudiates, while the label "humiliated and powerless" bestows Indians with a lack of authority. As I demonstrate in my reading of this collection, Indians are able to negotiate an identity that accommodates ethnic difference *and* authors agency for itself.

Smith also locates a dual imperative to this collection in its focus on the particularity of the Indian community and the ever-present threat posed by the structures of apartheid. I would add yet another thematic preoccupation: the interplay of nonwhite races in supposedly Indian areas. The sheer diversity of races, and the subjection of whites to foreigners and aliens, enables the articulation of an alternative mode of racial interaction, always incipient but never foregrounded in *The Emperor*: one that decenters whiteness and instead focuses on the relationship between Indians and other nonwhite constituencies. If *The Emperor* calls for the subordination of whiteness to the periphery of South African life, *The Hajji Musa* collection actually performs this relegation.

Essop is concerned with themes as varied as passing ("The Hajji" is about a character who leaves Fordsburg and is able to "cohabit with a white woman" [2] because of his fair skin and gray eyes), false prophets ("The Yogi" satirizes a man who claims to be a Hindu saint), female sexuality ("Two Sisters" examines the sexual psyches of two Indian women), and Indian gangsters ("The Visitation," a novella, spends most of its pages describing the relationship between Mr. Sufi and Gool the Goon). But I am not merely interested in a thematic recital of this collection; I am interested in how claims to Indian identity are curated in a way that may be peripheral to plot but are actively engaged with the macropolitics of life under apartheid.

As Essop maps the heterogeneity of Indians in Fordsburg, he describes the Indian settlement as a permeable culture in which people of different ethnicities interact so closely that it is often impossible to know who is of what race. In the story "The Hajji," the lead character travels to a white area for some work. Unnerved by his Otherness there, he climbs into the blacks-only section of the train back to Fordsburg: "In the coach with the blacks he felt at ease and regained his self-possession. He was among familiar faces, among people who respected him" (8). If home—represented through the idea of ease, belonging, and familiarity—exists for the Indian community, it is configured not as a return to an imaginary India, but among the "familiar faces" of the indigenous Africans.[20]

Imagine a person from India in the United States claiming citizenry through the idea that home is among the "familiar faces" of the Native Americans. Although Tilo, the protagonist in Chitra Banerjee Divakaruni's *The Mistress of Spices*, falls in love with Raven, a Native American, the novel pairs Tilo and Raven as victims of colonial dispossession rather than suggesting that Tilo becomes more American through her association with the original inhabitants of the land. Divakurani's short story collection, *Arranged Marriage*, also implies that Indian women often acquire belonging, agency, and empowerment through their relationships with white men.[21] The recognition that black Africans are the original owners and inhabitants of the land powerfully distinguishes the South African Indian diaspora from its Western counterpart, where whiteness is given ownership of space even as that authority is constantly challenged by the immigrant presence.

The affiliation with the African population is further emphasized in a story entitled "The Yogi," where the eponymous character, Yogi Krishnasiva, is persecuted under the Immorality Act for having sex with a white woman. The Indian community is outraged, not because of the Yogi's arraignment but because of the Yogi's penchant for white (rather than *black*) women: "I tell you he no like black woman. He black but he don' like black. He like wite goose meat" (30). Here, too, Indians situate themselves as black rather than Indian. In the story "Black and White," the main character, a young Indian woman named Shireen, taunts her white boyfriend by pointing to the sea of faces around her and proclaiming, "'I belong to everybody . . . to everybody, you understand. That is to blacks only, black boys only. Whites not allowed'" (93). In reversing the vocabulary of apartheid ("*whites* not allowed"), the title of the story ("Black and White") also reconstitutes race relations alongside a black-white axis, but one in which Indians refuse to succumb to the divisive nomenclature of apartheid that situated them in a separate racial category from blacks. This story also decenters whiteness. If Fordsburg is an allegory for South Africa, this is a South Africa where the different nonwhite races rejoice in their interplay and where the entry of white people into the scene of quotidian carnival is regulated.

Similarly, in "Gerty's Brother" the Indian narrator says that the street Vrededorp, "as everyone knows, is cleft in two by Delarey Street; on one side it is colonized by us blacks and on the other side by whites" (122).

This sentiment of "us" versus "them" originated from the Black Consciousness movement, which called for rejecting alliances with all white people. It suggests the remarkable commitment to South African life that Indians have and also underlines the kinship between Indian diasporic and African indigene, one that is marked by an alienation from whiteness and by similarity of oppression. As we have noted in *The Emperor*, the rejection of whiteness is an important characteristic of the Indian diaspora in South Africa, where, because whites are a minority, Indians can forswear alliances with Europeans even as they desire white economic privilege. However, what makes South Africa even more different is the *necessity* of alliance with black people.

While the Indian characters align themselves with the black heritage of South Africa, we are also pointed to the diversity of the Indian community in this collection. Essop thus observes the dialectic of Indian identity in South Africa: Not only does Indianness alter its nomenclature and selfhood in its intense affiliation with blackness, it also, as we have already noted in Reddy's story "The Marketplace," reveals how other South African ethnicities have been shaped by the Indian presence in their midst. In a story entitled "Dolly," the character Bibi is the daughter of an "Indian father and a Dutch mother" (38), and Mrs. Cassim in "Two Sisters" is "half-Chinese" (44), signaling the subterranean amalgamation of Indians with other races. These details are submerged within the main narrative and are not central to the mobilization of plot, but their thematic and political consequences cannot be denied: They disclose the impurity, rather than the inviolability, of Indian identity in South Africa.

Yet Indianness is never eclipsed in this collection. Story after story evokes the cultural changes that Indians have engineered in everyday South African life. Mr. Das Patel, a character who returns in many stories, owns an Indian café in Fordsburg. Essop describes this café as "eternally smelling of sweetmeats, sub-tropical fruit and spiced delicacies" (28). The phrase "eternally smelling" implies that Indians have brought their sights, smells, and sounds into South Africa forever. Characters with names like Soma, Aziz Khan, and Nazeem populate this establishment. The building that houses the café is called Orient Mansions. The slumlord Mr. Sufi in the novella "The Visitation" names his tenement Nirvana Mansions. The Hajji, in the story by the same title, affectionately recalls his days in the Islamic Institute (8). In "The Betrayal," possibly Essop's most politically fraught story, Dr. Kamal, who heads the Orient Front, has been schooled in India and has been a "professed disciple of Gandhi during his political life" (20). When the characters in "Two Sisters" dye their hair blonde, the narrator remarks that "they looked rather odd as blond hair did not accord with Eastern features" (40–41). Essop notices nothing untoward in the intermingling of Indians and Chinese, but *blonde* hair does not go well with "Eastern features." Essop stresses the artificiality involved in Indians trying to be white: They need to dye their hair blonde. While there is nothing "natural" in the Indian claim to whiteness, their claim to blackness is presented so matter-of-factly that it often fails to register on our consciousness.

In other stories, devout Muslims agitate against pictorial representation ("Film"), the corruption of Muslim women ("Aziz Khan"), and conduct Gandhian missions of passive resistance ("Ten Years"). In the story "Red Beard's Daughter," the character Red Beard "chews paan (betel-leaf). *He had never worn a Western suit in his life*. . . . When he was dressed, smelling of *attar* and with a red fez on his head, he looked like some sort of gnome" (99; emphasis added). Essop reveals how Indian identity is rigorously maintained in diaspora, but this identity is often juxtaposed with the articulation of a common black identity and therefore is rarely insular, as a similar projection of ethnic specificity might seem elsewhere.

Hindu cultural identity is similarly inserted into everyday culture. In "The Visitation," Mr. Sufi visits Yogi Krishnasiva, whose room is described as "faintly lit by a flame-bud burning in an altar table in a clay bowl, before a brass figurine of the dancing god Shiva. Several incense sticks bloomed and smoked from a small porcelain vase" (201). In another story, "Hindu fruit and vegetable hawkers were starting their old trucks in the yards, preparing to go out for the day to sell to suburban housewives" (3). However, when a sprightly young Indian publishes a magazine (*Glitter*) aimed exclusively at the Indian community, he is denounced by the Orient Front as being a pawn of the whites and *Glitter* is accused of being "a racist newspaper financed by whites to undermine and divide the blacks" (228). Like other apartheid-era Indian writers, Essop negotiates the dialectic of assimilation versus cultural specificity with aplomb.

Compiled during the height of the antiapartheid and Black Consciousness movements, Essop's earliest fiction suggests that Indians defied the strictures of apartheid by refusing to separate the races.[22] Theodore Sheckels claims that while Essop "advocates community and generosity," in *The Hajji Musa* collection he "shows characters and a community sadly rejecting them" (53). Yet Essop does celebrate community—the individualized Indian manifestation as well as the larger black political identity. Though Essop's narrative strategies may seem subservient to the trajectory of plot, they have political implications, revealing that even while Indians rarely erase their Indian identity, they seek social kinship by aligning themselves with the disenfranchised blacks.

By emphasizing effacement and revelation as political strategies that insist on the South Africanness of Indians as well as the Indianness of South Africa, this book sets the stage for Essop's subsequent narratives of Indian identity in African spaces. In making whiteness liminal, Essop points to the vibrancy of interracial exchange. This is an important departure from theories of hybridity that insistently focus on the joy of transforming whiteness and infusing it with a new vigor by the ethnic presence in its midst: Homi Bhabha's "interstitial Third Space" comes to mind here (*Location of Culture* 36).[23] Instead Essop argues that his nonwhites have no need for whites. Lest this sound almost like inverse racial prejudice, one should add that anticolonial resistance often operates on a continuum that starts with a rejection of those in power and what they represent. The later stage almost invariably involves a realization that a negotiation with the former oppressor is necessary. In his next collection, Essop revises his own stance on white people and actively absorbs them into the fabric of the nation.

Engaging Whiteness in *Noorjehan* and Other Stories

Noorjehan and Other Stories was published in 1990, the year that signaled the beginning of the end of apartheid. In this collection, very often, an Indian or Indian culture superintends political awakening in a white person.[24] This may bring to mind the "Magic Negro" paradigm in film. "The 'Magic Negro' is a term coined in the 1950s describing Hollywood's portrayal of black men as characters who, although disabled, have supernatural powers that allow them to save lost or broken white men" (Baldwin, abstract). The "Magic Negro" is never a textured character, existing only to evoke an epiphany in a white person. However, Essop's Indians are less altruistic. Not only do they exist as developed characters, but they also engineer awakening in white people in order to procure citizenship for *themselves*.

Essop thus affirms the contribution of Indians to the antiapartheid movement and also to the nascent nation. As Vasu Reddy points out, "*Noorjehan* shows the Indian in moments of politicization and crisis of conscience where questions of identity straddle the divide of the changing African landscape" (86). The significance of the publication date of this collection cannot be overemphasized. It is 1990. While apartheid is in the process of being dismantled, many South Africans are preoccupied with the question "Now what?" Almost everyone recognizes that for South Africa to be a multicultural "rainbow nation," whites—who constitute roughly 10 percent of the population—have to be brought into its purview.[25] Essop therefore rejects the racial insularity of the Black Consciousness movement—indeed, the racial insularity he himself advocated in his earlier work—and seeks solidarity with white people also.[26] In locating Indians as active agents of nation-making, Essop heralds their arrival into South African citizenry. Notice also how Indianness pivots from effacement to exhibition here. In Essop's earlier work, Indians proclaimed their South Africanness by dissolving Indian identity into a nonwhite melting pot. In *Noorjehan*, Essop suggests that Indianness sparks an epiphany in white people that makes Europeans more South African in their rejection of racial supremacy and by joining hands with the dispossessed to create a new South Africa. Thus, if Indianness—an ontological state that has been historically thought of as not belonging in South Africa—is used to make white people more South African, then Indianness itself is always already South African.

"The Metamorphosis," a crucial story in Essop's agenda of incorporating white people into the national domain, hinges on the radicalization of Naomi Rosenberg, a Jewish woman who finds spiritual solace in political opposition. She joins an organization called Pharos and becomes an active member of the antiapartheid movement. Naomi slowly develops a curiosity about South Africa's Indian community:

> Her interest in Gandhi led her into the worlds of Indian and Islamic history and culture. Mr. Habib, in compliance with the Islamic tenet that the quest for knowledge and its dissemination is a moral obligation, allowed her the use of his extensive collection of Oriental books. Her interests even embraced China and she read Confucius and Lao Tzu—and came to realize that Oriental civilizations were largely unknown to whites, just as African civilizations were unknown to them. (33)

Rescuing Islam from its negative connotations of fanaticism and militancy, Essop gives us another, less well-known aspect of Muslim theology: its dedication to the "quest for knowledge." More significantly, Essop brings together Oriental and African civilizations in a bond of mutual dispossession. As victims of white ignorance, both Asians and Africans represent the unknown that the whites have to learn about in order to earn, rather than simply acquire, citizenry in the new South Africa. This reverses the dialectic of diaspora encountered in some parts of the West, where the whites are the self-proclaimed autochthonous majority. In South Africa, whites are settlers *and* a minority; thus, like all other minorities, they need to be integrated into the auspices of the nation. The shepherding of one community into national belonging is often done by the larger community. The distinctiveness of Essop's effort lies in the fact that it is one minority that extends the privilege of citizenry to another, acquiring citizenship for itself in the process.[27]

This theme is reiterated in the story "East West," where, again, a white person comes into political consciousness through his interactions with the Indian community and with Indian belief systems. This story revolves around an Afrikaner security officer named Borg who enters the world of Tolstoy Farm and becomes a Hindu as well as an antiapartheid activist.[28] Founded by Gandhi to instill the values of nonviolence and passive resistance in its members, Tolstoy Farm sought to eradicate arbitrary categories of racial difference by welcoming the world into its confines. Ranjit, the spiritual head of Tolstoy Farm, tells Borg:

> "People who come to Tolstoy Farm eventually come to appreciate that the entire universe is a manifestation of the divine Creator and that those who see the world in terms of difference only end by making their own moral and spiritual development very difficult. I am sure you know something about Gandhi?" (62)

The name Gandhi always signals an awareness of political responsibility, particularly through nonviolence. Gandhi also represents self-realization, resistance to oppressive structures, and the erasure of difference. Once again, a white person undergoes a process of self-awakening with the help of Indians. Gandhi, Ranjit, and (despite its Russian name) Tolstoy Farm all facilitate the change in Borg.

In highlighting Borg's transformation, Essop underlines the importance of Indian spirituality on the psyche of white South Africans and the urgent need for a culture of love, tolerance, and nonviolence. In suggesting that the new South Africa be modeled along Gandhian principles of satyagraha, Essop claims that an Indian—indeed, the founder of the Indian nation—encapsulates the essence of the new South Africa. This suggests more broadly that Indians encapsulate the essence of South Africa, once again highlighting the Indianness of South Africa. Even though the title of the story foregrounds the usual binaries of East-West/nonwhite-white interaction, the unfolding of the story reshapes the dynamics of racial relationships along an *East-West-South* axis. Anywhere in the West, an Indian would probably not have been shepherding the white person into national citizenry; rather, it may have been the opposite. The agency Essop gives his Indians in nation-making emerges particularly from the South African context. Quoting Paulo Freire, Njabulo Ndebele says that "only the oppressed can free themselves and their oppressors from the shackles of the past. But for the oppressed to feel that the moral high ground belongs to them, they have to experience themselves as having the power to be magnanimous, generous and forgiving" (158). Even though Ndebele firmly believes that the oppressed do not "feel that power in our country at this point in our history" (158), Essop's characters not only reveal the ability to heal and reconcile but also the power that comes with being "magnanimous, generous and forgiving" (158).

However, the facilitation of whiteness into political awakening is not as easy as the conversions of Naomi and Borg intimate. In "Fossil," Jason, a liberal white English professor confronts the fate of whiteness in a manner suggestive of a nervous breakdown. A nameless, presumably Indian, student brings about Jason's radical realization. The student, who is described as "a handsome youth, with black curly hair . . . his face was dark brown in shade and his black eyes glittered" (103), wants to write a dissertation on Peter Abrahams. One of South Africa's best-known writers, Abrahams was catapulted into instant fame by his novel *Mine Boy* (1946), with its evocation of the gritty reality of mine life. That an Indian student claims Abrahams as the subject of his thesis is important: Once again, Indians identify themselves with the cultural heritage of South Africa. They refuse to succumb to the divisive taxonomy of apartheid as well as to the divisive taxonomy of the English canon. Jason, however, scoffs at the idea of a noncanonical writer like Abrahams being a worthy subject of scholarly discourse and rejects the student's proposal outright.

After the student leaves his office, Jason rushes after him, his mind a tumult of conflicting emotions:

> Jason's head was now throbbing in pain and was affecting his vision. In the foyer he did not find him and he rushed out to the portico. He was suddenly arrested by the bright sunlight that flooded the wide steep flight of steps at his feet. He put his hands on one of the columns to steady himself. The light on the steps fused them in a molten mass that seemed to come up like a threatening fire towards him, wave upon wave. (104)

In describing Jason's awareness of the limits of his own tolerance, Essop inverts the rhetoric of the apartheid state. The word "arrested" has powerful resonances in the South African psyche. The fact that Jason is "arrested by the bright sunlight" brings to mind the black people regularly arrested for crimes against the state. That it is "bright sunlight" that is the active agent of arresting suggests two contradictory things: Jason is confronting his whiteness and coming to terms with his complicity in the structures of apartheid that have imprisoned him and prevented him from seeing clearly, but "bright sunlight" could also allude to the dissipation of the cloud of apartheid and his realization that to live in this better world, Jason must abandon his lack of political commitment. The phrase "threatening fire" is also significant. Whites *will be* arrested and threatened by the new world order that the end of apartheid heralds, and they must come to terms with this loss of privilege through an acknowledgment not only of political culpability but also of political commitment. Even as Essop introduces a new rhetoric of inclusivity in this collection, which hinges between the apartheid and postapartheid periods, he indicates that Indians have already earned their place as national subjects and citizens; now it is the turn of the oppressors to prove their South Africanness.

Intensely preoccupied with the nature of race relations in South Africa, *Noorjehan and Other Stories* celebrates South Africa's imminent arrival into global citizenry by ending with the story "Pilgrimage." Upon embarking on a tour of Europe, the narrator encounters Liu Chih, a Chinese woman, in Greece. Together they survey the magnificence of the Parthenon: "As we climbed the steps and entered the colonnade, I looked up at the sky flecked with moving clouds and felt as if the temple was rising and carrying Liu Chih and me to the Orient—of Confucius, Buddha, Kalidasa and Shah Jehan (141). The triangulation of Europe, Asia, and Africa heralds South Africa's return to the international community after decades of isolation and also reflects back to the internal dynamics of South Africa (white/European, Indian/Asian, and African/black) that need to achieve a similar harmony. The collection may end on a note of hope, but familiarity with Essop's later work tinges the narrator's perception of being transported to the Orient with a prescient gloom.

Since their arrival in South Africa in 1860, Indians have been threatened with repatriation to India. In that context, the phrase "carrying Liu Chih and me to the Orient" is freighted with consequence. It is also significant that this triangulated harmony of the races can only take place *outside* of South Africa. Essop's later work describes the birth of a new South Africa in which the old issue of Indian "unbelonging" once again rears its ugly head. Even though Essop celebrates Indian arrival into South African citizenry in this collection, he also reveals the tenuousness of that claim to national belonging.

Noorjehan and Other Stories shows how Indians negotiate the politicization of white people, thereby further earning their place in the new nation. In drawing an expansive and egalitarian blueprint for the future, Essop imagines a new South Africa where even the former oppressor is welcome. Essop's Indians reject racial solidarity based purely on the commonality of oppression and instead incorporate white people into the purview of the nation. The *Noorjehan* collection celebrates the overt Indianness of the Indian community. Indeed, Essop suggests that it is this public evocation of Indianness, especially the Gandhian values of nonviolence and peaceful resistance, that will heal the nation. By having Indians evoke racial epiphanies in white characters using Asian associations such as Gandhi and Islamic scripture, Essop situates Indians, as well as the sensibilities and cultural effects of the subcontinent, as firmly entrenched in South Africa. Indians are South Africans not only because they have been disenfranchised or have fought against the apartheid movement, but also because they have helped integrate the nation by bringing white South Africans into its sanctum. *Noorjehan* reclaims an Indianness that was overshadowed by more pressing circumstances in Essop's earlier fiction and uses that Indianness to author national agency for its constituents. This transitional collection sets the stage for the elaborate open performance of Indian identity in the postapartheid period as well as subtly anticipates the breakdown of race relations in the democratic present.

A study of Essop's apartheid-era fiction reveals that segregation radicalized Indians, who found political voice, social agency, and national belonging by participating in the resistance movement. This will to power is highlighted in *The Emperor* and *The Hajji Musa* collection. The former explores the consequences of racial alienation on the psyche of those who allow themselves to be isolated. Voluntary isolation, Essop warns, furthers the separatist agenda of apartheid by fracturing the power of mass movements. The latter celebrates the vitality of interracial contact and the political potency that Indians accrue by affiliating themselves with the black population. The racial camaraderie articulated above, as well as Indian involvement in the antiapartheid movement, justifies their inclusion in the nation as fully empowered citizens, an empowerment even more deeply etched in the national psyche by their participation in nation-making as Indians, rather than as blacks, in *Noorjehan and Other Stories*.

By showing us how much Indianness shapes itself according to political circumstances, Essop's apartheid-era fiction reveals the extent to which Indians are invested in being full citizens of South Africa. Unlike the newer diasporas, which maintain links with the homeland through technology and elaborate networks of communication, we do not see a retreat into a mythic India in either Essop's fiction or South African Indian writing. Essop's apartheid-era prose demonstrates not only that Indianness is conditioned by political occasion, but also how its responsiveness to social context exposes the instability of ethnic identity. Diaspora theorists may have characterized Indian diasporas in non-Western geographies as sealed ethnic enclaves, but Essop questions the validity of this critique. That Indianness is characterized by flux also demonstrates that ethnic identity never fully comes into being; rather, it is always dependent on external stimulus for its existence. R. Radhakrishnan's comments on ethnicity are instructive here: "[I]dentities and ethnicities are not a matter of fixed and stable selves but rather the results and products of fortuitous travels and recontextualizations. . . . [H]ow identity relates to place is itself the expression of a shifting equilibrium. . . . [E]thnic identity is a strategic response to a shifting sense of time and place" (in Braziel and Mannur 121). Essop's fiction demonstrates that Indian identity *strategically* adapts to the demands of the moment, a fluidity that refuses to situate Indianness in absolutist models of being. Different political junctures require different manifestations of ethnic identity. Essop's fiction thus upholds the complex nexus between Indianness and South African political occasion. As the next chapter also demonstrates, it is precisely this fluidity that allows Indians to assert their rootedness in South Africa.

3

National Longing, Natural Belonging

Flux and Rootedness in
Achmat Dangor's *Kafka's Curse*

Achmat Dangor's *Kafka's Curse* (1997), a collection of five interlinked stories, is set during South Africa's transition from apartheid to multiracial democracy. While Ahmed Essop's fiction evokes the instability of Indian identity in the time of political change, Dangor extends this instability to South African identity as a whole, thus revealing the flux that marks societies on the brink of a radical transformation. A preoccupation with nation-making typically characterizes the literature of newly formed postcolonial states, with examples including Salman Rushdie's *Midnight's Children* (India, 1981), Bapsi Sidhwa's *Cracking India* (Pakistan, 1989), Chinua Achebe's *No Longer at Ease* (Nigeria, 1960) and *Anthills of the Savannah* (1987) and Ama Ata Aidoo's *No Sweetness Here* (Ghana, 1970) and *Our Sister Killjoy* (1977). While all the above-mentioned texts raise questions about the nature of the emergent nation as well as the rights and responsibilities of its citizens, Dangor reformulates "the national question" from an Indian perspective. *Kafka's Curse* represents diasporic minorities—rather than blacks or whites—as the new nation and questions what it means to be South African/Indian in the interregnum between segregation and universal franchise.[1]

Kafka's Curse also suggests a causal link between nation-making and the alleviation of diasporic psychic anxiety. In order to fulfill the promise of postcoloniality, a nation should incorporate even the most minor of minorities into its purview. However, Dangor does not conceive of a simple one-on-one relationship between text and nation. Instead, his work is suffused with a revolutionary momentum that not only reflects the nation but also anticipates and corrects its homogenizing impulses. "National allegory," to use Frederic Jameson's term, in *Kafka's Curse* does not merely mirror the political landscape, it also offers a vision of the perfect composition of the nation: one that bestows belonging upon outsiders and Others by enabling them to *become* the nation.[2]

Dangor allegorizes Indians-as-nation and their consequent empowerment through an elaborately conceived network of images that reveals how the intersection of apartheid and Indianness confuses the categories of postcoloniality and transnationalism. Each and every aspect of the text's symbolic configuration represents or foreshadows aspects of the public and political domain, both in terms of South Africa in general and the Indian community in particular. Symbolic morphology thus enables a useful reflection on some of the issues central to this book, such as the East-South model of diaspora, assimilation versus cultural specificity, the instability of South African identity, racial mixing, the Africanization of Indians, the Indianization of South Africa, and particularly the assertion of national belonging and the claiming of citizenry. Yet Dangor examines these issues differently from the other Indian writers we have encountered in this project.

For example, *Kafka's Curse* reflects on the trajectory of diaspora from not only India to South Africa but also *within* South Africa itself. This internal migration is represented through the protagonist's move from the nonwhite townships to the white suburbs. The blurred racial lines in Dangor's text further reveal an alternative history of Indian immigration to South Africa—that of slavery rather than of indenture or trade—thus redefining Indianness itself. Indian identity in *Kafka's Curse* is an intensely hybrid state of being that has intermingled with other races to such an extent that its "essence" has been forever lost. The Africanization of Indians encountered in *Kafka's Curse* is not a superficial blackness assumed for political expediency, but is located at the heart of one's biological being and created through extended cross-racial fertilization. Dangor's version of Indianness extends to the seventeenth century, when Indians first arrived in the Cape as slaves, unlike the indentured version of Indianness that originates in Natal from 1860 onward.

As stated earlier, *Kafka's Curse* is underpinned by dense imagery that allegorizes the state of transition that characterized South Africa in the early 1990s.³ The transition period spans the years between 1990 and 1994, when South Africans were celebrating the fall of apartheid but still awaiting universal franchise. As nearly everyone who has written on *Kafka's Curse* has pointed out, the thematic schema of the novel is dominated by the motifs of "racial mixture" (Sastry 276), metamorphosis, transgression, and border crossing.⁴ In its relentless documentation of the possibility of movement, *Kafka's Curse* reveals the untenable natures of taxonomies that depend on strict boundaries. Racial movement then reflects the changing political scenario of the transition period.

Dangor also uses intricate imagery to assert Indian belonging in South Africa. Dominant suggestions of rootedness and finding place include architecture, sculpture, birds, dust, and trees.⁵ The dual emphasis on movement and place is not contradictory; rather, movement and place assert the same political agenda. Flux suggests that national, diasporic, and individual identity operates on a continuum and is always subject to change. Belonging intimates that the Indian community has come of age in South Africa by nearing the end of the process of identity formation through the acquisition of South African citizenry.

Kafka's Curse represents not only the obvious shift in political sensibility, but also the less obvious shift in genre. Apartheid-era Indian writing is formally characterized by the proliferation of the short story and stylistically marked by gritty realism. Postapartheid Indian writing favors the novel as the dominant mode of literary expression and expands its thematic parameters outside of the story of political oppression. *Kafka's Curse*, as short story cycle/novel and as social document/magical realist fantasy, encapsulates the characteristics of both apartheid and postapartheid fiction and bursts the boundaries of genre, theme, and ideology. Fiction then provides a specular gateway to macropolitics as the transition period reveals literary sensibilities from both eras. Writing from the interregnum also shows us the impossibility of drawing lines between two supposedly discrete historical moments as each will always be inflected in the other.⁶

Dangor's impossible-to-categorize text consists of four linked stories and a novella, which appears right in the middle of the stories. The text invites us to collect the pieces as a whole even as each "story" stands comfortably on its own. However, the richness of *Kafka's Curse* emerges only after we configure the text in its entirety. Even though it is important to emphasize that this text is a sequence of short stories, it also aspires toward the textual cogency a novel promises. Here I foreground Jameson's claim that "all Third World texts are necessarily . . . national allegories"

(69) and Timothy Brennan's assertion that "it was the novel that historically accompanied the rise of nations by objectifying the 'one yet many' of national life, and by mimicking the structure of the nation, a clearly bordered jumble of languages and styles" ("National Longing" 44). The narrative unity of *Kafka's Curse* represents a desire for a larger national unity. The novel incorporates national allegory into the heart of its compositional structure to claim that the postcolonial nation must include all that has been excluded, oppressed, and marginalized into its imaginary. Thus, it is no coincidence that the Indian community finds voice at the very same historical juncture in which the democratic nation comes into being. Later chapters will demonstrate that Indians have the most agency and authority during the nation's nascence. As the boundaries of the new nation solidify, they also become more exclusionary, fortifying the discourses of Otherness and Self-Sameness that writers such as Dangor deconstruct so skillfully.

Despite this sense of alienation that persists even in the rainbow nation, Dangor's novel represents a community coming of age. Indians attaining majority in South Africa does not mean an external recognition of importance, but rather an internal awareness of a minority's rootedness in and centrality to the new South Africa. By showing how a text that is so invested in the specificity of Indianness can also allegorize the South African nation, Dangor reveals that Indians not only participate in the project of nation-making but also *are* the nation.

While Dangor's work focuses mostly on the "Coloured" experience under apartheid, *Kafka's Curse* articulates the particularity of Indo-Islamic anxieties in the transition period and the abiding interconnectedness of races.[7] The title alludes to Franz Kafka's "Metamorphosis," in which a man wakes up one day and finds himself changed into a beetle. At one level this novel—I am going to refer to it as such for the sake of convenience—is about a South African Muslim, Omar Khan, who transforms himself into Oscar Kahn, as Jewishness was a socially acceptable ethnicity in apartheid South Africa.[8] But *Kafka's Curse* also meditates on the nature of South African Indian identity, especially Muslim identity, in *postapartheid* South Africa and on what it means to occupy an alternative space, not only in the black-and-white world of South African race relations but also in a nation whose religious identity operates largely within the parameters of the Judeo-Christian tradition.

The title of the first story, "Moving to the Suburbs," deftly allegorizes the various kinds of racial movement articulated in *Kafka's Curse*. "Moving to the suburbs" suggests not just moving from slum to Arcadia but also, at once, an overdetermined transformation from dispossession to privilege, black to white, Islam to Judaism. As Loren Kruger argues, "Omar's passing into Oscar's territory is thus registered less in racial impersonation than in spatial and social dis- and re-location. . . . He moves from Khan to Kahn, township to suburb, coloured ancestry to Jewish pedigree, and perhaps also from Muslim probity to Judeo-Christian laxity (from Malik's point of view)" ("Black" 128). "Moving to the suburbs" also references the East-West diaspora that Indians must reject. If East-West migration suggests a movement from the hurly-burly of the third world to the manicured spaces of the first world, Omar's migration from the nonwhite townships to the white suburbs reinforces the East-West model of diaspora. However, the novel seeks an alternative trajectory of diasporic exchange: one that not only reconfigures migration across an East-South axis but also explodes the idea of geographic coordinates by demonstrating that all South Africans are marked by the alterity and flux usually associated with diasporic populations.

Omar's metamorphosis into Oscar is not just for material gain, social standing, or for victory in love. The answer lies somewhere in between. He reflects on the tragedy of miscegenation and passing:

> I cannot claim that Anna [his white English wife] brought this upon me, that for the love of her I broke the bonds of my beginnings and defied the ancient injunction not to desert the pride or clan, not to leave the village of rickety houses or climb out of the womb of our nation. . . . The fact is that I met Anna long after I changed my name from Omar to Oscar and, by reordering one letter of the alphabet, had changed the name of my father from Khan to Kahn. The ease, the casual sleight of hand with which you could change an entire history seems lost on those who are punishing me now. (32)

This is a summation of the paradox of maintaining Islamic purity in South Africa. Oscar is breaking "bonds of beginnings" that have already been broken by the first acts of migration: the great movement of Indians as slaves, indentured labor, and traders. The purity of Islamic identity, then, has already been irredeemably compromised. "The pride and the clan" have always already been abandoned. Dangor points to the untenable desire to maintain purity in diaspora, even if that diaspora took shape under colonialism and apartheid, systems that were nourished on the idea of absolute purity. In showing that all it takes is a rearrangement of letters to transform Omar Khan to Oscar Kahn, Dangor reveals the transmutability of racial and historical categories and the easy slippage of one mode of existence to another.

Although Islamic Indianness is the dominant identity that is staged, and desperately maintained, in this novel, Oscar is "a mixture, Javanese and Dutch and Indian and God knows what else, they would discover. He was the lovely hybrid whom Anna had fallen in love with, perhaps because of his hybridity" (14). Indianness is hatched and rehatched in South Africa to such an extent that it can never recuperate its purity. Yet *Afrindian* identity is articulated in another way here. If the term suggests the coupling of African and Indian, Dangor expands the constitutive parameters of the term to include Coloureds (as the Javanese would have been categorized) and whites (the Dutch). Dangor also moves away from the rhetoric of identification that characterized the apartheid period as well as his own earlier work. While he foregrounds the impurity of Indianness, in remembering Coloureds and whites as South Africans, he refuses to invoke the umbrella category of black as shorthand for all dispossessed South Africans. In highlighting the allegorical resonances of text as nation, Dangor reminds us that the transfer of power from white rule to black rule should not mean a transfer from one binary mode of racial thinking to another for in-betweenness must be incorporated into the body of the nation.

In-betweenness lies at the heart of Oscar's tragedy: "No, the antagonism was not between good and evil or between black and white. I'm still not sure why they became the poles between which I had to choose. I chose neither, of course, and that is when all this began" (50). Occupying an alternative place in the black-and-white map of South African race relations, Indianness is afflicted by a similar tragedy of unbelonging. Significantly, the night his illness begins, Oscar says he "was besieged by voices, cajoling voices, screaming, tormenting, vilifying, voices of unspeakable grief, maddening, beautiful. It took all my will-power . . . to keep me from rushing out into the darkness in search for their source, gurgling like a throat that had been cut" (54–55). Oscar has just revisited the township for the first time since his renegade conversion in order to attend his mother's funeral; the return to roots causes his haunting and then his strange sickness. We have already encountered Indians as disembodied spirits in Deena Padayachee's story "Ghosts," where the repressed return to stage their claim to South African belonging. Similarly, Omar's discarded Indian past will haunt Oscar until he recognizes its claims upon his sense of self. It is also significant that Indianness is described as "gurgling like a throat that had been cut." The violent erasure of the history of

Indians in the national register has reduced the articulation of Indianness to bloody babble.

National allegory is also configured through the chronological parameters of Oscar's existence: 1948–1996. Oscar is born the year that apartheid was institutionalized as political praxis; he dies two years after the end of the transition era, when an ANC government was firmly entrenched in the hallways of power. The violence inflicted on the psyche of nonwhite people who pass as white in order to purchase social capital manifests itself as a physical unnamable sickness. However, because Omar's dates render him an allegory for South Africa, Dangor suggests that South Africa itself has been passing as white for nearly fifty years and is now afflicted by the unnamable, incurable illness that racial passing necessarily entails.

The year 1996 also brought the first census in democratic South Africa. A census enumerates the inhabitants of a geographic space for demographic purposes. In other words, it makes a nation count *all* its citizens. The auditory resonances of census ("sense us") are particularly germane to South African Indians, who have been historically clamoring to be "sensed" by the nation makers. Oscar's death in 1996 can be seen as the coming of age of the Indian community *as Indians*. Indians who pass as white can no longer be numerically calibrated in the nation's composition. Significantly, when Oscar's brother Malik comes to collect his body, he finds nothing there except some fine powder. Oscar's clothes are folded on a chair: "a dark suit, white shirt and red tie, the soft white kofiya, very similar to the one he wore himself" (67). As the evocation of the kofiya (Islamic headgear) suggests, in death Oscar has reclaimed his Islamic Indianness even as Islamic Indianness reclaims him *by* death.[9]

In the South Africa of this novel, Jewishness is conflated with whiteness and becomes a form of social and racial mobility: "This oppressive country had next-to-Nazis in government, yet had a place a begrudged place but a place nevertheless for Jews. Can you believe it? For that eternally persecuted race? Because they were white" (33).[10] Whiteness absorbs Oscar so completely that he becomes inured to the racial practice of apartheid. He hops onto a whites-only bus without thinking twice about whom the bus leaves behind, becoming, as he says, "completely acclimatized" (34). However, boundary crossing is much more tentative than the social privilege attributed to it above suggests. Oscar marries a white girl of old Natal stock and is constantly uneasy lest "some manner or mannerism, a mispronounced word, a plural verb in the wrong place, some inherent fault-line in the crust of my being" gives him away (48). When Oscar's mother dies and he returns to his childhood home for the funeral ceremonies, he slips into the Islamic rites of passage with extreme ease. Significantly, he remarks as his brother waits to drive him home that he is headed to his "banishment" (54). Here lies the crux of Oscar's tragedy. The transgression of racial categories engenders not so much empowerment as much as the neurosis of exile. Oscar's Israel is not the Jewish Holy Land but the little community of Muslims in South Africa.

Kafka's Curse thus locates Indians such as Oscar in a "double diaspora" (Bharucha 67).[11] If the migration of subcontinentals to South Africa yields a model of diaspora unfurling across an East-South axis, the internal migration within South Africa—this time across an East-West axis *inside* an East-South paradigm—reproduces in Omar/Oscar the anxieties of assimilation, loss of culture, and transplantation that the state of diaspora traditionally generates.[12] Vilashini Cooppan points out that the "question of just how snugly South Africa fits into postcolonial paradigms is a vexed one" (348). Apartheid, in other words, troubles discourses of postcoloniality and transnationalism, its unique scaffolding necessitating a unique theoretical discourse. The need for a different hermeneutic lens with which to view the postcoloniality of South Africa is further enhanced by the Indian diaspora. The idea of an internal diaspora, for example, exacerbates the usual diasporic anxieties of place and belonging, thus requiring a new methodological approach—one that recognizes the dual boundary crossing that someone such as Omar undertakes.

The flux and instability that Oscar embodies are paradoxically reinforced by the rhetoric of belonging and finding place. Images of systematic construction fortify the nexus between Indianness and rootedness. Ian Baucom argues that "Englishness has consistently been defined through appeals to the identity-endowing properties of place. . . . [T]hese material places have been understood to literally shape the identities of the subjects inhabiting or passing through them" (4). Dangor uses places—including images of buildings, sculpture, and trees—to inscribe Indian identity into the South African land.

Significantly, Oscar first meets Anna in Durban's famous Indian locality, Grey Street, "Grey" appropriately conjuring up the indeterminate space between black and white that Indians inhabit.[13] An architect by profession, Oscar is sent to Durban to design a "huge tower with a revolving restaurant . . . near Grey Street. Alongside Muslim minarets and Hindu temples and Holy Roman Cathedrals would rise this phallus. Apartheid with its balls up" (44–45). The presence of Islam and Hinduism in Durban is asserted through architecture, a trope signifying permanence and place as well as permanence *of* place. While pointed to the religious diversity of Grey Street, we are also asked to consider the significance of the giant phallus emerging from the Durban skyline, allegorizing how apartheid thrusts itself into bustling, viable communities as well as hinting at the rape of those communities. Dangor has claimed that "apartheid . . . involved the slow destruction of Johannesburg as a city of communities" (in Judin 360).[14] The same can be said of Durban—indeed, of all South African cities. The communal harmony shared by the mosque, the temple, and the church is violently dispelled by the capitalist imperative behind apartheid.

That Oscar has been sent to forcibly insert a white edifice in the heart of an Indian area suggests not only that Oscar is (literally) an architect of apartheid, but also that Indians participated in the structures of segregation. If apartheid-era South African Indian writing exposes the density of allegiances between the oppressed, transitional and postapartheid writing reveals how fraught, and open to future rupture, those links always were. Even as *Kafka's Curse* celebrates the coming of age of the Indian community, it showcases the fragility of that arrival into selfhood.

The use of architecture to suggest national belonging is further asserted through Oscar's house in the white suburbs. Moving into the white suburbs means discarding the hustle and bustle of township life. But as *Kafka's Curse* constantly intimates, it is impossible to erase what has been left behind, for the repressed will always return. Significantly, Oscar's house is an amalgam of various artifacts, a hodgepodge in which he revels and that his white English wife's family scorns: "It's Oscar's choice, this mishmash of colours and dull shapes" (13). The mishmashed house represents the intersecting ethnicities in the New South Africa, the "dull shapes" signifying the discarded, the unused, and the ignored. Indianness, in other words, has lost its burnish because of Oscar's racial passing.

Yet the house remains standing even after the death and departure of its inhabitants, suggesting that, like architectural edifices, Indianness is a carefully assembled entity that remains in place even if its adherents abandon it. Indians can forsake Indian identity, but Indianness will stay rooted in the soil because of its gradual Africanization that fortifies its assertions of belonging. Significantly, parts of Oscar's house are reclaimed by his black servant Wilhelmina after his death, suggesting not just black Africans repossessing their land from whites but also the Africanization of Indianness.

The fountain of David standing resplendent in Oscar's house in the suburbs also claims belonging, even as David suggests Oscar's passing into whiteness. The statue, according to Oscar, "becomes the symbol of my resistance—the ramparts of my soul" (55). The description of the fountain further invites comparisons between Oscar and David:

> It was a simple structure. A young, boyish David had water piped up through his foot and out through his penis. The piping was made of metal and it rusted. Over time the rust coloured the water until he appeared to be peeing blood. . . . In a fit of shame and anger Simon took a garden spade and lopped David's penis off. David was left with a set of stone testicles and a gaping hole through which the bloody pee now gushed. (56)

Wendy Woodward argues that the "fountain statue of the castrated David . . . symbolizes Oscar's own demasculinised and deathly identity" (30). Castration suggests at once a horrific parody of circumcision, an initiation into Jewish identity—it is significant that David is a Jew—that can only come through pain.[15] As ancestor of Jesus and Christianity, David also embodies a normative religious history that Oscar is eager to own but can claim only through suffering. The broken male figure further brings to mind Saleem Sinai in *Midnight's Children*, whose crumbling body marks India's many partitions. Similarly, David's and Oscar's crumbling bodies represent the breakdown of South Africa itself because of the divisions of apartheid.

However, like David, Oscar's physical state of being remains a defiant testimony to the potency of boundary crossing. Keep in mind that David is not only castrated but also menstruating, a connection Dangor makes obvious when a character remarks that "David was peeing monthlies" (57). Menstruation suggests life—indeed, the possibility of a future birth rather than death. In evoking future births through the figure of the menstruating statue, *Kafka's Curse* suggests that Indianness is also a nascent presence waiting to be born. David also represents the boy-king waiting to claim his place in the sun. Dangor deploys the trope of boyhood to suggest that Indianness has been historically incipient in South Africa, but now, at the moment of transition, is *emergent* rather than *latent*. This assertion of growth through the figure of the boyish David is a significant departure from earlier South African Indian writers, who use the figure of the child, rather than that of the adolescent, to articulate their political purpose. By deploying the figure of an adolescent boy, Dangor extends Indianness to adolescence, thus suggesting that as a communal entity, Indianness is about to approach maturity. This coming of age is also proclaimed through the statue's paradoxical menstruation, a bodily change that suggests a transformation of the female from girl-child to woman.

While Dangor uses architectural symbols to assert the idea of Indianness as a carefully assembled rooted structure, he employs the trope of trees, particularly the humanity of trees and the treeness of humans, to carve a niche for Indians in South Africa and to showcase their coming of age in the new nation. After his mother's death, Oscar is struck by a strange sickness where he inhales carbon dioxide and exhales oxygen, ultimately metamorphosing into and dying as a tree. This literary inventiveness distinguishes *Kafka's Curse* from the straightforward narratives produced by apartheid-era writers such as Essop, Sam, and Reddy, who favor realism over magical fancy, putting him closer to Padayachee, who writes within the same time frame as Dangor. Postcolonial literature has always used magical realism—Gabriel Garcia Marquez, Salman Rushdie, Ben Okri, and Arundhati Roy come to mind here—a stylistic innovation that had been suppressed in apartheid South Africa and could only come into literary being under democracy. *Kafka's Curse* also heralds the South African Indian novel's arrival into postcoloniality, both in theme as well as in literary method.[16]

In the magical realist vein, the novel cross-references not just Kafka but also the Arabian legend of Majnoen, the gardener who is transformed into a tree as he pines for his rich lover, the beautiful Leila.[17] While Kafka and Majnoen are liminal figures conveying Omar's own peripheral status, Dangor uses Arabic mythology to structure this South African novel, showing us how South Africa consists of a network of crisscrossing races and cultures that not only share the same space but also bubble in the heat of centuries of cross-fertilization, a literary hybridity exemplified though the obvious references to Kafka and Ovid. Majnoen's transformation into—and rootedness as—a tree reflects the transformation and rootedness of Muslim identity in South Africa, indeed highlighting the rootedness of Muslim identity *through* its transformation into something as "naturally" African as a tree.

While inserting Islamic legend into the scheme of the novel, Oscar's metamorphosis into a tree also allegorizes his Islamic roots, which take him in a viselike grip and change him into something that is alive, yet isn't human. Such is the punishment, Malik reflects, for the sin of "his inability to accept his station in life, the takdier—the destiny—of religion, language, and people into which all humans are born" (64). However, it is also significant that Oscar turns into a tree whose roots are firmly entrenched in the white suburbs, anticipating not just the return of land to the repressed but also the putting forth of roots into mainstream South Africa by people of Indian and Islamic origin.

Critics have complained that the tree-turning in the text reveals Dangor's bleak prophecy for South Africa.[18] Woodward decries the pessimistic vision of *Kafka's Curse*, claiming that "the rigidity of the body-turned-tree symbolizes only the corporeal aspects of death and death cannot be regarded as a transformative possibility" (29). Devi Sarinjeive argues that Oscar "metamorphosises into a being resembling a depersonalised, dehumanized tree . . . his body shows the results of daily assault and emotional repression, the very antithesis of activism" (272). I interpret Oscar's death as not a death so much as another *metamorphosis* that changes him from human to tree. It is important to note that the *Indian* characters are compared to/become trees. Trees are a natural, organic part of the soil from which they have sprung. They grow roots in land, establishing their permanent bond with the earth. Dangor asserts that, like trees, Indians are a natural organic part of the South African landscape and have established their enduring presence in South Africa by setting down roots.

Anthropologist Liisa Malkki points out that "the naturalizing of links between people and place is routinely conceived in specifically botanical metaphors. . . . [P]eople often think of themselves as being rooted in place and as deriving their identity from that rootedness. The roots in question here are not just any kind of roots; very often they are specifically arborescent in form" (56). Similarly, Robin Cohen points out that "arboreal metaphors—like 'roots,' 'soils' and 'family trees'—are intimately related to [diasporic] ideas of kinship and national identity" (177). The proliferation of "horticultural images" (Cohen 177) in *Kafka's Curse* thus suggests a way of claiming national belonging through natural belonging.[19] Oscar's body becomes not only a site of trauma but also a locus of radical activism, especially in terms of the citizenship-seeking agenda that characterizes South African Indian fiction. Once planted, trees take years to grow to full size, just as South African Indians have taken years to acquire full citizenry. *Kafka's Curse* underscores the claim that Indians' acquiring belonging in South Africa is an extensive *process* spanning centuries and is only now nearing fruition.

The idea of trees as representing organic citizenry is also asserted through the colonization by foliage of Oscar's house in the suburbs:

> Trees that she [Anna] remembered as *innocuous shrubs had changed their character*, grown tall and intertwined their branches to hide the house from view. Even the wisteria creeper, an unimaginative plant

which bloomed briefly, and dutifully, each spring, seemed to have clambered up pillars and guttering and colonised the roof. Most mysterious of all was the foliage draped around David's torso like some emperor's cloak. (24–25; emphasis added)

If trees represent Indians and Indianness, then the shrubs wrapping themselves around David suggests colonization through foliage, a return to the repressed also asserted by the trees enfolding Oscar's house. Notice the metaphor of nature on a rampage here. The trees colonize the house in the white suburbs, ultimately hiding it—and its whiteness—from view. If Indians came to South Africa as "innocuous shrubs," they are now changing their characteristics to stand as fully grown trees, a progress through the stages of life also asserted through Dangor's use of the trope of adolescence rather than of childhood. This passage, then, shows us the coming of age of South Africa's diasporic Indian community. The phrase "colonised the roof" is also significant in its allegorical echoes. In the new South Africa, the oppressed will return to take over their land. The idea of nature colonizing man-made structures suggests that nature—which is the "true" inhabitant of land—will reclaim ownership over artificial, arbitrarily imposed structures.

Even though the motifs of flux and the symbols of belonging coalesce around Omar/Oscar, he is not the only character whose psychobiography reveals the twin themes of movement and finding place. Kafka's Curse, or the metamorphosis engendered by interracial contact, does not die with Oscar. It infects all who come into its ambit, including Oscar's doctrinaire politician brother, Malik, who adheres to a strict Islam. The third story, entitled "Malik-ul-Mout," is refracted through the consciousness of Malik, who, born in the watershed year of Indian independence (1947), allegorizes an absolutist Islamic Indianness in South Africa as well as its redemptive and traumatic possibilities:

> His white djellaba, worn summer and winter, swish-swished defiantly in the dull, brown-stone corridors where other leaders of the revolution acquired a studious sameness, blue shirts and red ties and black shoes that squeaked from their newness. His steadfast adherence to his religion and its customs—he never attended meetings on Thursday nights or during the Juma prayer hours on Friday, no matter how urgent—created a confidence in him, even with the primarily Christian coloured community which he represented. Malik Khan was a symbol of simple honesty, even among his opponents who called him Koelie Khan during

the bitter election campaign. Our people love the exotic, there's a bit of the pagan in us, they said good-humouredly. (80)

In an arena wrung into conformity by three hundred years of European colonization, where even indigenous Africans fade into the sameness of Western fashion, Malik's djellaba marks an alternative identity. Yasmin Hussain argues that "ethnicity [in diaspora] becomes overtly presented through dress, language and behavior . . . wearing traditional . . . dress signifies [allegiance] to the values and codes of behavior of [a] community" (30). Indo-Muslims refuse to give up their cultural claims, thus asserting their ability to hybridize the representational economy of postapartheid South Africa.

Significantly, Dangor does not italicize the word "djellaba," indicating the naturalization of Islamic words in the vocabulary of the new South Africa. Yet Indo-Muslims remain separate from South African society. Their appellations ("Koelie Khan") reflect the alternative history of indenture that other Africans do not share, and deep schisms exist between "our people" who love the exotic and "those" who are the exotic. Further complicating this analysis is the fact that Malik represents the "Christian coloured community," asserting the shared political relationship between Indian Muslims and other ethnicities and religions around them.

Thus, however absolutist he may appear to be, Malik also shows his ability to slide between categories. When looking at the remains of Oscar's body, Malik says, "'Ons mense begrawe nie hul dooies asof hulle op pad partyjie toe is nie' . . . his tone mocking. but the lilt of his words so pure . . . [that everyone stares]. . . . It was as if someone else had spoken those words, a ventriloquist hidden behind the conventional bearded Indian face that Malik wore like a mask" (67–68).[20] Malik's Indianness is described here as *worn* like a *mask,* suggesting that subcontinental identity is something that can be put on and taken off. The use of the word "ventriloquist" is also significant. That the ventriloquist is *"hidden behind the conventional bearded Indian face that Malik wore like a mask"* implies that under the mask lies not authentic selfhood but yet another series of performances.

The Indian identity to which Malik rigidly subscribes also veils the violent history of cross-breeding that allows for a "pure"—albeit performed—Afrikaans accent to emerge from the "bearded Indian face." Notice how this neatly flips his brother's role-playing, for under Oscar's "Jewish face" lies a submerged Islamic Indianness. The boundary crossing revealed here challenges constructions of the Indian diaspora in non-Western geographies as isolationist. In exposing the spillage from one race to another, Dangor reminds us that South Africa is a racial melting pot in which the essence of Indianness has been forever lost. If everyone is someone else and identity consists of performing one role after the other, then no one—or everyone—has claim to authentic citizenry and belonging. The unveiling of buried histories reveals that all South Africans are marked by someone else. Claiming citizenry through boundary crossing also contrasts significantly with apartheid-era South African Indian writers such as Agnes Sam, Ahmed Essop, and Jayapraga Reddy, who acquired citizenry by claiming a black identity, and postapartheid South African Indian writers such as Praba Moodley, who claim citizenship through place. Dangor instead asserts South African citizenry by appealing to the cross-fertilization that has taken place between Indians and other South African ethnicities, thus earning Indians a place in the annals of the nation.

Malik too abjures rigid racial boundaries by beginning an affair with Oscar's therapist, Amina Mandelstam, another hybrid of Islam and Judaism. At first Malik is skeptical of a dalliance with Amina, his unease arising from the inappropriateness of her name: "Amina Mandelstam. What a name to have to carry through life. At least Omar chose a name that did not jar: 'Oscar' had the same ring to it as 'Omar.' But Amina Mandelstam? What an aberration. That's what these bastard unions create" (78). But through Amina, Malik enters the world of hybridity—except his access to difference is through sex rather than subterfuge. Ute Kauer claims, "metamorphosis is presented as a strategy of survival, but on the other hand the very hybridity caused by this metamorphosis leads to destruction" (112). *Kafka's Curse* demonstrates that neither Indian nor South African identity was, is, or can ever be pure, and this adulteration of identity forges both cultural alienation and political manumission.[21]

Even as Malik is used to show how ethnic purists are also subject to racial flux and movement, his national belonging is further reinforced through the recurring symbol of birds.[22] Malik recalls seeing birds near Oscar's suburban home: "[H]e remembered only that they seemed such a fittingly funereal flock—had landed on the lawn the day he went to fetch Omar's body. They pecked at the grass with sharp, practiced beaks, impervious to the group of gloomy onlookers waiting, like Malik, for the police to finish their business" (89). At that point in the novel, the birds are also compared to the Sacred Ibis, a bird associated with Egypt. It is significant that the birds are pecking the impeccable lawns of Oscar's house in the white suburbs, suggesting that a "foreign order" is pecking away at the heart of whiteness, gradually remaking South Africa in its own image.

After his affair with Amina winds down, Malik dies. His death is described as a bird trying to take flight (148). That Malik is unable to take flight suggests that his roots trap him just as they trapped Omar. No matter how much you seek racial mobility—as Malik does with his affair with Amina or Omar does with his movement from township to white life—your roots will always hold you down. If trees suggest belonging and rootedness, then birds suggest movement or the desire to escape. But Malik is not able to achieve this birdlike state, intimating that even when South African Indians want to resist the demands of national anchorage, they still remain rooted to the South African soil from which they have sprung.[23] The bird imagery thus reveals the *impossibility* of Indian unbelonging in the new South Africa.

Although *Kafka's Curse* focuses on the psychic anxieties of two Indian Muslim brothers, it extends the motifs of racial movement and national anchorage to incorporate all South Africans, including women and other races. The theme of cultural alienation as a consequence of racial transgression also coalesces around the figure of Amina Mandelstam, who, as a female version of Oscar, is weighed down by the same hybrid nomenclature. Born and brought up a good Muslim girl but married to a Jewish European man, Amina embodies a neurosis of her own that is not her own:

> Since her return from abroad, she had constantly been confronted by this disapproval of her "foreign" accent, the loss of her native gestures and intonation. She had grown weary of telling even the most intelligent among her family that during her years away she had lived in places of exile—Dar es Salaam, Algiers, Toronto, Paris, New York—where she was also regarded as a foreigner because of her accent. She no longer knew, she told them, who "her" people were. (73–74)

If *Kafka's Curse* is a national allegory, one can see here the theme of the exiles' return and the sense of unbelonging they encounter when returning to a land that has changed dramatically in their absence. Amina represents not only the feminized aspect of Oscar's tragedy but also the exilic version of his dilemma. Oscar is exiled from the community of believers, while Amina is exiled from the community of South Africans—because of the erasure of their original culture through an act of migration. The intersection of apartheid and Indianness once again troubles the theorizing of postcoloniality and transnationalism by creating another kind of double diaspora. The neurosis engendered by migration in earlier centuries is further aggravated by the exile engendered by the apartheid regime, which arbitrarily rescinded the passports of any nonwhite South African deemed dissident. Thus, if the temporal longevity of Indians in South Africa assured their belonging in South Africa, the displacement of apartheid resituates Indians in the diaspora of political exile.[24] The second diaspora, however, becomes a way of acquiring citizenry, as it turns *all* other revolutionary South Africans into émigrés. The commonality of the diasporic experience, rather than its alterity, makes Indians more South African, even though exile, paradoxically, stripped dissidents of their South African citizenry.

South African commonality is further asserted not only through the intermixing of Indians with other ethnicities but also in Oscar's wife's white family. Patrick Wallace, Anna's father, has conducted a lifelong sexual dalliance with Fawzia, a Coloured woman with whom he has an even more racially mixed son named Azur:

> A boy stands between them, a honey-coloured, slimmer version of Martin and me, growing from baby to luscious man in photographs ranged like "the stages of man" in a natural history exhibition. He was more like Caroline, I thought. He grew androgynously lovelier in each of the photographs. Someone any man or woman could love with brutal abandon. And always the sea behind them. (178)

Dangor's use of water imagery—"always the sea behind them"—suggests that taxonomies and identities, even as they persistently surround and shape us, are, like the sea, always fluid. Anna's description of Azur as a darker version of Martin and herself suggests that all South Africans are versions of each other. That Azur is half white/half Coloured, half man/half woman shows us the transformation and transition that Dangor evokes through the trope of racial movement as well as the impossibility of absolute states of beings. As Vilashini Cooppan points out, "the interweaving of black, white, Indian and colored characters and voices in *Kafka's Curse* teaches us, through the preoccupations of the novelistic form, to reenvision the South African nation itself" (358). In recognizing that all South Africans—blacks, Coloured, Indians, and whites—are already "tainted" by other ontologies, Dangor claims that the new nation must abjure purist visions of its own identity.[25]

The history of racial interaction foregrounded in *Kafka's Curse* also has significant repercussions for this book's reconceptualization of diaspora discourse. It is commonly agreed that all diasporic identities are in a state of flux. South Africa's Indian population, however, reveals that diasporics intermingle with indigenes to such an extent that the composition of the receiving country changes dramatically as much as it seeks to rehabilitate diasporics in its own image. The name Azur further evokes the blueness—and fluidity—of both sky and sea. Blue also suggests a state of being that exists beyond "the color line." Even as blue explodes the idea of race, it evokes the latent Indianness of *all* South Africans by bringing to mind *Hindu* gods, who are traditionally painted blue.

Dangor, however, does not just locate racial boundary crossing in the transitional present, but also goes further back in time to trace the restless movement between racial categories that took place in South Africa, even before the establishment of the strictures of apartheid. Oscar and Malik's Afrikaner grandmother, Katryn, becomes Ouma Kulsum, erasing her Dutch heritage in anticipation *and* a reversal of her grandson's metamorphosis into Jewishness.[26] Sailaja Sastry reminds us that *Kafka's Curse* reveals that the "system thus contains alternative definitions of whiteness, whose presence demonstrates that whiteness as a category is neither pure nor fixed, but nebulous" (277). In its articulation of the various forms of passing available to all South Africans—from Afrikaner to Muslim, Muslim to Jew—the novel suggests that South Africa, with its politics of separation and segregation, not only invites this metamorphosis upon itself but also demonstrates that all categories are unstable and shifting. In marking each and every South African with mutability and unfixedness, *Kafka's Curse* claims that the *only* way to be South African in the moment of transition is to be characterized by change.

Yet Ouma Kulsum also exhibits the "neurosis of the converted," to appropriate V. S. Naipaul's memorable phrase:[27]

> Kulsum, rocking in her chair, read books in Afrikaans, listened to music that did not seem fitting for her home, smiling sadly when it was time to go. In the sealed-up shop below, abandoned spices (ingredients for Gujarati curries and medicinal balms) were stirring; pungent dhunnia leaves found solace in beds of red-leaved wara-bhaji spinach; baked by shafts of secret sun, kalonji onion seeds burst, their combustion soothed by char-magaj melon pips; illicit unions of fruit and flower, fenugreek and tymol, nelaphany roots and sprouted moong gave metamorphic birth to virile mongrel species each emitting a sweet scent of horror at lives so darkly conceived. (99)

Kulsum's unease at her own conversion reflects Omar's terror at his rebellion. Yet the quoted extract does much more. Dangor uses inanimate objects as a way of thinking about the idea of national allegory through interracial fertilization. The cross-breeding of the various spices and seeds represents the various levels of cross-breeding that South Africans undertake. However, this cross-pollination is at once "virile" and "mongrel," and it generates horror because of the awareness of its own transgression. Dangor's use of the word "mongrel" may echo Salman Rushdie's famous celebration of hybridity in *The Satanic Verses* as "a love song to our mongrel selves" (*Imaginary Homelands* 394). But South African Indian writers reveal the trauma of racial fusion, a fear that emerges from the secretive nature of the cultural transactions undertaken before and during apartheid. Thus, the idealized celebration of hybridity that often characterizes other migratory cultures does not hold true under apartheid.[28]

Dangor also invites a comparison between Indian food and racial movement here. Indian cooking is often about the mixing of spices. The Indian spices in Kulsum's husband's store have intergerminated to such an extent that the distinctiveness of each spice from the other has been erased. If spices in Indian cooking are meant to be mixed in order to create a dish (Indian food is regularly made with a fusion of spices), Dangor suggests that Indians themselves are meant to be mixed with other South Africans in order to realize the fullness of a complete dish. We have already encountered the trope of food in Deena Padayachee's fiction. Padayachee suggests that Indianness is like a recipe, just ingredients that need to be methodically brought together in order to realize the complexity of a full dish. Dangor uses food in a similar way, but extends the gastronomic metaphor to include other South Africans. Food allegory in *Kafka's Curse* suggests that *all* South Africans are spices (i.e., raw material) that need to be methodically brought together in order to realize the complexity of a full dish. If earlier South African Indian writers suggest that only Indian identity is incomplete, Dangor applies this formulation to all South Africans, claiming that to be South African is to have failed to have achieved self-actualization as apartheid deferred the fulfillment of national identity.

We can compare the South African nation to an Indian dish that cannot be composed with just one spice but instead needs the admixture of various spices to create something distinctive in flavor. Keep in mind that this is different from the melting pot/tossed salad culinary metaphor that has usually characterized other multiracial societies. While melting pot suggests that all difference has dissolved under the insignia of a unitary identity and tossed salad brings to mind different elements that are shaken together but still do not interact, the metaphor of spices fermenting in each other's aromatic heat conjures up a dish in which each and every item interacts together even while retaining *traces*, rather than the absolutist aspects, of its original identity. Yet because this mingling has been covert rather than overt, it has prevented the fruition of identity. As South Africa moves from apartheid to democracy, it also moves from hiding its mixed past to openly acknowledging its history of cross-fertilization and racial movement, thus paving the way for self-realization on national terms.

This violence of hidden cross-fertilization is also asserted through tracing the commonality of imperial encounters that all South Africans share:

> These unsaid things smarted in me all day, until I saw the Malik child. He could have been anyone, the product of a gene pool that is not unique, as intertwined as the history of our coming here, as slaves, as commercial subalterns of the white man's empires, as the fucklings of poor white women pressed into whoredom by impoverished families, nurtured on the sour grief of despoiled purity. (171)

Sastry states that in "narrating into existence the lives of Muslims, Indians and Jews, among others, *Kafka's Curse* reminds us of South Africa's position in a global circulation of peoples. The country is not a closed system, but subject to constant revision" (277). The phrase "constant revision" suggests that South Africa was always a meeting point of world cultures and therefore always marked by fluidity, flux, and change.

In announcing the diversity of Indian settlement in South Africa— "slaves, commercial subalterns, and fucklings of poor white women"— Dangor reminds us of the alternative story of Indian arrival in South Africa: as slaves. Few people know that in addition to migrating as indentured labor and traders in the late nineteenth century, Indians also arrived in South Africa as slaves in the seventeenth century.[29] Uncovering the story of Indian slavery also redefines the meaning of Indian as well as Coloured identity in South Africa. Kruger points to the existence of "apartheid-era geographical and ideological boundaries between the mostly Afrikaans-speaking Muslims officially resident in the Bo-Kaap [Cape Malay area in Cape Town] for three hundred years and the mostly English-speaking Gujarati Muslims" ("Minor" 71).

This distance is because the Indianness of the subcontinentals in the Cape has been hybridized so very significantly that it *seems* to have been erased by their incorporation into the Coloured population. According to

Kruger, "Dangor's characters . . . signify the trajectory of the earlier and unacknowledged forced migration from the area we now identify as India and the contribution of this diaspora to a syncretic South African identity, masked as well as marked by the name *coloured*" ("Black" 115). Dangor invites us to unpack the category of Coloured in order to sift through the synthetic intermingling that has gone into the making of mixed-race people. In exposing the common roots shared by the Indian and Coloured communities, *Kafka's Curse* shows us how the two races that exist between black and white actually have so much in common. Indian ties with the Coloured population also indicate that Indians don't appeal only to blacks to acquire citizenry, but also to that *other* shadowy group.

In recovering the forgotten stories of Indian slavery, Dangor asserts that the South African "gene pool" is an entangled one, making it impossible to separate black from white or brown or Muslim from Jew or Christian. *He could have been anyone.* AbdouMaliq Simone points out that "enslaved political prisoners from Indonesia, indentured labourers from India, diverted West African slaves, a highly diverse indigenous population, Arabs, English, Dutch, Portuguese all entered into the early colonial mix. All eventually engaged in various sexual combinations whose complexities only increased" (166). While few "host countries" have had Indian migrants biologically integrate so much that they become virtually indistinguishable from indigene, the novel also pleads for further integration. Since South Africans, black, white, and brown, share a history of colonial violence, it is impossible to separate them within the communal imaginary as much of the discourse in both apartheid and postapartheid South Africa has sought to do. *Kafka's Curse* encourages South Africans to look at their shadowy selves, for every white South African has a nonwhite cognate and every nonwhite South African seems to have yet another nonwhite cognate, but of a different race. Unveiling the buried story of racial movement has salutary repercussions for the new nation. In recognizing the interconnectedness of all South Africans, postapartheid society must not reject the Other, for the Self-Same is already constituted by its shadowy have-not. Dangor thus fortifies Indian claims to national belonging and composite citizenry by revealing the bloodlines between settler, diasporic, and indigene.

Appropriately, close to the end of *Kafka's Curse*, a white character has an epiphany about nature, Indianness, and South African belonging:

> Remember, Terry, during the drought that time in the Free State, when Ma had to cover everything with cloth—cutlery, cups, plates, food—or

this red powder would contaminate everything? And we still tasted it, fine, spicy, like curry-powder almost. These days that Rooigevaar is more daring, more dramatic. I saw photos of entire fields buried under the stuff, the sun blotted out . . . and here the hovels begin, the little cities in the veld, aptly named Rooiground. . . . I am almost home. (198)

According to the glossary, Rooigevaar means "red peril or the threat of communism" (224). The red peril is more of a brown peril in its association with curry powder, implying that the whites may cover everything, but this fine layer of powder will still spread itself out with an intense ubiquity. Significantly, when Marianne (Malik's son's Afrikaner girlfriend) sees "entire fields" covered with brown dust, she realizes that she is close to home. Think of how powerfully a subversive gesture this is: the association of something *Indian*, such as curry powder, makes the *Afrikaner* Marianne feel at home in postapartheid *South Africa*. Even more significantly, Marianne reimagines the Free State, "the heart of Afrikaner nationalism" (Cooppan 357), as being overtaken by Indians, an ironic fantasy considering Indians were banned from the Free State during the apartheid period. As a literary strategy, it reminds us of how Essop uses Indians to bring white people into the fold of the nation in *Noorjehan and Other Stories*, thereby carving a place for themselves in the archives of the new South Africa.

We are also invited to compare this dust with the fine powder Malik finds in place of Omar's body, suggesting that Omar has become the fine dust that settles all over South Africa. Notice also how similar this is to the timid shrubs that gradually colonize Anna and Oscar's garden, the birds pecking away at the manicured lawn of whiteness, and Malik defiantly wearing his djellaba to parliament. If Indians only tentatively articulated their claims to South African citizenry, as time goes on, they become more "daring" and "dramatic" in inserting their cultural claims into the South African imagination. While apartheid-era writers deploy images of ghosts, recipes, and children, Dangor reveals what happens when a community reaches self-actualization: It becomes bolder in the way it represents itself. This bold presentation even imagines Indianness, with all its connotations of flux and belonging, as a metaphor for South Africa itself. *Kafka's Curse* represents an increasing confidence in the articulation of Indian identity in democratic South Africa, a representational shift that is anticipated by the possibilities of the transition period and actualized—as well as ruptured—in the fiction produced in the postapartheid present.

4

The Point of Return

Backward Glances in Farida Karodia's *Other Secrets*

Despite the end of legislative apartheid in 1994, South Africans remained preoccupied with the segregationist past, especially with resurrecting the stories buried by the ideologically slanted record keeping of apartheid. While the Truth and Reconciliation Commission (TRC) is the prominent example of returning to the apartheid period, this backward glance can also be traced through literary production.[1] A survey of fiction published in South Africa over the last ten to fifteen years confirms this claim. *The Smell of Apples* (1995) by Mark Behr; *Deadly Truth: A Novel Based upon Actual Events in South Africa under Apartheid* (2000) by Israel Heller, Zelda Heller, and Janice Rothschild Blumberg; *Mother to Mother* (1998) by Sindiwe Magona; and *The Madonna of Excelsior* by Zakes Mda (2002) are only some examples of a long list of texts that go back to the apartheid past. According to Rob Nixon, "many writers feel that post-apartheid literature plays an invaluable role by preventing, through restless exploration, the closure of history's channels. . . . [T]o revisit history can be a regenerative endeavour. . . . [T]he result has been not just a return to the past but a return in a more personal key" ("Aftermaths" 76–77).

If return was an immediate consequence of the dismantling of the apartheid past, then another important repercussion of freedom was the innovation in literary production including generic experimentation, growing confidence in the articulation of minority issues, and an "excavation of . . . "repressed history" (Fainman-Frenkel, "Ordinary Secrets" 62). In opening the book's section on *postapartheid* fiction, this chapter uses Farida Karodia's novel *Other Secrets* (2000) to analyze the conceptual stakes involved in retrieving the *apartheid* past as well as the literary inventiveness made possible in the democratic present. While later chapters demonstrate even more changes in South African/Indian literary production as democracy takes hold, this chapter discusses the *initial* changes following the arrival of freedom.

One of these changes is the discovery of secret stories. Literature may serve as the custodian of untold histories, yet literary voices from the apartheid period have tended to be white and/or male.[2] The most famous examples that come to mind are Nadine Gordimer, André Brink, Athol Fugard, and J. M. Coetzee, writers recognized all over the world. The names of nonwhite men, such as Alex La Guma, Mark Mathabane, Zakes Mda, and others, could be added here. Nonwhite women's voices, doubly silenced by apartheid and patriarchy, are among the recently excavated Other underpinning postapartheid literature's revisionist impulse. But even this utopian project of recuperation is shot through with holes. According to Betty Govinden, "the theme of 'recovery,' of finding a voice, has underlined South African women's writing in recent years," yet "Indian women writers have to date been largely neglected" ("Against an African Sky" 84). Govinden claims that the process of recovery will always leave someone behind. Here Indian women are the forgotten figures, the other Others, in the public act of literary remembrance.

Govinden further points out that even the titles of postapartheid women's texts commemorate the uncovering of a hidden history.[3] *Other Secrets*, Karodia's most celebrated work and the primary focus of this chapter, unearths buried life stories. The "Other" in the title refers to the double Otherness of Indian women and pointedly underlines their erasure from apartheid discourse. "Secrets" refers not just to the secrets kept by the novel's main characters, but also to the secret that Indians constitute a viable community in South Africa and to the relative secret of their disaffection during the enactment of apartheid laws in the 1950s and 1960s. According to Ronit Fainman-Frenkel, "one of the 'secrets' that Apartheid attempted to conceal is the number of people who fell between, or formed the interstices of, its systems of classification on one level or another" ("Ordinary Secrets" 54). Yet another secret that the novel excavates is the precarious racial identity of people who do not belong to any of the rigid categories prescribed by apartheid.

Karodia's project of recovery, of uncovering the "secreted" voices of Indian women, is further complicated by the fact that her novel "unveils" the trauma of another disaffected group: Muslim Indian woman in segregationist South Africa.[4] While Muslim women's writing has become an increasingly important body of work in postcolonial literature—Monica Ali's *Brick Lane* (Britain and Bangladesh), Kamilla Shamsie's *Kartography* (Pakistan), the novels of Assia Djebar (Algeria) and Mariamma Ba (Senegal) are all important examples—the work of South African women of Islamic origin is virtually unknown internationally. Writers such as Karodia, Fatima Meer, and "Cape Malay" novelist Rayda Jacobs help fill this gap not only in South African literature but also in postcolonial studies in general.[5]

Other Secrets reveals the hidden history and psychic anxiety of the Islamic Indian community through the trope of return, a backward glance made possible by the opening up of South Africa following the end of apartheid. By rewriting her apartheid-era novella *Daughters of the Twilight* (1986) and transforming it into the postapartheid novel *Other Secrets* (2000), Karodia enacts a form of literary return. The difference and distance between her two novels also metaphorize some of the changes taking place in Indian fiction and identity following the end of segregation, especially the movement of the subcontinental sense of self from the childlike/adolescent state of being that we have seen in earlier South African Indian fiction to a multifarious *adult* identity.

Karodia altering her own narrative also suggests a new self-reflexivity and self-analysis that has characterized South Africa following the first elections of 1994. As Shaun Irlam remarks, "the literature of the New South Africa bears abundant witness [to] the emergence of a culture of introspection . . . [that] . . . records a steady retreat from the strident, public, and political character of writing to a more private, introspective, and confessional mode" (698). The apartheid period was marked by writing that often described and recorded oppression rather than analyzed its psychic ramifications. Karodia thus reworks her earlier novella in order to infuse her prior rendition of political oppression with the "introspection" associated with the arrival of freedom.

Literary return is also a methodological innovation closely associated with postcolonial literature: the rewriting of a canonical narrative in order to insert marginal perspectives or to correct its problematic politics. The most well-known examples include *Jane Eyre*/*Wide Sargasso Sea*, *Wuthering Heights*/*Windward Heights*, *Scarlet Letter*/*Holder of the World*, *She*/*Of One Blood* and, closer to the South African home,

Robinson Crusoe/Foe. Karodia reworks her own writing rather than a colonialist metanarrative; however, the effect of this rewriting is similar to the postcolonial project of appropriation, recovery, and rectification. In infusing *Other Secrets* with psychological reflection and fully fleshed-out characters, Karodia refuses to allow her later writing to subscribe to the formula of apartheid-era writing. She thus corrects the "mistake" of bland social realism.

The "introspective mode" fuels a historical sense of return. Karodia turns to the apartheid past in order to plug the holes in national memory. Again, this form of return is an immediate result of the changes in the political climate following the demise of segregation. Apartheid created a normative repository in which Indians were consistently erased, marginalized, *and* misrepresented. The postapartheid period allowed a critical reflection on the apartheid past as well as a resurrection of hidden histories. *Other Secrets* proffers an alternative archive, one that records the physical and psychic trauma of the unknown victims of apartheid. Irlam points out that the TRC asked "every South African" a crucial question: "[W]ho were you during the decades of apartheid?" (712). Portraying issues such as the fear of assimilation, adherence to an orthodox Islamic orientation, and the dual consciousness engendered by the tug of different cultures, religions, and value systems, Karodia answers this question *and* gives voice to a group whose everyday state of being has been virtually excised from national recollection. Thus, as Kruger claims, Karodia situates her characters "at the intersection of the collective experience of oppressed minorities and the autobiographical re-collection and gathering-in of that experience" ("Minor" 71).

Karodia's mediation of history is also anchored to this book's examination of Afrindian identity. Irlam calls for a "need to explore the articulations (and disarticulations) between recent autobiographical literature and emergent concepts of national identity" (712). By schematizing the psychic, cultural, and social lives of Indians under apartheid as well as revealing the biological intermingling of Indians with other races, Karodia's critical vigilance reveals how Indianness has altered itself to a South African context. This Africanized Indianness is infused with a sense of national belonging by its insertion into the postapartheid consciousness through the vehicle of the novel. Going back to the past is thus intimately tied to claiming citizenry as well as (re)defining South African national identity in the present.

Historical return further enables a reflection on how apartheid vexes our notions of diaspora, particularly themes such as the generation gap and the maintenance of religious and cultural identity. Karodia raises the issue of desire for assimilation on the part of second-generation diasporics in *Other Secrets* through her protagonist, Meena, and the sense of placelessness from which she suffers. Longing for belonging characterizes diasporas everywhere. In South Africa, the desire to belong in national terms is doubly aggravated by the structures of apartheid that denied a sense of "South Africanness" to nonwhites by separating them into ossified racial categories instead.

Other Secrets also frames the forgotten rehabilitation of Indians under the auspices of the infamous Group Areas Act.[6] The Group Areas Act forcibly expatriated many nonwhite communities from bustling, viable living spaces and moved them to arid, isolated quarters. While it was easy to segregate Indians in urban areas, semi-rural communities, like the one in which the Mohammed family lived, posed a problem, especially because nonurban Indians did not constitute large enough numbers to warrant corralling a location just for them. The act may have created an ethnically sealed space for Indians, yet, despite its best attempts, the segregationist government was unable to relocate semi-rural Indians, as they were too scattered a community to isolate in an "Asiatic" location. Plotting her narrative against the Group Areas Act allows Karodia to centralize the theme of return not only in order to rewrite the omissions, slips, and gaps in historical measurement but also to claim *place* for a community that had historically been denied a topography of its own.

The literal sense of return celebrates the exile's return to the homeland, a "coming home" embodied in the novel's protagonist and the novel itself and made possible by the change in political dispensation in the 1990s. The postapartheid period saw the return of the many exiles, Karodia included, whose passports had been arbitrarily rescinded by the white government. Meena's return from exile in *Other Secrets* allows her to reconfigure the various facets of her identity, thus enabling the emergence of a variegated self, the existence of which was often subsumed under the pressing exigencies of the antiapartheid imperative. Karodia's publishing history, shared by so many other nonwhite South Africans, confirms that the novel itself has been invested with the possibilities of return. *Daughters of the Twilight* was published by the London-based Women's Press. *Other Secrets*, however, was published by Penguin South Africa. In bringing the novel back to its origin, Karodia shows us how South African Indian fiction has also returned home.[7]

Literal return, like historical recovery, also reconfigures some of the normative assumptions of diaspora discourse across an East-South axis.

As an Indian, Meena is in a state of diaspora in South Africa. As an exile from the apartheid regime, she is also in a state of diaspora in England where she relocates. If a sense of displacement characterizes all diasporas, the circumstances of apartheid exacerbate the homelessness of Indians by creating yet another diaspora: that of political exile. In this double diaspora, home is not a mythic India but an everyday South Africa. *Other Secrets* reveals how the South African Indian diaspora is similar to Indian diasporas in the West, how those similarities—such as the generation gap, national anchorage, and minority unbelonging—are aggravated by apartheid, and how *radically different* the South African diaspora is from other diasporas.[8] These various traits of diaspora are not contradictory, but rather exist comfortably with each other. Even though the issues characterizing South African Indian life are framed by a larger rhetoric of migration, political circumstances simultaneously distinguish them from mainstream diasporic discourse.

Yet the novel's ending, in which Meena is suspended in an airplane somewhere between Africa and Europe, suggests that both text and character are unable to affiliate with any one location, a disavowal of anchorage that may locate Karodia within a dominant paradigm in postcolonial studies: that of the restless, rootless migrant. A rejection of place also distinguishes Karodia from other South African Indian writers who are harnessed firmly to South Africa, either by racial affiliation or by invoking their ties to the land. Analyzing the novel through the trope of return ultimately reveals not only the complexity but also the *impossibility* of return. Does the protagonist's inability to come home suggest the eternal unbelonging of Indians in South Africa? Or does it reveal, instead, recognition of the multiple loyalties engendered by the powerful intersection of apartheid, exile, and Indianness? *Other Secrets* invites us to explore how Afrindian identity complicates the act of rewriting, historical recovery, and the migrant's arrival home. Each aspect of return helps us unravel a different facet of Indianness in the immediate aftermath of freedom.

Rewriting Her Own Fictional Past: Othering Daughters

Almost a decade and a half after she published *Daughters of the Twilight*, Karodia published her magnum opus, *Other Secrets*. Both texts are narrated by Meena, an Indian Muslim girl growing up in apartheid South Africa. Novella and novel revolve around the strict adherence to Indo-

Islamic identity that Meena's father demands, the rape of her elder sister Yasmin by an Afrikaner, the family's forced relocation to the backwater of McBain, and Yasmin's decision to abandon the child of rape. *Daughters of the Twilight* ends at this point. *Other Secrets*, however, consists of a tripartite structure entitled "Daughters," "Mothers," and "Other Secrets." The "Daughters" section reworks *Daughters of the Twilight*, while the other two sections extend the dangling narrative of the earlier text.

After the death of her father, Abdul, Yasmin takes Soraya and Meena back to England. Following years of struggle, Meena becomes a successful romance writer. Following the dissolution of apartheid, she returns to South Africa, where she confronts the inevitable deracination that has resulted in her taking on an assimilated English identity. Meena stumbles upon the titular secret after her return home: Yasmin is not their father's daughter but rather the daughter of a white man whom her mother was unable to marry. *Other Secrets* pointedly highlights the racial cross-fertilization characterizing the apartheid era.

In traversing the distance between *Daughters of the Twilight* and *Other Secrets*, the most pressing question that comes to mind is why Karodia rewrote her own narrative.[9] Karodia has claimed that the "Daughters" section of *Other Secrets* preserves the structural integrity of its predecessor (*South African Indian Writings* 347). However, a careful mapping of one novel onto the other reveals changes that have important consequences for the thematic provenance of both texts. Minor differences include the age difference between the sisters. Yasmin is two years older than Meena in *Daughters*, but four years older in *Other Secrets*. The later novel emphasizes the gulf between Yasmin's worldview and Meena's, a gap enhanced by their difference in years.

Karodia also alters the father's background in the later novel. In *Daughters of the Twilight,* she states that Abdul was an indentured laborer (*Daughters* 24), but in *Other Secrets* his reasons for migrating to South Africa are unclear. The novel hints that Abdul was a passenger Indian who came to South Africa to trade rather than in servitude (*Other Secrets* 5). Passenger Indians were more likely to be Muslims than indentured Indians, who were primarily Hindu in religious orientation. Since adherence to Islamic orthodoxy is central to the conflict in the novel, altering Abdul's origins coheres better with the motor of Islamic identity.

Daughters of the Twilight is also less preoccupied with biological integration than its successor. We are not quite told of Yasmin's patrimony in any direct way in the earlier book. Karodia might have felt a greater need to foreground the theme of racial intermixing in the postapartheid climate in which *Other Secrets* was composed. The racial solidarity that characterized the apartheid period exploded after the end of segregation. Indians in particular were made to feel their foreignness even more. By adding the sexual boundary crossing undertaken by many South Africans in *Other Secrets*, Karodia argues for the deconstruction of divisions across ethnicities in the postapartheid period. Karodia, like Dangor, appeals to a common history of cross-fertilization that makes Indians uniquely South African. To be South African, according to these writers, is to always find the Other in your bloodline, heritage, and ancestry.

Meena also does not visit Johannesburg and encounter a group of young radicals in *Other Secrets*, as she does in *Daughters of the Twilight*. Although she meets South African activists in London, the later novel focuses on the emotional texture of its protagonist's psyche rather than on her overt politicization, thus signaling an important shift from the social realism of the apartheid period to the ruminative mode of the postapartheid era. Finally, *Daughters of the Twilight* contains a scene of reclassification, depicting in elaborate detail the humiliating procedure necessary for a change in racial categorization. In *Other Secrets*, Meena's reclassification is dismissed in a sentence: "I had finally decided to have myself reclassified as Coloured, in order to keep my teaching post" (185). By relegating the process of reclassification to a single terse phrase, Karodia refuses to give the agonizing procedure narrative space, thereby defusing its importance in her imaginative world. The negation of the significance of this boundary crossing also anticipates Meena's occasionally cavalier attitude toward her assuming an assimilated English identity. Paradoxically, it further signals Meena's repudiation of apartheid taxonomies by not taking ethnic categorization seriously *anywhere.*

According to Chetty, *Other Secrets* "explores the mother-daughter relationship in the running crisis of the apartheid situation, updating it to include new family alignments in the post-apartheid South Africa" (*Indias Abroad* 143). The "new family alignments" include the reimagined dynamics of not just the Mohammed family but also the family of Indians in South Africa. The relationship between Karodia's two novels allegorizes the initial stylistic and thematic changes in Indian fiction in the postapartheid period. As it was written in the 1980s, a decade that saw the urgent need to unite the nonwhite population in order to dismantle apartheid, *Daughters of the Twilight* relies on the effacement and strategic revelation of ethnic identity in order to garner political agency.[10] *Other Secrets* rarely imposes erasure on itself, especially in the later sections of the novel, even as it discusses the forced invisibility of Indians under apartheid. This is because the need to seek political franchise by absorbing Indians into a larger constituency is less urgent in the postapartheid era.

Acutely aware of the disavowal of Indians in the apartheid fantasy of racial ordering, Karodia inserts Indians into South African life by returning to the past and broadcasting their disaffection under apartheid in *Other Secrets*. Unlike its predecessor, *Other Secrets* demonstrates a confident, if conflicted, articulation of Afrindian identity, especially in the second half of the novel. This is reflected in a change in both style and tone. *Daughters of the Twilight* refuses to embrace narrative closure by leaving characters dangling. The later novel discusses not just the process of assembling a multifarious identity but also the final mosaic of identity itself. Thus, if Indian identity exists in a thwarted, unfulfilled state during apartheid, its particularity often negated by the need for racial solidarity, the postapartheid period reveals the multiple contradictory strands that compose this identity. Appropriately, *Daughters* focuses only on the figure of the girl-child. *Other Secrets* traces the growth of the girl-child to an adult woman, suggesting that Indian identity itself has grown up and assumed all the complexity of adult biographies. Literary return allows Karodia to trace the progression of this identity from past to present as well as hint at its future possibilities.

Because political change is less urgent, postapartheid fiction also often abandons social documentation and becomes more experimental stylistically, favoring genres such as magic realism and the comic style of the big nineteenth-century novel. Size matters too. Big books are hard to come by in apartheid-era prose, probably because all writing deemed to be subversive was banned and apt to be confiscated. Apartheid-era literature needed to be easily hidden. Moreover, certain ethical rationales determined its literary agenda. Political content could not be compromised by psychological meditation; the argument needed to be crisp and clearly stated. As Njabulo Ndebele argues:

> What is on display [in apartheid-era writing] is the spectacle of social absurdity. . . . The necessary ingredients of this display are precisely the triteness and barrenness of thought, the almost deliberate waste of intellectual energies on trivialities. It is, in fact, the "emptying out of interiority to the benefit of its exterior signs, [the] exhaustion of the content by the form." The overwhelming form is the method of displaying the culture of oppression to the utmost in bewilderment. (42)

Daughters of the Twilight, in keeping with other apartheid writing, may sacrifice "interiority" in order to foreground "exterior signs." *Other Secrets*, in keeping with postapartheid writing, reflects the changes that have taken place with the advent of democracy. Written in the psychologically realistic, emotionally finessed style of George Eliot, it runs 456 pages. *Daughter of the Twilight,* true to apartheid-era writing, is only 150 pages long. Anthropologist Thomas Hansen points out that in South African Indian drama, by "the early 1990s, the powerful trends towards either political satire or family farces began to reverse somewhat and more subtle and poetic work without explicit or didactic agendas began to re-emerge" ("Plays" 265). A similar shift can be charted in Karodia's fiction, perhaps even in South African Indian fiction as a whole. In reverting to its own narrative past, *Other Secrets* discards the *explicitly* political overtones of *Daughters of the Twilight,* even though political idiom fortifies its fictional structure. Indeed, after a point, *Other Secrets* ceases to be about either Indians or South Africans and instead exists in a timeless, placeless zone where the emotional contiguity between women seems to be the text's primary structuring thematic.[11]

The space between *Daughters of the Twilight* and *Other Secrets* does not merely showcase the distance traveled by Karodia as a writer; it also metonymically reveals some of the early aesthetic and thematic shifts in South African Indian fiction from the apartheid to the postapartheid period. As we have seen in the first section on apartheid-era prose, writers such as Jayapraga Reddy, Agnes Sam, Deena Padayachee, and Ahmed Essop favored the short story and the novella that were also written primarily in the mode of social realism. The need to assert solidarity with other nonwhite groups in order to combat segregation was the "categorical imperative" underpinning Indian literature. Even though writers like Padayachee attempted to infuse some fantasy and levity into their writing, psychological introspection was kept to a minimum.

It is in the transition period that we begin to note a change through novels such as *Kafka's Curse* that deploy magical realism and fantasy to discuss political transformation. Karodia takes this literary and generic turn even further by infusing her writing with intense psychological meditation. This shift—from documentary realism to introspection, from short prose to big books—is not only indicative of a shift in Indian writing but also suggests an increased confidence in the way that Indians have imagined their place in South Africa today. Karodia's backward glance at her fictional past in order to flesh out Indian identity reflects not only the growth of a writer but also the growth of a community in self-consciously literary ways.

Chapter 4
Excavating Buried Biographies: A Historical Return to the Segregationist Past

Literary rewriting further enables the project of historical return. The first two sections of *Other Secrets,* entitled "Daughters" and "Mothers," concentrate on revising the apartheid past in order to recover the complexity of Indian identity under segregation, unfurl diaspora across an East-South axis, and assert South African nationality for Indians in the postapartheid present. Karodia infuses the representation of Afrindian identity during apartheid with the psychological introspection that marks the postapartheid period, revealing not only the oppression of Indians but also the emotional and mental consequences of that victimization. Historical return enables the excavation of an Afrindian identity by exposing how Indianness, even as it struggles to maintain an absolutist sense of self, is never pure. Instead, Indianness actively engages with South African social structures and Africanizes itself. In revealing the history of interracial intimacy, Karodia also demonstrates the *biological* Africanization of Indian identity. *Other Secrets* claims Indian belonging in South Africa by remembering a shared story of suffering as well as cultural and cross-racial fertilization.

In *Other Secrets,* Indian selfhood is initially hesitant, tentative, and prone to erasure, even as this identity is rigorously maintained through the will of the father. That the protagonist is the child of an Indian Muslim father and a Coloured Christian mother also exposes the fragility of Indianness. The splitting of identity, religion, and culture engenders a bifurcated selfhood. Meena's "double consciousness" can be integrated only through the death of the father and a physical withdrawal from South Africa.[12] The identity Meena forges in the end, what she calls the "place which reflected the geography of my soul" (310), is rootless *and* composite, suggesting both the fragmentation and the restorative capacities of exile.

Other Secrets also raises questions about the place of Islamic Indianness in South Africa.[13] Meena's father, Abdul, who came to South Africa as a passenger Indian at the age of seventeen, "during the height of the Mahatma Gandhi inspired resistance campaigns" (5), is associated with the Islamic Indianness that the rest of the family struggles to maintain. For example, Abdul utters the Islamic benediction *bismillah* before meals (33). Meena and her family also observe Ramadan with the flourish of the devout: "during this month of fasting, like millions of other Muslims throughout the world, we were up before sunrise to prepare and eat the last meal of the day" (64). Here Meena yokes her family to the *ummah* or the global community of Islamic believers, extending her identity outside of South Africa not only to India, but also to a pan-Islamic confederacy. Do Indian Muslims jeopardize their already tenuous claims to citizenry by claiming affiliation with the worldwide federation of Islamic believers and asserting ties to an imagined India rather than the local habitation of South Africa? Can a pan-Islamic identity exist comfortably with a South African one, or do the two contradict each other in their demands for allegiance? How does a community already apart because of race, religion, and culture claim a South African identity without compromising its Indian past and without consolidating the demarcations established by apartheid? Abdul's tenacious clinging to an insular Islamic Indianness raises important questions in this novel and in South African Indian fiction in general.

The preservation of Indianness in diaspora thus often rests in private, especially familial, life. According to Thomas Hansen, "the most precious construction of all, the Indian family [is] the heart of every claim to the distinctiveness of Indian ethnicity in South Africa" ("Plays" 255). Meena's family is no exception in this regard. Ashwin Desai and Brij Maharaj claim that "the Indian family [in South Africa] continues to be very conservative and extremely authoritarian. The father-figure is inscribed very heavily as the decision-maker and disciplinarian. . . . [L]ike other patriarchs, the father's role is to enforce a morality aimed to produce 'acquiescent subjects'" ("Minorities in the Rainbow Nation").[14] Abdul thus submits to a rigid standard of social behavior, especially where his daughters are concerned.[15]

By giving narrative space to the Mohammed family's everyday state of being, Karodia interjects Indo-Islamic conflicts into public discourse. She also shows us how Indian identity alters, with the first generation that actually came from India clinging more tenaciously to its Indian roots than the generation that is born and brought up in South Africa. The tensions between Meena and her father also reveal that, though the South African Indian diaspora invites us to construct a new model of diasporic contact, some of its features, such as the generational conflict, are startlingly similar to diasporas everywhere.[16] In highlighting Meena's conflict and by emphasizing the fact the she is not comfortable adhering to a purist version of Islamic Indianness, Karodia creates a space for Meena as a South African.[17] To belong in South Africa, Indianness must be impure.

This impurity is often engendered inadvertently. For example, Meena's father supplies goods to the African community and Africanizes his store, revealing how even rigid adherence to religious and national codes is never absolute:

> Mohammed's General Store specialised in dry goods and catered to the African trade. The interior was filled with stacks of blankets which reached all the way to the ceiling; billy-cans hung from the doorway in tight bunches and the three-legged cast iron pots popular with the Africans for outdoor cooking were propped up against the door; beads and colourful bangles festooned shelves stacked with rows of plastic shoes. (46)

While the name Mohammed signals the Islamic orientation of its owner, the store's contents accommodate its African patrons. Meena tells us that "shopping was a major social event. . . . At Mohammed's General Store the African customers milled around the doorway or sat on the sidewalk" (47).

Trade propels Abdul not only to Africanize the store but also to defy the segregationist imperative by making the store into a venue where Indians interact, commercially and socially, with the Africans. The word "general," then, suggests not only the contents of the store but also a thwarting of apartheid rules by refusing to subscribe to racial specificity. Karodia demonstrates how Indians take on identities depending on material circumstances and geographic location as well as economic exigencies. Despite its obsessive record keeping, apartheid failed to archive Indian identity and its dialectic relationship with the land it inhabits. *Other Secrets* reveals how Indianness couldn't but help Africanize itself during the apartheid years, thus inserting this hybrid form of Indianness into public knowledge in the postapartheid period.

In going back in time, the novel also excavates other hidden histories of the Indian community, particularly highlighting interracial coupling. Much of the first section centers on Yasmin's rape by an Afrikaner youth. As in the violently racialized societies of the antebellum South or the slave-owning Caribbean, the rape of nonwhite women by white men was common in the apartheid period. In uncovering this history of violence, Karodia shows us how Indian women were also subject to sexual brutalization, thus underlining their affiliation with other disenfranchised communities through a shared story of pain.[18] When Yasmin's rape results in a pregnancy, she gives birth to a baby girl. The family debates over what to name the girl. They finally decide on "Soraya, after the Empress of Iran" (147).

The child's name is Persian, but given that Yasmin is not really Abdul's daughter but the daughter of a white man her mother was unable to marry, it is an exotic name for a child who has no Asian blood in her. The child's full name, Soraya Fatima Mohammed, emphasizes the connection with Yasmin's Indian "father." Abdul's last name is Mohammed and Fatima is the name of his mother. It is significant that the child is named after Empress Soraya, who led a somewhat fraught life. Also of biracial origin (Iranian father/German mother), Soraya married the Shah of Iran at the age of nineteen and was divorced for failing to produce an heir after seven years of marriage. She died an exile in 2001. Her biography touches the life narrative of the fictional Soraya with a prescient doom.[19]

The fact that the fictional Soraya is the daughter of a Coloured mother and a white father but passes as an Indian child is significant. Soraya's secret history reveals that *all* identity in South Africa is tenuous. The relentless segregation of apartheid invited covert racial mixing that irrevocably compromised efforts at maintaining purity.[20] The mixing of races also suggests that Indians have integrated into other South African ethnicities, blurring the lines drawn between communities. Karodia uncovers the buried stories of interracial sexual encounters and foregrounds the Africanness of Indians by emphasizing the degree of their biological integration with other South African ethnicities. As discussed in the chapter on *Kafka's Curse*, the evocation of racial cross-fertilization claims a different sort of citizenry: one that appeals to biological integration rather than racial affiliation or anchorage to land.

Through the story of the relationship between Meena's father (Indian) and Meena's mother (Coloured) and Yasmin's father (white) and Yasmin/Meena's mother (Coloured), *Other Secrets* depicts racial interaction not only as a rhetorical gesture whereby Indians identify with blacks, but also as sexual intimacy, a physical embracing of the Other that erases boundaries and hierarchies between nonwhite groups and fulfills Indian claims to South African belonging. The novel foregrounds the racial intermixing, ranging from rape to thwarted romantic liaisons, that characterized apartheid South Africa. A classic "race narrative," it also evokes the buried history of interracial relationships in other segregated societies such as those depicted in the novels of early twentieth-century African American writer Pauline Hopkins.

However, Indian belonging in South Africa is asserted not only through biological interaction but also by narrating the shared pain caused by legislation such as the Group Areas Act. Few people are cognizant of how much Indians suffered under the act. The first part of *Other Secrets* is set against this backdrop of relocation, with the government contemplating "moving Indian traders out of the small towns" (54). This picks up on another widely prevalent perception of Indians. Fainman-Frenkel explains that

> [e]xpropriation, forced removals, and disempowerment were just some of the historical hurdles that the South African Indian community faced under Apartheid as racist stereotyping designated Indians as unscrupulous business people, who posed a threat to white-owned commerce. This stereotype motivated government response and reinforced the division between groups. ("Ordinary Secrets" 60)

Indians were considered a threat to white prosperity and often banned from trading in white areas. According to Abdul's friend Cassimbhai, Indians had "become the Jews of Southern Africa, hated and envied . . . scapegoats" (67).[21] The comparison with Jews evokes Nazi Germany and the widespread perception of the Jewish community as alien others who had become rich at the expense of native Germans. Like the Jews, many Indians during the time of the Group Areas Act were also in a state of restless wandering, caught between the apartheid imperative to relocate and the regime's inability to find an area in which to confine this group.

The Group Areas Act, which mandated that each community live in zones of confinement with uncrossable lines drawn across racial categories, then serves as a metaphor for the unstable position that Indians occupied in the apartheid scheme. "Nana said that the rumours about a 'plan' to remove Indian traders from small towns to an area specifically created for them would have been laughable, if it hadn't been so frightening" (69). Karodia points to the irony in perceiving as a threat a community that constitutes less than 3 percent of the population, wields no political power, and is constantly rendered invisible. However, the idea of relocation is not as laughable as it initially seems. Meena and her family are removed from her childhood home; only afterward does the government realize the futility of trying to segregate Indians in their own "Bantustans."[22] As Meena says, "We had become the first victims of the government's grandiose scheme to move all Indians out of small towns into one central area, a task so impossible to implement that it eventually had to be abandoned. But for us it was too late. We had already been 'expropriated' and had lost everything" (98).

It is important to emphasize, then, that there was no *place* for Indians, literally and figuratively, in the apartheid imagination. Recovering the story of Indian suffering under the Group Areas Act allows Karodia to claim space for a community that had historically been denied a topography of its own. The small town Indian community, in all its scatteredness and diffusion, may have eluded governmental efforts at spatial confinement, but Meena's family's relocation and the isolation that follows function as powerful symbols of the tenuousness of the Indian community in a system that compartmentalized the world in black-and-white segments. The novel's referencing of the Group Areas Act emphasizes the twilight zone in which Indian identity unfolds, allows Indians to politically connect with other nonwhites through the rhetoric of disaffection, and carves a place for Indians in the South African imagination. In remembering their victimization by a totalitarian regime, Karodia articulates the ironic South Africanness of Indians.

Finding Home in Homelessness: The Impossibility of Return

The project of historical recovery ends with the first two sections. By the third section, entitled "Other Secrets," Abdul has died, and Yasmin comes back to South Africa to claim her daughter and to take Meena with her to England. Meena's South African passport is then revoked and she becomes an exile. The last third of the novel initiates the literal valence of return by tracing Meena's journey to England and her "coming home" to South Africa after many years of exile. The seamless passage from one section to another, from the twilight zone of apartheid South Africa to the supposedly liberating European cosmopolis, suggests new beginnings and old closures, but such transitions are never hermetic, as past spills into present and present leaks into every possibility of future. In the final section, Meena maps an alternative cartography of self while attempting to excise her Afrindian past from her memory.

Meena's move to London seemingly reinforces the South-North trajectory of diasporic exchange. However, apartheid blurs the categories of diaspora and postcoloniality. It is one thing to migrate west/northward; it is another thing to be *forced* to migrate west/northward *after* you have migrated southward from the east. The idea of double diaspora once again powerfully enters our consciousness. Here, the diaspora engendered by exile (South African Indians in London) is complicated by the fact that the diasporics are already in "exile" from elsewhere (Indians in South Africa). It is in this double diaspora that Meena realizes that South Africa—not

India—is her home. The second diaspora of enforced exile, then, subsumes the longing for India that is a consequence of the original act of migration from the subcontinent. In exile, Meena realizes that she is not Indian but South African.

London, however, does not yield its liberatory promise. Meena's apprehension that Yasmin and Soraya will become assimilated without ever being accepted in white English society brings back memories of her Nana's aphorisms: "[P]eople who went to England and became carbon copies of the English were like *brinjals*—aubergines [eggplants]. Dark on the outside and white on the inside. No matter how hard they tried to be white on the outside, they would always just be brinjals" (318).[23] Nana's imagistic strategies bring to mind American metaphors for racial confusion, such as Oreos, Twinkies, and Coconuts, demonstrating that Afrindian writing consistently raises issues that are "universal" to migratory selfhood even though identity formation is always complicated by political circumstance in South Africa. Like migrants everywhere, Meena must walk the tightrope between putting down roots and assimilating completely, a conflict that conjures her past life, where her allegiances vacillated between Indian Islam and Coloured Christianity.

Yasmin's daughter, Soraya, who has been born and brought up in South Africa, resents her forcible uprooting. She is initially disconnected from her English environs even as her mother slides into British society with relative ease. Meena thinks all of Soraya's problems can be cured by "the warm embrace of her family at McBain and under the heat of the African sun, she would recover her spirit" (344). The smallness of life in McBain and the authoritarian demands of the father once made Meena feel that her world was constricted. Even as Meena turns away from South Africa, she aches to return. When Meena is able to go home in 1992, she is overjoyed. "[W]hen my [South African] passport finally arrived I was ecstatic. I didn't know whether to laugh at the absurdity of the whole issue, or to cry with joy" (366). Return, Meena imagines, will resonate with the victory of reclaiming an identity and a history elided by the apartheid regime as well as by exilic deracination. "At the time I thought it was the single most significant act of my life. I was finally liberated. The old South African government had stolen my life, my history and my identity. . . . But I was returning. I was coming home. A mist had lifted and I could see the sun again" (367). For the exile home is always what is left behind, a place where deposited histories can be retrieved upon return. But coming home is not easy now that Meena is marked by her years in London. "There had been times when I ached to feel the warmth of the sun, to watch the night sky from our stoep—a scene which was uniquely ours. Yet now I wondered if I would want to live anywhere else. London had finally become home" (375). Once again, Meena is poised at the threshold between two worlds, unable to decide which one to step into. It is in the act of returning that Meena is able to find a place for her otherwise transient self.

Meena returns to South Africa following the death of her grandmother, which also necessitates her mother's departure from McBain. Realizing that she may never see McBain again, Meena is seized with nostalgia. She takes back to England "a bronze plaque with a Koranic verse in Arabic that hung in the front room. . . . The plaque was the only religious item in our house. When the morning sun caught it, the gold lettering still sparkled, highlighting the words. Papa told us that several of the letters had fallen off" (378). Meena's parents had disagreed about the placement of the plaque and her father had always insisted that "in a Muslim household this room [the front room] is the right and proper place for it" (378). By inserting Islamic iconography into her otherwise secular world, Meena finds the "right and proper place" for Islamic identity in her life. The fact that "several of the letters had fallen off" suggests that the Islam that is present in her life is an incomplete Islam, yet that the "gold lettering still sparkled" implies that the religion is still alight in Meena's life, albeit in a fragmented, impure way. In imbuing the plaque with talismanic properties, Meena is able to reconcile past and present:

> I studied the verse, thinking of my father and my grandmother and the way our lives had unraveled and then, by some miracle, had come together again. I thought about the years we had spent at McBain. There had been both good and bad times. Looking back then, even the bad times seemed to have been an integral part of growing up there. (379)

Meena's father and grandmother symbolize the claims of her Indian and Coloured roots. Meena can now synthesize the various aspects of her multifarious self. These include her Islamic, English, South African, and Indian identifications. The plural affiliations reveal the heterogeneous identity that is made possible by the intersection of apartheid, Indianness, and exile, a complex state of being that can only be appropriately showcased through the introspection and nuance associated with the postapartheid period.

With the death of her father, it might seem that Meena's Indo-Islamic identity has also died, especially because she leads a resolutely secular life in London. But Meena realizes that each shard of memory has gone into the making of her composite self and that she can never turn away from who she is. Karodia refuses to provide one single moment that engenders this realization; instead, she demonstrates how exile and return have steadily enabled this epiphany. In coming home after years of separation, Meena can integrate her diverse selves into a composite whole. As Meena herself states: "Perhaps McBain was the kind of place one had to leave in order to appreciate" (369).

Even though Meena might have fused her Indian past into her English present, a later comment about her connection to South Africa strikes a note of disquiet in the harmonious ordering of identities. When Meena's mother comments on how assimilated into English life Soraya really is, comparisons with Meena's own English integration surface:

> "Don't you have friends from other backgrounds? What about other South Africans, people who share our way of thinking?" Ma frowned.
> . . . It was difficult to make Ma understand that because we had lived abroad for such a long time, we had become assimilated into a different culture. *We were no longer South African.* It was only the childhood memories that kept us connected—and in my case, *it was a connection not to South Africa, but to McBain.* (426; emphasis added)

Meena realizes that she has been severed from her national origins and that she no longer identifies herself as South African. If the act of returning generates an epiphany on the role of Islam in Meena's life, paradoxically, it also shows her how disconnected she has become from her South African past.

Significantly, as her plane touches down at Johannesburg airport, Meena conjures up the memory of "the desolation at McBain: the pale-yellow sun-scorched veld dotted with dry scrub. A desolation that, ironically, I had yearned for in those dark days in London" (368–69). All it takes for Meena is to arrive in South Africa to realize the futility of her desire for return. Even though *Other Secrets* attempts to bestow South African citizenry on Indians, Meena's deracination and her eschewal of national identification may seem like a rejection of the South Africanness of Indians that other subcontinental writers, including Karodia herself, have claimed. However, *Other Secrets* also demonstrates the complexity of South African national identity, particularly how the powerful juxtaposition of exile and subcontinental affiliations subverts the idea of a homogenous South African self. To be a product of South Africa's unique history is to always be marked by other races, cultures, countries, and continents.

If Afrindian harmony exists, it remains a future possibility hinted through the promise of unlived lives. When Yasmin's daughter, Soraya, slips into a coma after a car accident, the family finds out that she is pregnant. Soraya, convinced that the baby was going to be a girl, already had a name in mind: "She wanted the baby named Ashleigh Fatima Mohammed" (453). Nomenclature is not accidental here, instead it foreshadows the many worlds the child will be required to intersect. Soraya's daughter will be brought up in England. Therefore, it is significant that her first name is Ashleigh, its distinctive spelling bestowing the name with a very English air. Yet the child's name also suggests her Indian heritage that can never be erased. Fatima was the name of Abdul's mother. It was also the name of the Prophet Mohammad's daughter, a call to the past that infuses Ashleigh's name with Islamic possibility. Mohammed is Abdul's last name, the last name of his daughters and the last name that Yasmin gives Soraya. The patriarchal line ends with matrilineal overtones as Yasmin not only keeps her own "maiden" name but also bestows that name on her daughter and granddaughter. That Yasmin herself is not Abdul's biological daughter, but rather the daughter of a non-Indian man, invests this final assertion of Indian identity with wider significance.

The ethnicities that Ashleigh Fatima Mohammed inhabits suggest that South Africans are intermixed to such an extent that it is impossible to separate Indian from Coloured or white. *Other Secrets* asserts further that Indians have participated so much in South African life that they cannot be distinguished from other South Africans and therefore have an equal claim to citizenship. That the child will be brought up in England suggests that this harmony can take place only *outside* of South Africa, thus anticipating the rupture of race relations in South Africa in the post-apartheid period.[24] Through the character of Ashleigh Fatima, the novel implies that Indians, paradoxically, become more South African when they are not physically situated in South Africa, an assertion already validated by Meena's recognizing South Africa as home when she is in exile and then realizing that she doesn't fit in when she returns.

Other Secrets ends with Meena returning to England on an airplane somewhere between Africa and Europe, eternally frozen in a state of limbo. The image of the plane also brings to mind what is often considered the emblematic novel of diaspora: Salman Rushdie's *The Satanic Verses*.[25] In *The Satanic Verses*, the plane in which the two diasporic protagonists are traveling to England crashes and the characters are washed up on the shores of England. Rushdie's use of the plane suggests that diaspora involves a violent crashing of one way of life into the other. Karodia refuses to bestow the classic tropes of shock and enigma on migratory arrival.[26] Arrival, instead, is seen as an *impossibility*. The fact that Meena is neither here nor there affirms the fundamental impurity of South African Indians as well as the untenable nature of the desire to belong in absolute terms.

It is also fitting that the novel concludes with Meena's letting go of her past and thinking about her future: "*Forbidden Love* was waiting. My publishers were waiting. *There could be no looking back*" (456; emphasis added). Earlier, Meena had asserted that "we all have our own places. I discovered mine much later—a place which reflected the geography of my soul" (310). We do not know what the contours of Meena's inner life look like, but we do know that the "geography of her soul" is suspended in the indeterminate space between England and South Africa. In her return to South Africa, Meena realizes that she is always returning somewhere else. When in England, she is always turning to South Africa; when in South Africa, she is always turning to England. The ending of the novel then suggests the impossibility of fulfilling the promise of return, especially in the sense of coming home and being at home.

Meena thus assumes the role of the cosmopolitan wanderer—a stock figure in diasporic fiction and theory produced about the East-West encounter—gliding between different geographies, histories, and cultures.[27] *Other Secrets* reveals some of the assumptions of mainstream diaspora studies even as it undoes the East-West/South-North model of migratory exchange. The reinforcing of dominant diasporic paradigms also raises the question of whether an East-South model of diasporic can only be assembled in fragments as Europe always intrudes to take center stage. Dipesh Chakrabarty's comments on the difficulty in "provincializing Europe" (241) are apposite here: "Europe remains the sovereign theoretical subject of all histories, including the ones we call 'Indian,' 'Chinese,' 'Kenyan' and so on" (223). Since Europe was the prime mover in forging the relationship between India and South Africa, England often assumes prominence in interactions between Indians and other South Africans weakening, though not dismantling, the East-South bridge that South African Indian fiction builds. However, the cosmopolitan "countryless" figure disrupts the totalizing imperatives of the African *and* European nation-state by refusing to adhere to a hegemonic—or single—form of national identification.[28] Karodia also reveals the multiple attachments that sustain communities whose roots are as tangled with different groups, histories, and nations as those of South African Indians.

That the novel closes with Meena reflecting on her writerliness further enhances her nebulous, though ultimately successful, quest for place. Meena's becoming a romance writer is significant, especially when this authorial activity is juxtaposed with what seems to be a rejection of her South African identity. Even though her retreat into fantasy suggests a turning away from immediate politicization and immediate realities, her novels, inspired as they are by the nonwhite men in her life and with titles—such as *Forbidden Love* and *Strangers in Love*—reflecting a defiance of apartheid law, are more steeped in South African reality than they initially seem to be.[29] Although her assertions suggest otherwise, Meena cannot erase her South African past. She may refuse to look back and refuse to return, but South Africa will always infuse her consciousness.

Analyzing *Other Secrets* through the tropes of return enables a reflection on some central issues in postcolonial and diaspora studies—hybrid identities, national anchorage, cosmopolitan affiliations, nostalgia, communal memory, and generational conflicts. The novel also demonstrates how these preoccupations of diasporic postcoloniality are *always* complicated by the central issues in South African studies such as apartheid, exile, minority identities, and the advent of democracy. The literary valence of return, exemplified in Karodia's rewriting of her earlier fiction, suggests the author's desire to accommodate early cultural shifts in the postapartheid present into a narrative about the apartheid past. This has important repercussions for the depiction of Afrindian identity in South Africa. Karodia points to the initial changes in Indian identity, particularly how Indianness is able to articulate itself without the reservations imposed by the antiapartheid imperative that necessitated an erasure of racial specificity in order to challenge the prescriptives of segregation.

Yet the identity that emerges in the novel is never a pure resurrection of Indianness. Instead, Karodia reveals how Indianness has pluralized, hybridized, and *Africanized* itself. The historical valence of return allows the postapartheid public to remember Indian disenfranchisement during the apartheid years as well as commemorate the Indian struggle to Africanize itself, thereby earning a place for subcontinentals in the annals of the nation. Finally, the character's return—the literal valence of coming home—explodes the idea of return itself, challenging absolutist notions of citizenship and identity. Being suspended in a nether zone somewhere between Europe and Africa may well be the price to pay for foregrounding a plural identity that nourishes itself on Europe, Africa, *and* Asia.

5

Lost in Transplantation

Recovering the History of
Indian Arrival in South Africa

The immediate consequence of the dismantling of apartheid was a relentless examination of the menace of the past; however, even greater literary experimentation was one of the inevitable, if later, repercussions of decolonization. Literature could now expand its frontiers in creative ways. South African writers such as Njabulo Ndebele were already addressing this issue in the 1980s, calling for a movement away from the "spectacle" to "rediscovering the ordinary" by focusing on the "daily lives" forgotten in the grand narrative of political struggle (57). Such a literary turn would foreground the fact that "the problems of the South African social formation are complex and all-embracing; that they cannot be reduced to a single, simple formulation" (57).

For South African fiction, the "rediscovery of the ordinary" opened up extraordinary possibilities in form, content, and tone. One such thematic change is revealed in the turn to the *preapartheid* past in order to showcase the multiplicity of the "South African social formation" and to make sense of the democratic present. Frantz Fanon describes this retreat into history as using the "the past with the intention of opening the future, as an invitation to action and a basis for hope" (210). Publications such as Anne Landsman's *The Devil's Chimney* (1997), Aziz Hassim's *The Lotus People* (2002), Elleke Boehmer's *Bloodlines* (2000), Ann Harries's *Manly*

Pursuits (1999), and Zoe Wicomb's *David's Story* (2001) are only a few examples of a postapartheid literary tendency to mine the trails of historical memory in order to activate the here and now.

The archiving of the preapartheid past suggests a paradigm shift in South African literature: one in which stories not directly related to the segregationist scenario can be discovered and narrated. As André Brink remarks:

> [C]ertain territories of experience . . . and certain regions of the past (notably those less obviously connected to the realities of apartheid) remain unvisited, or were visited only rarely, in much of South African literature, specifically in fiction. In the spectrum of possibilities now opening up to the writer in post-apartheid South Africa, these silent places invite exploration, almost as a condition for future flowering. . . . [U]nless the enquiries of the Truth and Reconciliation Commission (TRC) are extended, complicated, and intensified in the imaginings of literature, society cannot sufficiently come to terms with its past to face the future. ("Stories of History" 30)[1]

South African Indian fiction, shaped as it always is by broader literary developments, has also turned to the preapartheid past. However, the unique concerns of South African Indians, caught between the anxieties of diaspora on the one hand and the oppression of colonialism and apartheid on the other, engender a different form of literary retrieval: one that uncovers the story of Indian *arrival* in South Africa—as indentured laborers and traders—in order to assert national belonging in the present as well as offer all South Africans a vision of the diversity of their nation's origins.

To fulfill that project, Praba Moodley's *The Heart Knows No Colour* (2003) and Imraan Coovadia's *The Wedding* (2001) travel down history's passages to survey the migration of Indians to South Africa in the late nineteenth and early twentieth centuries. Since the worst of their battles were fought during the time of indenture, a period predating the institutionalization of apartheid in 1948, the experience of migrant Indians was expunged from a national memory so heavily focused on events following 1948. This invisibility was further exacerbated by the marginalization of Indians in a black and white national imaginary and the inevitable deracination of diaspora.

Betty Govinden laments the erasure of the story of Indian migration and delves into the cultural and phrenic consequences of indenture by posing the following questions: "What thoughts filled the early Indian migrant workers in their physical and emotional encounter and confrontation with the colonial masters and the new land? What 'counter-memories' . . . came into being? . . . The stifling and even absence of a literary tradition among Indians prevented us from reflecting on our psychic displacement ("Learning Myself Anew"). Geographic transplantation results in loss—of culture, nationality, and selfhood—necessitating a turn to the past in order to retrace the history that has been erased. Moodley and Coovadia take up Govinden's challenge to probe the history of indentured laborers and traders in order to expand the parameters of South African national identity today. In their triumphant proclamation of Indian arrival into South African citizenry, Moodley and Coovadia's fixation with the past not only heralds the present but also a future in which a nation recognizes the different strands that compose its prehistory, thus fulfilling its promise of democratic inclusivity.

The Heart Knows No Color and *The Wedding* help create a "national culture" in the expansive Fanonian sense of the term: "the whole body of efforts made by a people in the sphere of thought to describe, justify and praise the action through which that people created itself and keeps itself in existence" (Fanon 210). The hybrid past invoked by these texts "resist[s] the dangers of a new totalitarian national history" (Moslund 34) as well as counters a tendency apparent in most postcolonial societies to create a monolithic and romanticized precolonial era.[2] The two novels function as palliatives to the ethnocentrism of preapartheid, apartheid, and postapartheid repositories, a literary corrective that acts as a situational device for Indians *as Indians* in the postapartheid present.[3]

By showing South Africans the diversity of their history, Moodley and Coovadia participate in the project of nation-making. In her study of South African historical fiction, Annalisa Oboe claims that "at the origin of the nation we find a story of the nation's origin, in which history becomes a function of the foundational impulse. . . . Representations of the past become discursive productions of the narrating self, struggling not so much to have access to the 'real' world, *but over the right to representational authority in and for the present*" (175–76; emphasis added).[4] Oboe argues that in helping to create a "foundational" story of nation creation, denizens of a state acquire agency in the present.[5] Moodley and Coovadia inaugurate a new moment in South African Indian fiction: the birth of the historical novel tracing the extended periodicity of Indians in order to acquire agency in nation-making *and* to create an expansive South African identity that incorporates Indians into its spectrum.

The Heart Knows No Colour and *The Wedding* infuse Indianness with a sense of national belonging by demonstrating how subcontinental identity adapts to different phases in the migratory story. The novels reflect on the process and immediate consequences of migration, a thematic concern that underpins narratives of more recent Indian diasporas—particularly those in the West—but has only just entered the South African imagination as a result of the creative possibilities opened up by the end of apartheid. *The Heart Knows No Colour* and *The Wedding* are paradigmatic narratives of migration, but with key differences induced by the South African setting. Although issues that characterize diasporic communities everywhere are foregrounded, geography and history give us an alternative tale of diasporic interaction from those derived from East-West migratory stories. This *difference* in the migratory narrative allows us to trace South Africa's central role in shaping Indian identity. In focusing on the Africanization of Indianness by tracing its gradual progress through the stages of migration, diasporic contact is reconfigured across an East-South axis even as the showcasing of Afrindian identity asserts South African nationality.

Literary representations of diaspora often begin with the voyage from the home country, move to focus on the consequences of transplantation, and end with settling down in the host country. Moodley and Coovadia also schematize their novels within this paradigm of migration while showcasing the radical difference place produces. Though their diasporic narratives commence and culminate the same way, the material circumstances under which Moodley's indentured Indians migrate compared to those under which Coovadia's passenger Indians migrate create two very different texts absorbed with the same circumstances of geographic dispersal. In South Africa, the diasporic story immediately varies as the arc of diaspora bifurcates according to historical contingency: one part is concerned with indentured or labor experience and the other deals with the passenger or trader experience.

Phase one of the indenture narrative that emerges in Moodley's novel describes the voyage; phase two, the aftereffects of the voyage; and phase three, the process of settling down in South Africa. Since indenture was centered on a brutalizing servitude, its commemoration reflects that trauma. Phase one of the passenger narrative embedded in Coovadia's novel concentrates on the physical act of migration, the process of "getting there"; phase two concerns the loss of culture and nationality that haunts the migrant; and the final phase emphasizes the ritual of settling down and confronts the migrant's inevitable disconnect from the homeland.

Because passenger Indians were wealthier than indentured Indians, they could maintain emotional and cultural attachments to the subcontinent. *The Wedding*'s configuration of the Indian topos as a retrievable past reveals the class position of passenger Indians. Since the anxieties of indentured Indians centered on basic necessities like economic survival, Moodley does not record the stories of displacement and immigrant angst that Coovadia chronicles so superbly as the aftereffects of diasporic arrival. Coovadia's narration of the passenger experience is more focused on the psychic consequences of migration than Moodley's recovery of the indenture experience, which is governed by the physical violence of bonded labor.[6] Both novels also evoke a mythic India, but in different ways. Moodley creates an imagined India *in* South Africa by holding onto an absolutist vision of Indian identity in order to heal the traumas of indenture. Coovadia sets more than half his novel in India, a literary strategy that establishes connections between East and South over time. *The Wedding* recreates the Indian topos *itself* in order to claim that India and South Africa were always already present in each other.

The Heart Knows No Colour and *The Wedding* reveal that South African Indians experience similar anxieties that are articulated in differing ways based on the historical event that is being uncovered. For example, the labor diaspora came into being through the exploitative processes of empire, while the trader diaspora emerged through the economic opportunities provided by colonial capitalism. One set of Indians arrived in conditions of servitude with little choice or agency in their migration and another set arrived voluntarily and with relative wealth, engendering two very different narratives about Indian immigration to South Africa. Colonialism and capitalism play a structuring—yet radically different—role in the indenture and passenger consciousness.

Both novels, therefore, focus on wealth and money making. *The Heart Knows No Colour* depicts a preoccupation with the rags-to-riches narrative, while *The Wedding* discusses the commercial motives that underpinned the passenger voyage. Each text also demonstrates a fascination with imperialism. While *The Heart Knows No Colour* uses the rhetoric of the colonizer, especially in its representation of black Africans through a series of imperial-era tropes, *The Wedding*'s Orientalist imagery is suffused with an impish irony that distances the text from the colonialist vocabulary it deploys. The preoccupation with the British Empire reveals the dominance of the West in the making of Indian diasporic identities, even those assuming shape in an East-South formation. We have already noted the difficulty in "provincializing Europe" in Karodia's *Other Secrets*, thus revealing that alternative discourses of diaspora often centralize Europe in both literal and literary ways. This fascination with Europe, and the self-conscious and unconscious use of colonial rhetoric, stems from the fact that Indians are in South Africa because the British Empire grafted colonial subjects all over its domain. However, because these texts recover an era of imperial dominance—even as they seek to subvert that dominance—they often give Europe salience.

Foregrounding the prehistory of migration also asserts the difference between the passenger and indenture experience, thereby separating two different stories of identity formation that were amalgamated into a singular Indianness in the apartheid archive. It must be emphasized that descendants of indentured and passenger Indians *differently* articulate *similar* concerns, such as egalitarian citizenship, memory, hidden histories, relationships to the British Empire, the Indian contribution to South African life, their oppression preceding apartheid, affiliation with black Africans, and the emergence of Afrindian identities. Yet Moodley and Coovadia garner these tropes for a shared purpose: to affirm the South Africanness of Indians and the Indianness of South Africa. The South Africanness of Indians allows subcontinentals to claim belonging in the democratic present, while the Indianness of South Africa compels the nation to acknowledge its "rainbow" composition and the impact of neglected minorities on its cultural, political, and economic history.

Citizen Cane: The Rags to Riches Narrative of Praba Moodley's *The Heart Knows No Colour*

Praba Moodley's novel *The Heart Knows No Colour* (2003) is unique in its restoration of the historical density of indenture in order to bring it to public cognizance.[7] Ndebele points out that "there [exists] a disturbing silence in South African literature as far as peasants, as subjects of artistic attention, were concerned . . . seldom do we see peasants, *in their own right*, struggling to survive against the harsh conditions of nature or man-made injustice" (24–25). Moodley's novel thus fills a lacuna not only in the South African Indian literary imagination but also, more broadly, in South African cultural representation by endowing the indentured peasant experience with a "certain human validity" (Ndebele 25).

The Heart Knows No Colour also fulfils other agendas through its plotting of the various moments in the process of indentured migration:

Moodley links Indians to other dispossessed groups in South Africa, reminds her audience that apartheid was not the only mode of oppression, underlines the historicity of the Indian presence in South Africa, and justifies their inclusion as fully empowered citizens of the democratic nation. Moodley's alternate history of the struggles of Indian migrants who came to South Africa in conditions of near slavery emphasizes the psychical and physical suffering of the indentured laborers. Her novel cautions its readers to remember Indians, other victims in the struggle for equality, a struggle that predates the institutionalization of apartheid in 1948 and is therefore easy to forget.[8]

The plot of *The Heart Knows No Colour* is relatively straightforward: The novel's protagonist, Sita Suklal, comes to South Africa with her family as part of the great wave of labor migration in the late nineteenth century. Sita falls in love with Albert, the white brother-in-law of the plantation manager, and becomes pregnant with his baby. She marries an Indian man to confer legitimacy on the child. The rest of the novel deals with the consequences of Sita's secret, the child's hidden patrimony, and the upward mobility of the Suklal family, who flourish economically following their release from servitude. Moodley also records the trauma of indenture in meticulous detail.

In underlining Indian preoccupation with issues of oppression, both specifically Indian and generally South African, Moodley challenges stereotypical representations of Indians as apathetic and politically inert. However, the text occasionally espouses reactionary racial and class politics, even as its explicit agenda promises a radical reconceptualization of the South African past. Many of the Indians here are insular and politically quiescent. While the text's class politics are intimately tied to the rags-to-riches narrative that is predicated on the success of the "by your bootstraps" myth, the novel's racial hierarchies remain a puzzle, especially because an illicit interracial romance governs its thematic register. Even as Moodley uses the past to establish Afrindian connections, the identity she foregrounds is a conflicted one that is governed by Africanization through *place* rather than through *race*. Moodley's notion of Afrindian identities also disrupts the somewhat homogenous representation of racial interaction between Indians and blacks—of either solidarity or tension—by nearly erasing black Africans from the story.

Moodley constructs an emblematic narrative of diaspora by sketching the various phases in the arc of indentured migration. The text traces the movement of labor from India to South Africa in the late nineteenth century, the destitution of living conditions under indenture, the unfolding of the diverse life stories of Indians after the period of indenture had lapsed, the maintaining of cultural identities in diaspora, and, finally, the feeling of being at home. *Heart* opens in 1879, on the long nautical voyage undertaken by the Suklal family from India to South Africa, commencing the first phase of the indenture migratory arc: the process of getting there. The liminal space of the ocean suggests the liminal identities that South African Indians will occupy as they restlessly move between South Africa and India, while perhaps never quite belonging to either. Moodley captures the anxieties of indentured Indians and gives the ceremony of indenture due recognition: "Small boats had been sent out to the ships to bring the immigrants ashore. After a couple months of seasickness and bouts of terrible illness, which came with living on an overcrowded ship, relief was clearly written on their faces; in their haste to set foot on land, the newcomers virtually fell over one another" (16). Narrating the arduous journey of the labor diaspora gives Indians a Middle Passage of their own.[9] That indenture, like slavery, was a condition of absolute servitude is not widely known. Moodley inscribes this history of trauma into the South African collectivity by recognizing the horrors of the journey itself.

The forgotten trauma of the voyage can also be traced to the East-South diasporic encounters that this project foregrounds. The theme of the passage, "the voyage out," is not a major preoccupation of Western diasporas, obviously because these migratory formations mostly took shape in the days of air travel and were often journeys of choice made by relatively wealthy people. However, the *ordeal* of travel is an important aspect of diasporic stories that originate from the experience of indenture, marking the preoccupation with the voyage as a central characteristic of East-South migratory exchange, especially in context of the experience of indenture.[10]

Moodley goes on to describe the conditions of indenture by focusing on the living arrangements of the Suklal family after their incorporation into the labor economy. This reflects the second phase in the indenture trajectory, a concentration on the process of bonded labor rather than on the theme of national acculturation that characterizes the passenger migratory story and many other diasporic itineraries: "When her family first arrived at the plantation, they had been allocated rooms in a long building called a barracks, erected solely for the labourers. It was cramped and unhygienic and the Suklals, like the other labourers on the plantation, hated it" (29). As for the labor itself, Sewcharran, Sita's father, complains: "'We work like animals here. We have to be up before the sun rises in the east, and toil in these stupid fields until after the sun sets in the west, and they even expect us to work on a Sunday, without any extra pay!'" (18–19).[11]

While the above recitation might sound like a mere catalogue of horrors, the text achieves more than just the narration of a forgotten past.[12] Many diasporic stories focus on the deprofessionalization of skilled labor, alienation, assimilation, and racism by white society. Moodley demonstrates that such issues rarely infiltrated the psyche of the Indian laborer, whose life centered on the physical hardship of everyday life. By giving these stories a fictional layer, Moodley attempts to circulate them as widely as possible, endowing this forgotten trauma with a reach that historical repositories may not possess. In uncovering buried histories, Moodley etches them in South African public memory. The narrative reconstruction of the indentured past also stresses the contribution of Indian labor to the South African economy, emphasizing that the country's wealth was built on the backs of the economically dispossessed, including Indians. The historical recuperation analyzed above pursues this novel's agenda—and that of South African Indian fiction in general—of recognizing subcontinentals as indisputably South African.[13]

In revealing the horrors of indenture, Moodley articulates Indian arrival into South African citizenry through *land* rather than through communion with indigenes. Brinda Mehta asserts the importance of land in the indentured psyche in the Caribbean:

> [According to Khal Torabully] The first indentured immigrants were an agricultural labour force that toiled the land to make its first impression on non-native soil. The Indian identification with the land was twofold, symbolizing a metaphysical umbilical affiliation with the rural lands of India as well as a politicized inscription of memory on the land. . . . Earth-anchored memories promote a prismatic sensibility that reflects the earthy dynamism of the soil, *which [guarantees] permanence and continuity.* (144–45; emphasis added)

Similarly, Fijian politician Krishna Datt claims that "a symbiotic relationship of love and balance develops between the Indo-Fijian household and the land. For four generations of Indo-Fijians, that land has now acquired a very special, sentimental and religious significance . . . land holds me here, provides me with a sense of identity" (in Cohen 65).

Like their counterparts in the Caribbean and Fiji, indentured South African Indians were physically tied to the land and thus wrote their memories on and *through* its surface. Remember that indentured Indians, like slaves, tilled the land but could never claim ownership. Neither did they see any of the profits of their physically wrenching work. Moodley's carving of Afrindian identity through land becomes profoundly subversive in its reclaiming of the soil, an act Mehta describes as a "territorial repossession" (176). In emphasizing the backbreaking labor with which Indians sustained the soil, Moodley appropriates an essential part of South Africa—its land—and makes it uniquely Indian.

In another instance of "territorial repossession," Raymond, a friend of Sita's brother Gopi, tells him that he now owns, rather than works in, a banana plantation: "'I have owned this plantation for the last thirteen years,' Raymond stated. 'I have built it up from virtually nothing, and today I have a thriving business. I basically supply the whole country with bananas,' he added proudly" (190). Raymond's affirmation of *ownership* of the banana plantation evokes the Afrindian identity that emerges through land.[14] This Afrindian identity acquires national agency by its proprietary acquisition of the site of Indian labor. In seeking control through soil, Moodley also suggests that, like the earth, Indians are a natural, organic part of the South African landscape. Yet the assertion of an Afrindian identity through land rather than through people may create problems of its own. Land, after all, comes alive only through its inhabitants. Moodley's appropriation of the land on behalf of the indentured raises an important question: Who owns the land—those who broke their backs tilling the soil or those from whom the land was taken away in the first place? Moodley's reclaiming of place, especially by creating *plantation-owning* characters, might place her protagonists uncomfortably close to the white plantocracy.

This affiliation with Europeans rather than with Africans is simultaneously mirrored in the novel's plot. On the one hand, the story at the heart of *Heart* is of an illicit romance between Albert, the white plantation manager, and Sita, the daughter of indentured Indian immigrants, a schema challenging the racial boundaries consolidated by apartheid and imperialism. On the other hand, the novel is mostly silent about the presence of other nonwhites in general and black people in particular. Sita's crime is ultimately forgiven by her husband and by society, but it is significant that her lover is a white man. A similar crime may not have been sanctioned with a black man.[15] The narrative also seems preoccupied with skin color among the Indians themselves. Sita, the protagonist, is fair. We are told this repeatedly. Gopi's wife, Rani, is dark skinned: "[Gopi] looked past her dark skin: all he saw was the woman he loved" (70).

We are also told that "Rani toiled in the fields from dawn to dusk, and her once olive skin was now darkened. One had to look at her closely to appreciate the pretty features she possessed" (70). That Rani's skin has darkened by working on the land suggests a blackening that puts indentured Indians closer to Africans racially.[16] In tilling African soil, Indians have become African, a change in citizenship *and* racial status suggested by the darkening of their skin. Yet this fraternity is undercut by the assertion that "one had to look at her closely to appreciate the pretty features she possessed," a claim suggesting that dark skin hides "pretty features." If light skin is the acceptable sign of beauty in *The Heart Knows No Colour*, it further distances the characters from the darker black Africans. The preoccupation with fair skin reveals how a text that challenges racial boundaries often fails to challenge the aesthetic hierarchies acquired from European imperialism. In revealing that the heart *does* know color, the novel exposes the extent to which the indentured consciousness is implicated in the process of colonialism. Moodley interprets Indian-African relationships through the prism of imperial discourse even as the narrative disavows the potency of the colonizer through its appropriation of (what the colonizers thought to be their) land.

An ideological affiliation with white Europeans perhaps leads to problematic ties with black Africans. Sita's son, Mukesh, says: "We Indians are made of strong stuff. The white and the black man think that because we wear garlands and pray to statues we are weak and ignorant, but Gandhi has shown them differently. We don't need a rifle to fight, we have words and pen and paper" (240). While this foregrounds political commitment derived from Gandhian principles of nonviolence, it hinges on separatist rhetoric. *The Heart Knows No Colour* constructs a vision of Indianness based on not just community, but insular community that extends itself outward only to embrace whiteness.[17]

The novel is also characterized by a notable absence of fleshed-out black characters. *Heart's* representation of the few Africans that inhabit this text is, again, structured by Orientalist rhetoric. After Sita's daughter Rani is raped by Albert's son Joseph, she visits a Zulu witch doctress to induce an abortion:[18]

> She was greeted by a *wide, toothless smile and eyes that glinted in the light*. The wrinkled old lady had *colourful beads encircling her neck, arms and legs, and was wrapped in an equally bright blanket*. . . .
>
> *Grinning*, the old lady reached out and with *surprisingly gentle hands* touched Rani's tender breasts and slightly swollen belly. . . . *A wild shriek sprang from her throat as she ran backwards*. (257; emphasis added)

My italics point to the proliferation of Orientalist stereotypes in the extract. As we already know from the novel's color-coding of feminine beauty, Indians internalized European representations of other colonized people. There is nothing ironic or self-conscious in the depiction of the Zulu woman, suggesting, as it does, a fecund and feral nature. Even though Rani speaks to her in Zulu, the woman initially seems incapable of forming whole sentences and speaks in fragmented phrases. The black woman who cannot verbalize but instead uses an incoherent vocabulary of her own brings to mind Joseph Conrad's *Heart of Darkness*, once again showing us the extent to which Indians *even today* approach Africa and Africans through the hermeneutic lens provided by colonialism.[19] Since this is one of the few times a black character enters the novel, it is important to note that the text portrays her through a series of stock images that seem to be distinctly imperialist in origin.[20]

The representation of the inarticulate black woman demonstrates that Afrindian identity is never absolute; instead, it is full of gaps, fissures, and holes that may compromise the progressive charge that it historically sought to bestow upon itself.[21] The novel's racial schema also reveals the centrality of Europe in the making of Afrindian identities. Indians came to South Africa because of Europeans, they were deprived of their rights because of Europeans, and even now often respond to black people through the stereotypes of European colonialism. In revealing the limits of Afrindian identity, *The Heart Knows No Colour* suggests that *Euroafrindian*, rather than Afrindian, might be an apposite moniker for Indians in South Africa. No matter how rigorously we construct alternative trajectories of diasporic exchange, Europe often manages to reclaim center stage. Similarly, no matter how much Indians may disrupt the black-white paradigm of race relations in South Africa, the ideologies of whiteness often end up asserting their supremacy.

Moodley's choice of genre also demonstrates the influence of Western modes of perception. *The Heart Knows No Colour* can be classified as romantic fiction, even though it blurs literary categories as historical archive, social tract, and text of feminist awakening. In using the genre of romantic fiction (which Jane Bryce and Kari Dako describe in another context as a "devalued 'feminine' form") to excavate the hidden history of Indians in South Africa, Moodley "undermines masculinist presumptions of what constitutes an appropriate field for revolutionary action" (Bryce and Dako 160).[22] Yet the romance novel is a Western genre that is particularly complicit in the Orientalist project. As Bryce and Dako point out, romantic fiction was usually set amid "exotic locations and period settings [but] they rarely serve as more than a backdrop to the private drama of the white protagonists" (157). Substitute white protagonists for Indians and exotic locations for black South Africans, and we may arrive at the conclusion that South Africa and black South Africans exist only as background against which Indian psychic turmoil and the rags-to-riches story can unfold.[23] Even though Moodley's project of historical recovery undermines some conventions of the romance genre, the novel still subscribes to many of its central formulations.

Race relations in *The Heart Knows No Colour* signal a significant rupture from other South African Indian fiction encountered in the course of this project. But Moodley's novel also raises another question: Why do Indians *have to* assert belonging through affiliation with black Africans, despite having been in South Africa for 150 years? Moodley's refusal to stage these alliances exposes the fracture in the rhetoric of affiliation as well as heralds another moment of arrival: one where it may no longer be necessary to make gestures toward racial comity in order to inscribe Indian belonging in the South African psyche. Moodley's eschewal of links with black Africans also reflects the postapartheid political landscape in which the racial harmony of the past implodes. The interaction with whiteness often dominates racial exchange in Western diasporas. In East-South interactions, especially in South Africa, race relations become triangulated between white, black, and Indian. Indians have to grapple with the two races and where they fit in within that binary formulation. In refusing to negotiate with Africans in any *explicit* way, Moodley seems to reject the East-South paradigm of diasporic interaction that the migratory pattern in her novel validates.

Heart ends in 1919, a year that not only heralded the end of the First World War but also continued the severe restrictions on migration from the subcontinent to South Africa initiated in 1913. While many South African Indians remain mired in poverty, the Suklal family has risen in the world, thanks to the death of banana plantation owner Raymond, who leaves all his wealth to Gopi. The novel closes with a celebration of Indianness, with the Suklal family and all their friends gathered together to celebrate the seventy-fifth birthday of Chumpa, Sita's mother. Only one person, Mukesh, is politically active: "The family was a little terrified of his passion for politics: he had . . . turned into a serious man, who voiced his political views with such candour that it was frightening" (264).

Mukesh's political passion *terrifies* and *frightens* his family, who retreat into wealthy ethnic enclaves instead. If another way of inserting Indians into the spectrum of the nation is to claim their commitment to political equality, insular Indianness may compromise that radical intent. Diasporic identities often result in new hybrid forms of being that confirm the closure of the migratory arc through the process of settling down. Are the Indians in *Heart* unable to achieve this synthesis, not only because of their inability to forge kinship with other nonwhite South Africans but also because of their ultimate disavowal of political commitment, an ideological stance that was almost necessary for finding place and belonging in South Africa? Yet it bears repeating that this is another instance of postapartheid literary arrival, one in which asserting political commitment is no longer necessary for South African citizenship.

In the monetarist social order that the novel espouses, it is apposite the end showcases the paraphernalia of rich Indian life. This is where the complexity of historical recovery collides with the simplicity of the romance genre. *Heart*'s fantasy of upward mobility, with all the gaudy excesses of wealth, is very much in keeping with the genre of the romance novel that promises happy endings amid material splendor. Chumpa reflects on the rags-to-riches ambit of her biography: "She had come to Natal, against her wishes, scared out of her wits; today it was her home and she had raised her children here" (264). Moodley attempts to carve a place for indentured Indians in South Africa: "[T]oday it was her home" is a significant assertion. The suffering of the indentured laborers, and their commitment to remaining in South Africa by acquiring agency over the land, has earned them a place in the chronicles of the nation. Yet Indian social harmony seems to have been achieved through isolation. The concord depicted in the final pages of the novel suggests a separation from other South African communities:

> Her guests—family, friends, and business acquaintances—were dressed in simple yet elegant splendour. The ladies, adorned in rich silk saris, many with intricately designed gold jewellery, and their spouses in formal suits, some still wearing turbans but minus the dhotis . . . her guests had been given . . . [banana] leaves to eat off—the way they had done when they first arrived. (265–66)

In its focus on the richness of the saris and the delicacy of the gold jewelry, the novel paints a picture of Indians as *exotica*. In evoking their arrival in South Africa, the banana leaves also suggest that Indians remain frozen in that moment of time. Significantly, the men abandon their dhotis for "formal suits," implying their Westernization rather than their Africanization.

The novel's racial and class politics suggest that the Suklal family remains suspended in some sort of nether realm, clinging to an imagined and mythic India. Even though Vijay Mishra's description of the old diasporas as "diasporas of exclusivism" does not hold true of other South African Indian writers ("Diasporic Imaginary" 422), Moodley's depiction of the Suklal family at the end of her novel suggests that her Indians at least create "self-contained 'little Indias'" for themselves (Mishra 422). This retreat inward is perhaps a consequence of the anguish of indenture that necessitates a simpler, more fantastic narrative in order for its restorative vision to succeed. Indentured Indians were too poor to keep in touch with their Indian past, too illiterate to even write letters home. Their disconnect from the "homeland" was further vitiated by South Africa's isolation from the international community during apartheid. The only India that is available to Moodley is an India that is always already South Africanized and always already a romanticized fantasy, suggesting a "loss of the real" that is a tragic consequence of migration in general and indentured migration in particular.[24]

Frantz Fanon's comments on "cultural retrieval" may further enable a more nuanced interpretation of *The Heart Knows No Colour*. Fanon claims that a turn to the past is often "directed by the secret hope of discovering beyond the misery of today, beyond self-contempt, resignation and abjuration, some very beautiful and splendid era whose existence rehabilitates us both in regard to ourselves and in regard to others" (in Desai 200). Similarly, Robin Cohen states that throughout "the Indian labour diaspora, the success of petty entrepreneurship was to provide a role model for those emerging from rural impoverishment" (79). In turning to the "very beautiful era" of wealth and professional success, Moodley provides a healing communal vision as well as a "role model" for people traumatized by a brutal history.

Passages from India: Revisiting the Trader Experience in *The Wedding*

Imraan Coovadia's debut novel, *The Wedding* (2001), revises South Africa's history by resurrecting traces of the Indian presence in the making of early twentieth-century Durban.[25] The novel's buoyant, Rushdiesque prose provides a stylistic counterpoint to the bleaker narratives of Agnes Sam, Jayapraga Reddy, and the early Farida Karodia, although its use of humor resembles Ahmed Essop's sly wit. *The Wedding* is narrated by the nameless grandson of its central character, Ismet Nassin, who migrates to South Africa at the turn of the nineteenth century, dreaming of economic prosperity with his new bride, Khateja.

Coovadia creates history out of family lore, as events in the novel are inspired by stories he grew up listening to in Durban.[26] *The Wedding* reminds us not only of the nexus between the private and the political but also of a dialectic easily forgotten: Indians have a century-long presence in South Africa that has changed South Africa as much as South Africa has changed them. *The Wedding* thus celebrates the history of Indian beginnings in South Africa. That it is able to unearth these buried life stories without compromising its opulent sense of humor heralds yet another new moment in South African Indian literature: the genesis of the comic novel written with Dickensian aplomb. According to Elleke Boehmer, "in the South African novel as in sport, in language, the time for breaking the inherited rules is here, now. Writers need 'parameters' as broad as it is possible to have, for the metamorphoses that may unfold will, if nothing else, be unpredictable and astonishing" ("Endings" 55). *The Wedding* bursts the boundaries of the South African novel by refusing to take even its history-making moments seriously. The novelty of this novel rests in its ability to laugh at the grave events in human history as well as in its mining of the preapartheid past in order to recover the story of Indian arrival in South Africa.

Although Indians were transported to South Africa as indentured labor from 1860 onward, traders from the subcontinent began to arrive only a decade later. Passenger Indians, as they were called, came to South Africa to establish what they thought would be lucrative trading enterprises.[27] That Ismet belongs to this category of migrant Indians is repeatedly underlined in the early sections of the novel: "Ismet Nassin was a businessman at heart, an enthusiast of the economist Ricardo" (3). Later in the novel Ismet's wife, Khateja, describes him as a "businessman-capitalist" (92). Ismet is also "quite fond of these English and their elastic bands and their cricket balls and brussels sprouts. . . . Yes, the Englishman was a creature after his own heart" (4). This Anglophilia is not incidental. The fact that South Africa was also a British colony spurred many Indians to travel to the southernmost tip of the African continent. That trader Indians were often conversant in the English language facilitated their mercantilist agenda. Coovadia floods his texts with cultural codes situating Ismet in a particular historic juncture, explaining and justifying his migration southward.[28]

The Wedding provides an elaborate chronicle of its characters' lives preceding the migratory moment, thus deviating from the few other resurrections of Indian immigration to South Africa that focus only on life *after* the process of diasporic transference.[29] This is also an important distinction from other South African Indian fiction we have encountered in the course of this project. *The Wedding* is one of the few South African Indian novels set in India. The first half of the novel offers an account of Ismet's courtship of Khateja, their fraught relationship in India, and their consequent migration to South Africa. The preoccupation with India brings to mind migratory texts in recently formed diasporas, such as Bharati Mukherjee's *The Tiger's Daughter* (1972), Leena Dhingra's *Amritvela* (1988), Salman Rushdie's *The Satanic Verses* (1989), and Meena Alexander's *Fault Lines* (1992).[30] As first-generation immigrant narratives, these novels are as preoccupied with the home country as they are with the host country.

Coovadia's agenda is different from these texts. The India section in *The Wedding* does not merely breathe life into the prehistory of migration, although that is certainly one of its purposes; it also foreshadows Ismet's migration to South Africa as well as the inevitable merging of cultures that follows. Coovadia inserts South African cultural practices and historical moments into the India section and Indian cultural practices and historical moments into the South Africa section. This move anticipates the flowering of Afrindian identity in direct ways. If the term "Afrindian" suggests the dialectical possibilities of migration, Coovadia points to the "always already" aspect of relationships between East and South engendered not just by migration but also by recovering its forgotten history.

Coovadia thus uses the first section of the novel to fuse the disparate worlds of India and South Africa. *The Wedding* depicts Ismet's arrival in Khateja's village home though the vocabulary of intercultural contact: "Things seemed to have lost their concrete edges, their definitions. In this new climate would a *bharfee* be a *bharfee*, a three-cornered *samoosa*, a three-cornered *samoosa*?" (29). The "new climate" of migration leads to a blurring of the solid surfaces of past lives. This clouding of the past is ironically demonstrated in Coovadia's use of South African Indian spellings to describe Indian sweets and snacks, which are more usually spelled as *burfi* and *samosa*. Even when South African Indians attempt to retrieve the Indian past, it is never a pure evocation of the world they left behind; rather, it is always infused with the sensibilities of the South African present. The slippage foregrounds the South Africanness of Coovadia's novel even as the text attempts to recover the cultural ethos of India. Coovadia reveals the South African aspect of *his imagined* India paving the way for the Indianness of South Africa.

In another example of forging bonds between different histories and geographies, Ismet is sent hurtling across the train carriage when he first sets eyes on Khateja. However, Coovadia describes this phenomenon as if Ismet is about to be evicted from his carriage: "He'd caught sight of the woman through the window when he was swept from his seat and hurled across the width of the carriage by an invisible hand" (12). Coovadia further claims that "they were physical signs, brutal—to the extent they'd cast him across a railway carriage and bruised his two elbows to boot" (14). The above description obliquely recalls Gandhi's epiphanic eviction from a train in South Africa for sitting in a whites-only carriage. Gandhi as mobilizing trope emerges repeatedly in South African Indian literature. By paralleling Gandhi—the South African who returned to India—with Ismet—the Indian who goes to South Africa—Coovadia inscribes East into South and South into East, erasing differences between continents and cultures in the process.

The importance of India in this novel's schema is also anchored to the specificity of the passenger migratory experience. Passenger Indians could afford to maintain ties with India after migration, unlike indentured Indians, who did not have the financial wherewithal to even write letters, let alone make trips home in order to find "good Indian wives," the way their trader counterparts could. Thus the descendants of passenger Indians can claim an India to which they can imaginatively return. Their ability to go back—even only in literary ways—arises from the concatenation of attachments that passenger Indians have been able to forge because of the material exigencies under which they migrated. However, if bonds with India are often used to accuse Indians of a disloyalty to the host country, Coovadia's evocation of India makes his migrants more South African, not less. For South Africa and India were always connected—or so the novel claims.

In the second half of the novel, the paradigmatic arc of passenger migration—starting with the diasporic journey, moving to issues of national and cultural loss, and ending with the migrant's disconnection from the "homeland" and settlement in the "host" country—unfurls in organic progression. "So the two of them, beetle-backed migrants—bickering, feuding, mixing it up—disappeared from the face of India. They simply vanished. Somehow there's never enough ceremony at the migratory watershed" (129). Mother India has neglected to reclaim her wandering African children, who have instead "simply vanished" from her shores.

The novel styles itself as "the ceremony at the migratory watershed" by giving migration the space, the voice, and the history it deserves.

In chronicling the journey, Coovadia rehabilitates the forgotten narratives of passenger Indians and bestows their stories with a personalized cast: "With Khateja by his side, he saw himself forging a commercial empire, founding a dynasty, patronizing culture. A sea change. Riches, dragons, treasure barrels, roaring crowds, strange territory, trading delegations" (105). Ismet's desire to voyage out is underpinned by the imperialist fantasy of mastery, patronage, and commerce. In his search for "trading delegations" and "strange territory," Ismet harbors colonial desires of capitalist conquest. Conceiving of Africa as a blank slate, Ismet collapses the continent into a land without history:

> They set sail for Africa, a clean table of a continent: . . . Whenever one climbed off on a railway platform in history-free Africa, one wouldn't expect to stumble immediately upon a village. . . . There would be an untamed volcano, a chop-licking leopard circling around in the evening time, the poisoned darts of the bone-nosed natives whistling through the air to make sure they would always turn to the other for reassurance. (119–20)

Shades of *Heart of Darkness* again? While the extract quoted above is suffused with Coovadia's impish sense of humor, it also provides us with a useful example of how imperialist rhetoric was disseminated among the colonized. Ismet imagines Africa with all the tropes of empire, indeed as his civilizational Other. Indians immigrated to Africa not only to colonize with commerce but also with imperial preconceptions of the continent already firmly entrenched in their psyches. Betty Govinden remarks that Ismet "does not see his resolve imposed upon him by a larger reified colonial mentality" ("Performance" 161).[31] Yet Coovadia satirizes Ismet's complicity with the hierarchies of empire. Ulrich Broich points out that the "imperialist approach to history is often directly mentioned in [postcolonial] novels" (437). Coovadia not only showcases the "imperialist approach" that many nonwhites imbibed but also critiques colonial discourse by piling up one ludicrous stereotype after the other: "bone-nosed natives," "chop-licking leopard," "untamed volcano." This rhetorical strategy of excess then forces us to consider the ridiculousness of *all* stereotypes.

When Ismet arrives in South Africa, he realizes there isn't that much of a difference between India and South Africa, East and South, past and future, history-less and history-full. On their long voyage southward, Ismet and Khateja initially view the African coastline with trepidation. All their anxieties about entering a primitive world existing outside the parameters of time and history seem to be confirmed upon encountering "just the clear light and the plants and the birds and the water and the land" (135), a geography devoid of people. Once they see the city of Durban, the Orientalist binary collapses: "[L]o! there are railways heavy with locomotive and track, there are tall buildings, even a minaret, clean plaster houses by the hundred, sorry, thousands, there is a city tabled out on the hills, oh shining city!" (137). Ismet and Khateja's first impression of Durban situates the city as a beacon of immigrant hope that bustles with the modernizing effects of imperial commerce. The fact that even a minaret arches from the Durban skyline suggests that Islam already has a presence in South Africa. In collapsing differences between India and South Africa, here, by marking Durban with the recognizable familiarity of industry and Islam, Coovadia inscribes each into the other.

Ismet initially dreams of re-creating South Africa in an Indian image. He fantasizes that in South Africa he would help produce "a legion of children . . . a hundred, a thousand, peopling the vast land, young giants. . . . They would lounge on Ismet's knee, tumble about on the ground . . . raise cities from the tree and stone, fashion minarets, eat beef in the red" (120). While fashioning minarets is particularly germane to Ismet's grand design of populating South Africa with India and Indians, he is also ready to Africanize himself: "it would be a mistake to think that [Ismet] hadn't put some thought into the question of how the two of them were going to fit in, in South Africa. . . . Without some kind of adjustment on their part, progress was out of the question. . . . There is such a thing as customs and traditions you see" (149). Changing oneself as well as being the active agent of change are key aspects of the dialectical possibilities of migration. Ismet is most likely referring to the African traditions, which he must respect in order to belong, but he could also be thinking about his own traditions, which he must maintain in order to preserve his sense of self. Regardless, Coovadia reveals the tension between assimilation versus maintaining culture that migrants everywhere have to negotiate.

The next phase of migration is the aftermath of "getting there" and the migrant's inevitable confrontation with the problems of nationality, culture, and belonging. While these issues are complex anywhere, the unique racial situation in South Africa exacerbates migratory anxieties even more: "He hadn't realized how complicated and messy the situation of South Africa was, and he derided himself for it" (150). The novel points out that that nationality—indeed, the nation-state itself—comes into being in diaspora:

> Durban . . . one million strong: one-third black, one-third white and one-third Indian. Since Durban housed the largest number of Indians in a single place outside India, it was, excluding the subcontinent, the most rhetorical city in the world. (And thanks to its piebald multistriped composition, the municipality of Durban inculcated in the mind of the expatriate Mohandas Gandhi, who was currently residing there, the outrageous conviction that each disparate subcontinental belonged to the same nationality—and so, in a sense, Durban created the nation-state of India.) (142–43)

The city of Durban further splits the binary of black and white into a *trinary*. Coovadia also claims that the Indian presence in South Africa not only altered Durban beyond recognition, it also willed the Indian nation into existence.[32] Coovadia gives agency to South African Indians in the making of South Africa as well as in the making of India. In showing how India first came into existence in South Africa, Coovadia skillfully deconstructs national boundaries. But Durban does not just inaugurate India's accession into nationhood. It is in Durban that subcontinental South Africans proclaim their entrance into Indianness.[33] While this may be troubling in its anticipation of the divisive taxonomies of apartheid, it reflects the second phase of the diasporic arc: the migrant desire to cohere in clusters of national and cultural similarity, often forgoing the comforts of regional affiliation for a more globalized Indian identity.[34]

In keeping with his desire to Indianize South Africa, Ismet steadfastly maintains Indianness through what he consumes:

> India is a portable country, to some extent, which moves as people do, accommodating itself freely to new environments, but if they started off forsaking her, forgetting her in this and that detail, what would happen at the end of time?
>
> Ismet saw suppers, Sunday dinners, snacks on the weekend-time, curries, *biryanis*, *bhajias*, *pathas*, and *pooris* as the first essential step, the harbingers, the bringers of a new order among things and a new set of relations between men.
>
> Philosophically, what was a family if it didn't sit down together to table? Where was community to be found if not in the breaking of a *nan*, the passing round of a pickle dish? (157–58)

According to Kogila Moodley, "religion, music, customs, traditions, and distinctive food tastes [among Indians in South Africa] formed part of the reconstruction of a womb-like structure to act as a bulwark against a hostile environment" (459). Ismet's gustatory gusto enacts a sweep of substitutability in which food performs a synecdochic function by creating the Indian community forsaken by the act of migration.[35] Thus the second phase of the diasporic narrative—or the immigrants' struggle to recreate the culture left behind while adjusting in their new environs—envelops Ismet's everyday existence.

But the resolute emergence of Indianness articulated above also intersects with the African world it inhabits. Indianness is a compromised entity in diaspora, always inscribed by the geographic location in which it is inserted, even when it organizes itself into creation only through migration. No sooner is a pure Indian identity willed into existence than it is altered by place. While cooking Indian food for Ismet, Khateja douses the meal with "six bags red chili powder, twelve grated green chilies, a big glass bottle of black pepper . . . for good measure a fifth of a pint of Tabasco sauce in the prawns" (178). The fact that Indian food becomes too hot to handle is significant. In South Africa, the atmosphere is such that even the most ordinary efforts at maintaining identity are vitiated by the heat of political culture. The novel declares that no matter how vigorously Indians maintain ethnic identity, it is always infiltrated by the red-hot South African context. That Khateja uses Tabasco sauce—an American invention probably given to non-Westerners through colonial contact—in Indian culinary preparations underscores the presence of the West in the making of Afrindian culture.

Ismet slowly begins to adjust to life in South Africa, despite his efforts at maintaining an Indian identity. This is the final phase of the paradigmatic arc of migration: the process of settling down. "He was starting to feel perfectly at home. He looked at the blacks in blue overalls, light-bodied men sweating in the heat and moving boxes or grumbling, and he wanted to put his arms around them" (176). By claiming fraternity with the indigenous inhabitants of South Africa, rather than with the settler whites, Ismet is allowed to feel at home. Feeling at home results in an obliteration of contact with the homeland. Coovadia sketches this extirpation against events taking place in early twentieth-century Durban: "Around these star-spangled anti-lovers, South Africa started to burn, a slow ignition that would continue for the remainder of the twentieth century" (222).

Ismet and Khateja are gradually absorbed into the macropolitics of

South African life. Without knowing it, they find themselves "mentally denationalized": correspondence to and from India becomes rare and they begin to accept that their stay in South Africa is permanent. Apartheid catches up with them when they are forced to relocate to a "segregated suburb" outside of Durban:

> There were fewer letters back and forth to Bombay and Rashida—imagination, which is capable of joining together countries ten thousand miles apart, must be admitted to be a mercurial power. Like any deracinating system of forces and energies, the imagination sponsors moral and filial disorderedness. My grandparents got mentally denationalized, so to speak. (265)

The narrator claims that his grandparents were *denationalized* rather than *renationalized*, seemingly indicating that they were unable to tether their selfhood to South Africa and, like many other diasporics, remained trapped somewhere between past and present, home and host. Yet the word "denationalized" also evokes the systematic stripping away of citizenry—through the creation of Bantustans for black Africans, forced removals and depriving Indians of South African citizenry until 1961—to which all nonwhite South Africans were subject in some degree or the other. In underlining a common history of suffering through the simple use of the word "denationalized," Coovadia paradoxically renationalizes Ismet and Khateja: To be South African is to be trapped in its unique history of racism, violence and oppression.

In observing Ismet and Khateja's disconnect from India, Coovadia laments the failure of the imagination in connecting the past to the future. Yet the rejoining of India and South Africa through the mediating consciousness of the South African Indian novel invests the future with the possibilities of the past. As the narrator points out, the reason for telling his grandparents' story is important: "[T]he mask that's worn into my grandmother's face has a symbolic function: by rendering her more or less anonymous, more or less interchangeable, it indicates that her story is no longer really her own. It belongs to our common history" (267). The use of the phrase "common history" is referentially vague, and deliberately so. While the most obvious signified to the signifier "common history" is the collective subcontinental heritage that Ismet, Khateja, and other South African Indians share, "common" also expands to include the history of South Africa that Indians, Africans, and Europeans have created. Coovadia turns to the past to retrieve this shared history in order to create a space for Indians as South Africans in the collective imaginary of the present and to reveal to other South African ethnicities the Indian contribution in the making of South Africa. He thus offers us a more "optimistic view of history" than Broich credits most other "postcolonial historical fiction" with (438). According to Broich, "history is seen to be a heavy burden which deeply oppresses the present" (438). Yet, as Ndebele argues, "the past, no matter how horrible it has been, can redeem us. It can be the moral foundation on which to build the pillars of the future" (155). In Coovadia's view of history, the past *can* salvage the present; all we need to know is how to retrieve it.

6

Citizen Other

The Implosion of Racial Harmony in Postapartheid South Africa

Ahmed Essop's later fiction is fueled by a palpable unease at Indian, especially Indian Muslim disaffection, in democratic South Africa. Even though Essop is too skillful a writer to allow rage to overwhelm his prose, his postapartheid writing reveals an increasing anxiety about how democratic South Africa has stripped Indians of full citizenry. This chapter explores Essop's disquiet at the implosion of racial harmony in postapartheid South Africa, uncovering in the process what minority unbelonging tells us not only about national belonging and citizenship in the "new" South Africa, but also about the postcolonial nation itself. Essop thus takes up what Anthony O'Brien defines as "an opportunity to inquire into the role and the responsibility of the literary intellectual in constructing (establishing or *subverting*) a discourse of the nation, the new nation" (11; emphasis added).

While Essop's earlier writing is suffused with hope and promise, especially in his celebration of egalitarian racial interaction, his postapartheid fiction takes on a more ominous hue. Essop may depict interracial harmony in the apartheid years, yet *The King of Hearts* (1997) reflects the fraught relationship between Indians and the other races during the postapartheid era, while *The Third Prophecy* (2004) problematizes the accommodation of the Indo-Islamic community within the contours of a secular nation.[1]

Essop's articulation of Indian identity in contemporary South Africa demonstrates that Indians seemed to have more political franchise when they had no political franchise. As power changes hands from white to black, those inhabiting in-between states are assailed for being alien and foreign. The failure of multicultural democracy suffuses Essop's later work with a sadness that even the humor and satire that characterize all his fiction cannot eradicate.

However, despite the difference between his apartheid and postapartheid fiction, certain similarities run through all of Essop's writing. Essop is intensely preoccupied with how Indians fit into South Africa, the different roles they occupy at different political junctures, and the demands that a rapidly changing social milieu makes on Indian identity. As Lisa Lowe points out with reference to Asian American identity, "the processes that produce such identities are never complete and are always constituted in relation to historical and material differences" (in Braziel and Mannur 136). Closer to home, Thomas Hansen argues that "with a new freedom, which is also a moment of uncertainty, compounded by changing relations among local, regional, and global forces, everybody in the country was left to rethink themselves beyond that overpowering shadow and structuring power that apartheid had imposed on them for decades" ("Melancholia" 298). Apartheid, and the antiapartheid movement, created one set of determinants against which the Indian community developed a sense of self. The transition period (1990–1994) offered more guidelines for communal behavior. Finally, postcoloniality, with what many Indians consider its thwarted promise, is forging yet another aspect of Indian identity.

Even as South African Indian identity unfolds across multiple axes, it exposes the unique link between the sociocultural transformation of Indianness in South Africa and political reality. Essop's postapartheid fiction always comes back to the instability of ethnic identity in the time of rapid political change even as it foregrounds the theme of dispossession to expose the falsity of a nation's sense of self. Indian unbelonging in the postapartheid state reveals the difficulty—indeed, the impossibility—in fully settling down. As their *foreignness* is repeatedly used as a weapon against Indians, we are reminded that subcontinentals in South Africa remain suspended in a state of diaspora, with all the negative connotations of flux and instability that the term suggests.[2]

Thus, no matter how vigorously Indians asserted their belonging in South Africa in the past, their homelessness is reinforced in the postapartheid present. One of the questions Essop's later work raises is: How long does a migratory community have to continue to validate itself to indigenes in order to belong? In other words, when do diasporics stop being in a state of diaspora? Smitha Radhakrishnan argues that "South African Indians [now] face the political task of gaining recognition from the newly formed multicultural state as a key minority group" ("Time" 263). Essop's postapartheid fiction demonstrates the difficulty—perhaps even the impossibility—in "gaining recognition" as a viable minority. This desire for outside validation also raises further questions about self-empowerment. Is it enough for a disaffected group to acquire composite citizenry in its own eyes or do claims to citizenry need to be authenticated by the majority in order to have social and political effect? Is citizenship a matter of authentication—who validates claims to belonging being more important than who claims belonging—rather than simply due process of law?

Essop's sense of being "out of place," to use Ian Baucom's phrase, speaks to the instability of Indian identity and subcontinental claims to citizenship as well as to the instability of Essop's own fiction. Notice how Indians are *self-empowered* at a time when they did not have social authority, and how, at the moment of Amandla, Indians are dispossessed by the majority's inability to authorize their self-empowerment. Notice also how Essop's fiction moves from joy and celebration in the apartheid period to anxiety and then finally rage at Indian marginalization under the new regime.

The breakdown of racial solidarity also demonstrates how post-colonial states often replicate the behavioral paradigms of their imperial precursors. Indira Gandhi's Emergency in India, the military coups in Fiji and Pakistan, and the rise of African dictators, such as Idi Amin in Uganda and Joseph Mobutu in the Congo, may be extreme manifestations of the South African case but all reveal a colonialist tendency to shut down democracy, diversity, and dissent. Additionally, as scholars of postapartheid South Africa have pointed out, race continues to be a major interpretive lens through which South Africans approach each other (Radhakrishnan, "Time" 278; Desai 114; Muthal Naidoo 39). South African Indian Muslims—the primary focus of Essop's work—are subject to another level of alterity, furthering the neurosis of an identity already fractured by centuries of Otherness. So, for example, the celebratory staging of Indian identity—seen elsewhere in this project in the wearing of Indian clothes—reveals how sartorial difference can be a mark of radical Otherness rather than a proclamation of ethnic pride.

Essop's dramatic about-face in the postapartheid period also marks a significant shift in South African Indian fiction. Even though the rhetoric of racial affiliation may not be in circulation anymore, South African Indian fiction rarely engages with Indian-black hostility in such an explicit and direct way. Often, deteriorating race relations are blamed on the Indians in order to assert the necessity for "black" solidarity. In a significant departure from his own earlier prose—*The Emperor* comes to mind here—Essop also places the blame on the majority community: the black Africans. Essop does not uncritically censure black Africans, but rather attempts to comprehend the genesis of their anger against Indians. This also lends credibility to his critique of blacks, a charge that ordinarily might have been dismissed as racist had Essop already not demonstrated his antiracist credentials through his earlier work as well as through his refusal to assign blame to any one side.

Yet Essop's fiction does not simply show and satirize. He also uses Indian disaffection to seek change. Essop best expresses his literary agenda in an untitled essay in which he argues that "the work of writers may come to be seen not only as a testimony of the times and a revelation of the human condition with its potentials and possibilities, but as an important contribution to the metamorphosis of society into a rational, humane and compassionate one" (in Daymond, *Momentum* 21). As O'Brien points out, one of the central questions underpinning South African democratic discourse was "how to construct an expressive culture that springs from, responds to, and shapes visions of economic and political democracy deeper than ballot box democracy, parliamentary representation, liberal capitalism, cultural pluralism and the Enlightenment discourse of rights" (2–3). By questioning the practices of the new nation, Essop participates in an "expressive culture" that attempts to extend democracy, citizenship, and national belonging beyond "just" political freedom. Essop's later fiction thus places him close to South African writers such as Zoe Wicomb (*David's Story*), Ivan Vladislavic (*The Exploded View* and *The Restless Supermarket*), K. Sello Duiker (*The Quiet Violence of Dreams*), and Achmat Dangor (*Bitter Fruit*), all of whose works have expressed some sort of disaffection with the new order. In exposing the failure of multicultural democracy, postapartheid writing such as Essop's strains toward a radical transformation of South Africa into a truly democratic "nation-space" (Bhabha, *Nation and Narration* 299).

After Amandla: Otherness and Unbelonging in *The King of Hearts*

Although the new South Africa imagined itself as a tessellation of interlocking cultures, the shifting dynamic between Indians and blacks reflects the violence, hostility, and distrust amid the races after the abolition of apartheid. Freedom might have heralded a better world, but power still remained unequally distributed. Ralph Premdas's comments on the tension between Indians and blacks in Guyana can also be applied to a South African context: "[R]esidential, occupational, customary and racial cleavages together established a deeply divided state. Each group feared the other; each disparaged the other through a complex set of stereotypes. . . . [T]he . . . government never succeeded in re-aligning the ethnic vertical cleavages of race, religion, culture etc" (quoted in Mehta 93).

In South Africa, both Indians and Africans felt that the other community had greater access to the constellations of power. The Indians were thought to be invested with economic authority and the blacks with the political hegemony of the majority.[3] This hostility is part of a long culture of conflict between Zulus and Indians starting "from the riots in Durban in 1949, the destruction of Gandhi's Phoenix ashram in 1985, to the frequent accusations by Zulu leaders, intellectuals and artists that Indians are unpatriotic and racist" (Hansen, "Diasporic Dispositions").

It may be surprising that we don't often encounter the strained relationship between blacks and Indians in Essop's earlier fiction. However, it must be remembered that this conflict was given less importance, and may even have been glossed over, during the apartheid years because of the urgent need to unite against white sectarianism. Published in 1997, three years after the historic election of 1994, *The King of Hearts* abandons past representations of interracial solidarity, depicting instead the fraught relationships that emerge when ethnic unity is no longer a pressing compulsion.

The title story, "The King of Hearts," begins on the expectation of a better future. It narrates the story of Alexander King, a white heart surgeon—hence the title—who successfully performs the world's first heart transplant operation.[4] The story is set in a fictional nation called Saturnia. Originally belonging to the Sircon people, the country has been colonized by the settler Saturnians. King falls in love with a Sircon woman named Tasreen. Invoking the concord of the past, Essop does not distinguish the Sircons by racial categories (black, Coloured, Indian); instead, we are told that Tasreen is a Sircon woman. Only her Islamic name betrays her origin.

The metaphor of the heart takes center stage in this narrative. Essop imagines the country as a giant festering heart: "They were part of a social system that had become bloated and diseased. It seemed that the entire heart of Saturnia needed surgery—especially as its main artery had been poisoned by a social evil committed several centuries earlier" (2). Opportunity arrives at King's door when the president of the republic requires a new heart. The only heart obtainable is a Sircon one. The public face of apartheid now has a black heart. Gradually all the senators and lawmakers also need heart transplants (a clever conspiracy on the part of the president's wife, who hosts parties and makes them indulge in cholesterol-rich food) and King continues to replace white hearts with black ones. This is used later on to blackmail the lawmakers into yielding to the process of complete social change.[5] Essop abandons his own techniques of stark realism in this collection, thus registering an important shift from the apartheid to the postapartheid period. It is also significant that Essop employs the genre of fantasy to narrate this story of racial healing. Essop refuses to name the geographic terrain of his fabulist world as South Africa, suggesting that the real South Africa is incapable of sustaining a racial utopia.

The title story serves as an important caution to South Africans by serving them the perfect model toward which they should aspire. Like all perfect models, this too is a chimera. Frederic Jameson's comments on satire and utopia are instructive here: "Satire and the utopian impulse [are] two seemingly antithetical drives (and literary discourses), which in reality replicate each other such that each is always secretly active within the other's sphere of influence. . . . All utopias, no matter how serene or disembodied, are driven secretly by the satirist's rage at a fallen reality" (80).[6] In creating a utopia, Essop indirectly reveals his anger at the dystopic reality of the new South Africa.

Most of the other stories in the collection invoke deteriorating race relations more directly, particularly focusing on the implosive hostility between Indians and black Africans. Essop creates a bridge between his apartheid and postapartheid fiction by introducing characters from his earlier writing. This literary strategy—of showing how different social circumstances impact the same characters—allows us to observe how identity is changed by material and political happenstance. Essop also creates highly recognizable characters that embed themselves in our psyches by virtue of our having encountered them earlier. In the short story "Chess." The principal, Mr. Duma, also clashes with the English teacher Zenobia, whom we already encountered in the *Emperor*. Mr. Duma makes Zenobia's resistance to his dictates a matter of cultural difference: "He was incensed. Who else but Zenobia could have instigated the pupils to write the letter? No Christian would object to his sermons, but only a heathen Muslim woman who had challenged him to a game of chess which everyone knew was of Oriental heathen origin" (36). Mr. Duma also refers to Zenobia as the "woman in exotic clothing" and as "the Indian woman" (37).

Mr. Duma uses Zenobia's Indianness as a weapon against her. His obsession with her race reveals (a) that he is not Indian himself, giving his antagonism toward her an ethnic cast and (b) that he imagines Indians (their clothes, their religion, their pastimes) as heathen, exotic, and out of place in the everyday life of South Africa. The aural resonances of the name Zenobia also clamor to be heard. Scholars such as S. E. Dangor argue that "Indians were the first victims of xenophobia in South Africa" ("Negotiating" 256). Suggesting *xenophobia*, Zenobia becomes a symbol of indigenous hostility toward the foreign. The depiction of Indians as "'alien' par excellence; the ultimate 'Other'" (Brah 168) has characterized most Indian diasporas; indeed, all diasporics, before they settle down, are marked as foreign.[7] In South Africa, this Otherness takes on a tragedy of its own. It shows us not only the thwarted promise of postcoloniality but also how Indians still have not acquired composite citizenry despite 150 years in South Africa *and* their determined resistance to white oppression.

In resurrecting characters from the past, Essop rewrites his own fiction by imposing on it the consciousness of the present and warns us of the gathering tension between Indians and other nonwhite Africans, especially if the latter continue to view the former as exotic beings who can never belong in South Africa. Essop also shows us how postapartheid era sensibilities often reflect the rhetoric of the apartheid state. Thus, the new nation, even as it claims to herald a better world, is uncomfortably anchored to its segregationist history.

"The Silk Scarf" underlines the hostility between Indians and blacks even more emphatically than the stories discussed so far. Mrs. Nebo, a black African woman whose husband "had already been designated as the Foreign Affairs Minister in the new government to be established after the passing of the Apartheid era" (45), goes shopping in an Indian district. When purchasing a silk scarf she realizes that she doesn't have enough money to pay for it. She asks the shopkeeper, Mr. Sakur, to take a check. When he refuses to do so, she accuses him of racism. Likening him to the apartheid regime—"you make laws like the white government in this country without consulting the oppressed"—she claims that he is "behaving like the white government's whose time is up" (48). In her disavowal of Indians as oppressed, Mrs. Nebo constructs a dichotomous model of racial being consisting of the white/government and the black/oppressed. If Indians, as this book has consistently suggested, disturb the black-white model of race relations, here we observe a willed refusal to acknowledge that unsettling of binary categories. The phrase "time is up" signals the end of the solidarity of the past even as it evokes the fragility of Indian claims to South African citizenship in the postapartheid period.

Mrs. Nebo's companion then accuses Mr. Sakur of being drunk. When

Mr. Sakur tells her that he doesn't drink because he is a Muslim, she says "you are a fundamentalist . . . we won't have people like you when the new government takes over" (49). Islam and its imperatives are depicted as having no place in the new nation, a significant contrast to *Noorjehan and Other Stories*, where the Jewish Naomi Rosenberg is entitled to South African citizenry *through* her association with Indian Islam.

After Mrs. Nebo has been placated by other traders in the building, who pool their money and gift her the scarf, she tells Mr. Sakur: "[A]s for people like you there will be no place for them in the new democratic South Africa" (50). The interaction described above is a metaphor for contemporary race relations. It reveals the abuse of authority by those in power and their dismissal of Indians as a community whose "time is up" and whose alienation marks them as *subjects*, rather than as fully empowered citizens, of the new South Africa. If Indians stridently asserted their potential for citizenry in Essop's earlier fiction, we notice how citizenry is taken away from them in his later work. This raises important questions about national belonging: A marginal constituency may claim composite citizenry, like the Indian community has always done, but if those claims are not acknowledged by those in power (first whites and then blacks), then the empowering potential of such a gesture is undermined. It is not enough for a disaffected group to acquire composite citizenry in its own eyes; the majority must approve claims to citizenry in order for minority assertions of belonging to have social and political consequences.[8]

The story "Jihad" also reveals the lack of space for the Indo-Islamic point of view in the new order. Revolving around four revolutionaries engaged in military action, the story does not give the radicalized Indian a place in the political milieu. Zaid, a Muslim, expresses his disquiet at killing women and children because it goes against his idea of jihad. His leader, Mr. Fall, then dismisses Zaid's claim to a South African identity by telling him that "you have no claim to the land as the rest of us have. Indians are immigrants" (55). Mr. Fall secretly plots Zaid's murder with his wife and some other comrades. Although the racial identity of Mr. and Mrs. Fall is not revealed, the latter is described as "a light-skinned woman" (54), indicating that she is probably of mixed race. That Essop encrypts the race of many of the non-Indian characters in this collection suggests that it is not just blacks who see Indians as the alien, but also other South Africans. Collectively, these groups constitute more than 97 percent of the South African population, texturing the hostility toward Indians with pervasiveness, omnipresence, and menace.

The story ends with the murder of Zaid and with Mr. Fall proclaiming triumphantly "the word *jihad* has a new meaning. It means liquidating cowards and traitors" (56). The italicization of jihad is significant. Italics usually suggest difference, particularly the difference of the italicized word from its surroundings. Metaphorically speaking, Zaid himself is the italicized word, different from the surrounding norm of other South Africans. The italicization of jihad also implies that the concept has no room in the South African consciousness, intimating that the new South Africa will not accommodate the cultural practices of the Indo-Islamic community. Again, this speaks to the instability of Indian identity and the Indian desire for citizenship as well as to the instability of Essop's own fiction, which moves from joy and celebration in the apartheid period to anxiety and then finally sorrow and rage at Indian dispossession under the new dispensation.

But Essop also attempts to comprehend the genesis of this rage toward Indians. Black anger is often directed at the relative wealth of Indians, a wealth—so the assumption goes—earned through the exploitation of black people. In the story "The Councillor," Mr. Khamsin, a leading light in the South African Indian community, is an unscrupulous businessman.[9] Mr. Khamsin is nominated to the South African Indian Council (SAIC), a political elevation laden with consequence.[10] Members of the SAIC were invariably rich entrepreneurs, a "privileged group [from which] the apartheid system draws some support" (Ginwala 12). Political power begins to send forth its predetermined intoxication.[11] When Mr. Khamsin's employee, the narrator of the story, quits his job, Mr. Khamsin tries to persuade him that "the future of Indians lay with the whites. 'Politics is about power,' he ended. 'Those who wish to trade with morality will be defeated'" (111). Essop uses Mr. Khamsin as a figure around which racial hatred coalesces, for not only does Mr. Khamsin espouse racial hierarchies, but he also serves white capitalism. Essop does not uncritically assign blame to black Africans, but rather attempts to comprehend the genesis of this rage.

Mr. Khamsin's trajectory of upward mobility continues in the following story, entitled "The Banquet." As he ascends the social hierarchy, Mr. Khamsin begins to personify what Hansen refers to as the perception of the "vices of the Indian community: greed, excessive status consciousness, hypocritical family life, vanity and political opportunism" ("Plays" 258). In an effort at maintaining his upward mobility, Mr. Khamsin hosts a banquet at his home, where other leaders of the new South Africa congregate to elaborate on their vision for the future. A political chameleon, Mr. Khamsin now vociferously supports the new government.

The guests agree that democracy has to be Africanized to flourish in the continent. While everyone celebrates the fact that South Africa is "a rainbow nation that will set an example to the world with Afro-democracy" (115), no one questions in whose image democracy will be rehabilitated. Essop articulates his apprehension that the rainbow nation will be a black nation, with no room for the Indians. Shareef, the skeptical Indian introduced in this narrative, repeatedly tries to defuse the ethnocentric bombast circulating in the room. Professor Ramota argues that "whites have admired Oriental cultures but not African which they labeled primitive. It is now time to demand respect for what is truly African" (116). The assertion that "whites have admired Oriental cultures" hints at an affiliation between Indians and whites from which blacks are excluded. This erases any dispossession Indians might have suffered.

In claiming that it is time to respect the *truly African*, Ramota speaks in a discourse of apartheid-era purity that situates some groups as authentically African and others as not. We see how discourses that should have belonged to the apartheid past are resurrected in the postapartheid present. Here, a mode of thinking that supports rigid racial distinctions and asserts that Indians do not have a place in the new democratic South Africa is still alive in the national consciousness. Scholars of postapartheid South Africa often claim that apartheid still prevails in the distribution of wealth where fiscal power is clustered in the hands of the whites. Essop's articulation of Indian disenfranchisement reveals that if the whites have economic power and the blacks have political power, the Indians, caught in the middle, are powerless. Essop, however, doesn't merely illustrate this "truth." He also shows us how such revelations irredeemably compromise a democracy's claim to universal rights by making some citizens more equal than others.

Continuing the conversation, Mr. Hunter claims that "Africans built the pyramids, they invented hieroglyphics. They were the first prophets. Moses was an Ethiopian. Muhammad had black ancestry. Even the Buddha, I have examined his statues in the East. They have distinct negroid features" (116). Stephen Howe explains that "'strong' Afrocentrism is accompanied by a mass of invented traditions, by a mythical vision of the past, and by a body of racial pseudo-science . . . from all this follows extreme intellectual and cultural separatism" (2). In that separatist—a dangerous word in South Africa—vein, Mr. Hunter's sleight of hand reduces Africa to (and only for) blackness.

Yet the mythologizing of the precolonial past has characterized all postcolonial nation-building agendas, not just Afrocentric ones. As such, myth making serves as a powerful tool for engendering pride—what Howe calls "confidence-building or identity-affirming functions" (5)—in a historically downtrodden group. It is when mythology becomes exclusionary that its role in nation-making is compromised. Gayatri Gopinath reminds us that "the nation . . . is a nostalgic construction, one that evokes an archaic past and authentic communal identity" (in Braziel and Mannur 262). Here we see how some black Africans evoke an "authentic communal identity" by re-creating an African past that has no place for anyone other than black South Africans. The word "authenticity" always rings alarm bells for those who carry the burden of hybrid histories.

Shareef bristles at the willful Africanization of the Asian and responds that "we [should] speak of the cultural achievements of Homo sapiens in Africa, in Europe, in Asia" (116). As a figure outside the dominant racial paradigm, Shareef's challenge to an Afrocentric universe validates Homi Bhabha's assertion that "ambivalent margins . . . contest claims to cultural supremacy, whether these are made from the 'old' post-imperialist metropolitan nations, or on behalf of the 'new' independent nations of the periphery" (*Nation and Narration* 4). Indians' rejection of black identity contrasts dramatically with their prior affiliation with Africans in Essop's earlier fiction. We notice here how the rhetoric of affiliation shifts dramatically as Indians begin to think of themselves as Indians rather than as black. The Indian community may have come of age, but Essop also highlights the detrimental consequences of this arrival into selfhood. It almost always means a rupture in relationships with black Africans. Essop also cautions against the dangers of black ethnocentrism here. Historically, African ethnocentrism has spelled danger for Asians. The example of Uganda is foremost. Idi Amin expelled all Ugandan Asians in the 1970s, claiming that they were rapacious foreigners.[12] The rise of black nationalism in Kenya and Tanzania also led to the marginalization of the Asian community there. Essop warns us not to celebrate a historically disenfranchised community's will to power *uncritically,* especially if that power is asserted at the expense of another historically disenfranchised community.

After Shareef leaves the gathering, the people remaining plot to expel him from parliament. Claiming that "traitors are noted for their independent minds" (117), they accuse him of being a fundamentalist, based solely on his attire: "Some people say he is a fundamentalist. Observe his clothing" (117). Earlier Essop describes Shareef as "a tall man in a black robe and white turban, a small beard and an elegant moustache" (113). All this repeats Essop's fear that the accoutrements of Islam and its worldview will have no room in the new South Africa. Notice the movement in representational sensibility here. Malik in Achmat Dangor's *Kafka's Curse* defiantly wears his djellaba in public; indeed, Dangor's novel claims that the assertion of sartorial difference has profoundly subversive implications in its ability to hybridize public culture. Yet Essop shows us how clothes can also be a mark of Otherness. We can always locate agency in the assertion of the specificity of one's cultural identity. However, that agency is considerably undermined when people in power refuse to see sartorial flamboyance as a celebratory staging of difference and instead mark clothing as a fundamental civilizational difference that cannot be transcended.

The last words of the story are: "After several months Mr. Khamsin was called to parliament when a seat became vacant. Shareef Suhail resigned soon after the merchant's appointment" (118). The story ends on the elevation of a capitalist acolyte, who had profited during apartheid by aligning himself with the whites, to the highest legislative body in the land. As it is assailed for being alien, Indian identity, in Essop's later fiction, ends up becoming hesitant and tentative and *silenced*, as the eviction of Shareef from parliament suggests. That the racist succeeds and the man with the integrity to question the perils of ethnocentrism is punished reveals Essop's bleak vision for the nascent nation: In failing to incorporate minorities into its purview, the new South Africa has not upheld the promise of postcoloniality. Instead, postapartheid South Africa seems to repeat and preserve the mistakes of the past. Ashwin Desai points out that "many laboured under the illusion that apartheid-imposed identities would be broken off after that time. We were wrong. A racial language more insidious than apartheid was born. In its approach to race, development and nation it recodified much that the struggle had undone. It was the language of the rainbow nation" (*Arise* 114). Democratic South Africa thus maintains the race-obsessed discourse of its apartheid past.

Where Do Muslims Fit In? Religious Chaos in *The Third Prophecy*[13]

The stories in *The King of Hearts* set the stage for Essop's latest work, *The Third Prophecy* (2004). In the seven years between the publication of the two texts, the African National Congress further consolidated its power and Thabo Mbeki's government began to use the exclusionary rhetoric of an African Renaissance.[14] As Islamic militancy gained global notoriety, the position of Muslim Indians became even more tenuous in the new South Africa. *The Third Prophecy* evaluates the South African political psyche through the tropological consciousness of a single Indian Muslim and meditates on the nature of Islamic identity in South Africa as well as on the utopian possibilities of multinational democracy. This last, the novel seems to claim, will never achieve fruition unless it can incorporate the Indo-Islamic constituency within its parameters.[15]

Although Essop has depicted this crisis in religious accommodation in *The King of Hearts*, *The Third Prophecy* turns inward in much more detail in order to examine how Indian Muslims contribute to their estrangement from the folds of the nation. According to Islamic historian S. E. Dangor, "Indian Muslims are still vacillating between an Islamic and secular, South African identity" ("Negotiating" 264). Essop portrays this schizophrenia inherent in Indo-Islamic identity and also depicts the alienation of the secular Muslim from both mainstream (too Muslim) and margin (too secular).

Does the non-Islamic mainstream exclude Muslim Indians from democratic fulfillment because of their association with religious militancy and social vigilantism or are militancy and vigilantism fueled by Islamic occlusion from the norm? Essop doesn't answer these questions in any clear-cut way; instead, he suggests that this hostility is mutually reinforcing. The relationship between Muslims and other South Africans, then, is characterized by violence: not only violence in the way each community relates to the other but also a cognitive violence in the way each perceives the other.

Essop's depiction of the fraught encounter between the Muslims and the secularists has elaborate repercussions for understanding the composition of a multicultural nation that is nevertheless dominated by one race or ethnicity. Paul Gilroy's comments on ethnic fortification in an effort to consolidate national identity are apposite here:

> The intellectual heritage of Euro-American modernity determined and possibly still determines the manner in which nationality is understood within black political discourse. In particular, this legacy conditions the continuing aspiration to acquire a supposedly authentic, natural and stable "rooted" identity. This invariant identity is in turn the premise of a thinking "racial" self that is socialized and unified by its connection with other kindred souls usually, though not always, within the fortified frontiers of those discrete ethnic cultures which also happen to coincide with the contours of a sovereign nation-state that guarantees their continuity. (in Braziel and Mannur 66–67)

Black nationalist discourse, as Gilroy points out, mythologizes an anchored, uniform, organic picture of national identity. Thus, if national belonging is asserted through rootedness, purity, authenticity, and stability, even if Indians *think* they possess these qualities, other ethnicities refuse to assign these traits of belonging to them. Essop challenges what other South African writers before him have attempted to achieve by showing the impossibility of composite citizenry.

The Third Prophecy draws titular inspiration from three prophecies uttered on national television by the self-styled seer Mr. Roma, who predicts that a political star will be eclipsed, that the country will fall into chaos, and that it will emerge from this chaos only after a Muslim has been elected president (8). Essop traces the obsession of his Indian protagonist, Salman Khan, with the third prophecy—that a Muslim will become president—and his attempts to fulfill the prediction.[16] Set five years after the transition from apartheid to democracy (i.e., 1999), the novel opens with Salman celebrating his sixtieth birthday. Salman has been minister of education in the postapartheid government since its inauguration. One of ten Indians in parliament, his relationship with Indianness and Islam is ambivalent.[17]

Salman belongs to a political organization called the African Front, a party clearly modeled on the real-life African National Congress (ANC). Increasingly drawing criticism for its monopolistic grasp on South African polity and despite widely prevalent disaffection with its agenda, the ANC has nevertheless assumed an unassailable centrality in the national psyche. Essop invests the African Front with the same hegemonic impulses. Salman is accepted in the African Front because he is always attired in Western clothes rather than Islamic accoutrements and because he is a non-practicing Muslim, an atheist married to a woman named Elizabeth. In that context his disassociation from the Indian/Islamic community is political pragmatism. Despite his assimilation into a dominant image, Salman cannot believe that the prophecy refers to him: "[T]he black majority will not accept me at present. Perhaps in years to come" (10).

This sentiment, that the mainstream is not ready to accept a Muslim as president, compromises the nation's claim to have enshrined a representative democracy in its constitution, bringing to mind Gilroy's comments on "cultural insiderism":

> The essential trademark of cultural insiderism which also supplies the key to its popularity is *an absolute sense of ethnic difference*. This is maximized so that it distinguishes people from one another and at the same time acquires an incontestable priority over all other dimensions of their social and historical experience, cultures and identities. Characteristically, these claims are associated with the idea of national belonging or the aspiration to nationality and other more local but

equivalent forms of cultural kinship ... the forms of cultural insiderism [sanctioned] typically construct the nation as an ethnically homogenous object. (in Braziel and Mannur 52; emphasis added)

Essop's fiction reveals a similar manifestation of cultural insiderism. In order to belong, one must assign unbelonging to someone else—the "absolute sense of ethnic difference" that Gilroy mentions. Ethnic insiderism erases all other histories and affiliations in its effort to create a clearly demarcated body of difference and Self-Sameness. That Gilroy anchors ethnic insiderism to the idea of national belonging is significant. Black ethnic insiderism is used to assert a racial and cultural difference that at once becomes a national alterity. Essop points out how the new nation, despite all its rhetoric of inclusivity, still preserves an insider-outsider dichotomy. While ethnic insiderism is a characteristic of all nations, its presence in South Africa is particularly disturbing because democratic South Africa vowed to never repeat the mistakes of the past.

When a new dispensation assumes power following the second elections of 1999, Salman is demoted from his position of minister of education to the minister of prison, suggesting a movement from light (education/knowledge) to darkness (underworld/underground): "He had now fallen from meridian heights into 'dungeon darkness,' a phrase that recurred in his consciousness with searing dismal finality" (35). Prison also has powerful resonances in the South African psyche, bringing to mind the unjust incarceration of black activists by the white supremacist regime. Similarly, Salman's demotion also suggests the unjust incarceration of apartheid: this time one undertaken by the postapartheid government.

If education, especially in its postapartheid ANC manifestation, also represents secularism, then prison represents the other world secularists must confront in order to come to terms with the limits of their own tolerance. Essop interrogates the role of orthodox religious politics in a secular state, especially one in which the religious Other is also marked with racial difference. In that context, Salman's first name is no coincidence, evoking as he does a very famous figure whose novel *The Satanic Verses* grappled with similar questions about the nature of Islam, Islamic fundamentalism, and the secular possibilities of the Muslim religion. Essop mentions Salman Rushdie at least twice. The fictional Salman in many ways is like the real Salman: both secular Muslims who are trying to determine their relationship with the hard-line fringe of their religion. *The Satanic Verses* controversy was manipulated to declare that the British Muslims who protested against the "blasphemous" aspects of the novel were unassimilable, reinforcing another parallel between Salman and Salman even as Essop demonstrates how South African Indian fiction is molded by global literary trends as well as local ones.[18]

Mr. Bengali is the first orthodox Muslim Essop's Salman encounters. The antipodal opposite of Salman, Mr. Bengali is described as "always dressed in a white cotton shirt that reached his ankles and an embroidered white skull cap. His beard was black and long. He was an outlandish figure in the council chambers of legislators wearing suits" (26). Throughout the novel Mr. Bengali is a figure of fun, at least in the eyes of Salman. This is because he refuses to assimilate to the sartorial, cultural, and religious demands of the larger South African community. The visual difference of Muslims from other South Africans and their consequent alienation from the norm is a theme that we see running through Essop's fiction. The use of the word "outlandish" (out + landish) further implies that Muslims like Mr. Bengali are out of the land rather than in the land, highlighting once again the unbelonging of Indian Islam in South Africa. The name Bengali also suggests that Mr. Bengali belongs to Bengal rather than to South Africa, although in the earlier Essop, the name Bengali would have suggested that Bengal is *as much* a part of South Africa as KwaZulu Natal or Gauteng.

The passage quoted above also testifies to Salman's discomfiture with what he has turned his back on: a more conservative Islam. Later, Salman describes Mr. Bengali to Mr. Khamsin as "always the same, a discordant figure. He is an ambitious man and may have secret designs" (30). "Discordant" again suggests something out of place, while "secret designs" harbors connotations of latent militancy. Although no evidence in the novel suggests that Mr. Bengali has participated in any sort of religious violence, the significance of this conversation lies in the ease with which Salman can accuse Mr. Bengali of militancy based purely on his outward appearance. Through the failure of his own political ambitions, Salman later realizes that it is not just conservative Islam that has no place in South Africa, but also Islam in general..

As the encounter with Mr. Bengali reveals, Salman, the assimilated secular Indian, imposes the rhetoric of difference onto other Indians, obviously in an effort to make himself feel more at home and in place in South Africa. Thus for Indians to belong, they have to abjure their Indianness and embrace the dominant cultural identity. We get exactly the same message from Essop's apartheid-era novella *The Emperor*, in which Essop urges Indians to repudiate their Indianness and embrace blackness instead. However, in the postapartheid period, this rhetoric of affiliation takes on a dangerous tone, as it implies assimilating into the dominant majority. While affiliating with black Africans during apartheid was a gesture of agency and empowerment, in the postapartheid period it becomes a much more problematic assimilation as it erases the specificity of Indianness not for resistance against oppression but to create a homogenous South Africa.[19]

Later in the novel, a Muslim group called UMAC (Unity Movement Against Crime) begins "a campaign of opposition to the many gangs in the city and its environs" (41).[20] The city also erupts in violence. It is not clear that the UMAC is responsible for this spate of criminality, but the president of the republic blames the UMAC and, by deft legerdemain, all Muslims:

> This is an organization that is determined to establish a fundamentalist Islamic state. It claims that it is combating crime. It is the state's duty to combat crime, not a religious movement's. . . . [I]n fact these very people of Indian and Indonesian origin, voted during the second general election for the predominantly white racist parties, who are now in the ranks of the Opposition in parliament and against transformation. They are always critical of government attempts to redress the wrongs of the past. (41–42)

Even though many Indians voted for the white parties in the first elections in 1994, the election of 1999 saw Indians drift away from the National Party (Dhupelia-Mesthrie 27). As Ashwin Desai and Brij Maharaj point out, historically "two broad strands existed [among Indians]: one sought an exclusive Indian politics and collaboration with the white ruling class as a means for winning concessions for its mainly trader constituency, the other sought to build alliances with other disenfranchised groups, especially with the African National Congress (ANC) and rejected collaboration with the white rulers" ("Minorities in the Rainbow Nation"). There is no recognition of the various histories of Indian political affiliation in the consciousness of the mainstream. Once more a homogenizing link between Indians and apartheid ideology is made. The president's statement erases the participation of Indians in the antiapartheid movement and situates *all* Muslims, Indians, and "Malay" as participating in the same divisive ideology. The ambiguous "they" in the last sentence, referring either to the "white racist parties" or to the Indians who voted for them, further forges a connection between Indians and the architects of apartheid. Indians, particularly Muslim Indians, are yet again excluded from the fraternal umbrella of the nation. Essop warns against homogenizing the Indian community and its diffuse responses to political possibility.

Indeed, as Mr. Khamsin points out, "when there is turmoil in the state ... reason evaporates. All Muslims will be branded as fundamentalists" (45). As we stereotype and generalize, we reinforce parameters of Otherness and unbelonging.

If Essop establishes a binary between Salman (stridently secular) and UMAC (stridently religious), this dichotomy is interrupted by our reencounter with Shareef Suhail. In running through a list of all Indian Muslims who could possibly stake a claim to the presidency, Salman comes upon Shareef Suhail:

> In Apartheid times he had been imprisoned on Dragon Island for his political writing. ... He has not been afraid to criticize the party when necessary. He was a historian of repute with published work on imperialist expansion in the East, and comparative studies of Western and Eastern philosophy. ... Some newspaper editors said that he had perceived that the administration was moving in the direction of totalitarianism, clearly evident in the monolithic party structure that rejected opposition, or criticism and even descended to defamatory remarks. (72–73)

Shareef—the name means honest—is everything Salman is not. He did not flee the country during apartheid, but rather chose to dissent from within. Unlike Salman, who absorbed himself in medieval European history in the confines of Cambridge, Shareef's historical imperative is more cosmopolitan and less Western. He studied imperialism in the East as well as "comparative studies of Western and Eastern philosophy." Shareef is also not ready to be a lackey of the African Front/ANC.

Shareef represents the synthesis of the Indo-Islamic and the secular; however, he is allowed no space in the African Front, not only because of his criticism of its absolutist policies but also because he is a Muslim. In *The King of Hearts* Essop describes the plot against Shareef as being based on the perception that he is a "fundamentalist" simply because he speaks against black ethnocentrism (*King of Hearts* 117). In its horror of Islamic fundamentalism, the mainstream rejects even secular Muslims. That an Indian Muslim—Shareef, Mr. Bengali, and, in the black majority's refusal to accept a Muslim as president, even Salman himself—can always be suspected of harboring fundamentalist aspirations simply because he is Indian (an *ethnicity* not indigenous to South Africa) and Muslim (a *religion* not indigenous to South Africa) suggests the dual dispossession of subcontinental Muslims in the rainbow nation and underlines the temporality of Indo-Islamic identity in South Africa. This is a significant contrast to the somewhat more celebratory evocation of Islamic Indianness in Achmat Dangor's *Kafka's Curse*, where he emphasizes rootedness, belonging, and the reclaiming of South Africa by its Islamic Indian constituency. It's also important to situate these novels during the historical moment of their composition. *Kafka's Curse* was published just three years after the first election of 1994. *The Third Prophecy*, published ten years after the first election and five years after the second election in 1999, has had more time to reflect on South Africa's transition to multicultural democracy and the failure of its egalitarian vision.

However, a transformation comes upon Shareef, a transformation Salman remarks upon with wonder:

> In parliament Shareef had always looked very distinguished, in a black, dark blue or green Arabian mantle. He was now dressed in a flowing pearl-white shirt with an open neck that displayed his muscular torso and grey pants. His face was clean shaven; in parliament he had a neatly trimmed beard. His appearance surprised and unsettled Salman for a moment. (73)

Shareef's shedding of his Islamic garments can be interpreted in two conflicting ways. The first is that he rejects the "categorical imperative" of Islam by refusing to *look* Muslim. In doing so he supposedly turns his back on Islamic fundamentalism and fanaticism. Alternatively, Shareef decides not to *secularize* but to *assimilate* into mainstream South African society by discarding what marks him as different in the first place. Shareef's coded state of being (does he reject fundamentalism or does he integrate into the norm?) metonymically reveals the tenuous allegiances of Indo-Islamic identity in a nation where the confluence of religious and racial difference always means national difference. It emphasizes the illegibility of Indo-Islamic identity, its indecipherable nature giving discomfiture to those who cannot interpret it on their terms, further extending the circle of disaffection.

Just as Shareef and Salman represent different forms of Islamic being, so too are Salman and Mr. Khamsin constantly contrasted with each other. If Salman criticizes Indians for alienating themselves from the black mainstream, Mr. Khamsin fuels racial hatred of another sort by comparing black South Africans unfavorably with South African Indians:

> When Indians arrived in this province in the late nineteenth century they had little knowledge of the English language. The majority of them had been farmers in India, but that vocation was denied them by the

white rulers. . . . But the community looked ahead. The youth had to be educated. So they built their own schools, both secular and religious. . . . Now when this country was transferred into the hands of the indigenous people, there were no challenges to face. They found themselves in possession of a country with the best infrastructure on the continent, possessing great wealth. In such a situation there is no appreciation, foresight declines and we have what we have today. (98)

In contrasting Indian industry with black indolence, Mr. Khamsin revives apartheid-era stereotypes of African and Indian. The power of these stereotypes lingers even today, especially in the way these historically disenfranchised communities view each other. Dramatist Kessie Govender has spoken out against this tendency on the part of many Indians to "'help prop up the apartheid system. There is a rigid caste system here—no solidarities can be made in Chatsworth. There are Indians who look down upon the whites—never mind the Africans'" (quoted in Hansen, "Plays" 260).

Mr. Khamsin regurgitates apartheid ideology that claimed it was the white/Indian people who developed the land and if it were to be handed to black people, they would squander its resources. As Njabulo Ndebele points out, "individuals who have benefited from that flawed environment [apartheid] cannot deny responsibility. To deny responsibility is to affirm indirectly the perception that there has indeed been no change" (157). Essop demonstrates how minorities themselves can contribute to their disaffection by subscribing to the rhetoric of divisiveness. Thus, the allegiance and alliance that characterized the apartheid period is replaced by racial division instead.

The contrast between Salman and Mr. Khamsin is also developed when Salman consults the origins of the word "Khan" in the *Oxford Dictionary*: "Title of rulers and officials in Central Asia, Afghanistan, (Hist.) supreme ruler of Turkish, Tartar and Mongol tribes and emperor of China, in Middle Ages. (From Turki kãn lord)" (76). The origins of the word suggest that Khans belong as rulers elsewhere—in Turkey, China, and Mongolia perhaps, but not in South Africa. The word "Khamsin" means "Oppressive hot S or SE wind in Egypt for about fifty days in March, April and May (Arab 'kamsün' fifty")" (76). The association of Mr. Khamsin with oppression is significant in terms of his dogmatic political vision. The fact that Khamsin refers to a wind in Egypt (i.e., Africa) is even more important. Salman, whose ancestry can be traced back to India, China, and Turkey, has no African roots. Mr. Khamsin, whose lineage goes back to Egypt, is anchored to the continent in a way that Salman can never be.

Salman is then forced to realize that the third prophecy refers not to him, but rather to Mr. Khamsin:

> He had played no part in the liberation struggle, in fact had enriched himself in apartheid times. . . . He was not only a master of commerce but also a man who knew how to arrange things to his advantage . . . Mr. Khamsin was the man destiny had chosen to be the future president. He was a devout Muslim, buoyant in temperament, keenly perceptive of political realities, diplomatic in his relationship with others, prudent in making statements, calculating in action, convincing in argument. Above all he possessed the energy to advance towards whatever he wished to achieve. (155)

Mr. Khamsin may seem to have achieved the perfect balance between secular and spiritual imperatives, but his behavior in this novel and in *The King of Hearts* gives us pause.

Muslim politicians have to perform orthodoxy in order to placate the community they represent, but they also have to be slippery and flexible in their beliefs if they nurse larger political aspirations. This leads to a Janus-faced existence, a split consciousness.[21] *The Third Prophecy* intimates that there is no room for secular Islam, for even secular Islamists are never wholly accepted, despite their assimilation. Neither is there any room for an orthodox Islam. The only Islamist who can succeed in this regime is a consummate politician who can belong to both worlds (the secular and the Islamist) without really being committed to either one. This is not necessarily a bad thing. However, Mr. Khamsin's expediency, rather than devotion, as a politician and as a Muslim presages Essop's pessimistic vision for the Indo-Islamic community. Mr. Khamsin's duality reflects the instability of Indian identity; indeed, it suggests that in order for Indians to survive in a dispensation where one powerful group after the other denies them full belonging, subcontinentals have to take on a chameleon-like aspect in order to exist as viable political and social entities.

The novel ends on a bitter note, with Salman being removed from the cabinet and with Mr. Khamsin being elevated to the ministry of trade and industry. In the very last line of the novel, Salman collapses, a breakdown symbolic of the collapse of his political ambitions as well as the death of secular Islam. This echoes Shareef's eviction from parliament in *The King of Hearts*. We can also see this disenfranchisement of South African Indians in terms of C. L. R. James's reflections on citizenry in a Caribbean context: "[T]he good life . . . is that community between the individual and the state; the sense that he belongs to the state and the state belongs to him. . . . [T]he citizen's alive when he feels that he himself in his own national community is overcoming difficulty" (in Mehta 131). If an organic connection between individual and state makes the citizen feel alive and partaking of the "good life," Salman's collapse suggests the collapse of the nexus between citizen and state, particularly between Muslim citizen and secular state. That we don't know whether Salman survives further suggests the tenuousness of Islamic Indian identity in the postapartheid present.

In charting a shift in Indo-Islamic consciousness, historians of South African Islam, such as S. E. Dangor, claim that:

> There appears to be a gradually emerging consensus that Indian Muslims should develop a distinctive *South African Muslim* identity that is inclusive of all Muslims in South Africa while at the same time positioning themselves as an integral component of the broader South African citizenry with common objectives. It could be said that unlike British Muslims, Indian Muslims in South Africa no longer feel a sense of dislocation, and are on course for a transition from formal citizenship to what Bottomore calls "substantive citizenship." ("Negotiating" 265–66; emphasis in original)

If Indian Muslims have been able to carve a distinctively South African Muslim identity, the identity that survives is Mr. Khamsin's, not Salman's. This reveals Essop's bleak vision for Islamic identity in the rainbow nation. Essop's depiction of Indian Muslim identity challenges Dangor's optimism about the place of Islam in South Africa. Contrary to Dangor's celebration of "substantive citizenship," Indian Muslims seem more occluded from the national norm than before. *The Third Prophecy* laments the two strikes—of race and religion—against Indian Muslims and critiques the new nation for failing to live up to its own image of egalitarianism and inclusivity.

Indian disaffection in South Africa has somber consequences for the composition of the nation and for national and cultural identity in our postcolonial lives and times. Stuart Hall defines cultural identity as:

> [A] shared culture, a sort of collective "one true self," hiding inside the many other, more superficial or artificially imposed "selves," which people with a shared history and ancestry hold in common. Within the terms of this definition, our cultural identities reflect the common historical experiences and shared cultural codes which provide us, as

> "one people," with stable, unchanging and continuing frames of reference and meaning, beneath the shifting divisions . . . of our actual history. This "oneness" . . . [underlies] all the other more superficial difference. (234)

Hall highlights the "oneness" engendered by a common history based on a shared set of historical circumstances. This oneness makes citizens feel that they belong by giving them a sense of national solidarity. A common history should transcend the "fact" of race, especially in South Africa, where the story of political oppression binds dispossessed constituencies tightly. However, the tragedy foregrounded in Essop's work reveals that despite the commonality of oppression under apartheid, Indians and blacks are incapable of forging the unity woven by shared suffering. The dominant cultural identity in South Africa is a black one, and national identity is therefore also black.

Indian unbelonging underlines the fact that the new South Africa is not so new after all. The rainbow nation continues to preserve an absolutist sense of racial, ethnic, and national identity as it moves from Eurocentrism to Afrocentrism. Postapartheid South Africa is also infected by xenophobia, as its Indian population is still considered foreign, thus encountering the fear of the alien. Essop also marks the new South Africa's inability to accommodate the Indian presence, particularly the Indian Muslim presence, whose racial difference is exacerbated by religious difference. Essop's later fiction thus reveals a disturbing trend in postcolonial societies in general, where independence does not always herald a better world—especially for those still on the fringes of power.[22] Citing Pamela Johnston Conover, Pal Ahluwalia argues "that citizen identities are the defining elements which shape the character of communities. Such identities can be socially cohesive. However, when they are found to be lacking, *legitimacy itself becomes problematic*" (505; emphasis added). Similarly, Desair and Maharaj quote Y. Carrim to assert that "the ways in which and the degree to which Indians are integrated into the post-apartheid society will be a not unimportant measure of how successful a non-racial democracy South Africa has become" ("Minorities"). Indian alienation from the national norm in the postapartheid period casts doubts on South Africa's success in the projects of community building, intercultural reconciliation, and racial healing. South Africa's failure in these spheres compels us, then, to question its very "legitimacy" as a truly postcolonial nation.

New Directions or Same Old?

Afrindian Identity and Fiction Today

*A**frindian** Fictions* has focused on narrative acts, arguing that works of the imagination have powerful political implications for the citizenship-seeking agenda that characterizes South African Indian fiction. Yet the "fictionality" of fiction often reminds us of its distance from "reality," even as fiction not only springs from material and political conditions but also determines our perception of those material and political conditions. In this brief conclusion, based on my visit to South Africa in December 2005, I analyze the difference between "imagined" and "lived" Afrindian identity. During my time in South Africa, I noticed that many of the issues central to this book—the cross-fertilization of races, the hybridity of Indian identity, the intense affiliation with black Africans, a disavowal of mythic India over everyday South Africa—did not seem important to many of the Indians with whom I interacted.[1] Is South African Indian fiction really that removed from the world in which it is produced? Or is fiction aware of the problematic ideologies underpinning the lived experience and merely offering a vision of an alternative *better* universe? Analyzing Louis Althusser, Jeff Lewis states that "art and literature are capable of creating a critical distance by which the subject may at least partially escape the controlling power of the ideological imaginary. ... [T]he relationship between the imagined and real conditions of life ... can somehow fracture the substance of the ideology by making us 'see'" (97). South African Indian fiction is not only an escape from but also a corrective to the "controlling power" of quotidian ideology.

On December 28, 2005, Dr. Deena Padayachee organized a gathering of the South African Indian literary community in his Durban home.[2] Attendees included playwrights Ashwin Singh and Rajesh Gopie, scholar and community activist Ashwin Desai, literary critic Betty Govinden, first-time novelists and short story writers including Nazia Peer and Faezaa Simjee, poets, cartoonists, biographers, and scholars. In other words, the group represented the spectrum of South African Indian cultural expression. I asked the gathering to comment on the current state of Indianness in South Africa and the issues that animate Indian writing today. What followed was a lively discussion that was suffused with high emotion and the constant interjection of politics into a supposedly "literary" conversation. Initially I was frustrated. This was supposed to be a discussion on literature. What did the "ethnic cleansing" (a term repeatedly used by one of the two white men attending) of Indians and whites from the medical profession have to do with South African Indian literary production? I then realized that the repeated fusion of culture and politics only validated one of the central claims of this book: There is a direct and determinate relationship between political occasion and literary expression in South Africa, *even after* apartheid. Yet, as the conversation progressed, I was engrossed.

After having spoken to South African Indians at length during my stay in Durban and from the discussion at this gathering, I have concluded that Afrindian identity is underpinned by at least two antipodal political ideologies.[3] One group believes that Indians are now victims of Afrocentrism following decades of oppression by Eurocentrism. The rhetoric is similar to that used by opponents of affirmative action in the United States: It benefits unqualified Africans at the expense of qualified Asians and whites. I certainly saw the implosion of racial solidarity that Ahmed Essop describes in his later fiction. Some Indians feel strongly that Afrocentrism had shattered the solidarity of the past by collapsing nationality with race. For example, a retired professor attending the seminar said that he went to a meeting for "Africans" in Pretoria. The attendees were all black. When they told him the meeting was for Africans only, he responded, "What do you think I am?" Indians, therefore, resent their elimination from a race-based national identity, one which they had ironically fostered by uniting under the umbrella category "black" during apartheid.

The second group, consisting mostly of academics and activists, is more self-critical, focusing on the racism of Indians and arguing that affirmative action is necessary for black Africans, as they have suffered the most. In a recent e-mail, Mariam Akabor, author of a collection of stories entitled *Flat 9*, told me that among the most important issues "that Indians face in post-apartheid South Africa is how to deal with racism. The majority of Indians in SA are racist. It is sad but true. Many of the older generation Indian citizens became very used to the way life was during the apartheid days (especially the fact that in the race hierarchy, the Black people were below them) that they find it difficult to experience a total reverse in hierarchy since 1994" (May 23, 2006).

The political ideology of this liberal group of Indians echoes Parvathi Raman's comments in an essay on progressive Indians in the 1940s: "Their diasporic sense of self was thus also embedded in ideals of modern citizenship, freedom and equality and visions of membership in a democratic South Africa" (230). While identifying as, and even taking pride in being, Indian, the central issue for this community is that of creating an egalitarian nation-state and establishing solidarity across class lines rather than those of race. The new South Africa has seen the rapid rise of a nonwhite middle class, but the vast majority of South Africans, particularly blacks, remain mired in the vicious cycle of poverty. This poverty, the second group of Indians believes, is the issue requiring instant redress. If the apartheid regime was inordinately successful in dividing people across race, the new government has equally successfully split people across class.[4]

The highlights of the seminar were the personal stories I heard that helped me define—as well as redefine—Afrindian identity. For example, one of the writers mentioned that on a family trip to India—accompanied in true subcontinental style by many members of her clan—her parents' generation insisted on filling out Indian as their nationality on their immigration forms. The younger generation, of course, filled out South African as their nationality. The Indian immigration officer had to tell the older generation that their nationality was South African, not Indian.[5] Another writer pointed out that when she watches cricket with her father and India plays South Africa, she finds that they are cheering for different teams. Yet another participant came up to me during the break and said, "If you find out what South African Indian identity is, please tell us, for we don't know what we are." When I said this confusion ("Are we Indian or South African or both? And if we are both, how do we be both?") characterizes all Indian diasporas, she shook her head ruefully and said, "But in South Africa, it is worse." While it is clear that the older generation may still cling to the fantasy of return to a mythologized India, the younger generation, although confused and even disaffected, has anchored itself firmly to the everyday reality of South Africa. The older generation's holding on to the idea of a mythic India also complicates what we have seen in this book project where most of the writers analyzed, no matter what their age, are harnessed firmly to South Africa.

Part of this confusion regarding national and cultural affiliation emerges from the opening up of India as a source of diasporic retrieval following the end of apartheid. India is present everywhere in South African Indian life.[6] I noted this particularly in Durban, where a "Bollywoodized" Indian identity proliferates.[7] I saw young Indian women wearing the latest *kurtis*, listening to Indian music, and watching Hindi movies that I—Indian born and bred and a voracious Bollywood fan—had not even heard of, let alone seen. South African Indians have been cut off from India for so long that when India became available to them, as it always had been for Indian diasporas in the West, the intensity of that cultural retrieval was extraordinarily fierce.[8]

Thomas Hansen, for example, describes the vast number of subcontinentals who returned to India following the end of apartheid. As Hansen points out, many of them had an adverse reaction to India. They didn't expect it to be quite so dirty, backward, and third world—quite so "not-India," in other words:

> For the Pillays, as for so many others of their kind, their brush with India was an encounter with something disturbingly unknown, a place that made them feel very alien, *very South African* and very modern. It made them realise just how different they were, how "white" they were in their "work culture" and their habits, and how "inauthentic" their Indian-ness was. . . . Mrs. Pillay experienced India within a truly 'orientalist' framework: as authentic, a place imbued with a certain inner beauty and harmony, and a place that exuded history and timelessness. ("Diasporic Dispositions"; emphasis added)[9]

As we have observed in this book, South African Indians often approach Africa and Africans through the interpretive lens of Western colonialism. Here, Otherness is transposed onto what has always been historically apotheosized as the Self-Same: the "motherland" itself. The Pillays also collapse India into the stock stereotypes provided by Orientalist rhetoric: extreme poverty, timelessness, and spirituality.

The Pillays' response to India also underlines the permanent failure of return. Many South African Indians visited India thinking it would be a triumphant coming home. Instead, return, as it often does, firmly established India's essential difference and their South Africanness. In that vein, one man at our literary gathering even told me that he didn't think the "curries" he ate in India were as "authentic" as the South African ones. No matter how much South Africans may mythologize India, return always ruptures the fantasy of an idealized homeland as well as the very possibility of return itself. Ironically, this split from the Mother Country validates the South Africanness of Indians as their perception of the subcontinent is always inflected by South African history, culture, and politics.

Even though physical return exposes the hollowness of the myth of Mother India, many South African Indians—most of whom presumably have never been to India—adhere to a conservative, and therefore supposedly unsullied, Indianness in their daily lives. As a participant pointed out in the seminar, ties to India have lead to a retreat inward and to the creation of a community that cherishes a fantasy of India that would be unreal to many Indian Indians. The progressive politics engendered by apartheid have been supplanted by a fealty to a very conservative *filmi* aspect of Indian culture in South Africa.[10] From what I saw in Durban, many Indians are attempting to create a pure version of "Indian" identity, even though South African Indians can *only* reconstruct a South Africanized form of the Indian cultural past. The belatedness of this mythologizing of India, coming centuries after the original schism of migration, is an irony made possible by the isolation of South Africa during the apartheid years.

When the conversation eventually returned to literature, the most pressing question raised was: "What do we write about?" Many participants felt that the South African Indian experience was a local one and therefore did not resonate with the world outside. This explained the invisibility of South African Indian literature to those present at the gathering. I pointed out that the South African Indian experience is not necessarily local, but rather we allow Eurocentric aesthetics to determine our conceptions of local and global. We then had a lively discussion on whether Indians should write about their specificity of their own lives or "universalize" their voices. The published writers at the gathering said that ethically one has to be true to one's own voice, and the only way to do so was to write about issues animating one's life: In other words, the South African Indian experience should compass one's writing. Yet many writers also bristled at a narrow, race-based approach to literature, arguing that their work should be expansively South African rather than insularly Indian. Part of the problem in making that distinction, however, is to presume that to be Indian is somehow *not* to be South African, a negotiation of national collectivity and ethnic specificity that fiction has also struggled to maintain.

Most participants further believed that their writing performed an important communal and archival function by recording stories that are often forgotten or dismissed as unimportant. In its commitment to remember, literature corrects a collective amnesia on the part of the Indian community, a disavowal engendered by the pursuit of material wealth that marginalized stories of the community's struggle and rich history. It was with great sadness that I noted the disrepair into which the Durban Cultural and Documentation Centre had fallen. The centre was established to function both as an archive and a museum. It contains rare artifacts from the indentured past as well as a wealth of archival material. Unfortunately, the centre was almost unusable. I had to plead with the staff to be allowed in, even though the centre was open to visitors. It was thanks to the kindness of one of the curators that I was able to enter the archives. Once inside, the scenes were shocking. Nothing was catalogued. Reams and reams of valuable documentation were lying around unused. Precious old artifacts were gathering dust. The curator said that there is no interest among the Indian community or the administration to preserve the Indian past. This is ironic, given that the provincial minister of education was an Indian, but also perhaps reflecting a fear that to be openly proud of being Indian is to be susceptible to accusations of apartheid-era racial insularity. Indians in South Africa thus seem to be caught between their own apathy, the indifference of a government for whom they are just not important enough, and an anxiety among progressives that ethnic pride is dangerous in the racially charged climate of postapartheid South Africa.[11]

Another instance of a communal forgetting of the Indian past emerged during my visit to Phoenix, Gandhi's ashram in Durban. The ashram was uncurated and abandoned. The doors were open, and we were able to simply walk in to look at unguarded precious Gandhi memorabilia. Nor was this symptomatic only of Durban. When I visited Ahmed Essop in Johannesburg and found out that Gandhi's Tolstoy Farm was close to Lenasia, where Essop lives, I wanted to visit. Essop said that it had fallen into a state of absolute disrepair and that it was not safe to go there any more. "You'll probably be assaulted on your way there," he said grimly. I could not help but reflect on the irony that the road to the commune of the high priest of nonviolence was paved with the threat of violence. Parvathi Raman says that in the course of her "fieldwork in South Africa, many people seemed anxious to claim an association with Gandhi, however tenuous" (243, n12). That so many South African Indians take pride in Gandhi makes the neglect of the ashram and farm even more regrettable.

Paradoxically, ethnic pride proliferates among Indians, regularly manifesting itself through an exclusionary existence, racism toward black Africans, the mythologizing of the rags-to-riches history of Indians, and the "Bollywoodization" of Indian identity. Indianness in South Africa is polymorphous, full of gaps, fissures, and holes. My visit to South Africa, and my experience at the literary seminar conducted there, proved to me that there is no one, unified Indian voice and that disparate discourses influence Indian identity. It also reveals the structural determinacy of the apartheid past—political oppression, racial hermeneutics, national identity, and longing for belonging—that still prevails in the postapartheid period.

What, then, accounts for the distance between the literature analyzed in this book and the "reality" narrated above? If literature doesn't merely reflect reality but also creates and conditions our perceptions of reality, then the gap between South African Indian literary composition and "reality" can be explained as not a disconnect of literature from reality as much as a *corrective*. Indian fiction projects an alternative universe that rectifies the community's problematic ideologies. So, for example, fiction corrects the communal inability to archive the Indian past by proffering an alternative repository. Writers such as Farida Karodia, Imraan Coovadia, and Praba Moodley resurrect *and* memorialize the Indian past by returning to an erased history.[12] If many South African Indians cling to a mythologized India, fiction challenges this regressive impulse by anchoring itself to the everyday reality of South Africa. South African Indians have also been accused of racial and cultural insularity. Again, fiction showcases the centuries of racial intermingling undertaken by Indians.

The writers discussed in this book perform the function of "correction" and give us a progressive, albeit complex, version of Afrindian identity. Apartheid-era fiction articulates an intense solidarity with black South Africans and seeks citizenry through race. Even though Afrindian identity is never negated, it is usually *subsumed* by more pressing compulsions. The instability of subcontinental selfhood challenges the purist conception of South African Indian identity seen during my visit to Durban. That this fictional identity has a direct correspondence with South African political circumstances reveals that Indianness is not only influenced but also determined by the everyday reality of South African life. While all other postapartheid Indian writing is associated with a somewhat celebratory tone, it is only Ahmed Essop's later writing that comes close to the rhetoric of disaffection I encountered during my time in South Africa. *Afrindian Fictions* has argued that Indians proudly and defiantly assert their place in South Africa; closing with Ahmed Essop's latest fiction may expose the ultimate failure of that citizenship-seeking agenda.

Interviews

I conducted the following interviews in South Africa in December 2005 and January 2006. I am extremely grateful to the writers for their hospitality and their time. The interviews have been edited for length. Any changes and omissions from the original, usually because the audio in the original transcript was unintelligible, have been made in parentheses or with the use of ellipses.

I hope the interviews foster the book's project of listening to the unheard stories of South African Indians. I have included interviews with Aziz Hassim and Ronnie Govender, two very important South African Indian writers, whose work could not be studied in this project for reasons of space. The interviews with Hassim and Govender will serve as an introduction to their writing as well as give readers a fuller picture of the complexity and range of South African Indian fiction.

Interview with Deena Padayachee

DURBAN, DECEMBER 25, 2005

PR: Let's talk about why you write short stories rather than any other prose genre? Why does the short story work for you particularly?

DP: It appeals, because, basically of my time constraints. I have always found it very difficult to get my thoughts down on paper, to have the time to get [them] down, organized in the proper manner. Poetry also, I find, does not need as much time as a novel. I can concentrate on something and get it done properly. Also, I find short stories allow me to tackle a subject from many angles, and then I can analyze a situation. I usually focus on injustice, racism, humiliation, which is endemic to my country. And so I found that short stories allow me to do all this, but I find a novel much more difficult to write.

PR: And what about poetry?

DP: I love writing poetry, but poetry is more inspirational. I find that you have to have a certain feeling that will allow the poem to come out, so I can't dictate how a poem should be written. I can't sit down and say: "Oh, I'm going to write a poem today about something." But with the short story, I have the idea of a plot, and that's my main focus, that there's an idea and some issue that I want to really get to grips with. And in my short stories I like to be fair to all concerned. So I usually, or very often, make the villain of the piece the narrator, or I try to give his viewpoint first.

PR: ... How does your poetry differ from your fiction?

DP: Quite frankly, the poetry and the prose deal with the same things—it's injustice, basically—but, I find irrationality, irrationality of people and of life, the value systems, that's one of the things that drives me to write. I find again and again, especially growing up in a country like South Africa, so much that was irrational was taken as normal by highly educated people, a simple thing like putting a sign on the door that said "Europeans Only. No Dogs Allowed." Now, professors went along with it. They said this was fine. Professors of ethics. So it's that irrationality that I grew up with, that I needed to come to terms with in my own mind ... a lot of that writing came out of that need to clear things in my own mind about what was going on. Now, poetry, I find, you need to be very [critical] about each word that's in that poem, so I think poetry is very difficult to write, and I find prose much easier.

PR: What is the significance of titling your collection after Tina Turner's song *What's Love Got to Do with It?*

DP: I didn't do that. What happened was ... "What's Love Got to Do with It?" was the working title that I used for that short story, and when the Congress of South African Writers asked for my collection of short stories after what happened with the Nadine Gordimer Prize, then I sent over my collection to them, and they said that that was the best title. I didn't like it because of the song, but the publishers explained to me something that was pretty obvious, that every story was concerned with love: love of country, love of home, love of family, love of your career, love of life. So it was appropriate from that point of view, but I think it is a bit off-putting for some readers.

PR: Well, not really. . . . I really like the title, and it didn't occur to me that every story was necessarily connected with love, but I felt that the title . . . connected to a global black culture. And I do think that your collection was trying to connect with black oppression all over the world . . . it is significant that Tina Turner is a black singer. And the African American experience in the U.S. is very similar to what nonwhites have endured during apartheid, so I [thought] that the title was making this global connection between oppression [in various parts of the world].

DP: That's a nice way of putting it. Yes, I never thought about that, but I find this again and again. I find that readers of my work come to me and come up with fresh and new ideas . . . my writing is usually done very fast, like "Visitor" was written in half an hour—really quickly, just before the idea disappears from my head. I just want to get it done. It comes out exactly like that, and then I edit it obviously, over a couple of years sometimes, but very often when I'm writing it, I am not thinking about all the issues . . . that sometimes come to you later.

PR: And sometimes you are guided by your subconscious as much as by your conscious mind. You are really not completely in command of what you write.

DP: Exactly! You are not in command. There's something, I honestly believe—look, it's not only me, a lot of writers will feel this way—we seem to be tapping into something else . . . some sort of global consciousness, and so the words come . . . almost by themselves.

PR: So, do you agree with your publisher's assessment that all the stories have to do with love?

DP: Actually, I do. I do.

PR: Because my next question was—and I think it has been answered—can we use the song to interpret the stories in the collection?

DP: Yes, I think so. I find in the bigger picture, the love that is focused on in the book is the love that destroyed apartheid. Because apartheid nurtured and encouraged hatred between the cultures and colors, religions, and everything. So what destroyed apartheid was love.

PR: Let's talk a little about the individual stories. And let's talk about "The Visitor," which was one of my favorite stories. I want to talk a little about the significance of the figure of Gandhi. Clearly, the old man is the ghost of Gandhi and the spirit of Gandhi, a sign of Gandhi...

DP: And his values, yes.

PR: So, can you talk a little bit about the significance of the figure of Gandhi in this short story?

DP: ...[H]e was destroyed. I saw him being destroyed.

PR: And do you feel in some ways that what Gandhi represented was also destroyed?

DP: Yes. It was destroyed. We actually see that. The peace went out of this place. As a medical student I went there, because there was a free medical clinic and I used to go there to recharge my batteries. It was a place where I felt a great deal of peace. I read a great deal about Gandhi, and so I respected the person as the person who began the movement that shattered Western control of the world. So I adored him. I worshiped him. And so when I saw that the people he was trying to liberate were destroying a place of peace by violent means, it was very shattering for me. [*Padayachee is referring to the looting of Gandhi's ashram, Phoenix, during Indian-African riots in 1985.*]

PR: In that story Gandhi tells the looter, "'Look after these things,' he said in his gentle, squeaky voice. 'They're from Africa.'" This is my favorite line in the entire short story. But I wanted to talk a little bit about what he says, because among the things that the looter is looting is a copy of Gandhi's book and his desk. I want you to talk a little bit about what it means that Gandhi's things are of Africa, and therefore what Gandhi means for South Africans Indians as a community.

DP: Yes, his genesis as [mahatma] was here, and then Natal means birth, and so the birth of the movement to free the world began in Natal, and, ironically, this was the last place to be freed from colonial oppression. So it begins and ends here.... And he says: "Look after these things," because he has left a legacy. Unfortunately, I feel, it has been abused.

PR: Can you explain a little bit how?

DP: Well, the violence. The violence of this place—they were destroying his home and in a symbolic way they were destroying his legacy. Everything he stood [for] was being pulled apart in that ashram.

PR: So then it seems Gandhi is this really important person in the South African Indian psyche, because the fiction I read—Ahmed Essop, Farida Karodia, your work, Agnes Sam—all of you mention Gandhi one way or the other, and I was wondering whether you could just follow up a little more on the role that Gandhi plays for you and other South African Indian writers, and also for the community as a whole, the nonliterary community.

DP: What I'm going to say is not very nice, but the fact is that this is the effect of the writers, the intelligentsia. The general Indian populace, unfortunately, because of the brainwashing of Western education, has very little idea about Gandhi, and they don't follow his philosophies, and they become very materialistic, and there is much more violence now in the Indian community compared to a generation ago, and much more divorce, and much more disrespect between families, between parents and children, so I'm afraid, as far as the general Indian community is concerned, in my opinion, we have become very distant from the message of Gandhi.

PR: And why do you think the writers are also influenced by Gandhi in so many ways? Because even Christopher Heywood in his book says that one of the characteristics of Indian fiction is this incorporation of satyagraha.... Why do you think the writers themselves follow Gandhi?

DP: Because for us, who are aware of his message, we obviously feel the need to honor it. And we feel the need to spread his message among not just the Indian populace, but all sections of the South African population and the world population, about the goodness that was in that man.

PR: Let's move to "A Different Kind of Standard Four," which was again one of my favorite stories. Can you comment a little bit on the title?

DP: Yes, well, actually my father had a standard four [fourth-grade education] and he did so much with this standard four that it was an inspiration for us. So what we have is a situation where my father showed us in that story just what his generation had to go through, so that we could get an education. He enabled me to respect the older generation and the whole apartheid system taught disrespect and dishonor, so he turned everything on its head and that was really good.

PR: But . . . the father in the story is also talking about a different kind of education, because the apartheid system didn't give Indians or blacks their own history . . . it was basically Western history. So [he was] talking about a different kind of education also.

DP: Exactly . . . the concluding paragraphs focus on that. . . . And I'm afraid that even today we don't have much liberation history of countries, whether Vietnam, or India, or Arabia—we don't really know our own histories and so we have less pride in our heritage than the whites have. So that is still a major problem.

PR: So what would a perfect educational system look like?

DP: There is no perfect educational system, but if I had anything to do with it, I would say, know yourself first before you know the world. . . . I have met a lot of Indians from India—and they just have a different kind of quiet confidence, compared to us here. Indians here don't know their history. So they don't have that sense of respect for their own color, their own culture, their own heritage, even the educated ones.

PR: When you talk about "their own heritage, their own culture" what exactly do you mean? Do you mean the history of their arrival in South Africa?

DP: No, much more than that. I'm talking about Ashoka. I'm talking about the Ramayana. I'm talking about inventing the zero and technology and geology and algebra and plastic surgery, like the short story ["A Different Kind of Standard Four"] talks about . . . the Taj Mahal. These are things we need to know, and, unfortunately, many of us don't. They are part of our conquest.

PR: Do you think Indians don't know even much about their own history in South Africa?

DP: Oh, yes, that is a major problem. The generation that Gandhi worked with—when I read about the things he did with them, I marvel, because I couldn't do those things with the people today . . . they are so different from that time. And I find the same problem with my own children, because they don't want to know what happened to me when I was five years old and couldn't get to use this little boat in the paddling pool. They are not interested. . . . I can understand in a sense why they want to distance themselves from something which is quite painful, but at the same time I can see how a parent can have such problems getting a message down to their children. . . . So with books—especially, [if] our [Indian, non-white] books are prescribed at school—that makes it easier to get our message across. I think that will enable greater respect from the children towards the parents and from the parents towards the children. A lot of what we did when we were still teenagers was for our unborn children, and then it is very painful for us now to see our children turning away from our history. And that's because of the Western domination.

PR: And that's the purpose of "A Different Standard," which is for children to understand what their parents have done?

DP: Absolutely.

PR: And in a way . . . what you are pointing to is that the children who have grown up in the postapartheid era are taking their privileges for granted and don't understand what it was like to live [like] that.

DP: In a way it means we have succeeded . . . but then, beyond that, it also means that . . . we have a situation where we are in an environment which is fundamentally racist, because it is a Western-dominated environment that we are in, and the West immediately assumes third world inferiority. It immediately assumes cultural superiority, and so we look down on ourselves and we undermine our own culture.

PR: And what has Afrocentrism contributed to all of this? There has been a lot of tension between the Indians and the Africans, here in Natal particularly.

DP: Yes, well, that now is a different . . . aspect of things, obviously. See because I wouldn't call it Afrocentrism, but we are now faced with a problem that Africans have been empowered. Previously, the Europeans were empowered, so they did terrible things to us, and the Africans in their powerlessness also did terrible things to us, but now that they are empowered, we have affirmative action. So now what happens—I call it reparative action, rather than affirmative action—but at the same time we are now paying the price.

PR: Let's get back to your short stories. Many of your short stories use metaphor, and I really like that a lot about your [work] because I read a lot of short stories that were composed during the period of apartheid, and they tend to be much more straightforward . . . because their whole purpose is political, not literary, and I understand that and I sympathize with that. But what I like about your stories is that you are able to use these literary devices along with politics, so that the two go hand in hand. It's not that the literary is . . . considered subservient to the political, and one of the ways I see you do this is by using devices such as metaphor and allegory, like "A Pestilence in the Land," for example, which is about the subterranean vermin plotting a takeover, things like that. And so I was wondering whether you could talk a little bit about what function metaphors and allegories serve for you, because you use ghosts in "The Guests." You use the spirit of Gandhi in "The Visitor." . . . [T]here are so many instances in your book. . . . [W]hat purpose do they serve for you and why do you think they work better for you than straightforward narration?

DP: For me these things actually come naturally. I sort of conceive them in my head and quite frankly I never thought about them too much. I just wanted to write something interesting, entertaining, and to get a message across. And I find, as you said, that a straightforward narrative, for me anyway, would be boring. I have to like what I myself write, and if I don't like it then I don't publish it. So that is why I did that, because I obviously read a lot and I know what works for me. And for me allegory and metaphor work. That's why I use those devices. . . . And as far as the ghosts go, for me there is a spiritual dimension to life . . . and I also have scientific training, and in scientific training you do double-blind trials to work out whether something will work or not, whether it's a drug, medication, that kind of thing, and you use evidence-based results. . . . Now the spiritual dimension can't be quantified, and so I use the fact that there are forces beyond quantification, which need to be taken cognizance of, when we are perpetrating evil. So the wheel turns; there is karma, and that's why

I tend to use the figure of Gandhi, the spirit of Gandhi, then I use the ghosts in "The Guests," in the short story "The Guests," which for me is one of my little . . . joys. I feel so good that I wrote that story. I really love the fact that I wrote it . . . even though I wrote it thirty years ago. I come back to it and read it and say, "Hey, I really did something there!" And I feel good about it. I can also understand the pain of somebody who would read something like "A Letter to the Mayor" and feel very distressed, because he wouldn't want his children to study what he did to us. But I think it is so important that people study stories like this, so that in their lives, if they are ever persuaded to engage in evil, they would understand that they are dealing with human beings.

PR: So why do you have a little white boy as the protagonist in "The Ghosts"?

DP: Because he is innocent of this whole thing. It is important to get an innocent person to understand what his parents are doing. His parents know fully what they are doing, but he doesn't. He just sees a human being that he loves.

PR: And it's significant that the parents can't see her [Vimla, the ghost], obviously, because that's what allows them to perpetrate the evil in the first place, so they see don't see Indians as human beings. They [are] invisible. I think that's why the metaphor of "ghosts" works so well.

DP: And I also think that children are closer to God than us. That's just a feeling I have always had . . . and that's why I'll always be drawn to children, because children have a beauty . . . and they lose that beauty as they get older. But certainly as children they can sense a great deal that we can't.

PR: . . . Race relations between Indians and Africans seem to be an important theme in this collection, and you are very critical of Indian racial attitudes also in this book. . . . Can you talk a little about Indian racial attitudes and the way you represented them in your book?

DP: Yes, I think they got this thing from India, the caste system, the color consciousness thing, is something really deep in the Indian psyche, and so we have a situation where Indians worship the pale skin, and they almost are in fear and hate of the black skin. And I, as a very dark-skinned Indian, had to endure this my whole life. . . . [N]ow those attitudes have been transmitted unfortunately to the African people, and so I am very, very disturbed by this, because the Africans are the majority here, and if we are going to discriminate against the majority, and be racist towards them, then our children will have no future.

PR: Do you see Indians trying to be white during apartheid?

DP: Oh, yes. Even now. It is a very big phenomenon, the children as well. They're trying to be as Western as possible and they jettison a lot of Eastern values. They think they are important if they color their hair and use blue contact lenses.

PR: So what does the title story, then—"What's Love Got to Do with It?"—what does that tell us about African and Indian relationships, because the last line of the story is "Goddamn coolie marrying an Indian girl."

DP: Yes . . . the way we used "coolie" at medical school wasn't derogatory. We often called each other coolie . . . and we used it almost as a term of affection, but if a white person used it on us, we would be upset. But this African was our friend, and if he used it, it wasn't a problem. And what I say in this story is that it is possible for us all to be friends if we can just all better understand where we are coming from.

PR: How has politics shaped your writing?

DP: As I said in my e-mail to you, I think that if there was no apartheid in South Africa, then this would not have been . . . I probably would not have begun writing, because it was the sheer irrationality of my childhood that made me write, and my adulthood, because I had to come to terms with what was happening, and also in my writing I found that I was writing for myself. I was writing to understand the world around me, and I found myself coming up with thoughts and ideas that I didn't even know I was thinking, and I find the same with my *Sunday Times* column. I find very often that thoughts that suddenly come out of me that I was not aware of. So it is a lovely way to drench your own mind and analyze things, this ability to write.

PR: Do you think the postapartheid period has given you similar creative inspiration the way the apartheid period did?

DP: Well, apartheid did much more, but . . . I think certainly for myself that is true, one uses very little of one's brain in the course of one's normal daily activities, but when one writes, one uses much more of one's mind, and that for me is a joy. But now writing is much more difficult, because writers tend to be critical of what's happening—well, certainly my kind of writer is very critical about what's happening around him—and now when you criticize, you criticize an establishment in power . . . and so you are now criticizing sometimes the majority . . . and there is far less tolerance. There wasn't much tolerance in my time, but I think there might be even less tolerance nowadays. For instance, if I wrote abut the 1949 riots, or I wrote in a very critical way of affirmative action, I might get a bad reaction from the new people in power, and that can be very difficult. Or if I wrote about the crime; I certainly get that kind of reaction when I'm writing about the crime, because I've had people in power tell me: "Oh, there's crime all over the world, not just here." And I find that difficult, because I find that one must be truthful, and I think it is very wrong that people who have actually participated in the struggle, and who shed their blood, were incarcerated and all that, can now turn around and say false things to fellows who they are against.

PR: What are some of the major themes in your writing? You have touched upon irrationality and oppression, but could you talk a little bit about other [themes]?

DP: Yes. Racism, humiliation, the oppression of women, our history, our heritage, trying to bring our country to life at a particular time.

PR: What are some of your major literary influences?

DP: Khushwant Singh from India, who was editor of the *Illustrated Weekly of India*, something I read in the 1970s, because I used to get the *Illustrated Weekly of India*, I subscribed to it, and I loved his writing. . . . I enjoyed the lucid way in which he writes. He writes in a very clear, simple way, and I think reading, some kinds of reading, can be seen as for the highly educated and for the upper classes and that kind of thing, and I think it's just so important for reading to go to everybody and to write in a way that everybody can interpret and understand, and not just the highly sophisticated academics.

PR: And you try and write in that way?

DP: Yes. And the other writers who write like that and who I like very much are John Steinbeck and Berthold Brecht, and I think to an certain extent also Ahmed Essop, André Brink.

PR: Are there any South African Indian writers who influenced you?

DP: Ahmed Essop, yes. Other than Essop, not really ... [poets] ... Shabbir Banoobhai, yes. And the other writer [who] is very good and I like very much is Alan Patton.

PR: Why has South African Indian literature been largely ignored so far?

DP: There is something very deep in the Western psyche, which I think comes from the Greek experience, probably even more from the Roman experience.... So they see the East as a problem ... and so they still have this antagonism to us. And so they reject anything Eastern. So we find that, for instance, Indian music, Indian art, literature, religion, culture, dance is all marginalized in KwaZulu Natal.... Again, I wrote in my last column about the fact that when I was invited to Denmark, a large part of the delegation that was going was Indian, but what they did was, they had the Drakensberg Boys Choir—this is 1999—this is five years after Mandela comes to power, and so what happens is, you have the Drakensberg Boys Choir—this is happening in Durban, by the way, which has more Indians than whites—and you have African dancing but you don't have anything Indian done at an event before we go to Denmark.

PR: Is this changing, or is it still a problem for South African Indian writers to be published?

DP: Some Indian writers, I think, are in a very difficult situation. I find that publishers in KwaZulu Natal and throughout the country seem to be much more amenable to African writing than to Indian writing, so like, for instance, the University of Natal Press—I went to a book launch recently, and they published a large number of black writers, but not a single Indian writer. And I constantly get badgered by Indians who have manuscripts ready and can't get a publisher, so it's very, very difficult. And most of our Indian writers ... they're all printing their books themselves.

PR: Hasn't anyone thought of setting up a printing press?

DP: See, the problem is for it to be financially successful ... you need bookshops that need to be prepared to sell our books. . . . But we've got this major problem that we have what I call the prison system of the Western culture, [people who are] all for Western books to be sold, Western theater, Western movies, Western music. They see us as a problem. They don't want our books. . . . They are very hostile to Indian books. . . . There is no culture within the book trade with a passion for your own indigenous writing; there is a hostile attitude towards our writing, because our writing very often deals with the suffering from so-called civilized people, you see, and they don't like that. They get very upset when they see what we've written, and I can understand that, but at the same time we are South Africans, and we have the right to have our books in our own bookshops.

PR: So why do you think then that there is an interest in publishing books by Africans and not by Indians, because even the books by Africans would be addressing the same issues ["suffering from so-called civilized people"]?

DP: Well, that's very interesting, because the whites used to tell us around 1990, that we shouldn't write about apartheid; we should no longer write about racism, because it's all in the past. We shouldn't be bothered by it anymore. So, for instance, when we have the writer's festival in Durban, the Africans will come on and they are not talking about persecution and suffering, because they know the whites won't like it. Now the whites are publishing their books, and they will be talking about taking the bus to work and having a shower, and that's what they are reading. They won't be talking about what's affecting them really, in a deeper sense, in their country, so the whites are orchestrating what is being written, and when we want to write what we want to write, then there is a problem.

PR: And is it possible that they—the whites—don't consider Indian writing even important?

DP: Well, obviously, my whole life they made it seem like what I was writing was not worth publishing, but obviously that is a false perception. It's more that they feel threatened, and because they feel threatened by our writing, then they say that it is bad.

PR: But they will also probably say that: "Oh, you are such a minority, you are not important. [You] are only 3 percent of the population" and I wonder whether anything has to do with that?

DP: Well, in the past they used to say: " . . . Indians don't buy books." And so it's not even worth their while to put it in their bookshelves. But we know that our writing is of relevance, not just to South Africans, over 40 million of South Africans, but is relevant all over the world. So that argument doesn't hold water. . . . That's what they say. They are using any strategy.

PR: What would you like a scholarly audience to know about your work? A scholarly audience . . . that [may not] even know that there are Indians in South Africa. You have to start at a basic level. What would you like them to know about your work?

DP: That to me is a difficult question, because I write as a South African first, then I write as an Indian South African. I would like them to know that Gandhi actually lived here for twenty-one years, and I'd like them to know that the West has done a lot of good for South Africa, but there have been many aspects of Western impact on South Africa that have not been good for us and that if America wants to continue its hegemony in the world, then it has to be seen as a force for good. . . . [M]y writing has been very critical of the Western impact on the people of this continent, and I think it is important for people in other countries to know where they have gone wrong and what they've done to us. I think that answers the question.

PR: So your writing addresses this issue of what the West has done to South Africa and to the Indian people in Africa?

DP: Yes, because a lot of the whites are actually acting as representatives of England or America and Holland and Germany, for that matter. . . . Gandhi put it nicely. He said: "Western civilization. That would be a very good idea."

Interview with Ahmed Essop

LENASIA, DECEMBER 18, 2005

PR: Has there been a change from the apartheid to the postapartheid period in your fiction, particularly in terms of the way you have represented relationships between Indians and blacks—so *The Third Prophecy*, for example, it's not very optimistic about the relationship between

Indians and blacks, whereas something like *Noorjehan* or *Hajji Musa* tends to be much more optimistic about a viable relationship between Indians and blacks—so I'm wondering if you agree with that assessment of your fiction and if you think that you represent in your fiction this kind of decline in the relationship between Indians and blacks?

AE: Yes, well remember in the early apartheid era we were separated from blacks, they worked as servants, and in that era, of course, there wasn't really an idea that some changes were going to occur in the country and that one day there will be a democratic [South Africa] where you could live where you wish to and everything that goes with that. The new era is different in that I perceive this as an era where all the earlier restrictions against races have been removed, but I don't see it as one where essentially blacks and Indians cannot integrate or cannot live together. They are living together now to a small extent[:] in an area like Lenasia there are a few blacks who have homes. But what does keep them apart I think are the various cultures.... [T]he Indians tend to hold on to their cultures and the blacks have essentially lost their tribal cultures, they lost it over a hundred years ago, and as they move into cities and they become urbanized the tribal culture disappears and Western materialist culture takes over. And, of course, it is taking over among Indians as well, propagated by television, propagated by the newspapers, the new lifestyles that ... that we see now.

PR: So let's talk about *The Third Prophecy* still a little bit while we are on the subject of your later fiction. It seems to me that the recurring theme in *The Third Prophecy* is the fact that a Muslim cannot become president in this current dispensation. And I was wondering if you wanted to talk a little bit about this, about the role of Islam in South Africa now. Do you think the larger community, black and white, is ready to accept Muslims? Because that seems to be one of the fundamental themes of *The Third Prophecy*, that Salman has this anxiety of not being fully accepted, no matter how secular he is, because he's a Muslim.

AE: Well, look, the [Muslim] community is a small community in South Africa, right, in the first place. And with Salman Khan, it's a delusion he suffers from, the idea that he could become president, because he has been removed from a very important portfolio of education and reduced to one which he felt was a reduction of his status, that is, as minister of prisons, and he found that very hard and the only way he could now rise up would be one where the prophecy of Dr. Roma gets fulfilled. So he eventually comes to believe that well "I'm the man . . . who might be able to take part of that prophecy." He deludes himself in thinking that perhaps he is a descendant of Genghis Khan and Kublai Khan. . . . [H]e also believes his friend Mr. Khamsin, [who] says, "[P]erhaps you are the man" . . . so that is a delusion which he suffers from and it will never be realized in a country where the majority [is] predominantly black.

PR: And not Muslim.

AE: And not Muslim, it cannot be realized.

PR: So you think a Muslim will never be able to become president in South Africa?

AE: Well, I won't be very positive about that, one can't predict the future.

PR: You are not Mr. Roma.

AE: Yes that's it [*laughs*]. But the essence of the book is also where I deal with the nature of democracy. I see that there is a grave fault in [that] the politicians who run a country do not require any qualifications of any sort, neither intellectual nor moral, and there I think there is a very serious thing.

PR: Do you think Salman has the qualifications?

AE: I wouldn't say he has the qualifications, because there is a question of personality as well. And then . . . also people change when they hold positions of power, they are no longer the same ones. . . . [P]ower can corrupt an individual.

PR: Do you think your book is then a reflection on democracy in South Africa in the present?

AE: Yes, definitely I do think that. I'm also trying to show that the ideals that were set down by the political movements are no longer being realized, former communists have all become capitalists, and I made this judgment in one of my stories called "The Banquet."

PR: I remember that one and I do want to talk to you about that collection too. Moving on then, I've noticed that in much of your fiction, characters who we encounter in a previous text, we reencounter them in another text, so that in "The Banquet," for example, we encounter Mr. Khamsin, we encounter Shareef Suhail, and then in *The Emperor* we encounter Zenobia, and then we meet her again in *The King of Hearts* collection. So I wanted to talk to you about this as a literary strategy. Can you tell us why you do this, because I was really fascinated with the way these characters keep appearing in different books?

AE: Yes, what I consciously do is that, since I'm dealing with a particular locality and a particular range of people, the Indian community, many people in the Indian community, I like to integrate them in the stories. I feel that then the stories become part of a world. They become part of a world and I find great joy in bringing them back. Even Guru, who appears in the "Hajji" and dies in a story called "Labyrinth" in a motor accident, I bring him back to life in the novel *The Visitation*. I felt that I needed a man like that now, so I bring him back, and then he appears again, he's briefly mentioned again in *The Third Prophecy*. And he forms the background of a story called "The Novel," in which a local gangster in Fordsburg now says " . . . I am the man that you have portrayed in the novel 'The Visitation,'" and it is very comical.

PR: So you think, then, when you say that you like to integrate them within a particular world, in your mind . . . all your books taken together form this kind of unified world?

AE: And I also try to present them in different dimensions as they appear in different stories, like Shareef Suhail is now a fully matured character in *Third Prophecy* and he only appears very briefly in "The Banquet". . . . [H]e's the only man who ever resigns from parliament.

PR: If you read about Shareef Suhail in *The Third Prophecy*, his character in "The Banquet" takes on a different tone . . . so they both work with each other.

AE: And, remember, I bring Zenobia and Kamar back. [They are] old friends of Salman Khan, and Zenobia does pose a number of questions to him, in that "Why did you take away art from the school curriculum?" . . . She realizes that, well, he is very disturbed by his demotion, so-called demotion, from his minster of education [portfolio]. Then there is something new that I brought in Said . . . from the background of resistance against the drug dealers that have taken over the country now. . . . So, what I want to present is South Africa as it is now, South Africa as it is now, the present time, and moving away from the apartheid era, which is over and done with.

PR: Can you tell me why you write in the novel [form sometimes] and why sometimes you choose to write short stories. . . . [D]o you [think that] one idea works better in a novel and therefore it becomes a novel?

AE: First of all, I read many short stories. I liked Maupassant a great deal when I was young. And there was the South African writer Bosman, I enjoyed his stories, and I enjoyed various stories of English writers but I felt sometimes that a theme just doesn't carry into a novel, it cannot carry into a novel and that, again, the novel is one of a larger world, you see. The short story is, as I mentioned previously somewhere, that it is a very demanding kind of thing, I've got to reduce it, it's got to have an impact, which is brief but significant.

PR: Let me ask you another general question. Where, and again in terms of your fiction but even more generally, where do Indians fit in South Africa? Do you think South Africa has failed to live up to its promise as a "rainbow nation"? Do you think Indians are being excluded from it?

AE: No, I don't think they are being excluded, there are quite a number of Indians in parliament. But do you know what? Parliamentary debates seem essentially one where members of a party seem to have lost their critical intelligence . . . and the Indians who are part of the dominant party, they say nothing. They resent criticism of any sort and they make no criticism. And they will defend the ruling party, whatever they may do.

PR: But in "The Banquet," for example, they keep talking about Afrocentrism.

AE: Yes.

PR: And Shareef is the only one who says Afrocentrism might be worrying because it might end up being exclusive.

AE: Yes.

PR: So do you think that anxiety, that fear, has it come to realization in the new South Africa?

AE: No, I don't think so. I don't think so. Indians have now moved into the world of materialism, really. . . . All their views and their ideas seemed to be shaped by television and desire for material things such as motor cars and so on, mansions and big homes and . . . they are becoming Westernized. Though, of course, there are religious groups that are trying to hold on to the moral values.

PR: So you think South Africa has lived up to its promise of the "rainbow nation"? In terms of the government, has the government done everything that it should have done?

AE: Well, I don't think they have done very much. . . . I think crime has taken over the country.

PR: And what about . . . , for example, the Zulu singer [Ngema] who wrote that song "AmaNdiya," who said that Indians are more exploitative than the whites and that the real enemies are the Indians. . . . [T]here does some to be this kind of friction between Indians and blacks now in the new South Africa . . . particularly perhaps in Natal.

AE: It's not an open friction, it's not open friction, politicians fortunately have not made those sort of accusations.

PR: But do you think it is there at the level of ordinary people?

AE: It could be. . . . I don't have much knowledge of that level really, but there could be some friction, but I don't think it's very serious really. No. I don't see it as very serious. . . . If this government, the ANC government, collapses, it could become serious . . . where certain communities are seen to have prospered.

PR: Let's talk about South African Indian fiction. Why do you think South African Indian fiction has largely been ignored? And do you think now it's acquiring shape as a distinctive literary form?

AE: Let me say this: there were not many writers, Indian writers, in the first place even during the apartheid era. There are not many writers in the first place. And schools and universities were essentially colonial. In that literature meant English literature: Dickens, Conrad, Shakespeare, Hardy, Lawrence, and others, you see, it's colonial literature. And that also, secondly, at schools and universities all black literature was excised. . . .

[T]he government banned certain works by black writers—fortunately, my works [were] not banned, but they banned certain works by black writers—so students were not aware of black writing or Indian writing or of my own writing, they were not aware. . . . I do feel now, of course, that Indian writers have a better chance of having their works read at universities and schools.

PR: Like Deena Padayachee's, for example

AE: Yes.

PR: Let's talk a little bit about your major literary influences, you mentioned Maupassant but who were some of the other writers that have [influenced you]?

AE: The first was Dickens . . . followed by Conrad, followed by Shakespeare. And then, of course, I did a BA majoring in English and an honors course in English. So English literature was my background, right. Then I went on to read Indian writers: Narayan, Anita Desai, Ruth Prawer Jhabvala, Nayantara Sahgal, and Naipaul—and I read those, and I read some West Indian writers such as Wilson Harris. And black writers in Africa, Chinua Achebe and Naguib Mahfouz, translations of his work, Nadine Gordimer, and other South African writers: Coetzee and, of course, all the works of Olive Schreiner and Pauline Smith and Bosman.

PR: And have you read any other Indian South African writers?

AE: Well, I've read Deena Padayachee's work mainly, Achmat Dangor's writings, those two and unfortunately I've never seen the collection of Govender.

PR: Since you talked about Dickens, let's talk about satire, because . . . among the many things that I really like about your fiction is how you use satire and how you use wit and humor. Could you talk a little bit about that?

AE: Yes, well, one of my perceptions of literature is that I want to present many dimensions of life . . . the various dimensions of life. I don't want to focus on one aspect of life only. So I enjoy writing, looking at human beings, satirizing them, looking at them with some irony and sarcasm, and [seeing] their follies and their strengths and the humor of situations, such as in the story called "The Film." Essentially I'm a happy person. And I don't focus on misery only, as I think that John Coetzee does. And I think also those dimensions make literature interesting and enjoyable. It is important that one derives some delight from literature and those aspects give delight . . . for instance, George Orwell's *Animal Farm,* which I enjoyed very much, and Swift's *Gulliver's Travels;* when I was young I enjoyed *Gulliver's Travels* a great deal.

PR: You named your main character Salman in *The Third Prophecy* and you mentioned Salman Rushdie at least two or three times in *The Third Prophecy,* and I was wondering if Salman Rushdie himself has influenced your writing in any way?

AE: Well, look, he is a modernist, as he says, and there are a few modernist elements in *The Third Prophecy,* where there's an exchange of letters between the president and Shareef Suhail and also an essay on democracy by Shareef Suhail, which is also in there. I read *The Satanic Verses* and it's a very impressive piece of work, though I think that the strength of the satire cannot be appreciated, the strength of the satire on Islam cannot be appreciated, if one does not know the early history of the Prophet Mohammad. He satirizes him in sections 2 and 6 . . . and his own belief is that religious ideology is dictatorial. He believes that firmly. [As for] the name Salman Khan. Well, I needed the name Khan because Salman Khan believes that he is somewhere or another a descendant of Genghis Khan.

PR: Right, and he looks it up in the dictionary.

AE: He looks it up in the dictionary and so on. Well, Salman is quite a common name among Muslims. . . . [M]y mother's brother was known as Salman. . . . Really it's a corruption of Suleiman.

PR: We've already touched on it, but can you talk about it just a little more on what it was like to write as an Indian under apartheid.

AE: I came naturally to writing, in that, firstly, when young I was exposed to English literature. I was an English teacher and, looking in hindsight [at] the three years I spent at home, during which I prepared myself for a case against a department, I spent a lot of time reading and I could then . . . [sit] down to read and write, so that in a way was in certain senses favorable to me. . . . I've always enjoyed English literature, all my life.

PR: But did you encounter any difficulties under apartheid?

AE: No, I had no difficulties. I was very fortunate. There was a publishing firm, Ravan Press, able to place me and my work, and there were literary magazines that accepted my writing. Essentially, they were run by whites, all run by whites.

PR: Can you talk a bit about how . . . you and your fiction have evolved? So starting from, say, *Hajji Musa* and ending with *The Third Prophecy*, how have you grown as a writer? How have some of the themes and preoccupations of your work altered and shifted?

AE: Well, it hasn't really shifted. I've been interested in the human condition from the beginning. The stories in *The Hajji* take place around the fifties and sixties period . . . and the others move upwards, right upwards . . . to the present era. And I still wish just to look at the human condition and I'll continue to do that, I think. Taking into cognizance the new circumstances that arise, the new responsibilities, the new perceptions that have taken place in the community. I write about the Indian community because I'm still living in an Indian area and I know them best. Of course, there are some white characters, black characters in my novels as well, but to present life in the [Indian] community is what I can do best.

PR: How has politics shifted your fiction?

AE: Yes, it has, it has. I present the political realities in my fiction, right. But I am weary of all politicians. I am weary of all politicians because politicians hold power and power invariably corrupts them.

PR: What new [writing] are you now working on?

AE: Firstly, I have a collection of stories, new stories . . . some stories relate to the past, some relate to the present times and . . . I am also writing a novel at the moment, called *The Citadel*, relating to the present time, using the present as circumstances, but the story takes place in a different continent, or in a different state, not in South Africa.

PR: But it is a metaphor for South Africa in a way, like *The King of Hearts?*

AE: Yes, that is right, it is a metaphor for South Africa, but I'm writing that. I hope to write one more novel. And of course I've completed an essay on the story of the prophet Mahound in Salman Rushdie's *Satanic Verses,* looking at the satire and the symbolism and filling in the historical background of that story.... I hope somebody would publish that someday.

PR: My [last] question is that this [book] is going to be read by an audience ... who would know nothing about South African Indian fiction, so what would you like to [say] about your work in particular and South African Indian fiction in general?

AE: Well, I would say those that are interested in literature should be aware of, right, that firstly South Africa is a country that underwent a unique change in that power was handed over to a majority without the agony of a revolution. And that [people] should be interested not only in the history of South Africa, but also in the change that has taken place and how that change is reflected in my work.... [T]here are very few revolutions, I think, that have ended in the way ... they have in South Africa. Whether the change is going to benefit the people of the country ... the ordinary people, the people who are still steeped in poverty, I am unable to say. I cannot prophesize that. I am unable to say that. In that I see it moving dangerously towards a capitalist-oriented society, a society of capitalist orientation, where the poor become poorer and the rich become richer. It's a gloomy view, but at the present time this is how I see it.

PR: I think it really comes out very clearly ...

AE: In *The Third Prophecy.*

PR: In *The Third Prophecy* as well as in *The King of Hearts* collection.

Interview with Farida Karodia

JOHANNESBURG, DECEMBER 21, 2005

PR: Unlike someone like Ahmed Essop, you do not write of Indian themes exclusively. Some of [your works], *Coming Home,* for example, deals with a much broader spectrum of South African identity. Can you comment on [the] literary choices that you make?

FK: I hate being restricted to one theme. I like broadening my perspectives because I always thought that South Africa consists of many other races other than the Indians. And being from a sort of mixed race background myself, it has had a great influence on the themes I choose to write about. I write about white South Africans as well, and I'm not limited in how I write about them. I write about the people that I know . . . which [are] basically the Afrikaners, because I grew up among the Afrikaners. I also write about the Coloureds, because I grew up amongst them, and I write about the Indians, because I also grew up amongst them. And so . . . I draw on what I know, I draw on my background. I am also expanding my horizons and setting a story in Canada, and this is a story about a Canadian woman, a white Canadian woman, and so I also know the Canadians as well. I also know people who live in the Calgary area, and so I feel that I can write about them. . . . It might surprise people that I try to break free of race restrictions and write about so many different people, but I enjoy it and that stretched me in many ways as a writer.

PR: And that's what I really enjoy about your work, too, that there is such unexpectedness in terms of content. . . . *Other Secrets* [is] a great book, but I love all your other work, too, like your collection of short stories, . . . *Coming Home*, for example.

FK: *Coming Home* is a really old collection.

PR: Yes, but it is a great collection, because it . . . brings out the diversity of the South African experience. . . . [I]t is given to us in so many voices, the idea of coming home and the [context] of apartheid, and I really like that. I really like the fact that I am reading one story, say, from a white perspective, and I turn the page and I am reading a story from a Coloured perspective.

FK: And it's not something that I do. I do not sit down and plan it like that. A lot of times I do not plan my writing; the characters come to me and they are quite persistent. And I feel I need to write about them. An Afrikaner face might appear and someone from my past reminds me of that, and so that's my choice. I am going to write about them in the same way that I might write about a black experience, and here is one area that I am very limited in . . . the black experience, because I only have the black experience from the time when I was living in the small community and that was a very limited experience too. So I am not very familiar with the black culture. I am sorry that I'm not. I would have loved to speak an

African language, and I could have, because in the area that we grew up in, of course, I was being spoken to in Xhosa—it was the Xhosa area and I'm sorry and now I regret it. And it's too late for me, because when at my age you try to start learning a language it is enormously difficult.

PR: My next question is turning to *Daughters of the Twilight* and *Other Secrets*. . . . Can you talk a little bit about . . . why you turn to Indian identity in those two novels, because those are the two novels, out of all your work, those are the most preoccupied with the idea of being Indian in South Africa. So why did you choose to write those novels? What was the inspiration behind the novels?

FK: Perhaps the inspiration for those two novels was a little bit from my background. Having grown up as Indian, because my father was Indian, and that feeling of split identity is a preoccupation in the book, and probably, once again, originates from my own experience. But I didn't plan *Other Secrets*, and in fact Yasmin came to me quite unexpectedly, and I felt that I had to write about her and I needed the kind of setting for her that would propel her out of her situation. And so I chose to set it in the area in which I grew up, but I thought that Yasmin was a phenomenal individual . . . and it's not based on anyone that I know, so it's purely from my imagination.

PR: . . . I prefer Meena.

FK: Do you really?

PR: I feel like Meena never gets enough attention and that is obviously so much a part of the novel too . . . that it's always Yasmin, Yasmin, Yasmin, but she seems to be a finer and stronger character than Yasmin. Yasmin [is] everything you say she is, but there is this very selfish streak in her, I think.

FK: Yes, but she's also a fighter and that's something I admire . . . she has chutzpah, which is what Meena didn't have. And when I wrote *Daughters of the Twilight* . . . that was the beginning. I didn't think that the story would continue, but what happened was so many who had read *Daughters of the Twilight* came to me and said "Well, what happened to Yasmin . . . ?" And fortunately I had written the first novel, *Daughters of the Twilight*, in such a way that I had allowed . . . an opening for a continuation, and it wasn't intentional either. So I got tired of all these questions of what happened to Yasmin, and I thought I better expand this.

PR: But I like how *Other Secrets* also follows through on Meena's life, because I found all those things that Meena was going through also really interesting. Since we are talking about the relationship between *Other Secrets* and *Daughters of the Twilight*, some critical work that I read on those two works says that *Other Secrets* changed *Daughters* only in minor ways. Do you agree, or do you feel that [in] the first part of *Secrets* and the first part of *Daughters* there are some sort of major differences?

FK: No, I think there are major differences. . . . I couldn't write the entire novel just based exactly on *Daughters of the Twilight*. I had to change *Daughters* in order to continue the story. I mean this is an accepted fact.

PR: . . . I do think that there are major differences also. . . . One difference that I thought was interesting was . . . Abdul's origins, because in *Daughters* you say very clearly that he came as an indentured laborer and in *Other Secrets* you say that he came around the time of Mahatma Gandhi, but it's not that clear that he is an indentured laborer.

FK: . . . [D]id I say that in *Daughters*? I can't remember. I must actually take a look back and see, because it was never my intention to state that he came as an indentured laborer, and it was an easy explanation. I have had problems getting a publisher for this novel because they [said it was] too parochial. . . . I can't remember what the reason was for that, but I think it allowed me a lot more freedom in dealing with Abdul, because Abdul was a very real and powerful character in the book. Abdul was there, Abdul represented the male population in South Africa, although he was Indian. He represented the male who is actually quite voiceless.

PR: The nonwhite male?

FK: The nonwhite male. Abdul was as emasculated as the nonwhite men in South Africa were . . . powerless. There are all these things that happen to his family and he is powerless to stop it. I mean, he tries his little things but he doesn't have the power to stop it. I chose to represent Abdul in that way so that it reflects what happened to the male population in South Africa, and I think somewhere in the novel I do say that the men are emasculated.

PR: And even though he is powerless, he is still a major influence in the novel? And . . . because he is powerless in the public sphere, he has to enact this kind of power over his daughters and wife.

FK: Yes, [he is a] very patriarchal figure.

PR: And since we are talking about favorite characters, I have to say the character of Abdul just broke my heart. Especially the way he . . . goes in for an operation and then he dies on the operation table. . . . And I think in *Other Secrets* particularly there is this tenderness for this patriarchal domineering character.

FK: No, you're absolutely right about that, because in the private sphere he was the patriarch that ruled and he ruled his family that way.

PR: The change in the novel, does it reflect any change in your own writing? Does it depict any evolution on your part as the writer?

FK: Yes, the fact I moved Yasmin out of South Africa in to London, moved her overseas, it does not matter where, was an indication for me that my writing is moving, is going beyond South Africa into other spheres now. . . . And the collection of short stories that I am working on right now is set in all different countries, and I have one story set in India.

PR: But yet, in a way, in *Other Secrets*, South Africa never leaves the novel. . . . So, the characters can physically leave South Africa, but when Meena is in exile she keeps thinking about the warmth of McBain and [how] Soraya's problems might be cured if she could go back to McBain, so that South Africa remains still a strong structuring presence in the novel.

FK: . . . And it is the whole theory of not wanting to leave our home countries. I mean, a lot of Indian writers that I know in Canada, for example, write about their Indian backgrounds. But I have moved away now in many respects . . . and I had to keep away from South Africa. There is another novel about the daughter, the granddaughter [Ashleigh]. That will continue . . . and she will move back into the Indian community.

PR: Why did you write about the fifties [and sixties]? We have talked about how in a way it is based on life in your own community, but can you tell me why you focus on the fifties or the sixties? Why did you choose this particular slice of time?

FK: Because I think that was a period when apartheid was most rife in South Africa. Yes, the fifties and the sixties, when there were mass removals, when people were moved out of one area into another; lives were thrown into turmoil, there were upheavals, and even in *Other Secrets* there were families torn from their home and moved into the *veld*. This happened [in] South Africa during that period. In the seventies things started slightly changing. There were children. Children were on the march. There was the Black Consciousness movement. There [were] a lot of protests. . . . There was lot of resistance. In the fifties and sixties the resistance was minimal. I mean, there were pockets of resistance, but this was when the government really started its relocation programs.

PR: And that still goes back to the theme of powerlessness that you were writing about. That is obviously a major theme then in both these novels and that for you the fifties and the sixties represent this time of powerlessness and it is focalized in Abdul's powerlessness as the powerlessness of the community as a whole.

FK: There is also a strong female presence. The women were very strong, and this is true of that entire generation. Now, even now, the grandmothers are the strong ones in the family. They know everything that is going on, AIDS and all that. Grandmothers are the ones that have come up to bat. . . . They are there for the grandchildren. They are supporting the grandchildren; and taking care of them. . . . And in those days the women . . . weren't aggressive in any way but they had their own way of protesting. They were strong. The kitchen for me was like a base of strategy. This is where strategy was always planned and formulated. So the kitchen for me was a very important part of the house. And the women had a very important role in that kitchen; they were like the generals planning strategy in the kitchen [like Nana, for example].

PR: I want to talk a little bit about Islam in both the novels, because Abdul is clearly a very devout Muslim. . . . [C]ould [you] comment a little bit about Islam and what role does Islam play in the novel, because you write so much about it[?]

FK: I think it has an important role in the early development of the girls, but because there was this split, and it's not really common, because generally when there is an intercultural relationship or a marriage and a non-Muslim marries a Muslim, the non-Muslim converts to Islam, and in the mother's case she didn't really convert, so there was always this split. I mean, the kids went to a [Christian] religious concert . . . and at home they were devout Muslims and as far as I know there are a lot of families where this happened.... And so this is, in my mind, what happens in a few families, where you have this diversity battle.... The kids ... decide who they are culturally, where they fit culturally, and the sad thing about these families is that they weren't always accepted by either culture, and it was a rather sad situation in South Africa, but I think it happens all over ... where you have interracial marriages.

PR: And this is complicated by interreligious [marriages], and not just interracial.... [I]n *Other Secrets* there is this scene ... when Meena sees this Islamic plaque, and she looks at it and the letters are falling off, and then she remembers how her parents had fought about it and how her father had said that it should be in the front room, which was the right and proper place for it, and Meena says she is going to take it back with her to England. Is that Meena's way of remembering her father, or is that Meena's way of realizing that Islam is always going to play a role in her life?

FK: I think a little bit of both, because her father has such a strong influence in her life, not in Yasmin's ... and you realize in the end why Yasmin is what she is. But in Meena's life, her father has always been the focus, and this was something that she associated with her father. But also, the falling off of the letters is a signal in the novel for the falling off of religion....

PR: It seems like *Other Secrets* focuses more on the idea of hidden sexual encounters between different races than *Daughters of the Twilight*. *Daughters* really focuses primarily on the rape of Yasmin, but with *Other Secrets* you then get to see Yasmin's history: who her father is, the fact that Soraya has an affair with a white man too. Why did you choose to bring this out in the later book, because this would have been an issue even while you were writing *Daughters*; so why did it come out [then]?

FK: No, it came out then because it was at a point when—I mean, *Daughters* was an earlier novel—what was the date?

PR: Nineteen eighty-six.

FK: Nineteen eighty-six, yes, that was still the date of the apartheid ... and what changed was that we were no longer in that apartheid, but what I wanted to show [in *Other Secrets*] is the different reactions of the mother, the grandmother.... [T]he grandmother talks about the grandchildren and makes it black on the outside and white on the inside, yes, but also, given that it was Yasmin, I thought it would be unlikely for her to choose a nonwhite. Given her background, and given her rebellious nature. . . . And also to choose a married man first and then . . . it was kind of typical for her to do this. I thought it was [in] her character. . . .

PR: Can you talk a little bit about the significance of the Group Areas Act in both novels?

FK: Yes, it is a very important issue in both novels, because it was also during the time when relocation was taking place and this was one of the major issues in South Africa. People were being uprooted from their homes and from communities that have been their whole lives. . . . Generations have lived in the same communities. . . . I'm from that era, so I know what it was like to be uprooted and being thrown into an environment that was absolutely sterile. There was nothing. Some of those communities were so vibrant, so full of life, they were mixed communities. . . . You lived alongside an Indian; there was a white in the community; the Coloureds living [beside] you. And there was so much joy in these communities. Joy and life despite . . . despite apartheid, there was such a community spirit that prevailed, and all of this was destroyed when they moved people and uprooted them and separated them. The Indians in one area, the Coloureds in another, so they actually tore these communities apart. So . . . it was a very important issue and I wanted to show how it affected people by using this one family [as] a microcosm of what was happening inside South Africa that affected lives in such an enormous way.

PR: Exile seems to be an important theme, not only in this novel, but also in some of your other [work]. . . like *Coming Home*, for example. And yet . . . when she [Meena] does return home, she thinks this is going to be this triumphant return, but yet exile isn't. She feels like she wants to go back to London when she comes to South Africa, because she realizes London is her home. I wanted you to talk more about the ending of the novel, really. What does it mean that . . . *Other Secrets* . . . ends with Meena suspended in this nether zone? She is neither in London, nor in South Africa. She is in the airplane, in the middle of Europe and Africa.

FK: It reflects her feeling of not belonging anywhere, anymore. Having lived in London for so many years, having being exiled in London for so many years and coming back and finding that she has grown away from

South Africa, that people have grown away from her, there is nothing to hold her in South Africa any more. South Africa has changed so dramatically that she can no longer connect with it as it used to be. . . . I did this deliberately, because she doesn't belong anywhere.

PR: But then, why does she not belong in London again?

FK: She doesn't because, and it is a very difficult thing to explain, when something is taken away from you, you want it. You want what's been taken away from you, and you want it at any cost. So she came back to South Africa to get back what she wanted, and I know—I've gone through that—but going back it leaves you with a lot of unresolved [questions]. . . . Now she's got what she wants, or she's dreamed of, going back home, and now that she's home, the weird thing is that it's different. . . . [H]er mother is selling up. Her mother is going to London. It's no longer a base for her to return to. But she doesn't feel really that London is her home, either, even though she's going back there. She's just going back there because her family is going to be there, or she thinks everybody is going to be there. But she has the ability to change; that's why I have left her in the air. If she wants to come back to South Africa, she can do that.

PR: Why did you make her a romance novelist in particular . . . some of her titles, such as *Strangers in Love*, for example, or *Forbidden Love*, because . . . in an interesting sort of way, they seem to evoke apartheid-era [attitudes]. So I was wondering whether you could talk a little bit about that?

FK: Because she had nothing else to read, growing up, and there were always fly-spattered romance novels hanging in the windows of the shop. . . . This is something that she gravitated to . . . and finally realized that she could write one of them, because she had read so many of them. . . . Because Meena is who she was, this quiet, introverted [character], these romance novels were actually a form of escape for her. She could dream about these characters. She could dream about lost love and fabulous faces that she thought she would never see and connect in some romantic way with a life, a romantic life, that was nonexistent for her. . . . [S]he was the good girl; she was the one who stayed home and listened to her father, and this is her escape, because she never thought that she would find a lover or a man. . . . So that was her history, because she had a very bad self-image, and it is just a natural way for her to gravitate to [romance novels].

PR: But I have to say, I wanted you to be the romance novelist and let Meena marry Said and have a happy romance . . . it was so sad when he [Said, Meena's lover] died. I think that . . . was more satisfying in a literary way; it was the better thing to do in a literary way, otherwise it would have been too much of a romance novel, but there was this part of me that wanted her to be happy romantically. But let me ask you this, then: Why did you want her to be single at the end? Because she really is alone; she's only got her writing. Said is dead, she's feeling . . . cut off from her family, Soraya has died . . . so why did you isolate her like this in the end?

FK: I think for her to continue writing, I had to isolate her.

PR: Since we are talking about Meena at the end, this was one of my favorite sentences in the novel, where she says . . . : "We all have our own places. I discovered mine much later; a place which reflected the geography of my soul." What does the geography of Meena's soul look like?

FK: I think it's geography in a more figurative sense. . . . [I]n her mind she has this place that she belongs to, and this place has really not existed until she thinks that this is it, because she is willing now to settle for whatever falls her way. . . . She stopped, I think, at this point in her life, where so much is happening, Meena has decided that she's going to stop looking, and so she's settling for whatever there is now.

PR: Is the ending of the novel for you happy, sad, peaceful? What tone do you get when you read it?

FK: I think it is peaceful. Just peaceful. This is the geography of Meena's soul. She wants peace now. She has gone through all this turmoil and she finds in the plane that this calmness comes over her, and she picks up her manuscript. . . . Yes, so I think it is more peaceful than anything else.

PR: And through the act of writing she finds peace. Is that autobiographical in any way?

FK: I think so. Maybe a little bit. I would not have chosen to write romance novels . . . but I think it was a space for Meena. Making her a writer was a space for Meena to go to, to get away from her life, to live another life, and even though she is in England, I think this has always been Meena's fate: to become a writer, a romance writer, fine, but to become a writer, because of the way she grew up, in a family, but virtually alone.... [S]he was always spiritually alone. And she seemed to be quite happy in that solitude. Not happy, but peaceful.

PR: I think in many ways she seems to be the most restful character in the entire novel.

FK: And that's why when you asked me that question, that's the first thought that came to my mind, peace. And she tried to instill some of that restfulness in Yasmin....

PR: What does the name Ashleigh Fatima Mohammed signify? Because I find all your names are significant.... Soraya is named after the empress of Iran, and [she] was also biracial, and she lived in exile all her life, like Soraya did, and she died in exile. But so what does Ashleigh Fatima Mohammad mean?

FK: I tried to introduce a Western, non-Muslim name, which is significant, because I wanted to indicate that this is now going to be a non-Muslim child, growing up in a totally different environment; that's why I gave her a Christian name.

PR: But do the names Mohammed and Fatima suggest that even though the child is going to be non-Muslim, Islam is going to come into her life?

FK: Yes.

PR: Well, just in terms of whatever you are ready to say at this point about the book you are working on right now, [what] can you tell me?

FK: I am trying to work on a collection of short stories, like I mentioned, which I hope to have published in South Africa and a novella.... [T]he title of the collection will be called *Transitions*. And it is about change, so about people who have left the country, people who have come back, people who are planning to leave the country ... a lot of stories are set in other countries, like Canada, United States, India, England, and so on.

PR: How has your work evolved from your first book to your most recent ones? So, in other words, what are the changes that you have detected in your own work as a writer, thematically as well as aesthetically?

FK: This is a difficult question for me to answer.... The changes that I am aware of are that my work has moved outside of South Africa. That's a major change. Thematically I think my themes are broader than they were in South Africa, much broader. I have finished an early draft of a novel, which I am hoping to submit to a Canadian publisher. I'm having a bit of a problem with the voice. . . . I am sure you know that writers have that problem from time to time. But it's set in Alberta; it starts in India, goes to the UK, and ends up in Alberta.

PR: What makes you choose to write a novel versus a short story? Is it again something that's generally out of your control, or is it a conscious decision?

FK: I like writing short stories, and I like writing them in between my novels, in between big novels. . . . I find that often I am . . . sitting at an airport, for example, and I can get started on a short story, but I wouldn't dream of getting starting on a novel. And so, for me, it's more portable [the short story] and some of the short stories, I think three of the short stories that I will include in this collection have been published before, but in overseas publications. I'd like to keep them all together in one collection now.

PR: Do you yourself identify as a South African Indian writer?

FK: No. I don't want to be labeled. I am just a writer.

PR: Why has South African Indian fiction not been read or critically analyzed or written about? . . . Because right now black fiction is getting a lot of attention, and I wonder whether it is the same problem with South African Coloured fiction, too, that it doesn't get the same kind of attention that black or white writing gets.

FK: I agree with that. I don't know what the reason for that is now. I mean, if we were talking apartheid, this would be an easy question to answer, but I have no idea why this is happening. . . . [T]he literary audience is a very small one in South Africa. I mean, it's almost impossible for writers in South Africa to survive, because there are so few readers. Most people can't afford to buy the books; the people who can afford to buy the books, the middle class, are more electronically oriented. The white population is actually the reading population, and even there it is only a certain percentage of the white population that would read serious fiction. And so I think that is basically the problem. If you look at people like Rohinton Mistry, and Mukherjee, and Vassanji . . . they are phenomenally successful in Canada, and that's because people read. But here this is the problem, and unless a book goes into schools and schools are forced to buy them, writers . . . sell very few copies.

PR: Who are some of your major literary influences?

FK: I have such an eclectic taste in literature. I can read anything. I don't think I can claim anyone to be [a major influence]. I have always loved Salman Rushdie's work [and Zadie Smith]. But like I said, I have a very eclectic taste in reading, and I read quite a number of Indian writers too from time to time. I try to keep up with what's current out there.

Interview with Praba Moodley

DURBAN, DECEMBER 29, 2005

PR: I want to talk a little bit about why you chose to revisit the past. . . . [W]hy did you choose to go back to the indentured experience and write about the experience of the cane fields?

PM: When I was in matric [school] . . . I had to do a history assignment and I found there was such lack of information. Everything was documented . . . we read about it through textbooks, but there were no human feelings or anything of that sort. And during the process of my research for my assignment, I came across areas that I thought were fascinating. And I think it just planted a seed and it just grew.

PR: Let's talk about the research you conducted. . . . Where did you conduct it? What were some of the discoveries that you made about . . . the indentured background? What were some of the frustrations of doing this research? Some of the surprises? Some of the joys?

PM: The initial dry facts came out from the history textbooks. But there's the *Indian Opinion* [a newspaper]. . . . It has such a lot of stories. . . . It gives you such a rich feeling of a different time span, and you actually feel for people that lived in that time. . . . They're going through the same emotions and the same feelings and everything else that one would go through now. And that's what caught me, actually. That they may have lived in a different time frame, but everything that you go through is [the same] . . . it's just another generation.

PR: And what are some of those issues?

PM: They were personal issues that people had: personal problems, marriages were falling apart, people were having relationship issues, family problems.... The newspaper actually conveyed human feelings and emotions that you would never have picked up in the history textbooks.

PR: So what were some of the frustrations, because as you were saying ... there aren't all these stories available ... ?

PM: We [are] living in this modern era, and you take things for granted. And just going back to everything the way we, our forefathers, came through, and you actually feel their pain and realize that it was hardship that actually brought us where we were today.... One of the difficult things during writing this was that it took such a long time to actually get the material, the research. Whereas now, you just type something into Google on the Internet and you pick up a whole lot of info. So it was actually frustrating during the research period to double-check your facts and make sure that everything was right.

PR: Let's talk a little bit about specifically the novel. Why did you choose to use a love story as the center of your story?

PM: It wasn't supposed to be a love story. When I started the concept of the story, it was supposed to be about the lady that gave birth on the ship, because it was a new idea. They were coming to a new land. They just had a baby, the Pillays ... actually when you write you find that some characters come alive and some don't. And what happened was the lady that delivered the baby, Chumpa, when she started to come alive in my story, she had more to say and more to give to the story, and it was actually a family saga. If you look at it, it's a family saga because it's about her family and her children and the decisions they've made.

PR: Absolutely ... the novel ends on her, so it comes full circle.

PM: Yes. It starts with her giving this life. She's delivering a baby, and with her birthday at the end. And actually ... when I started it, it was supposed to be about this new couple that came in and their trials and tribulations, but the other family just grew.

PR: Can you talk a little bit about the fact that it did become a love story.

Particularly . . . an interracial love story. . . . [W]hy did you choose to focus on that?

PM: Because that came up when you do your research. As I said, the *Indian Opinion*, they had stories about people that had these relationship issues . . . and in those days often white men abused [non-white] women and one in a million would actually fall genuinely in love. And I thought that would be very good.

PR: And is there evidence of those genuine love relationships in the *Indian Opinion*?

PM: I can't honestly remember proper evidence of such, but it gave me the seed that I needed. I can't quote you names and families that I've come across in there.

PR: So, then, to the character of Albert, what were you trying to say and do? Because I do think . . . you are countering the stereotype of white men as always being the abuser. . . .

PM: But there were cases, you notice there's good and bad. . . . And there were good whites that took care of the indentured laborers and there were others that abused them and that came across in the story. So that I picked up from the reading and the research.

PR: Did you see, in your research, any kind of interracial relationships between Indians and blacks too at that time? Or did they not come into much contact, because there aren't too many black characters in your novel, right?

PM: I will be very honest. I have not come across that so I couldn't put down things that I didn't really feel strongly about or come across. But there was . . . I wouldn't say openly acknowledged, but you can see products from a mixed relationship in terms of a black and an Indian, but when I was writing my story I didn't pick that up, so I didn't use that too much in it.

PR: Did you pick up, during your research, any kind of interaction between Indians and blacks at that time, or were Indians basically working so hard on the plantation that they didn't have any time?

PM: They did have blacks, but . . . in my book, I mentioned that the blacks were not as hard-working as the Indians. And that happened. They just didn't want to work so hard. So there was this friendship that grew with the blacks, but I think also the Indians knew that they were more hard-working, and they were used because of that.

PR: How does going back to the past in your novel . . . help us understand Indian identity in the present-day South Africa?

PM: The reason why I actually decided to write this book was because I never found personally, for me, a book that educated people in an entertaining manner. And that's what I wanted to do, was just make a story that would give people reading [pleasure] and [make them] realize, "Hey, you know, we can't just take where we come from for granted. There was more to us." And I found that, strangely enough, people wrote back to me and contacted me and said, "Thank you for writing this. It actually made us appreciate where we come from, and we never realized just how difficult life really was."

PR: And do you think in any way you are trying emphasize also the Indian contribution to South African life?

PM: Yes, greatly so. Yes, I think we did contribute. We may not have received very much in the past. But as a community, joining together and building schools and building community halls and temples and mosques, that happened a lot in the past. . . . People did band together; the community banded together.

PR: Can you talk a little bit about why your focus [is] on so many different life stories. . . . [Y]ou begin with one family and that one family then splits into these different narrative arcs . . . you have Sita's story, Gopi's story, Chumpa's story, Rani's story, which leads to Gopi's story, Mukesh's story. So can you talk about . . . what you were trying to achieve with all these different narratives?

PM: If you look at a family, every person in the family has a story to tell. And that's what happens here. . . . *The Heart Knows No Colour* is actually a two-layer title . . . the first one is the interracial [relationship] between Albert and Sita. Then, within the home, it's the cultural issue. Gopi is Hindi and Rani is Tamil speaking . . . there is a color difference as well because I mention that she's dark skinned in the book. It shows you it doesn't matter. It doesn't have to be different race groups or different colors. Your emotions and your feelings are still the same.

PR: So, in a way, Rani and Gopi's story parallels Sita and Albert's story.

PM: And they made it. They married and they fought it. She [Sita] couldn't. She had to follow the traditional role. She fought against it in the beginning and then she accepted it. She became a good role model and a good mother. But she always, at the back of her mind, [knew] she was living a lie. And that had to come out in the end. So, basically, you cannot live your life with lies. . . . I say that everything you do has an effect in life. Every decision you make.

PR: So why did you choose to end [your novel] in 1919? Why did you decide not to go further or even earlier?

PM: My characters came to a close. All things tied up nicely at the end. And I like doing that. I like setting it, ending it, in a way [with] one era finishing off for me. I've got another one coming up but it's not a sequel . . . it starts in the early 1900s, but it ends in the 1930s. But what I like to do is build stories over time and say how society has changed, how the Indian community progressed.

PR: And how do you think the Indian community progressed in the time span of your novel . . . from the time that they came as indentured labor to the time that the novel ends?

PM: I think they make great progress, absolute great progress. If you think about the first five years of indenture, where they had to give everything, and in the process of giving, they also learned to save, and they were planning, planning a better life. And that's what happened in reality. People did that. They refused to carry on being indentured laborers. There were some that were very scared, the older generation that just lived and worked and died on sugar cane plantations. And then the others . . . who . . . came into the city and lived their lives and they got education, they worked, they married, they moved out of Durban, as well. People have moved away and that's how we found Indians moving up to Johannesburg . . . they worked in the diamond and gold mines, as well. So there was progress . . . they couldn't be stunted. I think that's where we have to be very grateful. That they spread their wings.

PR: What role do women play in this novel?

PM: I think women are often the backbone in a family. In Indian society, we tend to often give men more status in the home, but basically, I think it's often run by women. . . . [T]he man goes out and earns the income, comes home, but you'd find with the indentured laborers women worked and toiled in the field as well, and they had to run their homes.

PR: . . .[B]y the end of the novel there's this kind of happy ending. . . . Chumpa feels like Natal is finally her home. She's celebrating her seventy-fifth birthday amidst these riches. And Sita and Hemith have reconciled and Sita's secret has come out. But in the midst of this happy ending, I feel like the character of Mukesh strikes a somewhat discordant note . . . and I was wondering if you had to imagine him thirty, forty years, or even ten years later [what would he be like]?

PM: He is in my head . . . if I have to do a sequel, it will be based on him and his emotions . . . and how he adjusts to being a product of an interracial relationship.

PR: He'd be very confused. And angry. I think that was the dominant emotion that came to mind with Mukesh. That he is extremely angry. But who is he angry at? Is he angry with his mother? Is he angry with his biological father? Is he angry with the society that's done this to him?

PM: He's angry with his mother for living a lie. . . . [H]e has forgiven her because he loves her so much. . . . I think in all relationships, if you think of a product of an interracial relationship, it's a hard thing to [be] because now you're going to have a confused identity. You're brought up as Indian, but now you know for a fact you're not totally Indian. So where does the other part of you come from? And you want to find out more. So if I ever do a sequel, it will be a lot based on him.

PR: So why has he become so politically active? . . . [H]e is the only member of his family who is really politically active.

PM: Because now he's going to get to a point . . . you must remember he grew up with Hemith. And he [Hemith] was a man that looked at right and wrong, and he stood up for his society. So he grew up with . . . knowing you must fight for your rights. And now to know that you have part of white blood in you . . . where do you fall? It can confuse you.

PR: Do you think *Heart* was political?

PM: Yes, it was. My intention was that . . . it tells you where you come from and to educate the people in the sense of politics. But this one

[Moodley's next novel, *A Scent So Sweet*] is a little bit different. . . . You won't get a lot of political background, because now the situation is that they're second-generation Indian. They're more set in their ways. The families that I talk about are more well established. There are . . . the class differences within the community that I talk about. We're not drawing too much on the white oppression anymore. It's the choices you make in your own Indian community now. That's what's happening in this one, yes.

PR: Are you planning to write only novels, or are you thinking of writing . . . short stories or poetry?

PM: No, I enjoy doing novels. I did do a short story that was published many, many years ago in the *Natal Witness*. But I enjoy doing a novel. I like a story unfolding.

PR: Do you think you'll keep writing about the Indian community?

PM: I think it's important to write about what you know. I honestly can't say where I would go as a writer because you grow with each experience. I just found it interesting to write about the past and grow from there, just follow and see how the Indians have grown and what we've achieved and the stumbling blocks that we've had. We've had numerous stumbling blocks. I mean, up till now you still find we're stumbling a lot, although we've been given so many new opportunities. In all fairness, we have to give blacks a chance as well. They've been just as segregated as we were in the publishing [world]. And I think Kwela has done such a wonderful job, because they've opened up this whole avenue of nonwhite writers. They've really done so.

PR: What does India mean for you? What does it mean for your characters, and is the Indian identity we encounter in the novel . . . is it a South African Indian identity? So let me start with the first part: What does India mean for you?

PM: It's my motherland. I haven't been there, but I do find a sense of Indianness that comes across. It's just to say, this is where my ancestors have come from. . . . If I do visit the land, I can't tell you exactly how I would feel, whether I would feel a visitor or part of it, I don't know until I visit it. So that is a difficult part, but we watch . . . a lot of movies, and I see that there are such differences between Indian Indians and South African Indians. . . . In South Africa, we are truly South African Indians.

PR: Can you explain a little bit what that means, for you, what it means to be South African Indian?

PM: We actually brought about our own identity. We've learned from the land. We've come across people that have taught us differently. We learned so much . . . it's very difficult, actually, to speak our own language. I don't speak any of the Indian languages. I speak English and I can speak a little bit of Afrikaans. That's because we were brought up in this country as South Africans. So I see India as where I have come from . . . but not necessarily as being part of it totally, because I am South African.

PR: And what does it mean for your characters, then?

PM: In *Heart*, they still felt they were from India, and they were fighting for identity in this country. And I think by the end of the novel, after they passed their period of indenture . . . the characters began to feel very South African. . . . When you're actually born here, you become part of the country. I would say, as a South African Indian, I benefited a lot from the country. . . . In the past, our great-grandfathers may have found it very difficult. They've . . . had to fight for what they have. And we because of the fight, we benefited. And especially now, with the new democracy, it has also done a lot for Indians as well.

PR: And I think in this novel you're trying to show the fight that your ancestors fought, [the results of] which now your generation is enjoying.

PM: That's right . . . don't forget that the struggle was there and now we're reaping the rewards off it.

PR: The last part of that question was: is the Indian identity we encounter in this novel a South Africanized one? You've talked about how your own identity is a South African Indian one. Can we talk a little bit about that as it is represented in the novel?

PM: As I said, the South African identity in the novel grew. . . . [I]in the beginning they came in as indentured laborers. They had the opportunity to go back, and they chose . . . to stay and make this home. So they did become South African without losing their Indian identity. Because if you look at tradition, we may not be totally traditional in everything, but we have our culture kept intact.

PR: And do you think your characters are like that in some ways? In many ways?

PM: Yes, they never became totally Westernized. They may have become Westernized to improve their lifestyle, but the sense of family and tradition . . . it was still there, it was still there.

PR: Why has South African Indian writing been ignored for so long, both in South Africa as well as . . . abroad?

PM: I'm going to talk from my own personal experience and the feedback that I got when I submitted my work. I didn't only submit my work to South African publishers. I did try overseas publishers. And they said to me that there was no market for it. The story was very good, very exciting, very interesting, but there was no market. And I thought that was not fair. Because when you say no market, you're already saying Indian people don't read. And that I thought was highly insulting, because we very readily read books by white authors, African American authors, black, anything. I read from across the globe. I don't select, so I thought that was highly insulting. And I think they felt that Indians just don't [read] so there is no market. It's not worth publishing a book when they can't get financial gain from it.

PR: And this was publishers abroad or even South Africa?

PM: Both. I found the door locked . . . a lot in South Africa.

PR: That's what people said yesterday [at the seminar discussed in the conclusion] too. The same thing, that it's a perception that Indian writing . . . there's no market for it. And . . . that's an erroneous perception, and it's completely not true. . . . [A]ll the South African Indian fiction that I've read, it seems to appeal not just to an Indian audience, but to a much larger audience.

PM: I've got some e-mails from Afrikaner white males, African female students, male black students, Indian students, Coloured. They were so excited about the book because they weren't exposed to what the Indians went through. It was more an education while entertaining them. And it taught them about family values. . . . [I]f you look at the Afrikaner background, it's very similar to the way we Indians live, in the sense of family relationships and their struggle with the English in this country. So there was a sense of identifying and realizing it was just the color of your skin that we didn't relate to.

PR: What would you like a Western . . . as well as a scholarly audience, to know about your work . . . your writing?

PM: It's more to tell them wherever you go, whoever you are, if you leave your country and settle down into a new country, you must remember you're putting down roots. And it's going to be difficult, but if you persevere, and you decide that this is what you want to do, you will be successful.

PR: The one character I was quite fascinated with in your novel is not an Indian character and it's not Albert. It's this Zulu woman . . . and I was wondering if you could talk a little bit about her, and . . . why you chose to put her in the narrative. What does she stand for? How are we supposed to interpret her?

PM: I came to a point in my story where I wasn't sure what I wanted to do with Rani, whether she should have this baby or not. And surprisingly enough, this person [at] work—it's so interesting . . . your research gives you new opportunities to create new things, and educate people in your book. . . . I work in the science faculty, and somebody, one of the students, handed in a PhD thesis, and they talked about using herbs and natural products in terms of inducing labor. And I thought this was so wonderful. And I know that the African tradition . . . [i]t's an old [tradition], and now people in South African society are becoming more into herbal remedies. So it fitted into that. And Sangoma are a people that are highly respected in the Zulu community.

PR: Yet Rani seems a little scared of her?

PM: Yes, because if you meet a Sangoma for the first time, and you're not exposed to them. . . . [T]hey dress differently. They have all these colorful beads. And . . . it's an alien sight to an Indian. But they're actually harmless. And they have such wonderful character. And a Sangoma is somebody who is like blessed. They're gifted . . . and it just shows you that she comes from a different culture. And her intentions were not evil. . . . She was helping. It's a different way of saying I can help you. I come from a different world, a different society, but we can come together when there's a need. That's what it is actually saying. It doesn't matter which culture you come from.

Interview with Aziz Hassim

Aziz Hassim is the author of the epic novel The Lotus People *(2002). Hassim's novel has received much critical acclaim, including the 2001 Sanlam Literary Award for unpublished work.* The Lotus People *traces the lives of two Indian families through various generations. Set in Durban's Casbah, it captures the diverse spirit of this Indian area with its wide cast of characters as well as recovers the history of the Indian community in South Africa and its participation in the struggle against apartheid.*

DURBAN, DECEMBER 28, 2005

PR: What made you write [*The Lotus People*]? . . . [I]n terms of South African Indian fiction, this is the first novel that can be called an epic . . . because it spans generations, it has the long chronological sweep. So, what made you want to write an epic? Did you plan a big book that spans generations, or did it just take a life of its own?

AH: It took a life of its own. . . . I wanted to write about our people, about what life was like at the time, because I thought it was disappearing and I started off with that in mind and the book just grew on me. . . . I had no idea that it was going to be an epic. I was just writing a story. . . . [T]here is a misunderstanding of the Indians in this country . . . there is a belief here that they came here very much in the same way as the British came, as settlers. The difference, of course, is that the Indians who came here from India came and worked, if they owned a piece of land they bought it, if they put up a building, they built it with their own money. They didn't come with an empire behind them that gave them guns and cannons to take over, so they were not invaders.

PR: But people do see them as the invaders and aggressors, when they were actually the victims. And I think your book does a very, very wonderful job of showing the victimization of the Indians as well as how Indians fought against that victimization and that they were not just the passive victims, they actively agitated against their oppression.

AH: Yes. Mahatma Gandhi did a great job, I think he really revitalized things, but the resistance had started even before then, he gave it a sense of purpose.

PR: You've called this novel your "personal TRC". . . . [W]hat truth are you trying to tell and who are you trying to reconcile with?

AH: History is recorded by the victors, always. And in South Africa, the truth of the Indian people, the contribution to the freedom struggle, is recorded nowhere. You cannot go and research anything anywhere that will tell you these things; if you go to the old newspapers as a last resort, you'll find nothing. Because newspapers were all white-controlled, and they, of course, wrote what would please the masters. But I lived it. I'm seventy now so of the one hundred years that I've covered, 70 percent of it I was there, and I remember this is wrong, the story of our people has not been told in truth. I have a personal philosophy . . . I like to believe the truth that remains untold is the beginning of a lie, its just my own philosophy and I felt that this was a truth that had not been told, has never been written about and that's what I meant when I said it was my personal [TRC]. . . . Also . . . I've dedicated the book to Dr. Kesavaloo Goonam. Dr. Goonam was an enigmatic person, while she was very strong on her religion—she was a Hindu—she was a very open-minded person, she contributed greatly to the freedom struggle, which is forgotten, completely forgotten. That is another part of my own odyssey, so to speak, that how can you forget these people? They were the forerunners in the freedom struggle. And that is one of the reasons why I dedicated the [TV version of *The Lotus People*] series to her.

PR: The second part of my question is, then, who are you trying to then reconcile with? . . . Whites? Blacks? South Africans in general?

AH: I am Indian . . . very Indian. . . . I don't want it to seem as if I'm being ethnic, I'm not. I just feel as though there was a time when the Indian community was a very united community. If in the forties, 1940s, early fifties, if we were to have an election, we would have had a half a dozen Indian leaders that the whole community regardless of religious background would have voted for. I think we've lost that. We've lost the ethos of those days, in the sense that we all celebrated Diwali, we all celebrated Eid, we all celebrated Christmas. . . . [T]oday we've become a little distanced. If you go out into the townships like Phoenix, Chatsworth, that ethos still remains. But in the city, in the nearby suburbs, some of that is gone, and I am saying why, and I'm trying to reconcile people back to that ethos.

PR: Can you talk a little bit about the title of your novel, *The Lotus People*? Was it your title? Did the publishers give you the title?

AH: It is my title, in fact I was quite insistent that the title remain for several reasons: one, of course, is that the lotus flower is very Indian. . . . [I]t is the national flower of India. Secondly, from my understanding the lotus flower grows in the muck. But look what it blooms into and this was my analogy in a sense. To say the Indian in this country was kept totally down, wasn't allowed to having a decent living place or whatever, a sort of muck and look how he bloomed . . . then, of course, there is Greek mythology, where there were a group of people who were called the lotus people, I'm not quite sure of my facts here . . .

PR: There are the lotus eaters also . . .

AH: Lotus eaters, who apparently migrated, . . . believed in the truth, [then] they forgot their origins and forgot their philosophy of speaking the truth. So there was that influence too.

PR: What role does politics play in your writing? It seems to play a big role . . . and it seems that you are writing against the dominant political structure. But perhaps you could talk a little more about that.

AH: I was never a politician. . . . I was never involved in politics, in any area. I grew up in the streets. . . . I come from a family of traditional barbers from Porbander in Gujrat. Now, barbers, as you probably know, don't make a lot of money. And mine wasn't a wealthy family; we grew up in the streets. And I had far more pressing issues, such as making sure there was food on the table, than going out and getting involved in politics. So politics per se had no part in my life. But as the years went by, I became aware of the restrictions that were placed on the people. Of course I lived in a classified area. And as I said, as I grew, I had my own anger against the system, but it was a question of priorities. If I had a family that was self-sufficient, I might have got into politics. But I had greater priorities. I had to see to my family's security, as opposed to the security of my people in the community. So I never really got involved in politics, I was never a political activist myself. That wasn't me.

PR: But this book seems to be . . . an exercise in political activism because . . . it's a very political novel. It's about the political structures and how the Indian community has participated in politics. . . . [T]he act of writing has always been a political act . . . people think that writing is not political, like politics is always taking a slogan and board and going out in the streets but . . . writing is a political act. . . . I wonder if you agree that this is . . . a very political book . . .

AH: [*The Lotus People*] is very political. . . . I have this personal philosophy that says the truth that remains unspoken is the beginning of a lie. I like that and I like living by that. And there are too many truths that have not been spoken by this country. Even the TRC doesn't bring it out.... If a person was truly politically active, somewhere someone would have written about it, even if it was somewhere in the papers. These are the people that I thought were my icons.... I just felt that, I'm now seventy years old, when my generation is gone who will remember enough to write? ... And how many people [who] have lived during those times remember it, or care to remember it? And of those who remember, how many would write? So I thought, maybe do it while I can; fifty years from now it will be on somebody's shelf who will say, "Hang on, we didn't know this." Well, they will then know it. That was my prime purpose.

PR: You also show ... racial solidarity in your book ... with Indians joining hands with the blacks.... [I]s this again something that happened? Is this reality that you are depicting ... are you also trying to challenge ... the stereotypes that I have read about a great deal, that Indians ... secretly want to be white and they disparage the black people?

AH: Let me just say, what you have said is partly true. But it was a class thing, more than a philosophy ... insofar as the racial thing is concerned, you have to look at it as two groups of people. You have to look at the Indian, who was wealthy, who lived in ... suburbs and the majority of the Indians who lived down market, so to speak. That lot that lived down market, there was a very close relationship between the blacks and the Indians, extremely close. We who are from the streets have black friends that we are very, very close to, and we never saw them as being black. There was this philosophy in my days that you were a bru, a bru is a brother. See, that existed ... to an extent. It was when apartheid took root that it changed. They moved those blacks that were in the city center out of the city and moved whites [into the city].

PR: Let's move directly into the novel.... One of the things that I really liked was the language, that there [was] this particular dialect which you were using which seemed to capture the way South African Indians really speak, and there were certain words you used, for someone like me, who is not South African, which ... I didn't know. Like "lightee" and "larnee" and I had to figure those out.... Can you talk a little bit about the language? You seem to capture the spirit of the language and the way people really speak; is that again something you do consciously or is it something that just happened?

AH: I was writing about those times, I had to be true to time and that is how people spoke, even academics spoke in terms of lightees and larnees and that sort of thing.

PR: Two interesting comments in your novel and I just want to read them out and then we can talk about it a little bit more. On page 415, you say, "The women in our family, [Jake] said turning to Sam. . . . They are the real fighters, put them in the front line and the war." Then on page 440, Sam says, "[M]y God, these mothers of ours" and then he adds, "[P]ut the women in the front line, that's what Jake said that night, . . . will we ever learn?" And I was wondering what role women played in this novel?

AH: Indian women have mastered the art of leading by following. I really believe this because the men sat around the place . . . like a rooster in the barnyard, making a lot of noises, shouting and screaming and that sort of thing. But then, by the end of the day, it is a woman that quietly controls things from the background. It is what she says that is carried [out]. She allows him to rant and rave, make his fuss, and then she'll say, "You know what, this is how it's going to be."

PR: Let's move to children because that's the other thing I noticed that by the end of the novel it seems like the children almost are calling the shots. . . . I was wondering if you could comment on the end of the novel which was very powerful . . . it worked beautifully for me where the children seem to have taken over the battle of their parents and their parents are sort of on the [fence] . . . ultimately they decide to join the children but . . . they vacillate . . . a lot. And it's the children who say, "We've got to do this," and can you comment . . . about that, the end of the novel, with the balance of power . . . shifting to the children?

AH: In the eighties . . . the apartheid government was locking all the leaders up, either sending them in exile, sending them to Robben Island, or putting them in jails . . . and there was a vacuum which . . . was filled by the children, they decided then that they would form their own leadership. . . . There was this mistaken impression that they were fighting for better education. That was not the case; they were fighting for freedom. As I said, they found leaders from within themselves. They had a very good rallying point: the schools. . . . And this was throughout the country, Cape Town, Johannesburg, Durban, the children took up the cudgels, more so after Sharpeville, [when they] saw what was being done. The political icons, the political fighters, were as I said either in Robben Island or wherever they were . . . people like my characters, the Sams and Jasons of the world, were busy making a living, and the children were left to fill the gap.

PR: I'm going to read another quote from the book which I thought was interesting. This is Sam's mother telling Zain that he is an Indian first and foremost and I wanted to talk a little bit about that. . . . She says, "You my son are an Indian first and foremost, in this country the [others] . . . behave as if that is something you should be ashamed of, don't let that affect you . . . it's always a loser, the envious person who resorts to such tactics" (471). Can you talk a little bit about what you mean being an Indian first and foremost? And what it means to be an Indian in this novel as well as in South Africa in general?

AH: . . . If you attend any kind of a function, a Zulu will say, "I'm a Zulu, but I'm a South African." He won't say, "I'm a South African, but I'm a Zulu." An Afrikaner will say, "I'm an Afrikaner" meaning "I'm also a South African." So would the English: "I'm British originally, but now I'm South African." And so why can't I say, "I'm an Indian"? I'm also South African, but I'm an Indian of Indian origin, this is where I come from and I am proud of it. As an Afrikaner or a Zulu or whoever, and I mean, in that light, why can't I have the same right that they demand for themselves? And that is what I mean by saying, "I'm an Indian." I'm also suggesting that I'm of a different culture and this has got nothing to do with religion, you can't confuse a person's origins and his religion. . . . I gave a talk recently, where somebody asked me, "The way you write, I can't make up my mind whether you are Hindu, Muslim, Christian; you're so open about things. Are you Hindu, are you Muslim?" And I said, "Well, I suppose I'm a Muslim for the past one hundred years and I've been a Hindu for the [last] five thousand years." Which is where I'm coming from. . . . And I'm saying, "Yes, I'm an Indian." I make no apologies for it. I'm a South African, I will fight and give my life for South Africa, but . . . why can I not acknowledge where I came from? When it's acceptable for the Zulu to say he is a Zulu or the Afrikaner or the British or whoever, or the German, nobody objects.

PR: What you are doing in this book . . . [is] . . . trying to make the Indians proud of being Indians . . . because you're uncovering all these buried histories of courage, bravery, commitment.

AH: We have everything to be proud of. . . . I don't see why we should be ashamed of being Indians. But definitely, especially here in South Africa, [the idea exists] that to be an Indian is something to be ashamed of.

PR: Many of the most attractive characters—like I found Jake to be one of the most attractive characters . . . just this incredibly powerful and charismatic figure—they support violence as a form of resistance. I want to again read out something on page 510 . . . where you specifically talk about passive resistance and the need for some kind of nonpassive resistance, perhaps: "[T]he concept of passive resistance was born in this country, what was the government's response? You know the answer: they resorted to violence, imprisonment and murder." And then it says, "So responding to violence with violence is the only option . . . they used violence and force to stay in power, they are not democratically elected, they have no legitimacy as a government" . . . and there is this sense that . . . when you have this brutal oppressive government that doesn't understand any language other than violence you have to respond with violence. But I was wondering . . . how you would place that in context of passive resistance and Gandhi and nonviolence because those are values that the Indian community all over the world, not just in South Africa but even in India, hold very sacred and dear. . . . Could [you] talk about the role of violence as a means of winning freedom placed against this context of passive resistance?

AH: Know where you are coming from first. Taking the first part, the Indian philosophy of nonviolence always . . . that's me, that's my culture, that's where I'm coming from and I come from Porbander, which as far as I'm concerned is my Mecca . . . that's where Gandhi comes from. . . . And that is my ingrained philosophy. Then there is the philosophy I acquired out in the streets, where if you survive you fight. Survival required you to fight, you couldn't, if a man came to you in the night, you couldn't reason with him and say, "No, hang on, according to our philosophy we can settle this," I mean, they will kill you. . . . [T]he one is my culture and my people and . . . then [there's] the violent one in which I grew up in and [in] that environment in the short term, not the long term, but in the short term violence was more effective. In the long term, of course, it didn't help at all. So that part that you read, Jake is responding with "street-cred," which is where he grew up, but he's an Indian and as an Indian he's got that nonviolent philosophy. But he says, "no, but here it won't work, because we applied from the time of Gandhi right through almost one hundred years this philosophy of 'come let's talk, lets be civilized about it,' which got you nowhere." It suited the apartheid government, "You keep talking I'll keep taking." I mean, they're a bunch of looters. . . . Now, if it didn't work over those one hundred years then Jake is saying . . . "what do I do but wait another hundred years?" No, this guy has got to fight back. And that is why he responded so violently when they came home and invaded his home to issue that ejection notice, he went and shot the guy . . .

because earlier in the book when he is a little boy, he says, "The only way to handle this is you fight back." . . . "If you do that," Sandy says, "if you do that they'll deliver your body to us." That's very early in the book.

PR: And they do do that.

AH: Exactly that. I am saying that violence does not solve a problem. There is the hidden meaning that there is a guy who said it [that he will fight back with violence] when he was a kid and there you are, his body was delivered, violence did not solve anything. . . . Gandhi's philosophy of nonviolence is the only way, but how are you going to get that across to people who come out of the streets?

PR: Who come out of such a brutalized atmosphere.

PR: You've . . . touched on this . . . but if you could just summarize it for me, what role does India play in your literary imagination? So not being Indian in South Africa, but India in South Africa? Does it have a role?

AH: No . . . remember, I was born and bred in South Africa, right. My father was born here. India plays a role in the sense that . . . my ancestral home in Porbander is right next door . . . to Gandhi's home. My Granny and Gandhi were playmates. . . . Now I would listen to my Granny and she'd talk to me about Gandhi, right. . . . I grew up with this belief that I am an Indian first and foremost, and then of course I also became very South African. Because of my life and everything around me. My friends were both white, Coloured, African . . . that perhaps took a bit of the Indianness out of me. Made me more tolerant perhaps, I don't know. But you must understand . . . and I must be very honest, I'm not an academic, I'm not a philosopher, I wrote what my life was about at the time. Now how it comes out is now how I am, not as a result as some reasoned process

PR: How would you situate *Lotus People* within South African Indian literature as a whole . . . where would you place it . . . what do you think your contribution has been to South African literature?

AH: I've never thought of it like that . . . I was very chuffed when I got all the reviews . . . very glowing reviews in every newspaper you can think of, and the people who reviewed it were academics. There were some that said it was the first true Indian novel written by an Indian. There were others who said it's probably the best history, some call it a historical romance, a historical fiction . . . historically accurate. Stephen Gray, who is probably our greatest literary academic, he wrote at length about it. . . . I get very angry with some of the books that have been written by Indians [in South Africa]. I'm going to finish my second book by the end of January, but this time my character is coming out of the cane fields and the horrors of the cane fields. And I want to be really fair, that whilst the white settlers abused the Indians in the cane field, abused them badly, the Indian merchant class in Durban was equally as bad in the way they abused their own people who worked for them. So one has to be fair.

PR: Why has South African Indian literature traditionally been ignored and what is its future?

AH: Well, what has there been? What Indian literature has there been? I mean there are books like Dr. Goonam's book (*Coolie Doctor*) . . . [but there has been] a paucity of Indian writings really. I can't think of a book, say, twenty years ago, that was written by an Indian.

PR: Ahmed Essop has been writing for a while . . .

AH: Ahmed Essop has been writing for a long, long time. And he got his fair amount of fame or credit for his writing. . . . But we [are talking] about literature as opposed to "a" writer. You've got Ahmed Essop, but who else?

PR: Do you think that's changing, then?

AH: Very fast. It's changing very, very fast. . . . I went and got a group of businessmen together and I floated what is called the Ronnie Govender literary award, which is a annual award, it has a cash prize of 20,000 rand for anybody . . . I named it after Ronnie because, in fairness, besides the fact that Ronnie's my friend, I think he has done a lot. . . . [H]e's a great playwright and that's important. But I wanted a literary award and I named it after him.

PR: You say your next book is going to be finished in January [2006]; can you just summarize it in a sentence or two?

AH: You see, as you probably know, the Indians in South Africa have been classed into two categories: those who came as indentured servants and those who came as the business class. There is not much—well nothing, as far as I know, has ever been written of either class. But the indentured workers who went into the cane fields lived a life that was no better than the slaves in America. They were flogged, everything. And I don't think anybody has bothered to write about that and I don't know why. So one of my characters is coming out of the cane fields and the horrors of the cane fields. It's a fictional work, but again it's like *The Lotus People*, it is historically accurate. Anything I say in *The Lotus People* I can back up. Anything I am going to say in my second novel I'll be able to back up. See, historically it's accurate, but it's a work of fiction or historical fiction.

PR: And again it seems to be performing the same function as *The Lotus People*, which is trying to tell the truth before the silence becomes a lie.

AH: Exactly, exactly. And also to be very objective and fair. We keep saying the white man did this and the white man did that . . .

PR: But what did we do to ourselves . . .

AH: But what did we do to ourselves. . . . [I]n this context I'm referring to what I call the "Grey Street Businessman." Grey Street is, of course, our Durban's major street, business street. They had their own system of slavery but, of course, they . . . were . . . employing Indians and treating them as slaves. And saying . . . yes the whites were bad but some of our own guys . . . were not much better . . . and that's where my two characters are coming from and then they will meet. How it's going to end, I don't know. Although I'm a month away from completion, it's the completion part I'm at now. How *The Lotus People* ended, I never planned it, it just happens.

PR: What would you like a scholarly audience . . . to know about your work?

AH: No more than that they read it. . . . [I]f they read it, then they'll know where I'm coming from, which will tell them where all the Indians are coming from.

PR: What would you like . . . a reading audience in America to know about your work, even a nonscholarly audience?

AH: Well, I'd like them to know, first of all, that the Indian didn't come into this country as an exploiter. He came in this country and he built this country, he made a major contribution in spite of his small numbers. That he imbued this country with a philosophy; Gandhi's philosophy of nonviolence was formulated here in South Africa . . . satyagraha was conceived here. . . . I'd like people to know that. It has now become a philosophy that the world should live by.

PR: And which the world doesn't, of course . . .

AH: Doesn't, of course. But wasn't that great in itself that it was formulated here, in South Africa alright. And I think that alone speaks volumes. Here is an Indian, from India, comes to South Africa with the same philosophies that we Indians here live by, and he comes here and he says, "Hang on, I like what my brothers are doing, let me refine their thinking," and he then develops a philosophy of satyagraha. But here. That is what I would like people to know. That forget the greatness of Gandhi for a moment, and the man was great . . . and just look at where that greatness was nurtured: it was here. Prior to that, there was nothing. . . . But I'd like the world to know, the scholars to know, hang on if you think Gandhi's philosophy is great, don't you think you should see where it was nurtured? What brought it out? . . . South African Indians. This is what I believe gave birth, this was the fetus that gave birth [to Gandhi].

PR: This is where Gandhi became Gandhi or Gandhi became the Mahatma.

Interview with Ronnie Govender

Ronnie Govender can be credited with inaugurating the genre of South African Indian theater. Govender is the author of plays such as Beyond Calvary; The Lahnee's Pleasure, *also among South Africa's longest running plays; and* At the Edge and Other Cato Manor Stories, *a collection of short stories.* At the Edge *was published in 1996. The collection describes life in the community of Cato Manor before the Group Area removals; it was awarded the Commonwealth Writers' Prize for the best first book in the Africa region. Govender has also published a novel* Song of the Atman *(2006) and is working on his memoirs.*

CAPE TOWN, JANUARY 2, 2006

PR: How does your fiction differ from your plays? Do you tell the same stories in both mediums? . . . [H]ow are the pressures of writing drama different from the pressures of writing short stories?

RG: I would say that my experience with writing plays actually certainly stood me in good stead in writing these short stories [*At the Edge and Other Cato Manor Stories*]. For one . . . I think literature is about economy. And that is no more so than on the stage. . . . [Y]ou're presenting the whole world, a whole time span, in an hour and a half, or so. So that discipline assisted me in the writing of these short stories. But it is a different genre. It affords you so much more opportunity to explore . . . which, of course, . . . you can't do on stage. Stage you do the actual action . . . so that would, in essence, be . . . the linkage that there is from my playwriting past to my tackling fiction.

PR: And do you write about the same themes and the same issues . . . ?

RG: I've been called a political writer . . . and I make no apologies for that. I believe that a writer must have a political consciousness . . . that's apart from a very narrow, parochial kind of politics, politics dealing with personal power. . . . I think politics governs our entire lives. This is what it's all about. So if you don't have a kind of political consciousness, the characters and people in your work are in limbo. . . . [F]or them to be three dimensional . . . the backdrop, the landscape, the life that they live, and they grew up in, is political . . . between some of the accusations that have been leveled at me, conveniently by those people who have resented my works and who call themselves critics but who are actually upholders of the establishment viewpoint. . . . They found it convenient to label me as . . . as a protest writer. I am a protest writer, in a sense. But I'm not this one-dimensional pamphleteer or propaganda machine. And I tell the stories of people. I tell stories, essentially, but I don't ignore the fact that the people that I write about come from a certain milieu, a socioeconomic political reality. And you can't ignore that, you see, and if that shows through, then I would have succeeded. For in that, my writing is political.

PR: But there is an aesthetic element which seems to be important to you in your work . . . in your short stories?

RG: Very important. I think that is implicit in my work. I strive for that, and I hope I have achieved that . . . some time back there was a professor, a French professor, who incidentally, I think, translated my play, *The*

Lahnee's Pleasure, into French. And he noted the difference between the general kind of protest play that was extant in South Africa and my play *The Lahnee's Pleasure*. As far as he was concerned, it was a story, essentially, a story.

PR: I want to talk a little bit about the composition of these stories. . . . I understand that you composed these stories in the sixties? Was that the case?

RG: Well . . . the memories have been there from childhood and I reduced them to stories whenever I had the opportunity. Of course, I [wrote] in my spare time, it would mean at four o'clock in the morning because my day was packed with lots of other activities. And so, whenever I had the opportunity, I would tackle a story and put it away. And, not realizing that it would be published as a collection . . . the more important thing for me was to get these stories done . . . because Cato Manor was destroyed, willfully destroyed by human greed. And there were all these wonderful people, those wonderful memories. And I didn't want them to die.

PR: And you didn't want them to fade from record. So what was the period in which you were writing them?

RG: . . . Well, I think most of them were finished in the fifties . . . sixties.

PR: When you were going to publish these finally, did you revise them in any way? Did you rewrite them or rework them?

RG: Largely not. But I did tamper with them a little bit during publication. . . . I saw opportunities . . . to enhance the story a little bit here and there. . . . [O]ne of the things that one strives for is that the word becomes . . . [the] purveyor of everything, the feeling and all that.

PR: . . . Should I, as a reader, think of them . . . as about the apartheid period? Or while you were editing them in the postapartheid period, [did] a postapartheid consciousness ever enter the way that you edited them? Because I find it fascinating that these were written in the apartheid period, so reflecting . . . the sensibility of that time, but they were published only in the postapartheid period.

RG: . . . In this instance, I dramatized the stories in the early eighties.

So it was published in a sense ... [but] I didn't interfere with the sense of what I meant.... I would hesitate to designate it as an apartheid collection. I would much rather say it was about people ... living in the apartheid times.

PR: What does Cato Manor mean to you, in particular, and to the Indian community in general? So obviously as an entity, Cato Manor, as a community, occupies this really powerful meaning in your psyche, which is why you wanted to preserve these memories in literary form. So if you could talk about that meaning a little bit, both to you as a writer and as an Indian, and also, if it has any meaning to the Indian community in general.

RG: I was born and raised in Cato Manor. I was schooled in Cato Manor. And ... [there was] this traumatic experience of suddenly being forced out, families being kicked out. One hundred eighty thousand people, peremptorily kicked out at somebody's whim. It was soul crushing, of course. And for me, a devastating blow. It destroyed an entire community. A community that had made itself self-sufficient, picked itself up by its own bootstraps. I recall those things. I recall how they struggled against penury, despite apartheid, and succeeded against the odds. I mean, they built their own schools.... And produced people of outstanding caliber in the different fields: education, sport, in all walks of life. And then suddenly there was this wonderful community that was just shattered overnight. And ... this stays with me.... You're born in a place, and you're raised in a place, and you have an attachment to that place, but in life generally people go on. One place is just like the other. But when something like this happens, it gives you a very special kind of linkage to that place.

PR: It seemed like Cato Manor, for me, as a symbol, also represented ... the success of a community and the harmonious life that a community lead before it was ... exploited.

RG: Yeah, the burgeoning kind of racial interaction that was taking place, which, if left unhindered, it would have led to a South Africanism which we so dearly long for.

PR: The second part of my question was what role does Cato Manor play for the [Indian community]? ... Does it have any kind of significance in the mind of the Indian community ... as it does in your mind?

RG: I can't answer that question . . . in an objective way because . . . things like that have to be researched. . . . But interestingly, when I went out to schools to talk . . . and the kind of responses I had from children. . . . They're very . . . wonderful responses. Children responding to things they didn't know about and [that were] initially dead to them. And [those things were] suddenly coming alive and [they were] seeing this community and understanding where they, themselves, come from. It was wonderful. It was like an awakening for them. . . . And of course also the dispelling of all these distortions about ethnic culture, all that kind of nonsense.

PR: Moving into this collection now, I noticed that—this is just my observation—but the stories seem to get more political, obviously political, as they moved along. So we ended with the story about the Group Areas Act, "Over My Dead Body," which I think is the most obviously political story in the entire collection, though I think all the stories are political. But politics seem to be more of an undercurrent in some of the stories, and as we move along they seem to get more and more political till [the political tension] culminates in this story, which is about political upheaval and political oppression . . . but did you do this deliberately, this kind of progression where the last story is the most overtly political story?

RG: I think possibly I was governed by . . . again, the discipline that I gained from writing plays.

PR: So like a climax, usually.

RG: In a sense. . . . And I'm happy that it came over in a kind of organic fashion, rather than a kind of contrived, forced way.

PR: What is the significance of the title *At the Edge?* And I'm wondering if we can use this idea of being "at the edge" as a way of thinking about the collection as a whole.

RG: . . . I witnessed this incident of exorcism on my grandmother and the tremendous spiritual kind of power . . . I witnessed this, you see. And for me, that was, for me, [who had been] rebelling against all the myths and ritual and things like this as a young man; suddenly I had been brought up to the edge of . . . prevailing realities. And you suddenly were at the edge of another kind of consciousness. Perhaps this was also a metaphor for Cato Manor's destruction and people being pushed to the edge.

PR: And also Cato Manor itself, because it's being demolished. Existing on the edge of memory and reality. So there's always that. Again, I thought, as a title it really worked well for me. And I somehow had this idea of being at the edge constantly on my mind.

RG: It's a pity you didn't see the play.

PR: And the play was called At the Edge, too, right? And it was about the same story?

RG: ... I was concerned [when the play At the Edge was being performed] because I had been accused, also, of being culturally specific ... again, these terms come up ... when people like James Joyce or Chaucer or Shakespeare write about culturally specific things, we have to accept that—

PR: As universal.

RG: As universal. But when we do the same thing, perhaps with even greater clarity, we are looked down upon for being culturally specific. It's something that I always have resisted. So I was worried about that. And people here, who I think, to an extent, had been indoctrinated, who had lost their own souls in this Eurocentric kind of supremacist kind of atmosphere that you're brought up in ... the West is great [as is] the English language, which itself was procreated in terms of the conquest through the colonies. ... And I resisted this. I said no. I said, we have a legitimacy. Although I write in English, but I write about what is ours. ... But generally ... these people themselves had been so colonized in their thinking. And I then I myself got a bit concerned about it. But when it played in Edinburgh and I saw Scottish women weeping at the scene, the one where my grandmother tends to the sick lady. ... To me, that was a transformation ... here was something that was transported from a small little place in Cato Manor, and Scottish women in Edinburgh were reacting to it.

PR: The other thing that I really liked about this collection was the use of humor and satire so that even when ... you had these high tragic moments in your short stories, there was also this undercurrent—well, not undercurrent—I think it was a very obvious "overcurrent" of humor and satire. And I was wondering if you could talk a little bit about that.

Does that again come from your drama and is that again something you are consciously trying to do? And what does it achieve for you?

RG: . . . I come from a background that celebrated life. . . . I look at my uncles and they were boxing, great boxing, champions, and they were fishermen and things like that. And the women in our family are strong women . . . coping with all . . . the poverty around us, etc., the lack of opportunity, and all that. But they never lost the sense of themselves, their sense of humor. I was reared in that kind of thing. And it struck me quite consciously later . . . when you look back at many of the things you've done in the past, and what you will have considered embarrassing to the point of excruciatingly painful or even something that you were very upset with, you can look back at it from a distance and see the humor in it. At the end of the day . . . things pass. And so I think, it's to look at something in totality, not just in isolation.

PR: Let's talk about women. You already mentioned strong and powerful women, but I was wondering if you could talk a little bit about the women in your stories. Because I noticed many of your stories are women-centered, and your women characters are, to use a phrase that you just used, very three-dimensional. And they're very strong women characters who I think often challenge the stereotype that we have of Indian women—and not just in South Africa—but all over. So could you talk a little bit about the women characters and why you depict them the way that you do?

RG: You must understand one thing about so-called Indian culture . . . just look at the kind of sexism that exists. There's no denying that there's heavy sexism, again, entrenched through mythology. . . . But how women themselves have coped with this kind of heavy repression and not only just survived, I think, but have triumphed. . . . [T]o a great extent, Indian culture and religion have been manipulated to maintain a kind of sexism. And as opposed to that there have been these strong women that have really sought their own dignity and have achieved it. And I look at my grandmother. . . . When my grandfather died she was left with a huge family and how she not only just survived but . . . she was so strong culturally. She passed this on to her children and this is recalled a little bit in my book *Song of the Atman*. . . . It's passed on, the strength. And women are very much part of that. I look at my grandmother. I look at my mother, and I can think of the day when at the age of fifteen, I watched my mother, I stood and watched my mother making the bed, taking it for granted. . . . And then I had to look at myself and say . . . what a chauvinist I am.

And I must confess I do retain some of that chauvinism even up till now. Happily my daughter . . . is a member of parliament, and she grew to be very strong . . . and has been acknowledged as one of the strong gender activists in the country and internationally also.

PR: Moving on to children. I've noticed that many of your stories use the figure of the child . . . "Incomplete Human Being," "Heavy Weights," "The Cosmic Clash," "Call of the Muezzin," I loved those stories also. And [they all use] . . . boys barely out of adolescence . . . was it deliberate? And what does the figure of the child suggest and mean to you as a literary idea?

RG: We have these quaint notions as to what it is to be grown up. What does it mean to be grown up? Does it mean carrying on with some of the forced notions of the past, which we've fixed in convention? Sexism, for instance. We just accept that. . . . Even up till now, you go to an Indian function, you see the Indian women on one side and the men on the other, knocking it back, and the women in the kitchen. Sometimes this is done quite—to use this word again—naturally. But all those things continue. This subscribing to weird dogma. Is that grown up? And prejudices, racial prejudices and things like that. Is that grown up? Or fixed ideas. Is that grown up? . . . And then look at the child and the freedom in that child. . . . I look at my grandson, and I see this wonderful, this gregarious approach to life. And to me that's wonderful. That's a celebration of life.

PR: So you think the child is a celebration of life?

RG: . . . The child is so much closer to nature, and, this may be a cliché, but very much so.

PR: The next question is about Indian identity. . . . What kind of Indian identity are you presenting in this collection? Is it a pure Indian identity or a South Africanized Indian identity, and how is it South Africanized, if you do say it is so?

RG: I don't consciously set out to posit a specific kind of position on that aspect of identity. But, in thinking about it quite consciously, if you look at the forces that seek to make you an alien from the hearth that you were born in and should belong to, and then you look at the historical kind of processes from which you, yourself, emerge . . . we cannot deny that these things [such as identity] impact on our consciousness. And I suppose they play a major role in your affiliation to a society and a nation. And if you look at what happened after liberation—when the Natal Indian Congress had to go out of existence, in pursuit of its own aims of an egalitarian society [because] it was an anomaly to have an Indian people in the opposition. But [now] you're in the classic situation where the people themselves hadn't been conscientized against the very forces . . . that impacted on their lives . . . this kind of racial consciousness. So on the one hand, you have this theoretical kind of thing [the advent of democracy]. On the other hand, you have the reality of lingering prejudices and lingering habits. And it was a political thing. And you needed to address that. And what you had was immediately after liberation, when you had your first elections, and you had Indian people, who in the past had participated in the fight against colonialism—they actually led, in some instances—this massive uprising against colonialism and against apartheid. And they made huge sacrifices . . . and they joined in the liberation front. And suddenly they were voting right wing [in the postapartheid elections]. They were voting for the Democratic Party. What happened? What happened to this community during the [postapartheid] elections. During the Tricameral elections [in 1984; set up to divide the nonwhite groups], they returned a poll of under 4 percent. Probably a record in the world for an election of that kind. What happened? This struck me. What happened in the meanwhile [from the Tricameral elections to the postapartheid elections]? Did it happen because it was an Indian community, and such? Or did it happen [because they were] leaderless, in a sense? So . . . again now, because of this, it was a question of knowing who you are and what you are. . . . And there were disturbing tendencies, in which even within the Indian community you had very strong say Hindi movements, Tamil movements, Gujarati movements, Muslim movements . . . and that was very disturbing.

PR: And you think that the community that you present here in this book shows a more unified Indian community?

RG: Organically what was happening was that they were a people that were interacting, living together, getting to know each other, and understanding each other. And poor people, living cheek by jowl, begin to see each other . . . as they really are and form very strong bonds and relationships. It's bound to happen.

PR: We've talked about what role politics play in your writing. I'd like to flip that around and talk a little bit about what role art plays in political liberation, and how does fiction achieve this differently from drama?

RG: Let me answer by pointing to that fact that throughout history, in terms of conquest, you kill ideas. And you can [then] . . . subjugate a people. And art is all about ideas. Art is about challenging the frontiers of life, the conventions of life, looking for . . . meaning in things and trying to get to grips with this wonderful thing called life. And going beyond all those . . . self-imposed kind of barriers. So you stop a man thinking, and you can imprison him. You imprison his mind; you imprison his soul; you imprison his body. And so art can therefore be dangerous.

PR: So art is a very powerful force in political liberation?

RG: Very powerful. And in South Africa there was a conscious move to deny people their own sort of cultural development.

PR: And how do you think fiction achieves this political liberation differently from drama?

RG: I think drama [can inspire people], because of the fact that things happen before one on stage. And you're part of something that is happening. It has a great immediacy in that sense.

PR: What does fiction have that compensates for this sweeping in the moment?

RG: I would hesitate to box things, put things into neat little boxes because again . . . a few lines can be . . .

PR: Of poetry can stir you up.

RG: Can stir you . . . "Don't go soft into that good night. Rage, rage against the dying of the light."

PR: Why has South African Indian writing, across genres—I think theater has got more attention than fiction—but why has it been ignored for so long? Because people are now increasingly aware of the white writers—and I'm speaking from a western perspective, living in the U.S.—everyone knows Nadine Gordimer, J. M. Coetzee, André Brink, and Athol Fugard. Now . . . gradually people are getting to know black, as in African, writers more. Somehow South African Indian writers get left out. They got left out in the apartheid period, and they're getting left out even in the post-apartheid period. Can you comment on that?

RG: Well . . . speaking for myself, I've had to make choices. I was one of the pioneers of the cultural boycott. . . . [W]e felt that we should close ranks against this crime against humanity, which meant . . . a sacrifice in one form or the other. Comrades were dying so . . . for a writer, the best possible thing that can happen is exposure for your work, whether it's to stage a play to audiences or to get your work published. When my play *The Lahnee's Pleasure* in the seventies became South Africa's longest-running play [with] the most number of performances . . . I had to make a choice. I was invited to London with the possibility of that becoming a film, in which case it would have preceded *East Is East* by about three decades. And it's a similar thing . . . very based on the kind of dislocation of a community. And it's a comedy. Yes, I had to make a choice. If I went overseas I would have got more exposure as a young writer then, which . . . I think every writer needs . . . international exposure. I turned it down, consciously, as opposed to other people, some of the names you mentioned, who went overseas. And I'm not, for one moment, saying that they didn't do any good because . . . much of their work was seen outside and attention was drawn to the [injustice of the] country. . . . But . . . as a writer, you're not above the struggle. . . . In one way or the other, you have to be part of this completely, and so I had to make the choice. I spoke to Lewis Nkosi and . . . we were talking about it. And Lewis said, "no . . . you should have [shown] your work overseas." He had a view, you see, that was different from mine altogether. I don't know whether I did the wrong thing. It certainly deprived me of great exposure at that time, which would have meant . . . opportunities, etc. But that's the choice I had to make. I can't speak for the other writers. When we started our theater group, we started in a back room. We had nothing. We didn't have any kind of facilities, no funding whatsoever. And we were dealing with a community which was its own worst enemy. And we had to get them to believe in themselves. And this is why we consciously wrote plays that dealt with our lives . . . so I think that, in my case . . . support for the cultural boycott did, in fact, prevent my work from being seen by a white audience.

PR: What would you like an academic . . . audience to know about your work? Both your fiction as well as your [plays]?

RG: What any audience, anywhere in the world, [should know]: I would want them to be able to celebrate with me the people that I write about and experience their joys, their sorrows, their failures, their achievements. And to look with them and to see life from . . . the viewpoints of these very many people that I write about or create. [Also that] I'm deeply conscious of . . . the fact that part of the oppressive machinery is stereotype. And I think that the Indians have been particularly subjected to the stereotype. *Mississippi Masala*, I thought was a horrendous portrayal of the Indian stereotype. The Indian male was presented as a wimp. And . . . there are prejudices in the community . . . there are very strong prejudices also in the caste systems . . . but that doesn't mean that other communities do not have their own prejudices also. There's nothing very special about the Indian community . . . *Mississippi Masala* presents the Indian as a . . . weak, weak person, prone to this kind of racist behavior. And a wimp also . . .

PR: When it comes to theater, and also South African Indian theater and literature, you're very much the forerunner . . . you've really inaugurated South African Indians into theater. What would you say has been your contribution to the world of letters in general and to Indian writing in particular?

RG: I hope my writing speaks for itself . . . every writer wants . . . the widest possible audience.

PR: I think your work, your plays in particular—from all the Indian writers that I've spoken to—they really seem to have inspired other people to write and to know that . . . their stories are important and that people want to hear their stories.

RG: Whenever I hear this, it really . . . warms my heart. And I hear it quite often from young people, and when I go to schools, particularly, and children come up to me, saying things like . . . your work made me feel proud to be an Indian. Now . . . proud to be an Indian. What does that mean? . . . [T]he wonderful things that are there in our scriptural legacies, in our cultural legacies . . . the universality of the essence of Indian culture . . . the striving for *moksha* or liberation and this oneness of life. Those things mustn't remain hidden . . . nice cultural artifacts to be celebrated every now and then. They must be living, a living thing.

PR: And the last question is . . . your future projects. You say that you've written a novel that's going to come out in March [2006]. What else are you working on?

RG: I'm writing my memoirs. . . . It's kind of a rambling account of things I was involved in, various things, and my growing up. I'm quite enjoying it. I've attempted to write this in the third person. I don't know how that's going to work. . . . So I'm looking at this guy who gets himself into one mess after another. I'm calling it *In the Manure*.

Notes

Introduction

1. Meer's exact words were: "[W]e Indian South Africans have had to struggle hard to claim our South Africanness, and that is something we jealously guard.... We are not a diaspora of India" (quoted in Waldman).

2. Even though Indians in South Africa are also referred to as Indian South Africans, I refer to them as South African Indians in order to preserve the integrity of an identity that sees South Africa as a primary affiliation. Also see n27. I use the term "Indian" rather than "South Asian" to respect the self-identification of the Indian community in South Africa. I have never observed South African Indians—both in fiction and in "real life"—identifying themselves as South Asian.

   Part of the title of this chapter—"When Does a Subcontinental Become a Citizen?"—is adapted from the title of Mahmood Mamdani's essay: "When Does a Settler Become a Native? The Colonial Roots of Citizenship."

3. In her reading of Ahmed Essop, Arlene Elder argues that "native-born Indians, both in East and South Africa, are shown to have been treated as full citizens, neither during nor after colonialism" (138). Similarly, Sangeeta Ray uses the South African Indian context to discuss the "deterritorialization of borders that seek to withhold access to 'citizenship' for some of its members on the basis of the lack of certain credentials" (3). Also see Agnes Sam's introduction to *Jesus Is Indian*: "Indians may have been excluded from South Africa's history because of the temporary status intended for them. They may even have considered themselves temporarily resident in South Africa (9). This erasure from the national consciousness is precisely what drives the desire for citizenry in South African Indian fiction. As Parvathi

Raman points out in context of "the struggles over urban space," Indians have historically contested their lack of citizen rights (230), a struggle we can also locate in Indian fiction. I must also emphasize that my reference point is always fiction and not the so-called reality of South African Indian life, however much fiction and reality may influence each other.

4. Recently, I searched for the word "Afrindian" on Google. I found that it had been used in an unpublished PhD political science dissertation by Kumi Naidoo entitled "Class, Consciousness and Organisation: Indian Political Resistance in Durban, South Africa, 1979–1996" (Oxford: Magdalen College, 1997; available online at http://www.sahistory.org.za/pages/library-resources/thesis/kumi-naidoo/kumi-naidoo-index.htm, retrieved on July 14, 2007). Naidoo's use of the term seems similar to mine. She focuses on "the need for a development of an Afrindian identity, which encourages Indians to indigenise themselves to Africa without necessitating a need to negate their historical heritage." However, her work focuses on "political resistance" rather than on literature.

5. The term "contact zone" is Mary Louise Pratt's designation for intercultural exchange. See *Imperial Eyes* (6–7).

6. For an excellent analysis of Asian-black relationships, see Vijay Prashad's *Everybody Was Kung Fu Fighting: Afro-Asian Connections and the Myth of Cultural Purity*.

7. For example, Crane and Mohanram assert that the "canon . . . is continually questioned and opened up afresh by the postcolonial novel" (xiv).

8. In that vein, Loren Kruger argues for the "literary exploration of fictions that deconstruct or transform the 'major' or master narratives and the accompanying physical and political forces that have shaped South African lives to the present" ("Minor" 70). See also Barnard (8).

9. South African Indian self-expression can be traced back to newspapers such as the *Indian Opinion*, established in 1903 by Gandhi, and *Colonial News*, a competitor to *Indian Opinion* that was published from 1901 until 1904. These were followed by publications such as the Natal–based *Leader*, the *Graphic*, and *Indian Views* (Y. G. Reddy in Arkin et al., 196–97). In terms of cultural production, I base my assertion on the assumption that Indian indentured laborers sustained themselves on a rich body of myth and legend that they carried with them from the homeland in addition to testimonies of indentured labor found in texts such as *Documents of Indentured Labour* by Y. S. Meer, Marina Carter and Khal Torabully's *Coolitude*, and Surendra Bhana and Joy Brain's *Setting Down Roots: Indian Migrants in South Africa, 1860–1911*.

10. I am certainly not claiming that only Indians occupy this middle place between black and white. Groups such as the "Coloureds" and the "Cape Malays" also disturb the black-white paradigm of race relations. Each of these neglected communities deserves its own academic space. My project here is to study Indian literary production in South Africa and the impact that body of writing has on postcolonial studies. For a study of Coloured literature, see Grant Farred's *Midfielder's Moment*. Farred also focuses on how the Coloured community blurs racial binaries as well as on its contested relationship with blacks and whites. I should also point out that though I use the terms Coloureds, blacks, and whites throughout this book, I am

aware of their problematic connotations as well as their continued deployment by South Africans themselves.

11. The middle space occupied by Indians in the non-Western world has also been described by writers such as V. S. Naipaul and M. G. Vassanji. Ralph Singh in Naipaul's *The Mimic Men* (1967) claims that Indians in the fictional Caribbean island of Isabella (Trinidad) are "the late intruder, the picturesque Asiatic, linked to neither" ["slave-owner" or slave] (93). Vikram Lall, the narrator in Vassanji's appropriately titled *The In-Between World of Vikram Lall* (2003), is an Indian keenly aware of being caught between the black indigenes and the white settlers of Kenya.

12. V. S. Naipaul (Trinidad, England), Samuel Selvon (Trinidad, England), and M. G. Vassanji (Kenya, Tanzania, Canada) are examples of this phenomenon.

13. What follows is a summary of literary scholarship on South African Indians. Work has been done from ethnographic (Hansen, Radhakrishnan), historical (Dhupelia-Mesthrie, Ginwala, and Ebr.-Vally) and political (Desai, Ebr.-Vally) stances. Work has also been done on South African Indian theater (Hansen, Naidoo). However, there is a paucity of scholarship on fiction/literature.

14. For books on Gordimer, some representative examples include Judie Newman's *Nadine Gordimer* (New York: Routledge, 1988), Stephen Clingman's *The Novels of Nadine Gordimer* (Amherst: University of Massachusetts Press, 1986, 1992), and Dominic Head's *Nadine Gordimer* (Cambridge: Cambridge University Press, 1994). Representative examples of books on Coetzee include David Attwell's *J. M. Coetzee: South Africa and the Politics of Writing* (Berkeley: University of California Press, 1993), Sue Kossew's *Pen and Power: A Post-colonial Reading of J. M. Coetzee and André Brink* (Amsterdam: Rodopi, 1996), and Jane Poyner's edited collection *J. M. Coetzee and the Idea of the Public Intellectual* (Athens: Ohio University Press, 2006). Rosemary Jolly's *Colonization, Violence and Narration in White South African Writing: André Brink, Breyten Breytenbach, and J. M. Coetzee* (Athens: Ohio University Press, 1996) studies the work of Coetzee along with two other white writers.

15. In addition to the scholarship cited in the body of this chapter, some examples of books on black South African writers include *A Vision of Order: A Study of Black South African Literature in English, 1914–1980*, by Ursula A. Barnett (Amherst: University of Massachusetts Press, 1983); *Still Beating the Drum: Critical Perspectives on Lewis Nkosi*, edited by Lindy Stiebel and Liz Gunner (Amsterdam: Rodopi, 2005); and *Rewriting Modernity: Studies in Black South African Literary History*, by David Attwell (Scotsville, South Africa: University of KwaZulu-Natal Press, 2005).

16. See *MFS* [*Modern Fiction Studies*] 46.1 (Spring 2000). The postcolonial journal *Kunapipi* published a special issue on South African writing that included an interview with Achmat Dangor and an article by Meg Samuelson on rape in the South African imagination, which mentions Farida Karodia's *Other Secrets*. See *Kunapipi* 24, no. 1 & 2 (2002).

17. South African Indian writers such as Farouk Asvat, Shabbir Banoobhai, Achmat Dangor, Ahmed Essop, Reshard Gool, Farida Karodia, Indres Naidoo, Deena Padayachee, Essop Patel, Shobna Poona, and Jayapraga Reddy are listed in the bibliography of South African literature provided at the end of this text.

18. I am summarizing published work only. Two unpublished dissertations have been written on South African Indian literature: Madhavi Jaiswal's "Writing the 'Ordinary': Indian South African Writing as Womanist Prose" (Ahmed Essop, Jayapraga Reddy, Farida Karodia) (MA thesis, University of Alberta, 1991) and Ronit Fainman-Frenkel's "'On the Fringe of Dreamtime': South African Indian Literature, Race and the Boundaries of Scholarship" (PhD diss., University of Arizona, 2004). While Fainman-Frenkel also analyzes writers such as Dangor, Sam, Reddy, Karodia, and Coovadia, and uses the Indian presence to think beyond racial binaries, my focus is much more on diaspora and citizenship. Additionally, *Afrindian Fictions* also attempts to chart the themes and generic shifts in South African Indian literature, providing the reader with a broad overview of this body of work.

19. The books on Rushdie are too numerous to cite. Prominent and recent examples include Timothy Brennan's *Salman Rushdie and the Third World: Myths of the Nation* (London: Macmillan, 1989), Catherine Cundy's *Salman Rushdie: Contemporary World Writers* (Manchester: Manchester University Press, 1996), and Sabrina Hassumani's *Salman Rushdie: A Postmodern Reading of His Major Works* (Cranbury, NJ: Fairleigh Dickinson Press, 2002). The critical work on V. S. Naipaul is perhaps equally extensive. Some examples include Rob Nixon's *London Calling: V. S. Naipaul, Postcolonial Mandarin* (New York: Oxford University Press, 1992), Fawzia Mustafa's *V. S. Naipaul* (Cambridge: Cambridge University Press, 1995), and Helen Hayward's *The Enigma of V. S. Naipaul: Sources and Contexts* (New York: Palgrave Macmillan, 2002). For books on Bharati Mukherjee, see *Ways of Belonging: The Making of New Americans in the Fiction of Bharati Mukherjee* by Andrea Dlaska (Vienna: Braumuller, 1999) and *Bharati Mukherjee* by Fakrul Alam (New York: Twayne, 1996). John Hawley recently published *Amitav Ghosh: An Introduction* (New Delhi: Foundation Books, 2005). For books on Kureishi, see Kenneth C. Kaleta's *Hanif Kureishi: Postcolonial Storyteller* (Austin: University of Texas Press, 1998), Bart Moore-Gilbert's *Hanif Kureishi* (Manchester: Manchester University Press, 2001), and Susie Thomas's *Hanif Kureishi* (New York: Palgrave Macmillan, 2005). A search in July 2007 for Salman Rushdie in the MLA bibliography yielded 833 results, while a search for V. S. Naipaul yielded 573 results.

20. For example, see Susheila Nasta's *Home Truths: Fictions of the South Asian Diaspora in Britain* (Hampshire: Palgrave, 2002), Sukhdev Sandhu's *London Calling: How Black and Asian Writers Imagined a City* (London: HarperCollins, 2003), Rajini Srikanth's *The World Next Door: South Asian American Literature and the Idea of America* (Philadelphia: Temple University Press, 2004), Yasmin Hussain's *Writing Diaspora: South Asian Women, Culture, and Ethnicity* (Aldershot: Ashgate, 2005), Jigna Desai's *Beyond Bollywood: The Cultural Politics of South Asian Diasporic Film* (New York/London: Routledge, 2004), and Ruvani Ranasinha's *South Asian Writers in Twentieth-Century Britain: Culture in Translation* (Oxford: Oxford University Press, 2007).

21. Emmanuel S. Nelson's *Reworlding* and Ralph Crane and Radhika Mohanram's *Shifting Continents, Colliding Cultures* are examples of this tendency. Some very recent scholarship has examined the Indian diaspora in non-Western areas in comprehensive ways. See, for example, Shanthini Pillai's *Colonial Visions, Postcolonial Revisions: Images of the Indian Diaspora in Malaysia* (Newcastle: Cambridge

Scholars Publishing, 2007), and Vijay Mishra's *Literature of the Indian Diaspora: Theorizing the Diasporic Imaginary* (London and New York: Routledge, 2007). Mishra only briefly touches upon Indians in South Africa. Due to the recentness of these books, I have not been able to incorporate them in *Afrindian Fictions*. Also see François Lionnet's essay, entitled "Transcolonial Translations: Shakespeare in Mauritius," *Minor Transnationalism*, ed. Françoise Lionnet and Shu-mei Shih (Durham: Duke University Press, 2005), 201-221, and Sudesh Mishra's "From Sugar to Masala: Writing the Indian Diaspora," in *A History of Indian Literature in English*, ed. Arvind Krishna Mehrotra (New York: Columbia University Press, 2003) 276-294.

22. Also see Michael Chapman's thoughts on "South/South, South/North conversations" in his essay by that title (15) and Loren Kruger's *Post-Imperial Brecht*.

23. Much of the scholarship discussed above is necessarily circumscribed by the geographic or thematic range it sets for itself. In terms of literary study on South African Indians, I have found only a few essays that explore the cultural consequences of migration from the Indian subcontinent to South Africa. Some of these include Smith (1985); Munson, Page, and Johns (1987); Freed (1988); Van Niekerk (1992); Elder (1992); Ray (1994); Flockemann (1992, 1998); Hope and English (1998); Kruger (2001, 2003); Reddy (2001); Fainman-Frenkel (2004, 2008); Govinden (1995, 2000, 2004). These are mostly author-based studies—other than Reddy, who focuses on apartheid-era writing—and none undertakes a comprehensive analysis of South African Indian fiction as I do here. Rajendra Chetty's *South African Indian Writings in English* (2002) is a groundbreaking book, but it consists of anthologized extracts from South African Indian writing, even though it contains useful interviews with most of the South African Indian writers I study in this project.

24. See *Empire Writes Back* for more details; also see Jolly for a critique of this formulation.

25. This is not to claim that nonwhites do not interact with each other in complex ways in Western geographies. However, the interaction with whiteness often dominates race relations because whites are not only the most powerful group but also the most numerous. Moreover, this model of racial interaction (white/nonwhite) is very much the central paradigm in diaspora scholarship.

26. Thomas Hansen suggests that some of the additional concerns animating the South African Indian community are "imaginings of the motherland, the erosion of proper cultural practices, inter-generational conflicts, crime, worries about the westernization of youth and the corruption of sexual mores, internecine struggles between Tamils and Hindi speakers, and so on. Today, these debates revolve around how, and whether, a cultural 'we' can be maintained after the external imposition of a racial identity has disappeared" ("Melancholia" 302).

27. A poll conducted by Ebr.-Vally corroborates this assertion. Ebr.-Vally interviewed seventy South Africans of Indian origin for her research. One of the questions she asked was: "Which of the following would you use to describe yourself?" followed by a list of descriptive labels such as "Indian South African," "South African," "South African Indian," "South African of Indian origin," etc. Thirty-four percent of the interviewees identified themselves as "South African," 20 percent as "South African Indian," and 13 percent as "South African of Indian origin." Only 3 percent identified as Indian South African (176).

28. I am indebted to Surendra Bhana's work for the idea of a fluid Indianness in South Africa. For more on how Indianness adapted to changing social conditions in South Africa, see Bhana, "Indianness Reconfigured."

29. The "return to roots" narrative is an important diasporic urge. In his controversial essay detailing the "ideal type" of diaspora, William Safran argues that one of the important characteristics of diaspora is that diasporics "regard their ancestral homeland as their true ideal home and as the place to which they or their descendents would (or should) eventually return" (83–84). Examples of return, both permanent and temporary, include the "back to Africa" movement in African American history or the trips to Israel by many Jews. Literary exemplifications of this phenomenon include Richard Wright's *Black Power* (1954) and Pauline Hopkins's *Of One Blood* (1902–1903). In a South Asian context, some examples of return that come to mind include V. S. Naipaul's travelogues on India, Leila Dhingra's *Amritvela* (1988), Indi Rana's *Roller Birds of Rampur* (1993), and Jhumpa Lahiri's short story "The Interpreter of Maladies" (1999) in the collection by the same name.

30. Kruger's perceptive essay explains that the first Indians arrived in South Africa in the seventeenth century as slaves and that their Indianness was erased by centuries of intermingling as well as by the apartheid taxonomy that classified them as Coloured. Even though this is historically verifiable information (see Suleiman Dangor, "The Myth of the 1860 Settlers," for example), 1860 is generally considered to be the originary moment of Indian migration to South Africa. I discuss the expansion of the category of Indianness by highlighting the buried Indianness of many "Malays" in my chapter on Achmat Dangor, who is himself Cape Malay as well as has Indian ancestry, like many other Cape Malays.

31. Elder describes the various legislation enacted to disenfranchise the Indian community:

> [T]he Indian Immigration Act of 1895 in Natal and even harsher regulations in Transvaal. Gregory reports that Indians were not attracted to the Orange Free State because of the extreme discrimination that had existed there all along against all non-Europeans: "The constitution of 1854 expressly conferred the benefits of citizenship only on 'white persons' and Indians were subsequently regarded as 'coloured.' (128)" (117)

32. According to Bhana, "Given the NIC's emphasis on 'Indianness,' Africans did not fit the strategy. . . . The Indians considered themselves part of an advanced civilization deserving of equality. The NIC's best strategy, therefore, was to stress separation from other Blacks" ("Indianness Reconfigured" 101). For Gandhi's stay in South Africa and his vexed relationships with nonwhites and non-Indians, see the chapter entitled "Confronting Difference and Exclusion: Gandhi's Struggle for Recognition in South Africa," in Manfred Steger's *Gandhi's Dilemma* and Thiara (139–40).

33. Even though Gandhi spent some formative years in England, he isn't often appropriated by the South Asian–British diaspora. This could be because his stay in South Africa (twenty-one years) was much longer than his stay in England (three years). Additionally, even though England might have germinated Gandhi's political

consciousness, it was in South Africa that this activism really took root. This appropriation of Gandhi, of course, can often lead to an an uncritical idealization of the South African Gandhi. See also Ebr.-Vally (95–96).

34. South African Indian fiction often speaks of the pain of relocation forced by the Group Areas Act. See also Chetty, *South African Indian Writings* (11).

35. For more on how Indians acquired wealth and social standing in the 1980s, see Hansen, "Plays" (261) and "Diasporic Dispositions."

36. Kathrada was imprisoned with Nelson Mandela following the notorious Rivonia Trial in the early 1960s. Dadoo, as Muthal Naidoo points out, was the "leader of the South African Indian Congress during its most militant period of the Defiance Campaign in the 1950s, and Fatima Meer, also involved in the Defiance Campaign, [was] a founding member of the Federation of South African Women and author of a biography of Nelson Mandela" (29, n1).

37. For more information on the role of Indians during the apartheid period, see Ramamurthi's *Apartheid and Indian South Africans*. For more historical detail, see Ginwala, Dhupelia-Mesthrie, Ebr.-Vally, and Desai.

38. Anne-Marie Van Niekerk, for example, states that "in their opposition to these [apartheid] laws Indians have joined hands with the black majority . . . in . . . fighting for democratic change" (36).

39. Similarly, Muthal Naidoo claims that "the relative affluence of some of their members and their social position caught between the haves (mostly whites) and the have-nots (mostly black) made them targets of African resentment" (29). Robin Cohen describes the position of Indians under apartheid as a "V, not of their own making. Turn right, towards the white regime, and they were rejecting their fellow victims of apartheid; turn left, in the direction of black solidarity, and they became frightened of losing what status, rights and property they had acquired. Perhaps, not surprisingly, many remained uneasily where they were, like rabbits, trapped before the headlights of an oncoming car" (66).

40. Radhakrishnan further argues that "even the all-encompassing identification of South African, which is to unify all racial groups under a banner of national unity, presumes a singular Black/white division" ("Time" 273).

41. See Hansen: "[T]he future of Indians in South Africa is too insecure . . . and ridden with anxieties and animosities" ("Melancholia" 314).

42. James extends the idea of the "mass participation" in civic life to modern-day West Indies; I apply his formulations to contemporary South Africa.

43. Diana Brydon argues that

> [d]espite their significant differences and the complexity of their individual work, Bhabha, Spivak, and Said have come to be associated with a brand of postcolonialism that valorizes exilic, cosmopolitan, and diasporic perspectives. . . . Homi Bhabha's focus on the "transnational and translational sense of the hybridity of imagined communities" seems typical (5) . . . what readers have taken from his work tends to be his interest in cultural difference, migrant sensibilities, performances of identity, and the "unhomely" as "a paradigmatic colonial and post-colonial condition" (9).

Gayatri Spivak describes *A Critique of Postcolonial Reason: Toward a History of the Vanishing Present* as a book that "forages in the crease between global postcoloniality and postcolonial migrancy" (373). With Edward Said, Bhabha and Spivak agree in assigning a privileged role to the intellectual's position as exile. Paul Gilroy's *The Black Atlantic: Modernity and Double Consciousness* also helped to redirect analysis from nation-based study towards the consideration of multiple diasporic formations, travelling cultures and travelling theories, in the 1990s. Gilroy's theorization of 'the Black Atlantic as a counterculture of modernity' based on diaspora resonates with a general shift within the postcolonial field towards privileging mobility and deterritorialization. (699–700)

Also see Padmini Mongia's critique of hybridity in her introduction to *Contemporary Post-colonial Theory* as well as Kruger's model of "the syncretic" as opposed to the hybrid ("Minor" 70).

44. This is particularly true of the Indian migrants in the United States who regularly send money "home" and are members of radical organizations such as the VHP, RSS, etc. See, for example, Sangita Gopal's essay entitled "Hindu Buying/Hindu Being: Hindutva Online and the Commodity Logic of Cultural Nationalism" and Amit Rai's essay entitled "India Online: Electronic Bulletin Boards and the Construction of a Diasporic Hindu Identity."

45. I am in no way implying that Indians only used the short story during apartheid and novel in the postapartheid period. However, many, if not most, novels from the apartheid period tend more toward novellas for the same fiscal reasons that caused the short story to prevail.

46. A recent (2002) controversy sums up African hostility toward Indians. Zulu musician Mbongeni Ngema's song "AmaNdiya" (meaning Indians) claims that things were "better with whites" than with Indians.

47. Lest the binary between apartheid and postapartheid fiction seem absolute, it must be asserted that the transition from past to present is not hermetic, especially given that the fiction I study here spans a relatively short period of time (1978–2004). Often we see the possibilities of an Indianized South Africa as well as the racial tension of later times anticipated in the apartheid period. However, these divergences are usually subsumed by the antiapartheid imperative that was intensely focused on identifying Indians as black. Correspondingly, the rhetoric of identification that characterized the apartheid period occasionally surfaces in the postapartheid period, often to counter the charges of Indian racism by Africans.

48. Bhabha's work on mimicry may suggest that hybrid identities always fail at some level. His work on the "interstitial Third Space," however, describes hybridity as empowering and dynamic. See chapter 2 for a critique of Bhabha's celebration of hybridity.

49. While my survey of South African Indian fiction is comprehensive, it is certainly not complete. For example, I do not examine fiction such as Ansuyah Singh's *Behold the Earth Mourns* (1960), Reshard Gool's *Cape Town Coolie* (1990), Mewa Ramgobin's *Waiting to Live* (1986), Fayiza Dawood Khan's *The Sounds of Shadows*

(1995), Ronnie Govender's *At the Edge and Other Cato Manor Stories* (1996), Aziz Hassim's *The Lotus People* (2002), Pat Poovalingam's *Anand* (2003), Neela Govender's *Acacia Thorn in My Heart* (2000), Shamim Sarif's *The World Unseen* (2001), and Ishtiyaq Shakuri's *The Silent Minaret* (2005), among others. This is because I locate each text studied here not just as a text but also as exemplary of a certain literary moment in South African Indian fiction. My purpose, then, is to trace the evolution of the genre of South African Indian fiction, and how that enhances our understanding of diasporic cultures, rather than to provide a complete critical history of this body of work. That one single book cannot contain a critical genealogy of South African Indian fiction reveals the aesthetic density of this body of writing and how much work still needs to be done.

Chapter 1

1. See, for example, Wicomb, "South African Short Fiction"; Oliphant, "Fictions of Anticipation"; and Gray, "Introduction."

2. Indian issues were often reported in *Drum*, however. John Matshikiza recalls reading in *Drum* about "six Indian sisters, none of them more than teenagers, who had hanged themselves in a death pact in the back yard of their family home in Durban, rather than submit to arranged marriages" (ix–x).

3. "The mixture of gangsters, religious cranks, easy girls, roving males and the occasional white intellectual—all of whom are to be found in [Ahmed Essop's *Hajji*] stories—recall the mood of black short fiction of the fifties, originating in *Drum* magazine and set in Sophiatown" (Rowland Smith, quoted in Chetty, *South African Indian Writings* 20).

4. According to writer John Matshikiza, who grew up listening to *Drum* beats, "the startling thing is that there is no real dividing line between the two styles of writing: the journalistic and the fictional. Real life in the black townships has the monstrously stifling yet banal quality of a B-Grade horror film while the fictionalized accounts cannot escape from the relentless quality of realism" (x–xi). Also see Michael Chapman's essay "More Than Telling a Story: *Drum* and Its Significance in Black South African Writing" in the same collection. Chapman argues that "the entire *Drum* writing exercise forces us to examine assumptions about story-telling forms and purposes" (195).

5. Publishing in serials does not necessarily preclude the writing of novels. Charles Dickens is an obvious example of a novelist who flourished in the serial form. In apartheid South Africa, the "seriality" of magazine publication was constantly under threat because of a lack of funds, official censorship, and so on. Magazine publication could be highly irregular and could not guarantee the continuity a novel would require.

6. Andries Oliphant claims that "the short story, when compared to the novel, apart from its length, does not require the same degree of stability in the order of things, or continuity between past and present, for its operations. This makes it extremely flexible and enables it to focus on the fragments and fractions of everyday life without forfeiting any of the efficacy of narrative" ("Fictions").

7. Similarly, M. J. Daymond observes "that it [the 80s] was a decade of such harsh State opposition and such determined resistance by ordinary people that the 'history' one might expect to find is that of the alignments and conditions of armed racial conflict" ("Gender and 'History'" 192).

8. Examples from "black" South African literature touching directly or indirectly on these themes include: Bessie Head's *The Cardinals* (written 1960–62, published 1993) and *Maru* (1971), Mtutuzeli Matshoba's *Call Me Not A Man* (1979), Njabulo S. Ndebele's *Fools and Other Stories* (1983), Farida Karodia's *Coming Home and Other Stories* (1988), Richard Rive's *Buckingham Palace, District Six* (1986), Zoe Wicomb's *You Can't Get Lost in Cape Town* (1987), and Achmat Dangor's *Waiting for Leila* (1981) and *The Z Town Trilogy* (1990).

9. Progressive South African Jews, such as Joe Slovo, Ruth First, Albie Sachs, Rusty Goldberg, and Helen Suzman, also asserted solidarity with black Africans. While Jews were Other in many ways, their whiteness gave them a certain sense of place in apartheid South Africa that was denied to Indians. See the chapter on Achmat Dangor and *Kafka's Curse* for an extension of this argument.

10. As Margaret Daymond points out: the "necessity of founding individual self-identity in a collectivity" is "particularly relevant to South Africans" (Bardolph 183).

11. Here I echo Indian writer Amitav Ghosh's idea of the "shadow lines" as invisible lines of difference that make Other what was the Self-Same (228).

12. Amitava Kumar claims that "immigrants balance the conceit of a preserved heritage against the unanticipated and fairly uncanny elaboration of new identities that are liberating" (*Passport Photos* 229).

13. Born in 1948, the year apartheid was formalized as political praxis, Jayapraga Reddy suffered from spinal atrophy, a disease that bound her to a wheelchair. She died in 1996, before she completed her autobiography, *The Unbending Reed*. In addition to her collection of short stories, *On the Fringe of Dreamtime and Other Stories* (1987), she also wrote a play entitled *Web of Persuasion* (1984).

14. "The Love Beads," for example, depicts African culture in detail, particularly focusing on the beads that African women give to men when they are separated by the vagaries of the apartheid system. "Snatch the Wind and Run" discusses a relationship between a young Coloured boy and his white social worker. "The Stolen Hours" is written in the voice of a black maid working for a privileged white family. "A Dream at Sunset" is about a black female nurse whose mother is dying. Also see Van Niekerk (36).

15. Here, I am indebted to Toni Morrison's claim that language is always racialized. According to Morrison, "in a wholly racialized society, there is no escape from racially inflected language" (12–13).

16. For more on the relationship between immigrant and indigene, see Prashad.

17. Born in 1942, Sam, who is descended from indentured laborers, was raised in Port Elizabeth and educated at Roma, Lesotho, and Zimbabwe (Jaspal Singh 209). Like Farida Karodia, Sam lived in exile in England from 1973 onward. Sam's stories have been published in various magazines and journals; two of her plays have aired on BBC Radio. According to her Web site, Sam has finished a novel entitled *I Am Not Myself*. www.agnessam.com (retrieved March 30, 2008).

18. The secret practice of one religion while outwardly maintaining another

brings to mind the crypto-Jews. Like indentured Indians, crypto-Jews were often coerced into converting from Judaism to Islam in Persia and Catholicism in Spain and Portugal, but continued to practice Judaism in private ("Crypto-Judaism," http://en.wikipedia.org/wiki/Crypto-Judaism). I am grateful to Sharon Weltman for alerting me to their presence.

19. Indeed, Sam herself emphasizes the importance of the figure of Ruth in her collection: "It seems appropriate for the theme of this collection to be expressed in the following quotation from the Book of Ruth" (introduction to *Jesus Is Indian* 12). For "A South African Indian Womanist Reading of the Character of Ruth," see Sarojini Nadar's essay with the same title.

20. See Ray for more on Sam's use of Gandhi.

21. As Ray claims, "Angelina's narrativization of the present moment is constituted by simultaneously continuing and changing narratives emerging from incommensurable historical pasts and positing a future that is not naively rooted merely in future possibilities" (10).

22. Also see Flockemann on how Sam's work "suggests the possibility for . . . pragmatic cultural creolisations . . . as we move away from discourses of identity based on apartheid oppositions and engage with the tricky discourses of an apparently 'new' nationhood" ("Asian Diasporas" 83).

23. Bharati Mukherjee uses this phrase in her novel *The Holder of the World* to describe her narrator's desire to forge connections between two historically unconnected spaces: medieval India and Puritan New England (11).

24. See Ray for a detailed analysis of these stories and how they "function as oral history" (3–4).

25. Writing with reference to Sam and Jamaican writer Olive Senior, Flockemann argues that we can "detect a shift from representing Asian women as 'in-between' . . . to reclaiming their cultural 'difference'" ("Asian Diasporas" 75).

26. Fainman-Frenkel also analyzes some of these stories by Reddy and Sam. See her dissertation, "'On the Fringe of Dreamtime.'"

27. Born in 1953, Padayachee was trained as a medical doctor and currently practices in Durban. His compendium of short stories, *What's Love Got to Do with It?* is Padayachee's only collected work of fiction, although his work has appeared in other venues such as the prestigious South African newspaper the *Sunday Times*. Padayachee is also an accomplished poet whose verse and fiction have been widely anthologized. His collection of poetry, *A Voice from the Cauldron*, was published in 1986. In addition to winning the Nadine Gordimer Prize, Padayachee was also awarded the Olive Schriener Prize in 1994.

28. In her analysis of the Sikh diaspora in Canada, Kamala Elizabeth Nayar states that "the models that have been used to understand the change that occurs when two cultures meet are as follows: assimilation, acculturation, integration, separation, marginalization, and fusion" (253). Yasmin Hussain argues that "being in the diaspora means living in a cross-cultural context, one in which change, fusion and expansion are inevitable" (preface).

29. David Attwell points out that "assertions about the overwhelming prevalence of documentary realism all too frequently involve generalisations based on other critical statements with little or no discussion of the literature's actual qualities: its range, its idiosyncrasies, its very unfinishedness, and sadly, also its high points"

(172). Without minimizing the importance of "documentary realism," I too attempt to locate a structural complexity in South African Indian writing.

30. Citing R. Peck, Chetty argues that "the invasion of the private realm by politics meant that even writers who might have ignored politics were forced to deal with it. The personal relationships that might otherwise have been their focus were moved into the political realm" (*South African Indian Writings* 11).

Chapter 2

1. In the interview Essop states:

> Well, I felt that the human element had to be predominant in our writings. Apartheid formed one aspect of life. There are many other aspects of life. I was exposed to the different aspects of life in the community. There were humour, joy, marriages, funerals and so on. I felt that in my writings I should present a comprehensive whole. . . . (Chetty, *South African Indian Writings* 352)

2. Arlene Elder, for example, argues that the *Hajji Musa* tales "delight the reader in their sympathetic revelation of a variety of human foibles . . . but often frustrate by seeming to deflect intense engagement with the South African reality" (132). Elder concludes her study by stating that the "entire collection charms the reader with the author's skill at humorous depiction but leaves her eager for more of the political/historical, not just individual, context by which to explain Essop's characters" (137).

3. Vasu Reddy argues that Essop's writing "shows close connections to apartheid as the informing context but it is by no means his only point of reference" (86).

4. Because Essop's value system and aesthetic approach shifts so much, I think of him as two writers rather than one. Correspondingly, this chapter studies only Essop's apartheid-era prose and focuses on his novella *The Emperor* and his two short story collections, *Hajji Musa and the Hindu Fire-walker* and *Noorjehan and Other Stories*, while chapter 6 examines Essop's postapartheid writings.

5. Literary critics have traditionally celebrated the pluralism embodied in the East-West migratory exchange. For example, Yasmin Hussain credits Asian British filmmaker Gurinder Chadha for "re-defining British identities as culturally plural rather than fixed around some national, ethnic, racial or other absolute boundary and hence also explores ideas of diaspora, hybridity and cultural syncretism" (71).

6. South Asian American writer Bharati Mukherjee has been criticized for promoting an assimilationist credo in her work. Susan Koshy asserts that "Mukherjee's celebration of assimilation is an insufficient confrontation to the historical circumstances of ethnicity and race in the United States and of the complexities of diasporic subject-formation" (in Ponzanesi 42). Significantly, the eponymous character Jasmine in Mukherjee's novel *Jasmine* undergoes Americanization by often mingling with white characters and changing her name to Jane.

7. I am obviously echoing Gayatri Spivak's phrase "strategic essentialism" here. See *The Post-colonial Critic* for Spivak's sense of the term (11).

8. Timothy D. Taylor argues that "in most uses of the term 'hybridity,' the two cultures that hybridize are white and nonwhite Other, but the complex and multiple nature of the Other or Others is not always accounted for in the discourses of hybridity" (in Oren and Petro 234). Examples in literature of this white/nonwhite hybridity proliferate: Karim Amin in Hanif Kureishi's celebrated novel *The Buddha of Suburbia* is the child of an English mother and a Pakistani father. The main character in G. V. Desani's *All About H. Hatterr,* a novel said to have inspired Salman Rushdie himself, is "biologically . . . fifty-fifty of the species," an Anglo-Indian with British and Indian blood (1).

9. Avtar Brah argues that diasporas do not "normatively refer to temporary sojourns. Paradoxically, diasporic journeys are essentially about settling down, about putting roots 'elsewhere'" (182).

10. Rajendra Chetty states that South African Indian writers "like Farida Karodia, Ahmed Essop, Ronnie Govender, Indres Naidoo and Kesaveloo Goonam relocate the South African Indian as an integral part of the South African landscape. In demonstrating the unique position of the South African Indian as part of the oppressed and committed to the liberation of the country, these writers help to restore [credibility] to Indians" (*South African Indian Writings* 21).

11. For a detailed analysis of *The Emperor,* see Rowland Smith's "Living on the Fringe." Interestingly, far from criticizing Essop for not being political enough, Smith views the novella as "explicitly political," arguing that "the overriding political motif" makes the writing very "thin" (66).

12. It should be noted that for most scholars, the term "Aryan" is a meaningless category of analysis. Discarded by the thinking world as an empty signifier, it is significant that both Ashoka and the apartheid state attempt to resurrect the original value of the term.

13. Interestingly, Ashoka's features are described as "classically Dravidian" (2), associating him more with black people as well as the darker South Indians than with the supposedly light-skinned Aryans and North Indians. This is a classic tension in the novel: Ashoka wants to assume a normative whiteness but fails to realize his inner (and outer) blackness.

14. The kinship between Hindu social stricture and apartheid is reiterated at a public gathering of educators where the director of education makes a speech eulogizing the Indian community in South Africa: "Indians . . . have decided to jealously guard their racial and cultural identities that they have made such great strides in the educational world. We have one of the world's greatest universities in Durban, the Indian University of Westville, where you can find the best professors and lecturers in the southern hemisphere" (*Emperor* 136–37).

The director uses Indian professional achievement to argue for the success of apartheid. He manipulates the Indian desire to maintain a distinctive identity in African spaces as a tool with which to drive a wedge between the various disenfranchised communities. If "the jealous guarding of their racial and cultural identities" has led to Indian empowerment and uplift, then that clearly demonstrates the importance of segregation, or so the thinking goes. Again, Indian social organization is used not only to justify apartheid but also as an analogy for apartheid as both discourses claimed that separation would benefit rather than harm the races.

15. See, for example, Patrick Manning's *Migration in World History*:

> The social and cultural structure of a diaspora originates in the homeland from which people departed, either recently or long ago. Connections with the original culture across the diaspora can be retained through oral and written history, literature, and song. The linkages sustaining diaspora include family, religion, language, occupation, and traditions in dress, music, art and cuisine. (160)

16. The notion of carnival as a reordering of stratified social systems is most popularly associated with Russian formalist Mikhail Bakhtin. For more on the subversive prospects of carnival see Bakhtin's *Rabelais and His World*.

17. See Vijay Prashad's excellent book, *Everybody Was Kung Fu Fighting: Afro-Asian Connections and the Myth of Cultural Purity* for an analysis of Indian-black relationships in various parts of the world.

18. *Herrenvolk* means the master race. Its use is pejorative here.

19. I base my analysis of these texts partly on their publication dates. Although Essop mentioned to me that the *Hajji Musa* stories were set in the fifties and sixties (see my interview with Ahmed Essop in this book), it is not completely clear when they were composed. Since new material was added to this collection, the stories were probably edited before their publication in the seventies and eighties. It is likely, then, that they reveal the sensibilities of the time of setting, composition, and publication. Similarly the stories in the *Noojehan* collection are set in the seventies and eighties, but many reflect the beginning of the end of apartheid. See also Flockemann ("Asian Diasporas") on how Sam's stories that are set in the 1980s look forward to the new nation of the 1990s, and Jacobs (198).

20. Essop echoes Nadine Gordimer's thoughts in her early essay entitled "Where Do Whites Fit In?" (1959). Gordimer claims that "home is not necessarily where you belong ethnogenically, but rather the place you were born to, the faces you first saw around you, and the elements of the situation among your fellow men in which you found yourself and with which you have been struggling, politically, personally or artistically all your life" (*Essential Gesture* 34).

21. According to Jaspal Singh, "most so-called love stories about choice are represented in terms of sexual relationships between Indian women and white men . . . we have only recently started seeing the exploration of such racial intermixing in terms of black and Indian as spaces of empowerment or transcendence" (211).

22. Associated with activist Steve Biko, Black Consciousness urged the black community to free itself mentally and psychologically.

23. In *The Location of Culture*, Bhabha describes "the third space" as an "innovative energy" (315), transforming the binary narrative of the (Western) nation-state. Using the image of the stairwell, he further describes hybridity as an "interstitial passage between fixed identifications [that] opens up the possibility of a cultural hybridity that entertains difference without an assumed or imposed hierarchy" (5).

24. Many stories simply evoke the fullness of Indian life—with its cycle of birth, death, marriage, divorce, love, loss, joy, and anger. (Also see Smith 71–72.) Other stories, however, are so politically charged that taken together they articulate an

unambiguous message of social radicalization. Since my project in this chapter is to examine the relationship between transitional Indianness and political occasion, my analysis of *Noorjehan* focuses on how Essop endows Indians with political agency by bringing whites into the national fold.

25. Coined by Bishop Desmond Tutu, the term "rainbow nation" evokes the idea of a diverse, democratic South Africa. According to Sibusisiwe Nombuso Dlamini, the rainbow is "also an image associated with the premise of safety that followed the Biblical flood and thus is a symbol of reconciliation following a difficult period . . . the image of a rainbow nation, then, can be read to include recognition of South Africa's diverse population [and] the interconnectedness of people within this nation" (3). Essop's project of incorporating white people into the folds of the nation thus highlights this national interconnectedness.

26. Chetty points out that "the personae of *Noorjehan and Other Stories* transcend the barriers of race and ethnicity—perhaps in an attempt at coming to terms with a rapidly changing landscape. Many of Essop's narrators act as witnesses to historical events" (*South African Indian Writings* 20).

27. The title of the story ("Metamorphosis") further foregrounds the idea of empowerment through transformation. Its obvious echo of Kafka shows us how South African Indian literature is shaped not only by the various subfields of postcolonial literature but also by other international literary paradigms. Yet Essop makes Kafka's tale into his own. In Kafka's "Metamorphosis," Gregor Samsa wakes up to find himself transformed into a bug, something that is clearly subhuman. Naomi Rosenberg's movement from indifference to empathy gives her greater claim to humanity.

28. According to historian Surendra Bhana:

> The Tolstoy Farm was the second of its kind of experiments established by Gandhi. The first, the Phoenix settlement in Natal, was inspired in 1904 by a single reading of John Ruskin's *Unto This Last*, a work that extolled the virtues of the simple life of love, labour, and the dignity of human beings. Gandhi was not as personally involved in the daily running of the Phoenix settlement as he was to become in his stay of interrupted duration at the Tolstoy Farm which lasted for about four years. In part this was because the political struggle had shifted to the Transvaal after 1906, and he controlled it from its Johannesburg headquarters.
>
> To a large extent Gandhi's more intimate involvement at the Tolstoy Farm coincided with the heightened tempo of the passive resistance campaign, and the development of the Gandhian philosophy of the perfect individual in a perfect new order.
>
> The Tolstoy Farm was in part born out of practical necessity. Funds were running short, morale was sinking, and the movement missed the benefits that might accompany the establishment of a centre where its followers might assemble and coordinate their activities. The Transvaal settlement accommodated all three. Money was saved, morale was boosted, and the satyagrahis, according to Gandhi, received "training" that proved to be "of great use in the last fight."

For more on the Tolstoy Farm, see Bhana's essay "The Tolstoy Farm: Gandhi's Experiment in Cooperative Commonwealth."

Chapter 3

1. See Sailaja Sastry for the nexus between "the stories of interracial relationships" with "the project of nation-building" (276).

2. While Jameson's formulation—"all third world literatures are necessarily . . . national allegories" (69)—is totalizing in its sweep, it is broadly true that postcolonial literature tends to often metaphorize the nation. For a critique of Jameson, see Aijaz Ahmad's chapter entitled "Jameson's Rhetoric of Otherness and the National Allegory," in *In Theory*. For a critique and simultaneous rehabilitation of the term, see Imre Szeman's "Who's Afraid of National Allegory? Jameson, Literary Criticism, Globalization."

3. A note on the term "transition" as pertaining to the South African context is necessary here. Apartheid weakened in 1990 with the release of Nelson Mandela and the unbanning of the ANC. Universal franchise, however, became a reality only in 1994 when all South Africans went to the polls to elect a democratic government for the first time. Mandela's party, the African National Congress (ANC), overwhelmingly won the election and Mandela became the first president of democratic multiracial South Africa.

4. While most of the existing criticism on *Kafka's Curse* interprets the text as a commentary on transition, no work, however, studies the compositional complexities of the narrative in order to examine how they allegorize the "terrible beauty" of an imminent nation or the coming of age of South African Indians. Elaine Young, the critic whose work comes close to my hypothesis here, argues that the "individual mutations and crossings-over reflect the increasingly hybridized nature of South African society itself . . . the narrative structure of the novella is analogous to the multivocality and complexity of South African society after apartheid" (17). Young primarily focuses on the trope of "rampant transgression" (17) and does not explicitly foreground the theme of national allegory through symbolic morphology; neither does she pay attention to the text's articulation of Indo-Islamic desires and anxieties and the fruition of South African Indian selfhood. Vilashini Cooppan's argument resonates even more closely with mine. Linking "metamorphosis . . . as a metaphor for national transition" (361), she uses the term "national allegory" to describe Dangor's novel, arguing that "the body politic imagined in *Kafka's Curse*, with its polymorphous sexual crossings, physical alterations, and multiple social and linguistic metamorphoses, well deserves the label of national allegory" (362). Yet Cooppan does not focus on the text's symbolic configuration in order to foreground national allegory, even though she is attentive to form and structure. In an extremely brief discussion of *Kafka's Curse*, Christopher Heywood lists "the museum of houses, Islam, body parts . . . cooking ingredients, furnishings, architectural projects, and the social atrocity represented by group areas" (232) as part of the novel's thematic roster. Few of these critics, additionally, see national allegory as a form of minority empowerment.

5. This list of tropes and motifs is by no means exhaustive. Rather, it is simply an articulation of metaphors that I find significant to the novel's structural intent.

6. As Vilashini Cooppan observes, "the transformations that the novella describes are both political . . . and textual" (356).

7. Many critics see Dangor and Omar/Malik as Malay. However, because *Kafka's Curse* deliberately obfuscates the racial identity of its characters, there is no consensus on the race of the characters, which seems to be Dangor's point. Taking my cue from Loren Kruger, I consider the characters to also be Indian not only to excavate the buried Indian roots of many Cape Malays, but also because the characters often identify themselves as Indian. Moreover, because racial, cultural, and religious identity in Muslim communities is usually asserted through the line of the father, Indianness has been passed down to the Khan family—rather than erased—through Omar's grandfather, who came to South Africa as a contracted trader.

Kruger also claims that Dangor's "person and texts inhabit . . . in-between spaces in exemplary ways" ("Black" 114). Dangor's own racial identity thus seems as uncodeable as that of his characters in *Kafka's Curse*. He writes with such an intimate insider knowledge of Indian culture and language in *Kafka's Curse* that it is impossible for him not to have Indian ancestry. I also base this assertion on an Internet interview with Dangor where he states that he "was a racially hybrid child (Indian/ Javanese/ Dutch ancestry)," a heritage shared by Omar and Malik, his two protagonists in *Kafka's Curse* ("Interviews with South African Writers (Mike Nicol—Achmat Dangor—Bridget Pitt—Pamela Jooste—Peter Horn)." Retrieved October 28, 2006, http://www2.univ-reunion.fr/~ageof/text/74c21e88–337.html.

This is not to say that *Kafka's Curse* is autobiographical. The book, and Dangor's own tangled racial history, show us the extent to which Indians have integrated into South African society. Yet *Kafka's Curse* needs to be studied as an *Afrindian* text because the novel is intensely preoccupied with the role of Indianness, particularly Islamic Indianness, in the time of transition in South Africa.

8. Phillip Roth's novel *The Human Stain* (2000) echoes a similar premise: Coleman Silk is a black American who passes as a Jew. Notice how the titles of both texts describe racial passing as a stain and a curse.

9. The Truth and Reconciliation Commission (TRC) also began its work in 1996; its resurrection of the segregationist past can be seen as an excavation of the buried "truth" hidden by decades of white supremacy. I am grateful to Shane Graham for making this connection.

10. For more on how Jews enjoyed white privilege, as well as the fraught relationship between Muslims and Jews, see Ameen Akhalwaya's essay entitled "A Love-Hate Relationship: Jews and Muslims in South Africa." Akhalwaya claims that "Jews and Muslims have a strange love-hate relationship in which they are divided by two issues. First, Jews are classified white, while the majority of Muslims have been categorized 'Indian,' 'coloured,' 'black' or other sub-divisions under South Africa's now-scrapped race classification laws. And second, the question of Palestine" (17). Even though many progressive Jews, like Helen Suzman, rallied against apartheid, as "anti-white resentment began to build up . . . the perception grew that Jews were all too happy to take advantage of massive white privilege thus created by apartheid.

Jews were increasingly seen as silent partners in apartheid's oppression of Muslims and other South African blacks" (18).

Additionally, Milton Shain claims that in

> the 1950s and 1960s . . . communist and progressive Jews had criticized the Jewish establishment for not speaking out formally against apartheid . . . the moral high road [was] not taken during the apartheid era, at least not by the formal leadership, represented in the South African Jewish Board of Deputies.
>
> The question of Jewish behavior during the apartheid years remains a source of contention and moral questions will not disappear. (205)

11. Bharucha is referring to the Parsi diaspora in England, which is twice migrant: once from Persia and the second time from India.

12. In his discussion of black South African writing under apartheid, Attwell partly echoes this line of thought even though he doesn't use the term "diaspora":

> When European modernism registers spatial dislocations, it frequently does so in terms of the expatriate or exile. . . . This pattern is not absent from black South African writing . . . black South African writing can reflect a sense of dislocation *at home* . . . [which becomes] a place of permanent unease or unsettlement, a place where one experiences one's *dislocation* from rural life, economic independence, political representation and citizenship. (176; emphasis in original)

13. Grey Street is increasingly becoming an important setting in South African Indian writing. Aziz Hassim's novel *The Lotus People* (2002), Mariam Akabor's collection of short stories entitled *Flat 9* (2006), and Ashwin Singh's unpublished play *Spice 'N Stuff* all use Grey Street as both location and as a symbol for Indian identity. For a pioneering study of place in the works of writers such as Gordimer, Fugard, Tlali, and Mda, see Rita Barnard's excellent book *Apartheid and Beyond*.

14. For Achmat Dangor's comments on architecture and apartheid see his short piece "Apartheid and the Death of South African cities" in Judin.

15. I am grateful to Sharon Weltman for this interpretation.

16. Cooppan argues that the postcolonial novel has rendered magical realism into a "generic model" but concedes that magical realism in *Kafka's Curse* is more complicated in its effort to "find the middle ground" (359).

17. Dangor is not the only one to demonstrate an interest in Kafka. A story in Ahmed Essop's *Noorjehan* collection is entitled "Metamorphosis." It is also impossible to miss the reference to Kafka in J. M. Coetzee's *The Life and Times of Michael K* (1983). The truncated last name of Coetzee's protagonist, reduced here to a single barren letter, brings to mind Joseph K in Kafka's *The Trial* (1925). For a study of Kafka's influence on Coetzee see P. Joffe's "The Naming of Michael K: J. M. Coetzee's Life and Times of Michael K." Interestingly, both Michael K and Majnoen are gardeners, showing the influence of Coetzee on Dangor. See Cooppan for a study of Coetzee and Dangor, and for an analysis of *Kafka's Curse* and transnational influences.

18. Woodward also argues that trees "figure repeatedly in the novel, but never as fertile natural symbols" (30). Like much of the novel, even the tree-turning is ambiguous. Oscar's body may have "crumbled to dust," (*Kafka's Curse* 27) but rumor has it that the "shapeless form [Oscar's body] . . . was really a shrivelled tree" (69). Also, "in what had once been the main bedroom, a tree had thrust up through the floor" (28). This is the room in which Oscar's body is found:

> He knew the case was unusual, Sergeant Johnson told Malik, but people said that they saw this *thing* happening to the dead man, like it was part of his nature. He indicated with a wave of his hand to the room, the mould on the walls, the flowers, the tree growing in the middle of the room. (66)

In my interpretation, Oscar becomes the tree in the middle of the room, while the word "growing" attaches an immediate and active fertility to the image of the tree. The unnatural circumstances in which the tree is growing further suggests Indian achievment and growth in the unnatural circumstances of apartheid.

19. See Malkki for metaphors of soil, rootedness, and trees.

20. "Our people don't bury their dead as if they're on the way to a party" (*Kafka's Curse* 224).

21. This is also echoed by Cooppan, who argues that the novel "portrays metamorphosis as both curse and blessing" (358).

22. Amina's beauty becomes "beaklike" and "thrust out" (*Kafka's Curse* 125). Toward the end of his relationship with Amina and the end of his life, Malik begins to take on birdlike aspects: "[T]here is a lightness about him, the insubstantiality of wings, his skin as smooth as down . . . a beaked face" (145). Significantly, this metamorphosis occurs after Malik leaves the white part of town, where he has been living with Amina, and returns to the township, bringing to mind Omar's mysterious illness that strikes him after he goes back to the township for his mother's funeral.

23. Bird imagery also recurs in Dangor's novella *The Z Town Trilogy*. One of the characters is described as "[a] dark and terrifying bird swooping down from the hot blue sky upon her frightened prey" (29). In another instance, migratory birds from the country amaze Hillbrow with their appearance (55). Another character has a "strange affinity for birds, the uncanny manner in which she seemed capable of communicating with them" (59). That same character, Jane, like Malik in *Kafka's Curse*, feels that she is physically becoming a bird: "Jane saw a flutter of tiny wings, she felt a lightness in her body, as exquisite as death or flight" (86). Also see Kruger on bird imagery in *The Z Town Trilogy* ("Black" 125) and Woodward for "Malik's identification from childhood with birds" (29).

24. See Fainman-Frenkel, "'On the Fringe,'" for apartheid creating a diaspora of exile (142–43).

25. See Cooppan: "[T]he becoming-other of Dangor's characters describes that radical becoming-other which each South African citizen must allow if national culture is to emerge from the territorialzed, classification-mad history of apartheid" (361). Also see Sastry (281).

26. See Woodward for an analysis of Kulsum/Katryn.

27. Naipaul uses the term "the neurosis of the converted" to describe the psychic anxiety felt by non-Arabic converts to Islam, particularly the populations of Iran, Pakistan, Indonesia, and Malaysia, who always feel that they have to outperform the original Muslims (those of Arabic stock) in demonstrating their religious piety ("Questions for V.S. Naipaul on His Contentious Relationship to Islam," October 28, 2001, from http://www.racematters.org/vsnaipaulonislam.htm). Retrieved June 11, 2007. Also see *Among the Believers* and *Beyond Belief* for more of this hypothesis.

28. Similarly, Sastry argues that in South Africa "standard postcolonial nomenclature such as . . . hybridity may have to be adjusted or abandoned altogether" (277). See the rest of Sastry's essay for a critique of theories of hybridity.

29. Many of the slaves in the Cape were brought from the Indian Ocean area under the auspices of the Dutch East India Company from the seventeenth century onward. According to the Web site of the Slave Lodge, a museum dedicated to commemorating South African slavery in Cape Town:

> Although a few of the first slaves came from West Africa, most slaves came from societies around the Indian Ocean Basin. Slaves came from Madagascar, from Mozambique and the East African coast, from India and from the islands of the East Indies such as Sumatra, Java, the Celebes, Ternate and Timor. . . .
>
> The Indian subcontinent was the main source of slaves during the early part of the 18th century. Approximately 80% of slaves came from India during this period. A slaving station was established in Delagoa Bay (present-day Maputo) in 1721, but was abandoned in 1731. Between 1731 and 1765 more and more slaves were bought from Madagascar. ("Slave Routes to Cape Town," http://www.iziko.org.za/sh/resources/slavery/slavery_routes.html). Retrieved November 18, 2006

The Web site also describes the work performed by the slaves housed in the Slave Lodge:

> The slaves that belonged to Dutch East India Company (VOC) made an important contribution to the establishment, management and protection of the Dutch settlement at the Cape. . . . They were the largest group of slaves and were used for a variety of duties, from manual labour to skilled artisan work. In contrast to slaves in private ownership at the Cape, no strong division of labour based on sex existed for the Lodge slaves. In the first few years of the Dutch settlement's existence, the slaves worked as assistants to the VOC officials such as artisans, the gardener and the wood-cutters. Seventy-five slaves were listed in a letter dated 11 April 1658—a third worked in the Company's Garden while 19 were employed on the Company's farm. ("At Work," http://www.iziko.org.za/sh/resources/slavery/slavelodge_work.html). Retrieved November 18, 2006

For more on the arrival of Indians as slaves in South Africa, see S. E. Dangor's essay entitled "The Myth of the 1860 Settlers." Also see Loren Kruger's essay entitled "Black Atlantics, White Indians and Jews."

Chapter 4

1. See Govinden, "Against an African Sky" (82).

2. This is not to say that black women were not being published during the apartheid years. Bessie Head, Miriam Tlali, and Zoe Wicomb all come to mind as examples of nonwhite women writing during apartheid. Yet, as Govinden argues, "[b]lack women writers have been a marginalised group for the better part of this century, and only in recent years have they been given critical recognition" ("Against an African Sky" 84).

3. Examples Govinden cites include *"Let it be Told,* by Lauretta Ngcobo; *Breaking the Silence,* by Cecily Lockett; and *Raising the Blinds,* by Annemarie Van Niekerk" ("Against an African Sky" 84).

4. As with most other South African Indian writers, little biographical or literary information is available on Karodia. According to Anver Versi, Karodia's father was a Gujarati Indian "who settled in South Africa in 1920. Her mother was coloured. . . . They lived in one of those small Afrikaaner-dominated towns, Aliwal, in the Eastern Cape. 'We were the only Indians in the town' she [Karodia] recalls. But of course they were not entirely Indian since her mother was not one" (39). Karodia taught school for two years after studying at a teachers training college in Johannesburg (Versi 40). Her South African passport was revoked while teaching in Zambia, after which she migrated to Canada, where she embarked on her writing career. While she began her literary career by writing dramas for the Canadian Broadcasting Corporation, Karodia's first novel, *Daughters of the Twilight,* was published in 1986 (Versi 40). Even though *Daughters of the Twilight* confined itself to tracing the impact of relocation on the psyche of an Indian girl, Karodia refused to subscribe to ethnic mandates in subsequent fiction. Her first collection of short fiction, *Coming Home and Other Stories* (1988), approaches race relations through the prism of the diverse constituencies that inhabit South Africa—white, black, Indian and Coloured. After visiting India, Karodia made a TV film entitled *Midnight in Embers* (1992) about "the relationship between a retired British actress living in India and her Indian male servant" (Versi 40). Her next novel, *A Shattering of Silence* (1993), focuses on the insurgency in Mozambique. Following her return "home," Karodia wrote *Against an African Sky and Other Stories* (1995) where she explores the impact of the changing social milieu on everyday South African life. Her magnum opus, *Other Secrets,* was published in 2000. Karodia's most recent work, the novel *Boundaries* (2003), is set amid the mayhem caused by the arrival of a television crew in a small South African town. As the chronological summary of Karodia's work reveals, it was only with the publication of *Other Secrets* that Karodia returned to exploring issues of Afrindian identity.

5. See Loren Kruger's essay entitled "In a Minor Key" for an analysis of Jacobs and Karodia.

6. According to Frene Ginwala, the act:

> [V]aunted by former prime minister Dr Malan as embodying "the essence of apartheid policy" is the one piece of legislation whose application has had the greatest direct impact on the lives of Indian South Africans. Ostensibly non-racial, it makes provision for each group to be allocated to specific areas, thus segregating the country on rigid racial lines. The application of the Act, however, has been such as to complete the process of dispossession and the abrogation of almost all urban land to the white population, either individually, corporately or through state ownership.
>
> Between 1966 and August 1984, 83, 691 coloured, 40,067 Indian and 2418 white families had been moved under the provisions of the act. . . . Entire communities are uprooted and forced to leave behind not only long established homes and businesses but also schools, temples, mosques, clinics and community centres. . . . The people have been forced to settle outside the towns in areas with few amenities, without telephones, police, health or even postal services. (12)

7. Penguin South Africa is not an indigenous South African press like Kwela, Ravan, or David Philip. Yet, given how many South African Indian writers—including Karodia herself—were published abroad, it is significant that *Other Secrets* was published at home. The fact that the novel was published by the South African branch of a Western publishing house also, ironically, supports the point made later in this chapter: that Europe always manages to inveigle itself into the assertion of South African Indian identities.

8. The idea of a double diaspora is not just confined to Indians in South Africa. Ugandan Asians in Britain, Fijian Indians in Canada, and the growing number of Asian Africans in the United States are all examples of twice-migrants. It is, however, significantly different from the once-migrant Indian diasporas in the United States, the UK, and Canada. For more on "second banishment" (43) in the Fijian-Indian imagination, see Satendra Nandan's essay in Crane and Mohanram, eds., *Shifting Continents/Colliding Cultures*.

9. Meg Samuelson very briefly explores some of these changes although her focus is on rape of Yasmin and "racial mixing" (96).

10. Effacement and revelation refer to the articulation of a common black/nonwhite identity and a tentative Indian selfhood that we have traced in all apartheid-era writing.

11. While Flockemann also sees "the community of older women, mothers, grandmothers, and aunts [as] significant touchstones" in *Daughters*, the novella, unlike *Other Secrets*, rarely abandons political context to describe emotional relationships ("Not-Quite" 43).

12. W. E. B Du Bois' famous term "double consciousness" refers to the split in identity that living as Other in a violently racialized society engenders. The portability of the term to a South African context suggests the similarities between American segregation and apartheid.

13. Achmat Dangor raises this question in *Kafka's Curse*, while Ahmed Essop also explores how Muslims themselves contribute to their estrangement from the nation in *The Third Prophecy*.

14. This is generally true of all South Asian diasporas, where family often substitutes for the community left behind. As Robin Cohen points out, "the Indian family was gradually reconstituted [in the labor diaspora], often in an oppressive patriarchal form, but none the less in such a way as to provide a source of social cohesion and a site for reasserting communal life" (63).

15. For example, Abdul is skeptical of Yasmin's dancing, saying that a good Muslim girl has no business dancing (*Other Secrets* 119).

16. Yasmin Hussain considers "inter-generational conflict" to be a "central theme" of the writings of South Asian diaspora in Britain (15). Similarly, Mark Stein argues with reference to black British writing that "in the diasporic novel of transformation generational conflict often signifies a concurrent cultural conflict between a parental generation who migrated and the generation born in Britain" (xvii). In an American context, this is echoed by Wanni W. Anderson and Robert G. Lee, who describe "the generational conflict between immigrant Asians who, until the late 1940s and 1950s, were ineligible for naturalization and their American-born citizen children" (9).

17. Abdul's absolutism is further focalized when Meena contemplates going to Johannesburg to take up a teaching course. Her apprehension in approaching this matter with her father is justified. When she expresses her desire to leave McBain for the city, her father loses his temper:

> "Shut up!" he shouted. "I will not have you speaking to me so disrespectfully! I will not have you disgracing me the way your sister did. What is wrong with you girls? Is it so hard to be honorable? Do you have to be cheap? Muslim girls don't run around the country—they stay home with their families. They know what's right and wrong!"
>
> "So what are we? It's not our fault that we're not what you wanted us to be!" (*Other Secrets* 210)

Abdul holds autocratic beliefs about how Muslim girls should behave. His concept of honor—and of daughters as custodians of that honor—also reflects an orthodox Islamic perspective that seeks moral restitution in a profane world.

18. See Chetty, *South African Indian Writings* (21).

19. For more on the tragic resonances of Soraya's name, see Meg Samuelson:

> Once again, though, the child's name foregrounds this mixing. Her namesake, Princess Soraya . . . was of mixed Iranian and German descent. Divorced and banished, [Princess] Soraya's . . . story fits into the tragic mould, confirming the "tragedy of mixed blood" that has held sway over the South African imagination. . . . The children, so relentlessly inserted into the plot, are an insurmountable stumbling block as the substitution of mother for rape victim rearticulates the Apartheid discourses of blood purity enshrined in . . . the "pillars of apartheid."
> . . . The South African literary imagination has shown itself unable to extricate itself from this web of legislation. (96–97)

Loren Kruger further echoes this claim by arguing that Soraya's "inheritance as the child of a white rapist and the daughter and granddaughter of transgressing women of colour somehow dooms her to a sudden and implausible death by accident" ("Minor" 72).

20. Fainman-Frenkel aptly summarizes the novel's commentary on inter-racial contact: "Karodia is, therefore, narrating the everyday 'mix' of many South Africans that Apartheid attempted to conceal and regulate, while highlighting the arbitrary and artificial nature of Apartheid racial classification itself" ("Ordinary Secrets" 62).

21. Discussing the idea of "middleman minorities," Ashwin Desai and Brij Maharaj argue that "the role of middleman easily becomes the role of 'economic villain' especially at a time of economic crisis. Middleman minorities or people in the status gap are scapegoats per excellence. Scapegoats often deflect hostility away from the superior status group. Hilda Kuper, a social anthropologist, argued that like Jews in other countries, Indians in South Africa were being used as 'scapegoats' by the dominant ethnic groups" ("Minorities in the Rainbow Nation").

22. Of course, I am using Bantustans metaphorically here. Rehana Ebr.-Vally mentions a plan to create a Bantustan for Indians. Ironically titled "Hindustan," this homeland failed to materialize (99).

23. Karodia elaborates on the deracination of migration in a short story entitled "Crossmatch." The South African Indian protagonist, Sushila, lives in London, where her mother constantly worries that Sushila "might have abandoned her Hindu traditions" (*Against an African Sky* 90).

24. See Samuelson for a critique of the celebratory aspects of the child (96).

25. Timothy Brennan has described *The Satanic Verses* as "the most ambitious novel yet published to deal with the immigrant experience in Britain" (*Salman Rushdie* 149).

26. Here I echo the titles of two important texts of diasporic arrival: Meena Alexander's *The Shock of Arrival* (1996) and V. S. Naipaul's *The Enigma of Arrival* (1987).

27. The most important figure, as well as theorist, of exile is Edward Said. The title of Said's autobiography, *Out of Place*, suggests the sense of placelessness that the cosmopolitan wanderer invokes. See Aijaz Ahmad's *In Theory* for a critique of cosmopolitans such as Said and Rushdie in particular and literary migrancy in general. Further examples of cosmopolitan migrants include Saladin Chamcha in *The Satanic Verses*, Tara in Bharati Mukherjee's *The Tiger's Daughter*, and Karim Amin in Hanif Kureishi's *The Buddha of Suburbia*. Sandhya Shukla also sees Ila in Amitav Ghosh's *Shadowlines* as a "cosmopolitan-migrant" (150).

28. Cosmopolitanism as multiple allegiances that disrupt homogenous categories of classification, such as nation, race, and citizenship, has been theorized by Bruce Robbins, Pheng Cheah, and James Clifford, among others. See Clifford's *Routes: Travel and Translation in the Twentieth Century* and Robbins and Cheah's *Cosmopolitics: Thinking and Feeling beyond the Nation* for more on the pluralizing possibilities of cosmopolitanism. Sandhya Shukla further echoes the idea of migrant identities destabilizing hegemonic codes: "[B]y looking at how migrant discourses have created India abroad, we can challenge the assumed centrality of 'America' and 'England' in the lives of people who inhabit the spaces of the United States and Britain" (5). She further adds that "Indians' connections to each other and to

places that traverse the boundaries of countries of settlement are often formulated in languages that straddle conceptual categories of race, ethnicity and nation" (9). Paul Gilroy makes a similar argument in *The Black Atlantic*, a book that destabilizes territorial and spatial boundaries through the idea of diaspora.

29. Loren Kruger interprets the titles of the novels that Meena reads as "shorthand comparisons between Meena . . . and the heroines of romance novels with titles like *Cast Adrift* and *Storms of Passion* [that] register irony as well as empathy" ("Minor" 72). I am, of course, referring to the romance novels that Meena writes.

Chapter 5

1. Similarly Sten Moslund argues that "many South Africans have a history of being misrepresented or obliterated by institutionalized histories and, being denied the access to participate in the making of institutionalized histories, literature has often assumed the function of being an aperture for self-expression and self-assertion" (21).

2. John McLeod argues that "Negritude is nostalgic for a mythic African past. Negritude often posited a 'golden age' of pre-colonial Africa from which black peoples had been separated by colonialism and to which they must return. . . . [T]hese 'returns' depended upon the construction of a mythic African pre-colonial past before the time of colonialism which was free from the ills of the present. But did such a 'golden age' of perfection ever really exist?" (82).

3. Moslund points out that "counter-histories involve a conscious attempt to regain the command of one's own reality. . . . Accordingly the distribution of other myths of origin . . . or the expression of a marginalized perspective may comprise a complex 'vital human strategy for sustaining a sense of agency in the face of disempowering circumstances' (Jackson, 2002, 4). Counter-histories may rework and restructure the past psychologically, socially and metaphorically to change our experience and perception of truths and the limits of reality" (16).

4. Lukács's formulations on the historical novel are useful to foreground here. As Michael Green points out, "Lukács . . . shifted the basis for his identification of the 'historical novel' from the realm of empty formalism and ahistorical classification to the materiality of the moment from which the form emerged" (123).

5. Similarly, Ulrich Broich argues that the "historical writing could have been useful to create . . . a national identity" (421).

6. Indians came to the Caribbean, Mauritius, Guyana, Fiji, and South Africa as indentured labor in the mid- to late nineteenth century. Due to the recentness of migration to the United Kingdom and United States, there is no dearth of fiction commemorating the diasporic voyage to the West. Accounts of voyaging to the Caribbean are fewer: David Dabydeen's *The Counting House* (1996) is one of the few texts that reimagines the passage of indentured Indians to colonial Guyana. Dabydeen's collection of poems entitled *The Coolie Odyssey* (1988) revives the indentured past. Indo-Trinidadian writer Ramabai Espinet's novel *The Swinging Bridge* (2003) also narrates the indentured experience. The anthology *Coolitude*, edited by

Khal Torabully and Marina Carter, attempts to excavate a distinctive "coolie" consciousness, but confines itself to poetry, as does the Noor Kabir edited collection, *The Still Cry: Personal Accounts of East Indians in Trinidad and Tobago during Indentureship, 1845–1917*. However, literary accounts of Indian migration to Africa are exceedingly rare. Recently, Pat Poovalingam's novel *Anand* (2003) partially recovered the indenture experience in South Africa. When I was in Durban in 2005, I had the opportunity to watch Rajesh Gopie's new play, entitled *Coolie Odyssey*, which sought to fill precisely this gap in South African Indian literature. Additionally, Aziz Hassim, author of the novel *The Lotus People*, told me that his next novel was to be set in, and about a character who emerges from, the cane fields.

7. The singular presence of apartheid in the national psyche often erased other histories of oppression—such as the experience of indentured labor—and prevented an examination of their psychic ramifications. Since the British who brought indentured Indians to South Africa were inveterate record keepers, it is easy to garner primary documentation of indentured migration. However, literary narrations of indenture are much rarer, even though, as Frene Ginwala estimates, "more than 90 percent [of South African Indians] are the descendants of indentured labourers" (4).

8. Moodley is currently an admissions officer in the Faculty of Science at the University of KwaZulu Natal. *The Heart Knows No Colour* is Moodley's first published work. Her second novel, *A Scent so Sweet*, was published in 2006.

9. Paul Gilroy's notion of the slave ship as "chronotope" is instructive here (Braziel and Mannur 49, 52–53, 64). The ship represents cultural interaction, albeit violent. Similarly, one can see the indentured ship, in keeping with the Middle Passage image, as a facilitator of cross-cultural movement. Indo-Caribbean scholar Ron Ramdin also uses the term "Other Middle Passage" to describe the movement of indentured laborers from India to various places in the British Empire. See also Mishra ("Diasporic Imaginary" 423, 429) on the importance of the ship in the indentured imagination.

10. According to Surendra Bhana and Joy Brain, the "first ship bringing indentured Indians from Madras was the *Truro*, which arrived in Durban on 16 November 1860. There were 340 men, women and children on board" (28). Brought by the British, who administered India in addition to the South African province of Natal, indentured Indians were to fill the labor shortage in "new and labour-intensive plantation crops like coffee, tea, or sugar along the coastal belt" (24). These immigrants were usually agrarian, illiterate, and destitute. Uma Dhupelia-Mesthrie states that "Natal would receive a total of 152 184 indentured immigrants (62 % men, 25 % women and 13 % children). Of these, 101 468 came from Southern India . . . while others came from the northern and north-eastern areas of India. . . . The majority were Hindus, some 2 % Christians and less than 12% Muslims" (10).

11. Moodley here directly echoes historian Uma Dhupelia-Mesthrie's account of "the six to six" schedule of Indian laborers:

> Being an indentured labourer meant that one was not quite a slave (a permanent piece of property) but neither was one a free soul. Indentured workers were bound by contract for five years and there was

incentive for a second contract for a further five years with the offer of a free return passage to India or the grant of some land; the land grant was eventually dropped in 1891. Food, clothing, and accommodation were provided. A minimum wage of ten shillings per month was provided for males, females received half this amount and children's wages were determined by their age. During the period of bondage there was little freedom. The contract stipulated a nine-hour working day but agricultural workers in Natal found that 'from sunrise to sunset' or 'six to six' was the norm. No worker could leave the estate without a pass. (11)

12. In another marking of the glossed-over physical trauma of indenture, Chumpa (Sita's mother) says that "I have helped deliver babies in the field and their mothers are back at work in a day" (*Heart* 52). Another indentured laborer is "flogged . . . in front of his wife and children and the other people from his barracks" because he had been afflicted with "diarrhea after drinking the water from the drums" (53). Even pregnant women were not given a respite. "Her job, like most of the other women on the estate, was to put the cane into bundles, ready to be carted off to the mills for crushing . . . being pregnant did not make it any easier" (36–37).

13. In addition to exploring the horrors of indenture, the second phase of the indenture migratory arc also traces the aftereffects of indenture. By sending Gopi, Sita's brother, to the city, Moodley follows the life stories of many Indians who left for Durban after their indenture had ended:

> The Indian labourers who were now free had many different plans for the future. Some, like Gopi, decided to go their own way. Some large and extended families, having saved very hard and pooled their resources, made tentative inquiries about purchasing land to start their own little farms. Then there were those who decided that they had had enough of this land, and used their money to purchase a passage back to India. Finally, the older generation, who were too tired and terrified to make any major changes in their lives, settled for a small increase in wages and succumbed to the call of the sugar-cane fields. (71)

The biographies of Indians after indenture diverged significantly from each other. In following Gopi as he makes his fortune in the city, Moodley charts one of the various trajectories across which the lives of the indentured laborers unfolded. The text shifts in tone once it moves to Durban. There we are exposed to the lives of Indians after the period of indenture has lapsed. The section in the city reflects the gritty reality of working-class urban Indian life. Moodley shows us that Indians have a long presence not only in the South African plantation economy but also in urban South Africa, where they contributed to the financial culture of the city in significant ways.

14. The economic uplift articulated above goes hand-in-hand with political commitment. Sita's eldest son, Mukesh, for example, "was forever talking about his political hero, Gandhi . . . he was not afraid to speak his mind about the oppression of the burgeoning Indian community" (*Heart* 192). Sita's other brother, Bharath, had

"died so tragically young after catching tuberculosis, helping the injured soldiers during the Anglo-Boer war. *Like so many young Indian men* he had served under the simple yet forthright politician, Gandhi, as a stretcher-bearer" (195; emphasis added). These moments in the narrative are elaborate strategies in fulfilling the text's political destination. While sketching the economic progress of many Indians following the end of indenture, Moodley emphasizes their politicization and commitment to an egalitarian South Africa. The story of Bharath, while recuperating a history hidden in the margins, also reminds us of the sacrifices that South African Indians made for a nation that would grant them citizenship only in 1961, 101 years after the arrival of the first wave of indentured labor. Moodley's meticulous reconstruction of the past enables us to understand the extent to which Indians have lived, suffered, and contributed to South Africa.

15. Hansen remarks that the "upwards snobbery in the racial hierarchy made relationships of Indians to whites more central and complex" ("Plays" 264).

16. The literal blackening of Indian identity here brings to mind the metaphorical blackening that Jayapraga Reddy evokes through the image of the "blackened ruin" in her short story "On the Fringe of Dreamtime."

17. In that vein of parochial commitment, Sita's daughter, Rani's future husband, Balu Pillai, is sent abroad for his studies. "Master Sheldon had seen a need for an Indian doctor in the community, and Balu had jumped at the opportunity to go to medical school. Now he had returned to serve his people" (*Heart* 220).

18. Note that there are two Ranis in this novel: Gopi's wife and Sita's daughter. The latter is named after the former, who is the wife of her mother's brother.

19. In his scathing critique of *Heart of Darkness*, Nigerian novelist Chinua Achebe decries the representation of black Africans as inarticulate Others. Discussing Kurtz's African mistress, Achebe argues that "it is clearly not part of Conrad's purpose to confer language on the 'rudimentary souls' of Africa" ("Image of Africa"). Commenting on South African Indian dramatist Rajesh Gopie's play *Out of Bounds,* Hansen says, "a deeply sedimented colonial conceptualization of the native world . . . still is . . . widespread among Indians in South Africa" ("Melancholia" 308).

20. Vilashini Cooppan points out with reference to Friday in J. M. Coetzee's *Foe* that "faced with the South African white writer's perennial problem of how to record the spoken discourse of black characters in such a way as to mark that speech's difference without altogether exoticizing it as a species of, quite literally, local color, Coetzee in *Foe* chooses what Gayatri Spivak and others characterize as a Derridean aporia of silence" (353).

21. Moodley could also be simply echoing the fraught relationships between Indians and blacks in the aftermath of indenture. Robin Cohen claims that "indentured labourers and their offspring developed a troubled and often hostile relationship with the indigenous people and other migrant groups. The inter-ethnic tensions in countries like Guyana, Fiji, Uganda and South Africa provide cases in point" (64).

22. I am extrapolating here. Bryce and Dako's subjects are black postcolonial writers such as Joan Riley and Ama Ata Aidoo.

23. Again, this is exactly the criticism that Achebe levels at *Heart of Darkness*:

Africa as setting and backdrop . . . eliminates the African as human factor. Africa as a metaphysical battlefield devoid of all recognizable humanity, into which the wandering European enters at his peril. Can nobody see the preposterous and perverse arrogance in thus reducing Africa to the role of props for the break-up of one petty European mind? But that is not even the point. The real question is the dehumanization of Africa and Africans which this age-long attitude has fostered and continues to foster in the world. ("Image of Africa")

See also Barnard (26–32).

24. Vijay Mishra aptly points out that "all that remained [in the indentured consciousness] was the memory of the passage and a loss that could only be sustained through the categories of myth" ("Diasporic Imaginary" 429) and that "in the old Indian diaspora this absence [of India] had become a true fantasy as India had no real, tangible existence in the socio-political consciousness of the people" (442).

25. The biographical information provided in this chapter is taken from the novel and the Internet. The only published scholarly study I have found is Govinden's essay "The Performance of Post-colonial Writing." Imraan Coovadia was born in Durban, South Africa, educated in the United States, and now teaches at the University of Cape Town. *The Wedding* is his first published novel. His second novel also deals with the South African Indian community: *Green-Eyed Thieves* was published in South Africa in 2006.

26. Coovadia spent a great deal of time shadowing his mother and his aunt so that he could accurately record the rhythms of South African Indian speech patterns in his text ("Green-Eyed Thieves: Imraan Coovadia." Retrieved July 13, 2007, http://www.tonight.co.za/index.php?fArticleId=3306330&fSectionId=375&fSetId=204).

27. According to Uma Dhupelia-Mesthrie:

> Of the Indian population of 41,142 in Natal in 1891 some 5500 were passenger Indians. News spread in the villages and towns of India and many immigrants to South Africa came from closely connected villages. . . . While the big merchants dominated the scene, many Hindus and Muslims from the west coast of India started small shops in Durban and also in the smaller rural towns of Natal. Others took to hawking in the hope of better things to come. The smaller traders, many of whom were inexperienced and lived in very humble and precarious economic circumstances, relied on the wholesale merchants with whom they ran up substantial debts. . . . Traders also cornered the African market, supplying clothing, blankets, trinkets and other goods. . . . Gandhi suggests that the white traders subjected African customers to poor treatment, while the Indian trader allowed the African into his shop and permitted him to handle his goods. (12)

Frene Ginwala states that "the majority were from peasant families who had been unable to maintain their traditional place in the Indian economy" (5). In a brief recapitulation of the history of passenger Indians, so called because they paid for their own passage to South Africa, sociologist Ravi K. Thiara explains:

> Passenger Indians arrived mainly between 1875 and 1897, thereafter their entry was restricted and finally abolished in 1913. They came from the north-west of India and were predominantly Gujarati-speaking Muslims (Memons) and Hindus (Banias), a few Urdu-speaking Muslims, Marathis and Ismailis. . . . With the expansion of opportunities they moved to the Transvaal and the Cape but were legally excluded from the Orange Free State. By 1911, an estimated 30,000 in number, they were present in most of the major towns and cities in South Africa. (129)

28. *The Wedding*'s structure is obviously influenced by Salman Rushdie's collection of short stories *East West* (1994), which is divided into three sections: East, West and East-West. Coovadia's novel consists of a similar tripartite arrangement around geographic coordinates: East, South, and North.

29. According to Betty Govinden, "apart from descriptions of indentured migration in the form of historical documentation, autobiographical writing of this history in South Africa follows a predictable pattern. For example, Neela Govender's story of her grand uncle *Acacia Thorn in My Heart* [2000] or Zuleikha Mayat's *A Treasure Trove of Memories* [1996] span a wide trajectory of events in the life of new immigrants from India" ("Performance" 158).

30. Appropriately, a diasporic character in Indo-American writer Sanjay Nigam's novel *The Transplanted Man* assesses the impact of India on its diaspora by claiming that "the shadow of India still hangs over us like hurricane clouds" (231).

31. See the section entitled "Images and Constructions of Africa" in Govinden's essay "Performance" for more.

32. Govinden ("Performance" 165) and Fainman-Frenkel ("'On the Fringe'" 152) make similar points about this passage.

33. Similarly, Vikram, Ismet's neighbor, tells Ismet to relinquish any nostalgia for region as the troubled situation in South Africa dictates that "in this country you must not come with stories if you are this Bombay-Indian or that one Tamil, one what-what Gujarati Indian . . . no, my friend, what is essential is we must stand together united as one, that is my point" (*Wedding* 150). Ismet, however, bristles at the forced referentiality of an imagined India: "What India did this Vikram imagine was there? The only India he had seen was a million squabbling fiefdoms and hostile tribes quarrelling over land. Where were these 'united as one man' Indians going to come from?" (189).

34. As P. Pratap Kumar remarks, "the Indians who came to South Africa came from various backgrounds: linguistic, religious, cultural and social . . . the nature of the ritual integration among Hindus, commercial co-operation between Hindus and Muslims—all demonstrate that the Indian is capable of negotiating the competing values in an effort to forge unity" (in Jacobsen and Kumar 389). Social scientist Goolam Vahed claims that "while a number of identities based on language, class, religion, and customs co-existed within the category 'Indian,' during critical periods of political and economic pressure, disparate community members were brought closer together and a common identity of 'Indian' emerged in relation to Africans and whites" (125).

35. For more on food in Coovadia, see Fainman-Frenkel ("'On the Fringe'" 151).

Chapter 6

1. Although Essop's fiction deals mostly with the Indian Muslim population, very often my analysis of the status of Indian Muslims in postapartheid South Africa reflects the disaffection felt by the Indian community as a whole. In those cases, I use the term "Indian" rather than "Indian Muslim." Yet this alienation perceived by the Indian population in general is aggravated greatly for Indian Muslims. While Hindu Indians may also suffer from the twin strikes of religious and ethnic difference, Hinduism is generally not collapsed with religious fundamentalism the way Islam is and can often be easily incorporated into the discourse of the rainbow nation.

2. Kruger points out with reference to *Kafka's Curse* that "the condition of diaspora, deterritorialization and uprootedness, attributed to the Jews, applies to other minorities as well, even in a possibly postapartheid moment of the 1990s" ("Black" 132).

3. Desai and Maharaj also note that "many Indians believed they would not benefit from the ANC's affirmative action policies. These perceptions appeared to gain currency as the elections approached and fear and vulnerability became pervasive. Indians began to retreat into their ethnic and cultural shell" ("Minorities in the Rainbow Nation").

4. Dr. King is obviously modeled on Christiaan Barnard (1922–2001), the South African doctor who conducted the pioneering heart transplant procedure in Cape Town in 1967.

5. The heart metaphor is not a trivial one. Essop underlines the need for "social surgery" (*King of Hearts* 13) in South Africa. He also suggests that the heart of humanity is the same despite outward differences, indicating that race is a constructed rather than real category. Dr. King asserts that "if one of the most vital organs in the body is that of a Sircon then they can no longer claim that they are pure Saturnians" (16). This implies an abjuration of purity and a synchronous desire to make Saturnians into Sircons by injecting them with blackness. It also forces the whites to recognize the futility of rejecting change. If a body rejects a transplanted heart, it dies. Similarly, in order to survive, whites must not reject the inevitable shift in social dynamics. Gradually the oppressive machinery of racial differentiation grinds to a halt. The country's name is even changed to Sircon-Saturnia (28), a necessary fusion of black and white for a viable political future.

6. Jameson is commenting on critic Robert C. Elliot's work on satire and utopia here.

7. Discussing Asian Indians in Britain, Avtar Brah argues that "a characteristic feature of [British] racism has been its focus on cultural difference as the primary signifier of a supposed immutable boundary" (168) and that "politicians such as Enoch Powell, being fully aware of the potency of cultural symbolism, made speeches which consistently used metaphors that evoked images of the Asian as the archetypal 'alien'" (27).

8. As early as 1959, Nadine Gordimer had presciently raised these questions vis-à-vis the white community: "[B]elonging to a society implies two factors, which are outside reason: the desire to belong, on the one part, and acceptance, on the other part. The new Africa, may with luck, grant us our legal rights, full citizenship,

and the vote, but I don't think it will accept us in the way we're hankering after" (*Essential Gesture* 32).

Azadeh Moaveni also raises the same concerns about belonging, but in different circumstances, in her return-to-roots memoir *Lipstick Jihad*. An Iranian American who has come back to Iran to seek a place there, Moaveni laments that even though she feels Iranian, the Iranians never validate her as such:

> I thought of my family in California and superimposed the question onto them. What if they woke up one day, and decided they were really American? Even if they felt it with all the force of their being, did that mean Americans would suddenly stop considering them foreign? Maybe identity, to an extent, was an interior condition. But wasn't it also in the eye of the beholder? . . . What percentage of identity was exterior, what percentage self-defined? (115)

9. "Unlike the Assyrian kings his wealth did not consist of conquered territory but money—money conquered by his retail and wholesale shops in the city" (*King of Hearts* 104). The use of the word "conquered" suggests the nexus between Indian trade and the exploitative process of colonialism, a connection further enhanced by the description of Mr. Khamsin's business interests as "a commercial empire" (106).

10. According to Frene Ginwala, the South African Indian Council (SAIC) "was established as a nominated body in 1964 and became an elected institution in 1981. However with 80 percent of the [Indian] community boycotting the elections, even the Council's creators and participant members did not claim that it was representative" (10).

11. Mr. Khamsin spouts the rhetoric of racial absolutism at a gathering of wealthy business and political interests and launches into a discussion of separate development: "What would happen if the races began to mix indiscriminately? We would have chaos. Even the great Shakespeare stood for order in human affairs" (*King of Hearts* 107).

12. In 1970, Uganda housed 76,000 Indians. Following the expulsions in 1972, the number of Indians in Uganda had fallen to 430 by 1980 (Cohen 60).

13. My subtitle here echoes Nadine Gordimer's well-known essay "Where do Whites Fit In?" (1958). In keeping with the argument of this chapter, Gordimer appropriately answers her own question: "*Nowhere* [in Africa], I am inclined to say in my gloomier and least courageous moods" (*Essential Gesture* 31).

14. According to Daniel Herwitz, "the African renaissance [associated with Mbeki] explicitly eschews racial language while implicitly courting it. It explicitly opens South Africa to a multiplicity of citizens in the manner of the South African constitution while implicitly returning to images of a glorious black Africanist past—the past of the great decolonizing struggles and, earlier still, to that of a utopia before colonialism, which ultimately means before the white man" (70). For more on the African Renaissance, see the chapter entitled "Afro-Medici: Thabo Mbeki's African Renaissance" in Herwitz's book *Race and Reconciliation*.

15. Unless otherwise indicated, my use of the term "Muslim" refers to "Indian Muslims." Having said that, it is important to remember that the Muslim constituency in South Africa is much larger than its Indo-Islamic adherents. While a study

of Islam in the Cape may lead to different conclusions about minority unbelonging, for reasons of focus, the subject of this chapter is Indian Muslims only. According to S. E. Dangor:

> While official statistics put the number [of Muslims in South Africa] at 500,000 unofficial estimates range from 750,000 to one million. The overwhelming majority of South African Muslims have their origins in South East Asia, with about equal numbers from India and the East Indies. Muslims of Malay origin constitute about 45 per cent of this population and reside mainly in the Western Cape; a similar percentage is of Indian origin and resides mainly in KwaZulu-Natal, Gauteng and Mpumalanga. A small percentage has roots in Africa. ("Negotiating" 244–45)

16. Even though Essop clearly satirizes his protagonist, Salman Khan, and his overweening ambition, the novel also critiques the *reasons* for Salman's failure as much as it censures Salman himself. My analysis focuses more on why Salman fails to fulfill his ambitions than on Essop's critique of Salman, although the two are obviously related.

17. Only another Indian from parliament, Mr. Khamsin, previously encountered in *The King of Hearts* collection, is invited to the celebrations. "There were other Indians in Parliament, but he had not invited them as none of them, he felt, measured up to his academic eminence" (*Third Prophecy* 1). Later we are told that "there were eight other Indians, besides Mr. Khamsin, in parliament, but Salman had refrained from becoming friendly with them" (26). An intellectual elitist, Salman's distance from the Indian community is highlighted here, an estrangement that also takes on a physical quality, "his eyes blue and his face pale so that in appearance he looked more European than Eastern" (2).

18. According to Humayun Ansari, "the call for a ban on *The Satanic Verses* and a change in the blasphemy law failed because they were unable to convince the non-Muslim majority of the validity of their case in an idiom and in ways which that majority could understand. While actively seeking a more sympathetic hearing for these religious grievances, Muslims did not seem to be engaging constructively with British political, social and cultural institutions" (233).

19. The narrative thus transfers this imaginative failure—the willed refusal to offer belonging to those who should own it—to Salman. Essop criticizes Salman's strident secularism, a secularism he has acquired by living overseas. As Minister of Prisons, Salman refuses to allow a contingent of Muslims to preach religion to Muslim men in jails. One of the men from the group says to him, "You come from overseas and you make laws against us" (*Third Prophecy* 28). A reference, of course, to the white community legislating discriminatory laws against blacks and Indians, it also situates the group of Indian Muslims conversing with Salman as *not* coming from overseas, an unequivocal assertion of the Africanness of Indian identity, indeed of the Africanness of conservative Indian Muslim identity. Later Mr. Khamsin tells Salman that "in life one must make compromises . . . you know what happened to Salman Rushdie" (29). Like Rushdie, Salman too lives by a secularism that holds no sensitivity for those who believe differently from him. That is the problem not only with Salman, but also with the secular government he represents. Once again

this reveals important aspects of national identity in the postcolonial state. One is accepted as belonging only if one adheres to dominant patterns of religious, moral, sexual, and social affiliations. Alterity is not welcomed, even in the rainbow nation.

20. Just as the African Front is a thinly disguised manifestation of the ANC, the UMAC is a thinly disguised manifestation of PAGAD, or People Against Gangsterism and Drugs:

> PAGAD was formed in 1996 as a community anticrime group fighting drugs and violence in the Cape Flats section of Cape Town but by early 1998 had also become antigovernment and anti-Western. PAGAD and its Islamic ally Qibla view the South African Government as a threat to Islamic values and consequently promote greater political voice for South African Muslims. The group is led by Abdus Salaam Ebrahim. PAGAD's G-Force (Gun Force) operates in small cells and is believed responsible for carrying out acts of terrorism. PAGAD uses several front names, including Muslims Against Global Oppression (MAGO) and Muslims Against Illegitimate Leaders (MAIL), when launching anti-Western protests and campaigns. ("People Against Gangsterism and Drugs [PAGAD]". Retrieved June 12, 2007, http://www.nps.edu/Library/Research/SubjectGuides/SpecialTopics/TerroristProfile/Prior/PeopleAgainstGangsterismandDrugs.html).

21. I am repeating, and diverging from, Homi Bhabha's description of the "Janus-faced discourse of the nation" (*Nation and Narration* 3).

22. For example, Ama Ata Aidoo's collection of short stories *No Sweetness Here* reflects on the failure of postcoloniality. The short story "For Whom Things Did Not Change" is about an old man who is still waiting for the benefits of independence and ends powerfully with the words: "what does Independence mean?" (29). Similarly Chinua Achebe's *Anthills of the Savannah* mourns postcolonial Nigeria's decline into dictatorship, and Khushwant Singh's *Train to Pakistan*, written only nine years after Indian independence, forecasts the corruption of the Indian state and the meaninglessness of political freedom for impoverished agrarian communities.

Conclusion

1. Some of my findings here echo the excellent ethnographic work done by Thomas Hansen and Smitha Radhakrishnan. See particularly Hansen's "Diasporic Dispositions" and Radhakrishnan's "Time to Show Our True Colors."

2. One of the consequences of the gathering was the decision to establish a support group for South African Indian writers. According to Padayachee, the "Writer's Network," as it is now called, is flourishing.

3. See Radhakrishnan for an ethnographic analysis of these two strands of South African Indian identity ("Time" 268, 274). For more on the range of Indian political affiliation see Desai and Maharaj.

4. See Patrick Bond's *Elite Transition: From Apartheid to Neoliberalism in South Africa* for more on the failure of the ANC government to alleviate some of the most pressing economic concerns of South Africa, particularly those of racialized poverty. Also see Radhakrishnan, "Time" (277) and Irlam (697).

5. See also Dhupelia-Mesthrie (9).

6. Recently, the South African Broadcasting Corporation (SABC) even started showing Bollywood films on Saturday night.

7. See Hansen, "Melancholia" (302–303), on the prevalence of Bollywood among Indians in South Africa.

8. Sangeeta Ray asserts that the "majority of Indians in the United States have very close ties with the homeland to which they periodically return.... Most South African Indians ... have almost no connection with their native land" (5).

9. This is not an unusual response even from Indians located in non-Western diasporas. The Indo-Trinidadian writer V. S. Naipaul wrote bitter, scathing narratives upon encountering an India radically different from the one encountered through the communal diasporic imagination. The titles of the texts speak for themselves: *An Area of Darkness* and *India: A Wounded Civilization*. Betty Govinden cites a similar incident in Dr. Goonam's autobiography, *Coolie Doctor*, when Goonam's family visits India: "My father and I were soon munching away in peasant-like abandonment, but not my mother and sister, the stuff was not hygienically handled, cellophane wrapped and hermetically sealed for them" (quoted in "Against an African Sky" 91).

10. *Filmi* is an Indian neologism and refers disparagingly to Bollywood films. Also see Jaspal Singh's essay for the role of Hindi film in constructing diasporic Indian identity and how "Indians abroad ... become ... more 'Indian' than Indians in India" (203).

11. An interesting contrast to the Durban Centre was the Jewish Museum in Cape Town. Jews in South Africa number approximately seventy-five thousand, compared to the 1.1 million Indians there. The museum was impeccably maintained and filled with visitors from all over the world. Clearly there was a pride in the Jewish presence in South Africa and its contribution to South African life, as well as in its rich history of resistance to apartheid that seemed to be missing among Indians.

12. See Ray on how "postcolonial writings are ... on the side of memory, their oppositionality a function of anamnesia" (7).

Bibliography

Abrahams, Peter. *Mine Boy*. 1946. Reprint, Oxford: Heinemann, 1963.
Achebe, Chinua. *Anthills of the Savannah*. Oxford: Heinemann, 1987.
———. "An Image of Africa: Racism in Conrad's *Heart of Darkness*." *Massachusetts Review* 18 (1977). Retrieved October 5, 2006, from http://social.chass.ncsu.edu/wyrick/debclass/achcon.htm.
———. *No Longer at Ease*. Oxford: Heinemann, 1963.
Adhikari, Mohamed. *Not White Enough, Not Black Enough: Racial Identity in the South African Coloured Community*. Athens: Ohio University Press, 2005.
Ahluwalia, Pal. "When Does a Settler Become a Native?: Citizenship and Identity in a Settler Society." In *Postcolonialisms: An Anthology of Cultural Theory and Criticism*, edited by Gaurav Desai and Supriya Nair, 500–13. New Brunswick, NJ: Rutgers University Press, 2005.
Ahmad, Aijaz. *In Theory: Classes, Nations, Literatures*. London: Verso, 1992.
Aidoo, Ama Ata. *No Sweetness Here*. London: Longman, 1970.
———. *Our Sister Killjoy or Reflections from a Black-eyed Squint*. New York: Longman, 1977.
Akhalwaya, Ameen. "A Love-Hate Relationship: Jews and Muslims in South Africa." *Jewish Quarterly* 40 (Spring 1993): 17–19.
Alexander, Meena. *Fault Lines: A Memoir*. New York: Feminist Press, 1993.
———. *The Shock of Arrival*. Boston: South End Press, 1996.
Anderson, Wanni Wibulswasdi, and Robert G. Lee. *Displacements and Diasporas: Asians in the Americas*. New Brunswick, NJ: Rutgers University Press, 2005.
Ansari, Humayun. *The Infidel Within: Muslims in Britain Since 1800*. London: C. Hurst, 2004.
Arkin, A. J., K. P. Magyar, and G. J. Pillay, eds. *The Indian South Africans: A Contemporary Profile*. Pinetown, South Africa: Owen Burgess, 1989.
Ashcroft, Bill, Gareth Griffith, and Helen Tiffin, eds. *The Empire Writes Back: Theory and Practice in Post-colonial Literatures*. London: Routledge, 1989.
Attridge, Derek, and Rosemary Jolly, eds. *Writing South Africa: Literature, Apartheid, and Democracy, 1970–1995*. Cambridge: Cambridge University Press, 1998.
Attwell, David. *Rewriting Modernity: Studies in Black South African Literary History*. Scotsville, South Africa: University of KwaZulu-Natal Press, 2005.
Baldwin, Gayle R. "What a Difference a Gay Makes: Queering the Magic Negro." *Journal*

of Religion and Popular Culture 5 (Fall 2003). Retrieved July 2, 2005, from http://www.usask.ca/relst/jrpc/art5-whatagay.html.
Bakhtin, Mikhail. *Rabelais and His World.* Bloomington: Indiana University Press, 1984.
Bardolph, Jacqueline, ed. *Telling Stories: Postcolonial Short Fiction in English.* Amsterdam and Atlanta: Rodopi, 2001.
Barnard, Rita. *Apartheid and Beyond: South African Writers and the Politics of Place.* New York: Oxford University Press, 2007.
Baucom, Ian. *Out of Place: Englishness, Empire and the Locations of Identity.* Princeton, NJ: Princeton University Press, 1999.
Behr, Mark. *The Smell of Apples.* New York: Picador, 1995.
Benhabib, Seyla. *The Rights of Others: Aliens, Residents and Citizens.* Cambridge: Cambridge University Press, 2004.
Bhabha, Homi. *The Location of Culture.* 1994. London and New York: Routledge, 2004.
———, ed. *Nation and Narration.* London and New York: Routledge, 1990.
Bhana, Surendra. "Indianness Reconfigured, 1944–1960: The Natal Indian Congress in South Africa." *Comparative Studies of South Asia, Africa and the Middle East* 17, no. 2 (1997): 100–106.
———. "The Tolstoy Farm: Gandhi's Experiment in 'Cooperative Commonwealth.'" *South African Historical Journal* 7 (November 1975). Retrieved July 11, 2007, from http://www.anc.org.za/ancdocs/history/people/gandhi/bhana.html.
Bhana, Surendra, and Joy B. Brain. *Setting Down Roots: Indian Migrants in South Africa, 1860–1911.* Johannesburg: Witwatersrand University Press, 1990.
Bhana, Surendra, and Bhoola Kusum K. *Introducing South Africa, or Dialogue of Two Friends.* Durban: Local History Museum, 2005.
Bharucha, Nilufer. "Imagining the Parsi Diaspora: Narratives on the Wings of Fire." In *Shifting Continents/Colliding Cultures: Diaspora Writing of the Indian Subcontinent,* edited by Ralph J. Crane and Radhika Mohanram, 55–82. Amsterdam and Atlanta: Rodopi, 2000.
Blunt, Alison, and Gillian Rose, eds. *Writing Women and Space: Colonial and Postcolonial Geographies.* New York: Guilford Press, 1994.
Boehmer, Elleke. *Bloodlines.* Cape Town: David Philip, 2000.
———. "Endings and New Beginning: South African Fiction in Transition." In *Writing South Africa: Literature, Apartheid and Democracy, 1970–1995,* edited by Derek Attridge and Rosemary Jolly, 43–56. Cambridge: Cambridge University Press, 1998.
Bond, Patrick. *Elite Transition: From Apartheid to Neoliberalism in South Africa.* London: Pluto Press, 2000.
Bose, Sugata. *A Hundred Horizons: The Indian Ocean in the Age of Empire.* Cambridge, MA: Harvard University Press, 2006.
Brah, Avtar. *Cartographies of Diaspora: Contesting Identities.* London: Routledge, 1996.
Braziel, Jana Evans, and Anita Mannur, eds. *Theorizing Diaspora: A Reader.* Malden, MA, and Oxford: Blackwell, 2003.
Brennan, Timothy J. "The National Longing for Form." In *Nation and Narration,* edited by Homi K. Bhabha, 44–70. London: Routledge, 1990.
———. *Salman Rushdie and the Third World: Myths of the Nation.* New York: St. Martin's Press, 1989.
Brink, André. "Interrogating Silence: New Possibilities Faced by South African Literature." In *Writing South Africa: Literature, Apartheid and Democracy, 1970–1995,* edited by Derek Attridge and Rosemary Jolly, 14–28. Cambridge: Cambridge University Press, 1998.
———. "Stories of History: Reimagining the Past in Post-apartheid Narrative." In *Negotiating the Past: The Making of Memory in South Africa,* edited by Sarah Nuttall and Carli Coetzee, 29–42. Cape Town: Oxford University Press, 1998.
Broich, Ulrich. "Memory and National Identity in Postcolonial Historical Fiction." In *Intercultural Encounters—Studies in English Literatures: Essays Presented to Rüdiger Ahrens on the Occasion of His Sixtieth Birthday,* edited by Heinz Antor and Kevin L. Cope, 421–38. Heidelberg: Universitätsverlag C. Winter, 1999.

Bryce, Jane, and Kari Dako. "Textual Deviancy and Cultural Syncretism: Romantic Fiction as a Subversive Strain in Black Women's Fiction." *Matatu: Journal for African Culture and Society* 21–22 (2000): 155–64.

Brydon, Diana. "Postcolonialism Now: Autonomy, Cosmopolitanism, and Diaspora." *University of Toronto Quarterly* 73, no. 2 (Spring 2004): 691–706.

Carter, Marina. *Voices from Indenture: Experiences of Indian Migrants in the British Empire.* London and New York: Leicester University Press, 1996.

Carter, Marina, and Khal Torabully. *Coolitude: An Anthology of the Indian Labour Diaspora.* London: Anthem Press, 2002.

Chakrabarty, Dipesh. "Postcoloniality and the Artifice of History: Who Speaks for 'Indian' Pasts?" In *Contemporary Postcolonial Theory*, edited by Padmini Mongia, 223–47. London: Arnold, 1996.

Chapman, Michael, ed. *The Drum Decade: Stories from the 1950s.* Pietermaritzburg, South Africa: University of Natal Press, 2001.

———. "More Than Telling a Story: *Drum* and Its Significance in Black South African Writing." In *The Drum Decade: Stories from the 1950s*, edited by Michael Chapman, 183–232. Pietermaritzburg, South Africa: University of Natal Press, 2001.

———. "South/South, South/North Conversations: South Africa, India, the West." *Comparatist* 26 (2002): 5–16.

———. *Southern African Literatures.* London and New York: Longman, 1996.

Cheah, Pheng, and Bruce Robbins, eds. *Cosmopolitics: Thinking and Feeling beyond the Nation.* Minneapolis: University of Minnesota Press, 1998.

Chetty, Rajendra, ed. *South African Indian Writings in English.* Durban: Madiba, 2002.

Chetty, Rajendra, and Pier Paolo Piciucco, eds. *Indias Abroad: The Diaspora Writes Back.* Johannesburg: STE, 2004.

Chrisman, Laura. *Postcolonial Contraventions: Cultural Readings of Race, Imperialism and Transnationalism.* Manchester: Manchester University Press, 2003.

Clarke, Colin, Ceri Peach, and Steven Vertovec, eds. *South Asians Overseas: Migration and Ethnicity.* Cambridge: Cambridge University Press, 1990.

Clifford, James. *Routes: Travel and Translation in the Late Twentieth Century.* Cambridge: Harvard University Press, 1997.

Coetzee, J. M. *The Life and Times of Michael K.* Harmondsworth: Penguin, 1983.

Cohen, Robin. *Global Diasporas: An Introduction.* London: UCL Press/Seattle: University of Washington Press, 1997.

Cooppan, Vilashini. "National Literature in Transnational Times: Writing Transition in the 'New' South Africa." In *Nation, Language, and the Ethics of Translation*, edited by Sandra Bermann and Michael Wood, 346–69. Princeton, NJ: Princeton University Press, 2005.

Coovadia, Imraan. *The Wedding.* New York: Picador, 2001.

Crane, Ralph J., and Radhika Mohanram, eds. "Introduction." *Shifting Continents, Colliding Cultures: Diaspora Writing of the Indian Subcontinent*, vii–xv. Amsterdam and Atlanta: Rodopi, 2000.

Dangarembga, Tsitsi. *Nervous Conditions.* Seattle: Seal Press, 1988.

Dangor, Achmat. "Apartheid and the Death of South African Cities." In Hilton Judin and Ivan Vladislavic, eds. *Blank ___: Architecture, Apartheid and After*, 359–61. Rotterdam: NAi, 1998.

———. *Bitter Fruit.* Cape Town: Kwela, 2001.

———. *Kafka's Curse.* New York: Vintage, 2000.

———. *The Z Town Trilogy.* Johannesburg: Ravan Press, 1990.

Dangor, S. E. "The Myth of the 1860 Settlers." *Africa Quarterly* 32, no. 1–4 (1993): 73–80.

———. "Negotiating Identities: The Case of Indian Muslims in South Africa." In *South Asians in the Diaspora: Histories and Religious Traditions*, edited by Knut A. Jacobsen and P. Pratap Kumar, 243–68. Leiden: Brill, 2004.

Darian-Smith, Kate, Liz Gunner, and Sarah Nuttall, eds. *Text, Theory, Space: Land, Literature and History in South Africa and Australia.* London and New York: Routledge, 1996.

Daymond, M. J. "Bodies of Writing: Recovering the Past in Zoë Wicomb's *David's Story* and Elleke Boehmer's *Bloodlines*." *Kunapipi* 24, no. 1–2 (2002): 25–38.

———. "Complementary Oral and Written Narrative Conventions: Sindiwe Magona's Autobiography and Short Story Sequence, 'Women at Work.'" *Journal of Southern African Studies* 28, no. 2 (2002): 331–46.

———. "Gender and 'History': 1980s South African Women's Stories in English." *Ariel: A Review of International English Literature* 27, no. 1 (January 1996): 191–213.

Daymond, M. J., J. U. Jacobs, and Margaret Lenta, eds. *Momentum: On Recent South African Writing*. Pietermaritzburg, South Africa: University of Natal Press, 1984.

Deleuze, Gilles, and Felix Guattari. *Kafka: Towards a Minor Literature*. Translated by Dana Polan. Minneapolis: University of Minnesota Press, 1986.

Desai, Ashwin. *Arise Ye Coolies: Apartheid and the Indian, 1960–1995*. Johannesburg: Impact Africa Publishing, 1996.

Desai, Ashwin, and Brij Maharaj. "Minorities in the Rainbow Nation: The Indian Vote in 1994." *South African Journal of Sociology* 27, no. 4 (November 1996): 118–25. Retrieved August 14, 2007, from http://www.lib.lsu.edu/apps/onoffcampus.php?url=http://search.ebscohost.com/login.aspx?direct=true&db=aph&AN=9705234694&site=ehost-live&scope=site.

Desani, G. V. *All About H. Hatterr*. 1948. Reprint, New York: Farrar, Straus and Giroux, 1970.

Dhingra, Leena. *Amritvela*. London: Women's Press, 1988.

Dhupelia-Mesthrie, Uma. *From Cane Fields to Freedom: A Chronicle of Indian South African Life*. Cape Town: Kwela, 2000.

Diesel, Alleyn. "Hinduism in KwaZulu-Natal South Africa." In *Culture and Economy in the Indian Diaspora*, edited by Bhikhu Parekh, Gurhar Palsingh, and Steven Vertovec, 33–50. London: Routledge, 2003.

Divakaruni, Chitra Banerjee. *Arranged Marriage: Stories*. New York: Anchor, 1995.

———. *The Mistress of Spices*. New York: Anchor, 1997.

Dlamini, Sibusisiwe Nombuso. *Youth and Identity Politics in South Africa, 1990–1994*. Toronto: University of Toronto Press, 2005.

Dubey, Ajay. *Indian Diaspora: Global Identity*. New Delhi: Kalinga, 2003.

DuBois, W. E. B. *The Souls of Black Folk*. 1903. Mineola: Dover publications, 1994.

Duiker, K. Sello. *The Quiet Violence of Dreams*. Cape Town: Kwela, 2001.

Ebr.-Vally, Rehana. *Kala Pani: Caste and Colour in South Africa*. Colorado Springs: International Academic Publishers, 2001.

Elder, Arlene A. "Indian Writing in East and South Africa: Multiple Approaches to Colonialism and Apartheid." In *Reworlding: The Literature of the Indian Diaspora*, edited by Emmanuel S. Nelson, 115–39. Westport, CT: Greenwood, 1992.

Erasmus, Zimitri, ed. *Coloured by History, Shaped by Place: New Perspectives on Coloured Identities in Cape Town*. Cape Town: Kwela, 2001.

Essop, Ahmed. *The Emperor*. Johannesburg: Ravan Press, 1984.

———. *Hajji Musa and the Hindu Fire-Walker*. London: Readers International, 1988.

———. *The King of Hearts and Other Stories*. Johannesburg: Ravan, 1997.

———. *Noorjehan and Other Stories*. Johannesburg: Ravan, 1990.

———. *The Third Prophecy*. Johannesburg: Picador Africa, 2004.

Fainman-Frenkel, Ronit. "'On the Fringe of Dreamtime': South African Indian Literature, Race, and the Boundaries of Scholarship." Ph.D. dissertation, University of Arizona, 2004.

———. "Ordinary Secrets and the Bounds of Memory: Traversing the Truth and Reconciliation Commission in Farida Karodia's *Other Secrets* and Beverley Naidoo's *Out of Bounds*." *Research in African Literatures* 35, no. 4 (Winter 2004): 52–65.

Fanon, Franz. "On National Culture." In *Postcolonialisms: An Anthology of Cultural Theory*, edited by Gaurav Desai and Supriya Nair, 198–219. New Brunswick: Rutgers University Press, 2005.

Farred, Grant. *Midfielder's Moment: Coloured Literature and Culture in Contemporary South Africa*. Boulder: Westview Press, 2000.

Flockemann, Miki. "Asian Diasporas, Contending Identities and New Configurations: Stories by Agnes Sam and Olive Senior." *English in Africa* 25, no. 1 (May 1998): 71–86.

———. "'Not-Quite Insiders and Not-Quite Outsiders': The 'Process of Womanhood' in *Beka Lamb, Nervous Conditions* and *Daughters of the Twilight*." *Journal of Commonwealth Literature* 27, no. 1 (1992): 37–47.

Freed, Eugenie R. "Mr. Sufi Climbs the Stairs: The Quest and the Ideal in Ahmed Essop's 'The Visitation.'" *Theoria* 71 (May 1988): 1–13.

Frenkel, Ronit. "Performing Race, Reconsidering History: Achmat Dangor's Recent Fiction." *Research in African Literatures* 39, no. 1 (Spring 2008): 149–65.

Ghosh, Amitav. *The Shadow Lines*. 1988. New York: Mariner, 2005.

Gilroy, Paul. *The Black Atlantic: Modernity and Double Consciousness*. London: Verso, 1993.

———. "The Black Atlantic as a Counterculture of Modernity." In *Theorizing Diaspora: A Reader*, edited by Jana Evans Braziel and Anita Mannur, 49–80. Oxford: Blackwell Publishing Ltd., 2003.

Ginwala, Frene. *Indian South Africans*. London: Minority Rights Group, 1985.

Gopal, Sangita. "Hindu Buying/Hindu Being: Hindutva Online and the Commodity Logic of Cultural Nationalism." *South Asian Review* 24, no. 1 (2003): 161–79.

Gopinath, Gayatri. "Nostalgia, Desire, Diaspora: South Asian Sexualities in Motion." In *Theorizing Diaspora*, edited by Jana Evans Braziel and Anita Mannur, 261–79. Malden, MA, and Oxford: Blackwell Publishing Ltd., 2003.

Gordimer, Nadine. "Where Do Whites Fit In?" In *The Essential Gesture: Writing, Politics and Places*, edited by Stephen Clingman, 31–37. New York: Penguin, 1989.

Govender, Ronnie. *At the Edge and Other Cato Manor Stories*. Pretoria: Manx, 1996.

Govinden, Betty. "Against an African Sky: *Coolie Doctor: An Autobiography*." In *The Literature of the Indian Diaspora: Essays in Criticism*, edited by A. L. McLeod, 82–99. New Delhi: Sterling, 2000.

———. "Learning Myself Anew." *Alternation: International Journal for the Study of South African Literatures and Languages* 2, no. 2 (1995): 170–83. Retrieved June 15, 2007, http://singh.reshma.tripod.com/alternation/alternation2_2/13govin.htm.

———. "The Performance of Post-colonial Writing: An Analysis of Imraan Coovadia's *The Wedding*." In *Indias Abroad: The Diaspora Writes Back*, edited by Rajendra Chetty and Pier Paolo Piciucco, 158–69. Johannesburg: STE, 2004.

Gray, Stephen. "Introduction." In *The Penguin Book of Contemporary South African Short Stories*, 1–4. Johannesburg: Penguin, 1993.

Gready, Paul. "The South African Experience of Home and Homecoming." *World Literature Today* 68, no. 3 (Summer 1994): 509–15.

Green, Michael. "Social History, Literary History and Historical Fiction in South Africa." *Journal of African Cultural Studies* 12, no. 2 (December 1999): 121–36.

Hall, Stuart. "Cultural Identity and Diaspora." In *Theorizing Diaspora: A Reader*, edited by Jana Evans Braziel and Anita Mannur, 233–46. Malden, MA, and Oxford: Blackwell Publishing Ltd., 2003.

Hansen, Thomas Blom. "Diasporic Dispositions." *Himal: South Asian* (December 2002). Retrieved December 25, 2004, from http://www.himal.mag.com/december/essay.htm

———. "Melancholia of Freedom: Humour and Nostalgia among Indians in South Africa." *Modern Drama* 48, no. 2 (Summer 2005): 297–315.

———. "Plays, Politics and Cultural Identity among Indians in Durban." *Journal of Southern African Studies* 26, no. 2 (June 2000): 255–69.

Harries, Ann. *Manly Pursuits*. London: Bloomsbury, 1999.

Hassim, Aziz. *The Lotus People*. Johannesburg: STE, 2002.

Heller, Israel, Zelda Heller, and Janice Rothschild Blumberg. *Deadly Truth: A Novel Based upon Actual Events in South Africa under Apartheid*. Bloomington: First Books Library, 2000.

Herwitz, Daniel. *Race and Reconciliation: Essays from the New South Africa*. Minneapolis: University of Minnesota Press, 2003.

Heywood, Christopher. *A History of South African Literature*. Cambridge: Cambridge University Press, 2004.
Hiremath, Jagdish R. *Summering in South Africa: Diary of an Indian Indian*. New Delhi: Wiley Eastern, 1993.
Hodge, Merle. *Crick Crack Monkey*. London: Heinemann, 1981.
Honig, Bonnie. "Ruth the Model Émigré: Mourning and the Symbolic Politics of Immigration." In *Cosmopolitics: Thinking and Feeling beyond the Nation*, edited by Pheng Cheah and Bruce Robbins, 192–215. Minneapolis: University of Minnesota Press, 1998.
Hope, Christopher, and Robyn English. "'Good Books': Ahmed Essop's *The Visitation*." *English in Africa* 25, no. 1 (May 1998): 99–103.
Howe, Stephen. *Afrocentrism: Mythical Pasts and Imagined Homes*. London: Verso, 1998.
Huggan, Graham. "India, South Asia and the Diaspora." *Wasafiri* 21 (Spring 1995): 42–44.
Hussain, Yasmin. *Writing Diaspora: South Asian Women, Culture, and Ethnicity*. Aldershot, UK: Ashgate, 2005.
Irlam, Shaun. "Unraveling the Rainbow: The Remission of Nation in Post-apartheid Literature." *South Atlantic Quarterly* 103, no. 4 (Fall 2004): 695–718.
Jacobs, J. U. "Finding a Safe House of Fiction in Nadine Gordimer's *Jump and Other Stories*." In *Telling Stories: Postcolonial Short Fiction in English*, edited by Jacqueline Bardolph, 197–204. Amsterdam and Atlanta: Rodopi, 2001.
Jacobsen, Knut A., and P. Pratap Kumar, eds. *South Asians in the Diaspora: Histories and Religious Traditions*. Leiden: Brill, 2004.
Jain, Ravindra K. *Indian Communities Abroad: Themes and Literature*. New Delhi: Manohar, 1993.
Jameson, Frederic. "Third World Literature in the Era of Multinational Capitalism." *Social Text* 15 (Fall 1986): 65–88.
Joffe, P. "The Naming of Michael K: J. M. Coetzee's Life and Times of Michael K." *Nomina Africana: Journal of the Names Society of Southern Africa* 4, no. 1 (April 1990): 89–98.
Jolly, Rosemary. "Rehearsals of Liberation: Contemporary Postcolonial Discourse and the New South Africa." In *Contemporary Postcolonial Theory*, edited by Padmini Mongia, 365–82. London: Arnold, 1996.
Judin, Hilton, and Ivan Vladislavic, eds. *Blank ____: Architecture, Apartheid and After*. Rotterdam: NAi, 1998.
Kannan, Lakshmi. "From South Africa to South India." *Indian Literature* 28, no. 5 (September–October 1985): 187–92.
Karodia, Farida. *Against An African Sky*. 1995. Toronto: TSAR, 1997.
———. *Daughters of the Twilight*. London: Women's Press, 1986.
———. *Other Secrets*. Johannesburg: Penguin, 2000.
Kauer, Ute. "Nation and Gender: Female Identity in Contemporary South African Writing." *Current Writing* 15, no. 2 (2003): 106–16.
Kearney, Jack. "Representations of Islamic Belief and Practice in a South African Context: Reflections on the Fictional Work of Ahmed Essop, Aziz Hasism, Achmat Dangor and Rayda Jacobs." *Journal of Literary Studies* 22, nos. 1–2 (June 2006): 138–57.
Killam, Douglas, and Ruth Rowe, eds. *The Companion to African Literature*. Oxford: James Currey, 2000.
Kincaid, Jamaica. *Annie John*. New York: Farrar, Straus and Giroux, 1985.
Kruger, Loren. "Black Atlantics, White Indians, and Jews: Locations, Locutions, and Syncretic Identities in the Fiction of Achmat Dangor and Others." *South Atlantic Quarterly* 100, no. 1 (2001): 111–43.
———. "In a Minor Key: Narrative Desire and Minority Discourses in Some Recent South African Fiction." *Scrutiny 2*. 8, no. 1 (2003): 70–74.
———. *Post-Imperial Brecht: Politics and Performance, East and South*. Cambridge: Cambridge University Press.
Kumar, Amitava. *Away: The Indian Writer as an Expatriate*. London and New York: Routledge, 2004.

———. *Bombay, London, New York*. London and New York: Routledge, 2002.
———. *Passport Photos*. Berkeley and Los Angeles: University of California Press, 2000.
Kunjbehari, Ganesh. *Stories about My People*. Durban: Ratna, 1974.
Kureishi, Hanif. *The Buddha of Suburbia*. New York: Viking, 1990.
Landsman, Anne. *The Devil's Chimney*. New York: Soho, 1997.
Langa, Mandla. *The Memory of Stones*. Cape Town: David Philip, 2000.
Lewis, Jeff. *Cultural Studies: The Basics*. London: Sage, 2002.
Lionnet, François. "Transcolonial Translations: Shakespeare in Mauritius." In *Minor Transnationalism*, edited by Françoise Lionnet and Shu-mei Shih, 201–22. Durham: Duke University Press, 2005.
Lowe, Lisa. "Heterogeneity, Hybridity, Multiplicity: Marking Asian-American Differences." In *Theorizing Diaspora: A Reader*, edited by Jana Evans Braziel and Anita Mannur, 132–55. Malden, MA, and Oxford: Blackwell Publishing, Ltd., 2003.
MacKenzie, Craig. "Short Fiction in the Making: The Case of Bessie Head." *English in Africa* 16, no. 1 (May 1989): 17–28.
Magona, Sindiwe. *Mother to Mother*. Claremont, South Africa: David Philip, 1998.
Mahabir, Noor Kumar. *The Still Cry: Personal Accounts of East Indians in Trinidad and Tobago during Indentureship, 1845–1917*. Tacarigua, Trinidad, and Ithaca, NY: Calaloux, 1985.
Malkki, Liisa. "National Geographic: The Rooting of Peoples and the Territorialization of National Identity among Scholars and Refugees." In *Culture, Power, Place: Explorations in Critical Anthropology*, edited by Akhil Gupta and James Ferguson, 52–74. Durham, NC: Duke University Press, 1997.
Mamdani, Mahmood. "When Does a Settler Become a Native? The Colonial Roots of Citizenship." *Pretexts: Studies in Writing and Culture* 7, no. 2 (1998): 249–58.
Manning, Patrick. *Migration in World History*. New York and London: Routledge, 2005.
Marais, Sue. "Getting Lost in Cape Town: Spatial and Temporal Dislocation in the South African Short Fiction Cycle." *English in Africa* 22, no. 2 (October 1995): 29–43.
———. "Ivan Vladislavic's Re-vision of the South African Story Cycle." *Current Writing: Text and Reception in Southern Africa* 4, no. 1 (1992): 41–56.
Matshikiza, John. "Introduction." In *The Drum Decade: Stories from the 1950s*, edited by Michael Chapman, ix–xii. Pietermaritzburg, South Africa: University of Natal Press, 2001.
Matsuoka, Atsuko, and John Sorenson. "Ghosts and Shadows: Memory and Resilience in the Eritrean Diaspora." In *Diaspora, Memory, and Identity: A Search for Home*, edited by Vijay Agnew, 151–69. Toronto: University of Toronto Press, 2005.
Mayat, Zuleikha. *A Treasure Trove of Memories: A Reflection on the Experiences of the Peoples of Potchefstroom*. Durban: Madiba, 1996.
McClintock, Anne, and Rob Nixon. "No Names Apart: The Separation of Word and History in Derrida's 'Le Dernier Mot du Racisme.'" In *"Race," Writing, and Difference*, edited by Henry Louis Gates Jr., 339–53. Chicago: University of Chicago Press, 1986.
McLeod, John. *Beginning Postcolonialism*. Manchester: Manchester University Press, 2000.
Mda, Zakes. *Madonna of Excelsior*. Oxford: Oxford University Press, 2002.
Meer, Ismail. *A Fortunate Man*. Cape Town: Zebra Press, 2002.
Meer, Y. S. *Documents of Indentured Labour: Natal 1851–1917*. Durban: Institute of Black Research, 1980.
Mehta, Brinda. *Diasporic (Dis)Locations: Indo-Caribbean Women Writers Negotiate the Kala Pani*. Kingston, Jamaica: University of West Indies Press, 2004.
Mishra, Sudesh. "From Sugar to Masala: Writing the Indian Diaspora." In *A History of Indian Literature in English*, edited by Arvind Krishna Mehrotra, 276–94. New York: Columbia University Press, 2003.
Mishra, Vijay. "The Diasporic Imaginary: Theorizing the Indian Diaspora." *Textual Practice* 10, no. 3 (1996): 421–47.
———. *The Literature of the Indian Diaspora: Theorizing the Diasporic Imaginary*. Oxford and New York: Routledge, 2007.

Moaveni, Azadeh. *Lipstick Jihad: A Memoir of Growing Up Iranian in America and American in Iran*. New York: Public Affairs, 2005.
Mongia, Padmini. *Contemporary Postcolonial Theory: A Reader*. London: Arnold, 1996.
Moodley, Praba. *The Heart Knows No Colour*. Cape Town: Kwela Books, 2003.
Moodley, Kogila. "The Ambivalence of Survival Politics in Indian-African Relations." In *South Africa's Indians: The Evolution of a Minority*, edited by B. Pachai, 441–63. Washington, DC: University Press of America, 1979.
Morrison, Toni. *Playing in the Dark: Whiteness and the Literary Imagination*. Cambridge, MA: Harvard University Press, 1992.
Moslund, Sten Pultz. *Making Use of History in New South African Fiction: Historical Perspectives in Three Post-apartheid Novels*. Copenhagen: Museum Tusculanum Press, 2003.
Motwani, Jagat K., and Jyoti Barot-Motwani. *Global Migration of Indians: Saga of Adventure, Enterprise, Identity and Integration*. Released as a commemorative volume at the First Global Convention of People of Indian Origin. New York: National Federation of Indian-American Associations, 1989.
Mukherjee, Bharati. *The Holder of the World*. New York: Knopf, 1993.
———. *Jasmine*. New York: Grove Weidenfeld, 1989.
———. *The Tiger's Daughter*. Boston: Houghton Mifflin, 1972.
Munson, Rita, Burley Page, and Sheridan Johns. "South African Literature in the Seventies and Eighties: A Conversation with Achmat Dangor." *Polygraph* 1 (Fall 1987): 48–52.
Murray, Sally-Ann. "Telling Stories." *Current Writing* 3, no. 1 (1991): 184–92.
Nadar, Sarojini. "A South African Indian Womanist Reading of the Character of Ruth." In *Other Ways of Reading—African Women and the Bible*, edited by M. W. Dube, 159–75. Geneva: Society of Biblical Literature, 2001.
Naidoo, Jay. *Coolie Location*. London: SA Writers, 1990.
Naidoo, Muthal. "The Search for a Cultural Identity: A Personal View of South African 'Indian' Theatre." *Theatre Journal* 49, no. 1 (March 1997): 29–39.
Naipaul, V. S. *Among the Believers: An Islamic Journey*. London: Andre Deutsch, 1981.
———. *An Area of Darkness*. London: Andre Deutsch, 1964.
———. *Beyond Belief: Islamic Excursions among the Converted Peoples*. London: Little, Brown, 1998.
———. *The Enigma of Arrival*. New York: Knopf, 1987.
———. *India: A Wounded Civilization*. London: Andre Deutsch, 1977.
———. *The Mimic Men*. London: Andre Deutsch, 1967.
Nandan, Satendra. "Migration, Dispossession, Exile and the Diasporic Consciousness: The Body Politic of Fiji." In *Shifting Continents/Colliding Cultures: Diaspora Writing of the Indian Subcontinent*, edited by Ralph J. Crane and Radhika Mohanram, 35–54. Amsterdam, Atlanta: Rodopi, 2000.
Nayar, Kamala Elizabeth. *The Sikh Diaspora in Vancouver: Three Generations Amid Tradition, Modernity, and Multiculturalism*. Toronto: University of Toronto Press, 2004.
Ndebele, Njabulo S. *South African Literature and Culture: Rediscovery of the Ordinary*. Manchester: Manchester University Press, 1994.
Nelson, Emmanuel S., ed. *Reworlding: The Literature of the Indian Diaspora*. Westport, CT: Greenwood, 1992.
Ngcobo, Lauretta. *And They Didn't Die*. London: Virago, 1990.
Nigam, Sanjay. *Transplanted Man*. New York: William Morrow, 2002.
Nixon, Rob. "Aftermaths." *Transition*, issue 72 (Winter 1996): 64–78.
Nuttall, Sarah, and Carli Coetzee, eds. *Negotiating the Past: The Making of Memory in South Africa*. Cape Town: Oxford University Press, 1998.
Oboe, Annalisa. *Fiction, History and Nation in South Africa*. Padova, Italy: Supernova, 1994.
O'Brien, Anthony. *Against Normalization: Writing Radical Democracy in South Africa*. Durham, NC: Duke University Press, 2001.
Okri, Ben. *The Famished Road*. 1991. New York: N.A. Talese, 1992.
Oliphant, Andries Walter. "Fictions of Anticipation: Perspectives on Some Recent South

African Short Stories in English." *World Literature Today* 70, no. 1 (Winter 1996): 59–62. Retrieved August 17, 2007, from http://web.ebscohost.com.libezp.lib.1su.edu/ehost/detail?vid=4&hid=108&sid=167c761a-3eaa-4ae5-a1e5-12ad5dd7c680%40sessionmgr108.

Oliphant, Andries, and Ivan Vladislavic, eds. *Ten Years of Staffrider 1978–1988*. Johannesburg: Ravan Press, 1988.

Oren, Tasha G., and Patrice Petro. *Global Currents: Media and Technology Now*. New Brunswick, NJ: Rutgers University Press, 2004.

Padayachee, Deena. *What's Love Got To Do with It? and Other Stories*. Johannesburg: COSAW, 1992.

Paranjape, Makarand, ed. "Introduction: Displaced Relations: Diasporas, Empires, Homelands." In *Diaspora: Theories, Histories, Texts*, 1–14. New Delhi: Indialog, 2001.

Petievich, Carla. *The Expanding Landscape: South Asians and the Diaspora*. New Delhi: Manohar, 1999.

Pillai, Shanthini. *Colonial Visions, Postcolonial Revisions: Images of the Indian Diaspora in Malaysia*. Newcastle: Cambridge Scholars Press, 2007.

Ponzanesi, Sandra. *Paradoxes of Postcolonial Culture: Contemporary Women's Writing of the Indian and Afro-Italian Diaspora*. Albany: State University of New York Press, 2004.

Prashad, Vijay. *Everybody Was Kung Fu Fighting: Afro-Asian Connections and the Myth of Cultural Purity*. Boston: Beacon Press, 2001.

Pratt, Mary Louise. *Imperial Eyes: Travel Writing and Transculturation*. London: Routledge, 1992.

Radhakrishnan, R. "Ethnicity in an Age of Diaspora." In *Theorizing Diaspora: A Reader*, edited by Jana Evans Braziel and Anita Mannur, 119–31. Malden, MA, and Oxford: Blackwell Publishing Ltd., 2003.

Radhakrishnan, Smitha. "African Dream: The Imaginary of Nation, Race and Gender in South African Intercultural Dance." *Feminist Studies* 29, no. 3 (2003): 529–37.

———. "'Time to Show Our True Colors': The Gendered Politics of 'Indianness' in South Africa." *Gender and Society* 19, no. 2 (April 2005): 262–81.

Rai, Amit S. "India Online: Electronic Bulletin Boards and the Construction of a Diasporic Hindu Identity." *Diaspora* 4, no. 1 (Spring 1995): 31–57.

Ramamurthi, T. G. *Apartheid and Indian South Africans: A Study of the Role of Ethnic Indians in the Struggle against Apartheid in South Africa*. New Delhi: Reliance, 1995.

Raman, Parvathi. "Yusuf Dadoo: A Son of South Africa." In *South Africa's 1940s: Worlds of Possibilities*, edited by Saul Dubow and Alan Jeeves, 227–45. Cape Town: Double Storey, 2005.

Ramdin, Ron. *The Other Middle Passage: Journal of a Voyage from Calcutta to Trinidad 1858*. London: Hansib, 1994.

Rastogi, Pallavi. "Citizen Other: Islamic Indianness and the Implosion of Racial Harmony in Postapartheid South Africa." *Research in African Literatures* 39, no. 1 (Spring 2008): 107–24.

———. "From South Asia to South Africa: Locating Other Post-colonial Diasporas." *Modern Fiction Studies* 51, no. 3 (Fall 2005): 536–60.

Ray, Sangeeta. "Crossing Thresholds: Imaginative Geographies in Agnes Sam." *South Asian Review* 18, no. 15 (December 1994): 1–14.

Reddy, Jayapraga. *On the Fringe of Dreamtime and Other Stories*. Johannesburg: Skotaville, 1987.

Reddy, Vasu. "History and Memory: Writing by Indian Writers." In *Apartheid Narratives*, edited by Nahem Yousaf, 81–99. Amsterdam: Rodopi, 2001.

Rushdie, Salman. *East-West: Stories*. New York: Pantheon, 1994.

———. *Imaginary Homelands: Essays and Criticisms 1981–1991*. London: Granta, 1991.

———. *Midnight's Children*. New York: Knopf, 1981.

———. *The Satanic Verses*. New York: Viking, 1988.

Safran, William. "Diaspora in Modern Societies: Myths of Homeland and Return." *Diaspora: A Journal of Transnational Culture* 1, no. 1 (Spring 1991): 83–99.

Said, Edward. *Orientalism*. London: Routledge and Kegan Paul, 1978.

———. *Out of Place*. London: Granta, 1999.
Sam, Agnes. *Jesus Is Indian and Other South African Stories*. London: Women's Press, 1989.
Samuelson, Meg. "The Rainbow Womb: Rape and Race in South African Fiction of the Transition." *Kunapipi* 24, no. 1–2 (2002): 88–100.
Sarif, Shamim. *The World Unseen*. London: Women's Press, 2001.
Sarinjeive, Devi, "Transgressions/Transitions in Three Post-1994 South African Texts: Pamela Jooste's *Dance with a Poor Man's Daughter*, Bridget Pitt's *Unbroken Wing* and Achmat Dangor's *Kafka's Curse*." *Journal of Literary Studies* 18, no. 3–4 (December 2002): 259–74.
Sastry, Sailaja. "Assuming Identities: *Kafka's Curse* and the Unsilenced Voice." *Journal of Literary Studies* 18, no. 3–4 (December 2002): 275–83.
Shain, Milton. "Marginality, Memory and Identity: Jewish Literature and the Ambiguities of Jewish Life in Apartheid South Africa." *Pretexts: Literary and Cultural Studies* 11, no. 2 (2002): 205–10.
Sheckels, Theodore F. *The Lion on the Freeway: A Thematic Introduction to Contemporary South African Literature in English*. New York: Peter Lang, 1996.
Shukla, Sandhya. *India Abroad: Diasporic Cultures of Postwar America and England*. Princeton, NJ: Princeton University Press, 2003.
Sidhwa, Bapsi. *Cracking India*. Minneapolis: Milkweed Editions, 1989.
Simone, AbdouMaliq. "In the Mix: Remaking Coloured Identities." *Africa Insight* 24, no. 3 (1994): 161–73.
Singh, Jaspal Kaur. "Representing the Poetics of Resistance in Transnational South Asian Women's Fiction and Film." *South Asian Review* 24, no. 1 (2003): 202–19.
Singh, Khushwant. *Train to Pakistan*. New York: Grove Press, 1956.
Singh, Sarva Daman, and Mahavir Singh, eds. *Indians Abroad*. Gurgaon and London: Hope India/Greenwich Millennium, 2003.
Smith, Rowland. "Living on the Fringe: The World of Ahmed Essop." *Commonwealth Essays and Studies* 8, no. 1 (Autumn 1985): 64–72.
South Africa Census. 1996. Retrieved December 8, 2003, from statssa.gov.za/RelatedInversesSites/census96/HTML/CIB/Population/213.htm.
"South Africa Grows to 44.8 Million." Retrieved April 11, 2008, from http://www.southafrica.info/ess_info/sa_glance/demographics/census-main.htm.
Spivak, Gayatri Chakravorty. "Criticism, Feminism and the Institution: Interview with Elizabeth Grosz." In *The Post-colonial Critic*, edited by Sarah Harasym, 1–16. London, New York: Routledge, 1990.
Steger, Manfred. *Gandhi's Dilemma: Nonviolent Principles and Nationalist Power*. New York: Palgrave/St. Martin's Press, 2000.
Stein, Mark. *Black British Literature: Novels of Transformation*. Columbus: The Ohio State University Press, 2004.
Szeman, Imre. "Who's Afraid of National Allegory? Jameson, Literary Criticism, Globalization." *South Atlantic Quarterly* 100, no. 3 (Summer 2001): 803–27.
Thiara, Ravi K. "Imagining? Ethnic Identity and Indians in South Africa." In *Community, Empire and Migration: South Asians in Diaspora*, edited by Crispin Bates, 123–52. Hampshire, UK: Palgrave, 2001.
Vahed, Goolam. "Race or Class? Community and Conflict amongst Indian Municipal Employees in Durban, 1914–1949." *Journal of Southern African Studies* 27, no. 1 (March 2001): 105–25.
Vandenbosch, Amry. "Brown South Africans and the Proposed New Constitution." *Journal of Politics* 41 (1979): 566–88.
Van Niekerk, Annemarie. "Aspects of Race, Class and Gender in Jayapraga Reddy's *On the Fringe of Dreamtime and Other Stories*." *Unisa English Studies* 30, no. 2 (September 1992): 35–40.
———. "Introduction." In Annemarie Van Niekerk, ed. *Raising the Blinds: A Century of South African Women's Writing*, 11–28. Pretoria, South Africa: AD Donker, 1990.
Vassanji, M. G. *The In-between World of Vikram Lall*. Toronto: Doubleday Canada, 2003.

Versi, Anver. "Not at Home, At Home: Novelist Farida Karodia." *New African* 318 (1994): 39–40.
Viola, André, Jacqueline Bardolph, and Denise Coussy, eds. *New Fiction in English from Africa: West, East and South.* Amsterdam: Rodopi, 1998.
Vladislavic, Ivan. *The Exploded View.* Johannesburg: Random House, 2004.
———. *The Restless Supermarket.* Cape Town: David Philip, 2001.
Waldman, Amy. "India Harvests Fruits of a Diaspora." *New York Times,* January 12, 2003. Retrieved August 14, 2007, from http://www.indianembassy.org/US_Media/2003/jan/India%20Harvests%20Fruits%200f%20a%20Diaspora.htm.
Wicomb, Zoe. *David's Story.* CapeTown: Kwela, 2000.
———. "South African Short Fiction and Orality." In *Telling Stories: Postcolonial Short Fiction in English,* edited by Jacqueline Bardolph, 157–70. Amsterdam and Atlanta: Rodopi, 2001.
Woodward, Wendy. "Beyond Fixed Geographies of the Self: Counterhegemonic Selves and Symbolic Spaces in Achmat Dangor's 'Kafka's Curse' and Anne Landsman's *The Devil's Chimney.*" *Current Writing* 12, no. 2 (2000): 21–37.
Wong, Mitali P., and Zia Hasan. *The Fiction of South Asians in North America and the Caribbean.* Jefferson, NC: McFarland, 2004.
Worcester, Kent. *C.L.R. James: A Political Biography.* Albany: State University of New York Press, 1996.
Yousaf, Nahem, ed. *Apartheid Narratives.* Amsterdam: Rodopi, 2001.
Young, Elaine. "Cursing and Celebrating Metamorphosis: Achmat Dangor's 'Kafka's Curse.'" *Current Writing Text and Reception in Southern Africa* 12, no. 1 (April 2000): 17–30.

Index

Abrahams, Peter, 66
Achebe, Chinua, 70, 187, 262n19, 263n23, 268n22
affirmative action, 15, 162, 175, 178, 265n3
Africa, 2, 8, 9, 11, 41, 47, 48, 97, 106, 111, 113, 121, 125, 132, 147, 148, 157, 164, 171, 181, 187, 197, 222, 236n4, 240n29, 254n29, 259n2, 260n6, 262n19, 263n23, 264n31, 265n8, 266n13, 267n15
African, 2, 4, 8, 11, 12, 14, 15, 16, 18, 27, 30, 31, 32, 33, 34, 36, 38, 39, 40, 41, 42, 44, 45, 49, 50, 51, 55, 60, 61, 63, 64, 67, 75, 80, 90, 103, 104, 108, 112, 124, 129, 131, 133, 135, 140, 144, 147, 148, 149, 151, 154, 155, 157, 171, 177, 179, 192, 210, 211, 219, 231, 241n39, 242n46, 244n14, 247n14, 254n29, 259n2, 262n19, 263n23, 263n27, 266n14, 268n20
African American, 105, 170, 210, 240n29
African National Congress (ANC), 149, 151, 154, 250n3, 265n3, 268n20, 269n4
African Renaissance, 149, 266n14
Africanization, 2, 10, 18, 23, 26, 30, 31, 39, 40, 42, 44, 45, 46, 71, 78, 102, 104, 113, 117, 120, 127, 133, 148
Afrikaans, 5, 36, 83, 87, 209
Afrikaner, 65, 87, 91, 98, 104, 191, 210, 217

Afrindian identity, 1, 18, 20, 23, 27, 30, 33, 45, 46, 50, 57, 75, 95, 97, 100, 102, 107, 108, 111, 113, 117, 119, 123, 125, 130, 135, 161, 162, 163, 167, 236n4, 251n7, 255n4
Afrocentrism, 21, 147, 160, 162, 174–75, 185
Ahluwalia, Pal 16, 160
Ahmad, Aijaz, 250n2, 258n27
Aidoo, Ama Ata, 70, 262n22, 268n22
Akabor, Mariam, 163, 252n13
Akhalwaya, Ameen, 251n10
Alexander, Meena, 130, 258n26
allegory, 28, 29, 30, 42, 45, 51, 53, 57, 59, 60, 71, 72, 73, 75, 76, 78, 80, 82, 85, 88, 99, 175, 250n2, 250–51n4. See also National Allegory
Althusser, Louis, 161
AmaNdiya, 186, 242n46. See also Ngema, Mbongeni
Amandla, 140, 141
Amin, Idi, 140, 148
Anderson, Wanni W., and Robert G. Lee, 257n16
Anglophilia, 129
Ansari, Humayun, 267n18
antiapartheid, 1, 3–4, 13, 18–19, 23, 26, 28–29, 42, 44, 49, 51, 62–65, 68, 96, 113, 139, 154, 242n47
architecture, 48, 72, 77–78, 80, 250n4, 252n14
Aryan, 52, 247n12, 247n13

Ashoka (Indian king), 51, 58, 173
Asian British, 240n33, 246n5
assimilation, 5, 9, 19, 35, 49, 56, 62, 71, 77, 95–96, 122, 133, 151, 154, 158, 245n28, 246n6
Asvat, Farouk, 237n17
Attridge, Derek, 6
Attwell, David, 3, 237n15, 246n29, 252n12

Bakhtin, Mikhail, 248n16. See also carnival
Banoobhai, Shabir, 179, 237n17
Bantustans, 106, 136, 258n22. See also Hindustan.
Barnard, Christiaan, 265n4
Barnard, Rita, 236n8, 252n13, 263n23
Barnett, Ursula A., 237n15
Baucom, Ian, 77, 140
Bhabha, Homi, 20, 43, 63, 141, 148, 241–42n43, 242n48, 248n23, 268n21
Bhana, Surendra, 12, 236n9, 240n28, 240n32, 249–50n28, 260n10
Bharucha, Nilufer, 77
Biko, Steve. 248n22. See also Black Consciousness
bird imagery, 72, 84–85, 91, 133, 253n22, 253n23
Black British, 32, 257n16
Black Consciousness, 34, 61, 62, 64, 195, 248n22. See also Biko, Steve
black nationalism, 148
Boehmer, Elleke, 114, 129
Bollywood, 164, 167, 269n6, 269n7, 269n10
Bond, Patrick, 269n4
Brah, Avtar, 32, 144, 247n9, 265n7
Brennan, Timothy, 73, 238n19, 258n25
Brink, Andre, 93, 115, 179, 231, 237n14
British empire, 7, 12, 20, 118–19, 260n9. See also colonialism; empire
Broich, Ulrich, 132, 137, 259n5
Bryce, Jane, and Kari Dako, 125, 262n22
Brydon, Diana, 241n43

Canada, 2, 4, 43, 49, 191, 194, 200, 202, 237n12, 245n28, 255n4, 256n8
Cape Malay, 7, 89, 94, 236n10, 240n30, 251n7
Cape Town, 89, 216, 242n49, 244n8, 254n29, 263n25, 265n4, 268n20, 269n11
Caribbean, 1, 2, 6, 48, 104, 122, 158, 237n11, 259n6, 260n9

carnival, 55, 60, 248n16. See also Bakhtin, Mikhail
Carrim, Y., 160
Carter, Marina, 6–8, 236n9, 260n6
caste, 52, 157, 176, 233
Cato Manor, 14, 222–27, 242n49
Chakrabarty, Dipesh, 112
Chapman, Michael, 5, 239n22, 243n4
Cheah, Pheng, and Bruce Robbins, 258n28
Chetty, Rajendra, 29, 47, 99, 239n23, 241n34, 243n3, 246n30, 246n1, 247n10, 249n26, 257n18
child/childhood, 29–30, 32–33, 35–38, 43, 46, 79–80, 82, 89, 91, 94, 98, 100, 102, 105, 106, 110–11, 120, 127, 131, 133, 145, 172, 174, 176–77, 195–96, 200, 203, 216, 224, 226, 228, 229, 233, 247n8, 251n7, 253n23, 257n16, 257n19, 258n24, 260n10, 261n11, 261n12
Clifford, James, 258n28
Clingman, Stephen, 237n14
clothes/clothing, 15, 27, 32, 76, 90, 140, 143–44, 148–49, 151, 261n11, 263n27. See also dress
citizen, 1, 13, 16, 19, 32, 48, 53, 67, 68, 70, 76, 120, 145, 147, 159, 160, 163, 234–35n2, 236n3, 253n25, 257n16, 266n14
citizenry, 16–19, 32, 34, 39–41, 46, 50, 60, 64–65, 67, 71, 72, 81, 84, 86, 90–91, 95, 103, 105, 110, 116, 122, 136, 138, 144–45, 151, 158–59, 167, 235n3
citizenship, 1, 9, 13–14, 16, 18, 20, 27, 45–46, 50, 56, 63, 65, 81, 84, 111, 113, 119, 124, 127, 138, 140–41, 144, 146, 159, 161, 163, 167, 235n2, 235n3, 238n18, 240n31, 252n12, 258n28, 262n14, 265n8
Coetzee, J. M., 3, 5, 93, 187–88, 231, 237n14, 252n17, 262n20
Cohen, Robin, 81, 122, 128, 241n39, 257n14, 262n21, 266n12
collectivity, 19, 23, 26–29, 31, 34, 39–40, 45–46, 121, 165, 244n10
Colonial News, 236n9
colonialism, 9, 11, 74, 115, 118, 124, 125, 164, 230, 235n3, 259n2, 266n9, 266n14. See also British empire; empire
color, 52, 85, 87, 123–25, 173, 176–77, 205, 211, 262n20

Index

Coloured/Coloureds, 7, 10, 13, 27, 29, 40, 44, 50, 73–74, 75, 82–83, 86, 89–90, 99, 102, 105, 108–9, 111, 142, 191, 197, 201, 210, 219, 236n10, 240n30, 240n31, 244n14, 251n10, 255n4, 256n6
composite citizenry, 9, 16, 90, 140, 144–45, 151
Conover, Pamela Johnston, 160
Conrad, Joseph, 125, 186, 262n19
coolitude, 6–8, 236n9, 259n6
Cooppan, Vilashini, 77, 86, 91, 250n4, 251n6, 252n16, 252n17, 253n21, 253n25, 262n20
Coovadia, Imraan, 20, 115–19, 167, 238n18, 263n25, 263n26, 264n35; *Green-Eyed Thieves*, 263n25, 263n26; *The Wedding*, 20, 115–18, 128–37, 263n25, 264n28, 264n33
COSAW (Congress of South African Writers), 24, 170
cosmopolitan/cosmopolitanism, 17, 112–13, 155, 241n43, 258n27, 258n28
counter-histories, 259n3
Crane, Ralph, and Radhika Mohanram, 236n7, 238n21, 256n8
crypto-Jews, 245n18
cultural insiderism, 151–52
Cundy, Catherine, 238n19

Dabydeen, David, 259n6
Dadoo, Yusuf, 13, 241n36
daily, 30, 34, 36, 47, 55, 56, 81, 114, 165, 178, 249n28
Dangor, Achmat, 6, 24, 99, 141, 187, 237n16, 237n17, 238n18, 240n30, 244n8, 244n9, 252n14, 252n17; *Bitter Fruit*, 141; *Kafka's Curse*, 19, 70–91, 101, 105, 148, 156, 244n9, 250n4, 251n7, 252n16, 252n17, 253n18, 253n20, 253n22, 253n23, 256n13, 265n2; *Waiting for Leila*, 244n8; *Z Town Trilogy*, 244n8, 253n23
Dangor, S. E. (Suleiman), 144, 150, 159, 240n30, 254n29, 267n15
David (King), 78–79, 82
Daymond, M. J., 141, 244n7, 244n10
deracination, 98, 108, 110, 115, 258n23
Desai, Ashwin, 14–15, 103, 140, 149, 154, 162, 237n13, 241n37, 258n21, 265n3, 268n3
Desai, Jigna, 238n20
Desani, G. V., 247n8
Dhingra, Leena, 130, 240n29

Dhupelia-Mesthrie, Uma, 14–15, 154, 237n13, 241n37, 260n10, 260–61n11, 263n27, 269n5
diaspora, 1, 2, 107, 112, 117, 130, 134, 135, 139, 140, 164, 235n1, 238n18, 238n20, 238–39n21, 240n29, 240n33, 242n43, 245n28, 246n5, 247n9, 248n15, 252n11, 257n16, 259n28, 264n30, 265n2, 269n9; anxieties/issues of, 5, 9, 19, 25, 28, 77, 95–97, 113, 115; arc of, 117, 120–21, 127, 131, 134, 135, 261n13; criticism/discourse/scholarship/studies, 2, 5, 6, 17, 20, 46, 86, 97, 113, 119, 239n25; double diaspora, 77, 85, 107, 256n8; East-South, 2, 7, 9, 18, 23, 31, 33, 36, 50, 56, 71, 74, 77, 96, 102, 112, 117, 118, 121, 126; East-West, 2, 17, 65, 74, 77, 112, 117, 246n5; of exile, 86, 97, 107–8, 253n24; and ghosts, 43; and home, 43; identity in, 62, 103, 121; Indian, 1, 4, 5, 7, 12, 41, 117, 144, 256n8, 263n24; internal, 71, 77; labor, 8, 118, 121, 128, 257n14; nationalism, 17; non-Western, 48–49, 83; old/older, 10, 49, 128, 263n24; religion, 27; South African Indian 5–6, 8, 10, 12, 41, 49, 56, 60, 61, 90, 96–97, 103; South Asian, 1, 6, 7, 9, 20, 257n14, 257n16; theorists of, 20, 69; and unbelonging, 46; Western, 5, 49, 56, 60, 64, 68, 97, 117, 126, 164; women in, 39. *See also* migration.
diasporic exchange, 2, 6, 54, 56, 74, 107, 125
Dickens, Charles, 129, 186–87, 243n5
Divakaruni, Chitra Banerjee, 60
Dlamini, Sibusisiwe Nombuso, 249n25
Dlaska, Andrea, 238n19
dress, 32–33, 62, 83, 127, 153, 156, 211, 248n15. *See also* clothes.
Drum magazine, 24, 237n15, 243n2, 243n3, 243n4. *See also* Matshikiza, John
Du Bois, W. E. B., 256n12
Duiker, K. Sello, 141
Durban, 21, 30, 77–78, 128–29, 133–36, 142, 164–68, 179–80, 202, 206, 212, 216, 220–21, 236n4, 243n2, 245n27, 247n14, 260n6, 260n10, 261n13, 263n25, 263n27, 269n11
Durban Cultural and Documentation Centre, 166, 269n11

East-South, 2, 7, 9, 18, 23, 28, 31, 33, 36, 50, 56, 71, 74, 77, 96, 102, 112, 117, 118, 121, 126
Ebr.-Vally, Rehana, 13, 237n13, 239n27, 241n33, 241n37, 258n22
effacement, 23, 58, 63, 64, 99
Egypt, 84, 157
Elder, Arlene, 11, 235n3, 239n23, 246n2
elections (1994), 14, 17, 72, 92, 94, 142, 154, 156, 163, 230, 250n3
elections (1999), 14, 15, 151, 152, 154, 156, 179
Eliot, George, 101
Emperor, The (Essop), 19, 48, 50, 51–58, 59, 61, 68, 141, 143, 153, 184, 246n4, 247n11, 247n14
empire, 7, 8, 12, 20, 51, 89, 118–19, 132, 212, 239n24, 260n9, 266n9. *See also* British empire; colonialism
English, Robyn, 48, 239n23
Espinet, Ramabai, 259n6
Essop, Ahmed, 6, 19, 21, 24, 47–50, 70, 80, 84, 91, 101, 129, 138–41, 160, 162, 166, 167, 172, 179, 190, 220, 235n3, 237n17, 238n18, 243n3, 246n1, 246n2, 246n3, 246n4, 247n10, 247n11, 248n19, 249n24, 249n25, 249n26, 249n27, 252n17, 256n13, 265n1, 265n5, 267n16, 267n19; *The Emperor*, 19, 48, 50, 51–58, 59, 61, 68, 141, 143, 153, 184, 246n4, 247n11, 247n14; *Hajji Musa and the Hindu Fire-Walker*, 19, 48, 50, 58–63, 68, 182, 189, 243n3, 246n2, 246n4, 248n19; interview with, 181–90; *The King of Hearts and Other Stories*, 21, 138, 141–49, 150, 155, 158, 184, 189, 190, 265n5, 266n9, 266n11, 267n17; *Noorjehan and Other Stories*, 19, 48, 50, 63–68, 91, 145, 182, 246n4, 249n24, 249n26, 252n17, 252n27; *The Third Prophecy*, 21, 138, 149–59, 181, 182, 184, 188, 189, 190, 256n13, 267n17, 267n19
ethnocentrism, 17, 39, 52, 116, 147–49, 155
Euroafrindian, 125
Eurocentrism, 160, 162
Europe, 67, 97, 111, 112, 113, 118, 119, 125, 148, 197, 256n7
exile, 20, 43, 77, 85–86, 96–97, 102, 105, 107–11, 113, 194, 197, 200, 216, 242n43, 244n17, 252n12, 253n24, 258n27

Fainman-Frenkel, Ronit (Frenkel), 93, 106, 238n18, 239n23, 245n26, 253n24, 258n20, 264n32, 264n35
Fanon, Frantz, 114, 116, 128
fantasy, 54, 72, 91, 100, 101, 113, 127, 128, 132, 143, 163, 165, 263n24
Farred, Grant, 236n10
Fiji, 1, 48, 122, 140, 256n8, 259n6, 262n21
Flockemann, Miki, 30, 33, 35, 37, 38, 239n23, 245n22, 245n25, 248n19, 256n11
flux, 19, 49, 50, 69, 70, 72, 74, 77, 82, 84, 86, 89, 91, 139
food (imagery), 27, 88, 90, 135, 143, 214, 261n11, 264n35
Fordsburg, 19, 59–61, 184
Free State, 90–91, 240n31, 264n27
freedom, 4, 92–94, 97, 139, 141, 163, 193, 213, 216, 218, 229, 261n11, 268n22

Gandhi, Indira, 140
Gandhi, Mohandas Karamchand, 11–12, 14, 37, 41, 43, 61–62, 64–65, 68, 102, 124, 131, 134, 142, 166, 171–72, 174, 175–76, 181, 193, 212, 218, 219, 222, 236n9, 240n32, 240–41n33, 245n20, 249–50n28, 261–62n14, 263n27
gender, 6, 11, 29, 30, 32, 34, 36, 38, 77, 229. *See also* women
generational conflict, 3, 5, 103, 113, 239n26, 257n16
genre, 17, 23–25, 28, 30, 32, 34, 39, 42, 46, 57, 72, 100, 125–27, 143, 168, 222, 223, 231, 243n49
Ghosh, Amitav, 6, 238n19, 244n11, 258n27
ghosts, 41–43, 46, 75, 91, 171, 175–76
Gilroy, Paul, 150–52, 242n43, 259n28, 260n9
Ginwala, Frene, 146, 237n13, 241n37, 255n6, 260n7, 263n27, 266n10
Gool, Reshard, 237n17, 242n49
Gopal, Sangita, 242n44
Gopie, Rajesh, 162, 260n6, 262n19
Gopinath, Gayatri, 148
Gordimer, Nadine, 3, 5, 40, 93, 170, 187, 231, 237n14, 245n27, 248n20, 252n13, 265n8, 266n13
Govender, Kessie, 157
Govender, Ronnie, 168, 187, 220, 222, 242n49, 247n10; *At the Edge and Other Cato Manor Stories*, 222, 223,

226–27, 242n49; interview with, 222–34
Govinden, Betty (Devarakshanam), 5, 93, 115, 116, 132, 162, 239n23, 255n1, 255n2, 255n3, 263n25, 264n29, 264n31, 264n32, 269n9
Graham, Shane, 251n9
Green, Michael, 259n4
Grey Street, 77–78, 221, 252n13
Group Areas Act, 13, 25, 31, 42, 96, 105–7, 197, 226, 241n34
Gujarati, 11, 87, 89, 230, 255n4, 264n27, 264n33
Guyana, 142, 259n6, 262n21

Hajji Musa and the Hindu Fire-Walker (Essop), 19, 48, 50, 58–63, 68, 182, 189, 243n3, 246n2, 246n4, 248n19
Hall, Stuart, 159–60
Hansen, Thomas Blom, 15, 101, 103, 139, 142, 146, 157, 164, 237n13, 239n26, 241n35, 241n41, 262n19, 268n1, 269n7
Harries, Ann, 115
Hassim, Aziz, 168, 242–43n49, 252n13, 260n6; interview with, 212–22; *The Lotus People*, 114, 212–14, 219, 221, 243n49, 252n13, 260n6
Hassumani, Sabrina, 238n19
Hawley, John, 238n19
Hayward, Helen, 238n19
Head, Bessie, 244n8, 255n2
Head, Dominic, 237n14
Heart Knows No Colour (Moodley), 20, 115–28, 205, 207, 209, 260n8, 261n12, 261n13, 261–62n14, 262n17
Herrenvolk, 58, 248n18
Herwitz, Daniel, 266n14
Heywood, Christopher, 5, 12, 172, 250n4
Hindu, 11, 27, 30, 31, 35–36, 52, 59, 62, 65, 77, 87, 98, 213, 217, 242n44, 247n14, 258n23, 265n1
Hinduism, 51, 77, 265n1
Hindustan, 258n22. *See also* Bantustan
history, 5, 6, 9, 11, 14, 15, 18, 20, 27, 30, 31, 35, 39, 41, 42, 43, 51, 52, 58, 64, 66, 71, 74, 75, 79, 83, 86, 89, 90, 92, 93, 94, 95, 96, 99, 102, 104, 105, 108, 111, 114–17, 119, 120–21, 125, 128, 129, 130, 132–33, 136–37, 144, 155, 159–60, 164, 165, 166, 167, 173–74, 178, 188, 190, 196, 198, 202, 203, 212–13, 219, 231, 235n3, 240n29, 243n49, 244n7, 245n24,

248n15, 251n7, 253n25, 259n1, 262n14, 263n27, 264n29, 269n11
historical novel, 20, 116, 259n4
home/house, 20, 25, 29, 31, 42, 43, 55, 58, 68, 78, 84, 87, 91, 96–98, 106–13, 127, 128, 130, 146, 153, 162, 164, 170, 172
Honig, Bonnie, 36
Hope, Christopher, 47–48, 239n23
Hopkins, Pauline, 105, 240n29
Howe, Stephen, 147
Hussain, Yasmin, 83, 245n28, 246n5, 257n16
hybrid/hybridity, 18, 19, 34, 42, 50, 63, 71, 75, 80, 83–85, 88–89, 104, 113, 116, 127, 148–49, 161, 241–42n43, 242n48, 246n5, 247n8, 248n23, 250n4, 251n7, 254n28

indenture, 9, 11–12, 39, 71, 83, 115, 117–22, 128, 206, 209, 260n6, 260n7, 261n12, 261n13, 262n14, 262n21
indentured labor, 3, 13, 20, 74, 89, 129, 206, 236n9, 259n6, 260n7, 262n14
India, 3, 10, 11, 12, 25, 28, 29, 30, 39, 41–42, 43, 51, 52, 53, 54, 60–61, 67, 68, 70, 71, 90, 97, 103, 108, 112, 118, 120, 121, 122, 128, 130–32, 133, 134, 136, 140, 156, 157, 161, 163–65, 167, 173, 176, 178, 194, 200–201, 208–9, 212, 213, 218, 219, 222, 235n1, 240n29, 242n44, 245n23, 252n11, 254n29, 255n4, 258n28, 260n9, 260n10, 261n11, 261n13, 263n24, 263–64n27, 264n29, 264n30, 264n33, 267n15, 269n9, 269n10
Indian Opinion, 12, 202, 204, 236n9
Indianization (of South Africa), 2, 10, 28, 30–31, 46, 71, 134, 242n47
Indianness, 2, 5, 9, 10, 12, 18–21, 25–26, 29, 31, 33, 34, 35–36, 42, 49–51, 53, 54, 61, 63, 64, 65, 68–69, 71, 73, 75–76, 77–80, 82–85, 87–91, 95, 97, 102–4, 109, 113, 117, 119, 124, 126–27, 131, 134–35, 139, 143, 151, 153–54, 162, 165, 167, 208, 219, 240n28, 240n30, 240n32, 249n24, 251n7
Immorality Act, 13, 60
imperialism, 118, 123, 124, 155
instability (identity, selfhood etc), 19, 21, 24, 31, 49, 69, 70, 71, 77, 139, 140, 146, 167
interracial relationships, 17, 41, 55, 63,

68, 82, 88, 102, 104–5, 120, 138, 142, 196, 204, 205, 207, 250n1
Irlam, Shaun, 94–95, 269n4
Islam, 48, 64, 74, 78, 82, 84, 108–10, 133, 145, 148, 151–53, 156, 158–59, 182, 188, 195–96, 200, 245n18, 250n4, 254n27, 265n1, 267n15. See also Muslims
Islamic Indianness, 75, 76, 82, 83, 102–3, 156, 251n7
italics/italicization, 10, 36, 83, 125, 146

Jacobs, J. U., 40, 43, 248n19
Jacobs, Rayda, 94, 255n5
Jaiswal, Madhavi, 238n18
James, C. L. R., 16, 158, 241n42
Jameson, Frederic, 71, 72, 143, 250n2, 265n6
Janus-faced, 158, 268n21
Jesus Is Indian (Sam), 18, 34–40, 235n3, 245n19
Jewish, 64, 73–74, 76, 77, 79, 83, 85, 87, 106, 145, 252n10, 269n11
Jews, 76, 89, 106, 240n29, 244n9, 244–45n18, 251–52n10, 255n29
Joffe, P., 252n17
Johannesburg, 54, 59, 78, 99, 110, 166, 190, 206, 216, 249n28, 255n4, 257n17
Jolly, Rosemary, 4, 6, 237n14, 239n24

Kafka, Franz, 80, 249n27, 252n17
Kafka's Curse (Dangor), 19, 70–91, 101, 105, 148, 156, 244n9, 250n4, 251n7, 252n16, 252n17, 253n18, 253n20, 253n22, 253n23, 256n13, 265n2
Kaleta, Kenneth C., 238n19
Karodia, Farida, 20, 129, 167, 172, 237n17, 238n18, 244n8, 244n17, 247n10, 255n4, 255n5, 256n7, 258n20; *Against an African Sky*, 255n4, 258n23; *Daughters of the Twilight*, 20, 94, 96–102, 192–93, 206, 255n4, 256n11; interview with, 190–202; *Other Secrets*, 20, 92–113, 118, 191–97, 237n16, 255n4, 256n7, 256n11, 257n15, 257n17
Kathrada, Ahmed, 13, 241n36. See also Rivonia Trial
Kauer, Ute, 84
King of Hearts and Other Stories (Essop), 21, 138, 141–49, 150, 155, 158, 184, 189, 190, 265n5, 266n9, 266n11, 267n17
Koshy, Susan, 246n6

Kossew, Sue, 237n14
Kruger, Loren, 3, 5, 7, 11, 29, 74, 89, 90, 95, 236n8, 239n22, 239n23, 240n30, 242n43, 251n7, 253n23, 255n5, 255n29, 257n19, 259n29, 265n2
Kumar, Amitava, 244n12
Kumar, P. Pratap, 264n34
Kunapipi, 237n16
Kureishi, Hanif, 3, 6, 238n19, 247n8, 258n27
KwaZulu Natal, 14, 15, 153, 179, 260, 267. See also Natal

La Guma, Alex, 3, 93
land, 2, 8, 9, 11, 13, 18, 31, 34, 44, 54, 60, 77, 78, 80, 81, 82, 85, 97, 104, 105, 116, 121, 122–24, 127, 132, 133, 135, 149, 153, 157, 203, 208, 209, 212, 256n6, 261n11, 261n13, 264n33, 269n8
Landsman, Anne, 32, 114
Lenasia, 51, 166, 181, 182
Lewis, Jeff, 161
Lionnet, François, 239n21
Lowe, Lisa, 139
Lukács, George, 259n4

Magic Negro, 63
magical realism, 72, 80, 100, 101, 252n16
Magona, Sindiwe, 92
Maharaj, Brij, 14, 103, 154, 160, 258n21, 265n3, 268n3
Malkki, Liisa, 81, 253n19
Mamdani, Mahmood, 235n2
Mandela, Nelson, 15, 50, 179, 241n36, 250n3
Manning, Patrick, 248n15
Marais, Sue, 27
Matshikiza, John. 243n2, 243n4. See also *Drum* magazine
Matshoba, Mtutuzeli, 244n8
Matsuoka, Atsuko, and John Sorenson, 43
Mauritius, 1, 239n21, 259n6
Mbeki, Thabo, 15, 149, 266n14
McLeod, John, 259n2
McClintock, Anne, 13
Mda, Zakes, 3, 92, 93, 252n13
Meer, Fatima, 1, 5, 13, 94, 241n36
Mehta, Brinda, 6–7, 16, 122, 123, 142, 159
metamorphosis, 19, 72, 74, 80–82, 84, 87, 129, 141, 249n27, 250n4, 252n17, 253n21, 253n22
Middle Passage, 121, 260n9
middleman minorities, 258n21
migrants, 5, 7, 9, 28, 56, 90, 97, 108,

115, 116, 117, 118, 120, 129, 131, 133, 134, 241n43, 242n44, 252n11, 256n8, 258n27, 262n21

migration, 2, 5, 9, 11, 19, 20, 25, 26, 36, 49, 71, 74, 77, 85, 90, 97, 108, 115, 117–20, 126, 128, 129–33, 135, 165, 239n23, 240n30, 248n15, 259–60n6, 260n7, 264n29. *See also* diaspora

Mishra, Sudesh, 239n21

Mishra, Vijay, 4, 7, 49, 128, 239n21, 260n9, 263n24

mixed-race, 6, 10, 48, 90, 145

Moaveni, Azadeh, 266n8

Mobutu, Joseph, 140

Modern Fiction Studies (MFS), 6, 237n16

Mongia, Padmini, 242n43

Moodley, Kogila, 13, 135

Moodley, Praba, 20, 84, 115–19, 167, 260n8, 261n13, 262n14; *The Heart Knows No Colour*, 20, 115–28, 205, 207, 209, 260n8, 261n12, 261n13, 261–62n14, 262n17, 262n18; interview with, 202–11

Moore-Gilbert, Bart, 238n19

Morrison, Toni, 33, 244n15

Moslund, Sten, 116, 259n1

Mother India, 131, 165

Mukherjee, Bharati, 3, 6, 130, 201, 238n19, 245n23, 246n6, 258n27

Muslims, 11, 27, 44–45, 62, 64, 73, 74, 77, 83, 85, 87, 89, 90, 94, 97, 98, 102–3, 109, 138, 140, 143, 145, 149–56, 158–60, 182–83, 188, 195, 200, 217, 230, 251n7, 251–52n10, 254n27, 256n13, 257n15, 257n17, 260n10, 263–64n27, 264n34, 265n1, 266–67n15, 267n18, 267n19, 268n20. *See also* Islam

Mustafa, Fawzia, 238n19

myth/mythology, 10, 27, 28, 39, 43, 53, 68, 80, 97, 118, 120, 128, 147, 150, 161, 163, 164, 165, 167, 214, 226, 228, 236n9, 259n2, 259n3, 263n24

Nadar, Sarojini, 245n19

Naicker, Monty, 13

Naidoo, Indres, 13

Naidoo, Kumi, 236n4

Naidoo, Muthal, 9, 140, 237n13, 241n36, 241n39

Naipaul, V. S., 1, 6, 87, 187, 237n11, 237n12, 238n19, 240n29, 254n27, 258n26, 269n9

Nandan, Satendra, 256n8

Nasta, Susheila, 238n20

Natal, 11–15, 71, 76, 127, 153, 172, 174, 179, 186, 207–8, 230, 236n9, 240n31, 249n28, 260n8, 260n10, 261n11, 263n27. *See* KwaZulu Natal.

Natal Indian Congress, 12, 230

nation-making, 50, 64, 65, 68, 70, 73, 116, 148

national allegory, 71, 73, 85, 88, 250n2, 250n4. *See also* allegory

national belonging, 9, 11, 16–19, 31, 49, 65, 67, 68, 71, 78, 81, 84, 90, 95, 115, 117, 138, 141, 145, 150–52

National Party, 13, 14, 154

nature/natural, 80, 81, 82, 86, 90, 119, 123, 125, 150, 211, 229, 253n18

Nayar, Kamala Elizabeth, 245n28

Ndebele, Njabulo S., 65–66, 100, 114, 119, 137, 157, 244n8

Negritude, 259n2

Nelson, Emmanuel S., 5, 238n21

new South Africa, 6, 16, 18, 48, 64, 65, 67, 73, 82, 85, 91, 138, 141, 143, 145, 146, 148, 149, 160, 163, 185, 186

Newman, Judie, 237n14

Ngema, Mbongeni, 186, 242n46. *See also* AmaNdiya

Nigam, Sanjay, 264n30

Nixon, Rob, 13, 92, 238n19

nomenclature, 27, 44, 56, 60, 61, 85, 111, 254n28

nonwhite, 2, 4, 9, 13, 19, 23, 24, 25, 27, 28, 29, 32, 33, 34, 48, 49, 50, 54, 56, 59, 60, 63, 64, 65, 71, 74, 76, 86, 90, 93, 96, 99, 99, 101, 104, 105, 107, 113, 123, 127, 132, 136, 144, 163, 170, 193, 197, 208, 230, 239n25, 240n32, 247n8, 255n2, 256n10

Noorjehan and Other Stories (Essop), 19, 48, 50, 63–68, 91, 145, 182, 246n4, 249n24, 249n26, 252n17, 252n27

O'Brien, Anthony, 138, 141

Oliphant, Andries, 24, 26, 42, 243n1, 243n6

On the Fringe of Dreamtime (Reddy), 18, 28–34, 244n13, 262n16

organic citizenry, 81

Orientalist, 56, 118, 124, 125, 133, 164

Other Secrets (Karodia), 20, 92–113, 118, 191–97, 237n16, 255n4, 256n7, 256n11, 257n15, 257n17

Otherness, 15, 31, 59, 73, 93, 140, 141, 144, 149, 155, 164, 250n2

Padayachee, Deena, 18, 23, 46, 52, 56, 75, 80, 88, 101, 162, 187, 237n17,

245n27; interview with, 168–81; *What's Love Got to Do with It?*, 18, 40–45, 169–70, 177, 245n27; Writer's Network, 268n2
Paranjape, Makarand, 4, 7, 10
Parsi, 252n11
Passenger Indians, 11, 20, 98, 117–19, 121, 129, 131–32, 263–64n27
past, 8, 15, 21, 28, 35, 39, 43, 66, 89, 95, 100, 101,107, 108, 109, 110, 111, 112, 113, 114, 116, 118, 120, 122, 126, 130, 132, 136–37, 139, 142, 144, 147–48, 149, 152, 154, 162, 180, 181, 189, 191, 202, 205, 208, 209, 217, 223, 228, 229, 230, 242n47, 243n6, 245n21, 259n2, 259n3, 259n6, 262n14, 266n14; apartheid, 20, 45, 92, 93, 95, 102, 113, 145, 149, 167, 251n9; Indian, 21, 51, 75, 103, 110, 128, 130, 166, 167; preapartheid, 114, 115, 129
Patel, Essop, 237n17
People Against Gangsterism and Drugs (PAGAD), 268n20
Pegging Act, 13
Penguin South Africa, 96, 256n7
Phoenix, 14, 41, 142, 166, 171, 213, 249n28
Pillai, Shanthini, 238n21
place, 18, 43, 69, 72, 76, 77, 81, 82, 84, 96, 97, 106, 107–10, 112, 113, 117, 120, 123, 127, 135, 140, 153, 164, 167, 199, 214, 225, 227, 240n29, 248n20, 252n12, 252n13, 258n27. *See also* space
plantation, 120, 121, 123, 126, 204, 260n10, 261n13
politics, 4, 9, 12, 18, 26–29, 45, 47–49, 51, 53–54, 57, 58, 87, 94, 120, 126, 146, 152, 154, 162, 165, 175, 177, 189, 207, 214, 223, 226, 230, 246n30
Poona, Shobna, 237n17
postcolonial: literature, 2, 3, 21, 80, 94, 249n27, 250n2; nation, 18, 73, 138, 147, 160; societies, 116, 160; studies, 3, 7, 49, 94, 97, 236n10
postcoloniality, 2, 21, 71, 77, 80, 85, 107, 113, 139, 144, 149, 242n43, 268n22
Poyner, Jane, 237n14
Prashad, Vijay, 236n6, 244n16, 248n17
Pratt, Mary-Louise, 236n5

race, 2, 3, 7, 8, 9, 10, 18, 21, 27, 30, 33, 34, 36, 38, 44, 48–49, 55, 59, 60, 67, 68, 73, 75, 76, 84, 87, 90, 103, 105, 111, 120, 125, 126, 140, 142, 143, 144, 145, 149, 150, 159, 160, 162, 163, 165, 167, 176, 191, 205, 236n10, 238n17, 239n25, 246n6, 248n18, 249n26, 251n7, 251n10, 255n4, 258–59n28, 265n5, 266n14
race relations, 2, 3, 9, 18, 21, 27, 33, 36, 44, 60, 67, 68, 73, 75, 111, 125, 126, 140, 143, 144, 145, 176, 236n10, 239n25, 255n4
racial: binaries, 23, 34, 65, 236n10, 238n18; hatred, 146, 156, 171; mixing, 49, 71, 86, 88, 98, 105, 248n21, 256n9, 257n19
Radhakrishnan, R., 69
Radhakrishnan, Smitha, 14, 16, 140, 237n13, 268n1, 268n3, 269n4
Rai, Amit, 242n44
Rainbow Nation, 15, 21, 63, 73, 103, 147, 149, 155, 159, 160, 185, 186, 249n25, 265n1, 268n19
Raman, Parvathi, 163, 166, 235–36n3
Ranasinha, Ruvani, 238n20
rape, 78, 98, 104–5, 196, 237n16, 256n9, 257n19
Ray, Sangeeta, 36, 40, 235n3, 239n23, 245n20, 245n21, 245n24, 269n8, 269n12
realism, 72, 80, 95, 99, 100, 101, 143, 243n4, 245–46n29, 252n16
recipes, 43, 46, 88, 91
reclassification, 99
Reddy, Jayapraga, 18, 23, 24, 38, 40, 43, 44, 45, 46, 52, 56, 61, 80, 84, 101, 128, 237n17, 238n18, 244n13, 245n26, 262n16; *On the Fringe of Dreamtime*, 18, 28–34, 244n13, 262n16
Reddy, Vasu, 63, 239n23
return, 3, 10, 20, 53, 58, 60, 67, 75, 78, 80, 82, 85, 92, 94–98, 100, 102, 107–8, 110, 112–13, 131, 163–65, 197–98, 240n29, 255n4, 259n2, 261n11, 266n8, 269n8
Rive, Richard, 244n8
Rivonia Trial, 241n36. *See also* Kathrada, Ahmed
romantic fiction/romance novel, 17, 98, 113, 125–27, 198–99, 220, 259n29
romanticized, 116, 128
rootedness, 18, 43, 50, 69, 72, 73, 77, 80, 81, 85, 150, 156, 253n19
Roth, Phillip, 251n8

Rushdie, Salman, 3, 6, 20, 80, 128, 152, 188, 238n19, 247n8, 258n27, 267n19; *East-West*, 264n28; *Imaginary Homelands*, 88; *Midnight's Children*, 29, 70; *The Satanic Verses*, 88, 111, 130, 152, 188, 190, 202, 258n25, 258n27
Ruth (figure of), 36, 245n19

Safran, William, 240n29
Said, Edward, 241–42n43, 258n27
Sam, Agnes, 23, 40, 45, 46, 52, 80, 84, 101, 128, 172, 216, 238n18, 244n17, 245n19, 245n25, 245n26; *Jesus Is Indian*, 18, 34–40, 235n3, 245n19
Samuelson, Meg, 237n16, 256n9, 257n19, 258n24
Sandhu, Sukhdev, 238n20
Sarinjeive, Devi, 81
Sastry, Sailaja, 72, 87, 89, 250n1, 253n25, 254n28
satire, 47–48, 53, 59, 101, 132, 139, 141, 143, 187–88, 190, 227, 265n6, 267n16
satyagraha, 12, 37, 65, 172, 222
secularism, 12, 21, 109, 138, 150, 152–53, 155, 157–59, 182, 267–68n19
Selvon, Sam, 237n12
Shain, Milton, 252n10
Sheckels, Theodore, 6, 62
Shukla, Sandhya, 258n27, 258n28
Sidhwa, Bapsi, 29, 70
Simone, AbdouMaliq, 50, 90
Singh, Ashwin, 252n13
Singh, Jaspal, 39, 244n17, 248n21, 269n10
Singh, Khushwant, 178, 268n22
Slave Lodge (Cape Town), 254n29
Smith, Rowland, 53, 59, 239n23, 243n3, 247n11, 248n24
solidarity, 3, 8, 9, 14, 17, 21, 26, 29, 32, 39, 40, 45, 46, 48, 50, 52, 53, 64, 68, 98, 100, 101, 120, 140, 141, 142, 144, 160, 162, 163, 167, 215, 241n39, 244n9
South Africa census, 12, 76
South African Indian Council (SAIC), 146, 266n10
South African Indians: biological integration, 18, 71, 90, 95, 98, 102, 105, 111, 207; citizenship, 1, 9, 13–14, 16, 18, 20, 27, 45–46, 50, 56, 63, 65, 81, 84, 111, 113, 119, 124, 127, 138, 140–41, 144, 146, 159, 161, 163, 167, 235n2, 235n3, 238n18, 240n31, 252n12, 258n28, 262n14; nomenclature, 27, 44, 56, 60, 61, 85, 111; novel, 17, 19, 24, 51, 57–58, 72–76, 80, 84, 86, 87, 90, 93–100, 103, 104, 105, 107, 111–13, 116–19, 124–32, 134–36, 148, 149, 151–54, 158, 162, 169, 184, 185, 189, 192–95, 197, 199–201, 203–9, 211, 212–17, 219, 221, 222, 233, 242n45, 244n17, 247n13, 250n4, 251n7, 252n13, 252n16, 253n18, 253n21, 255n4, 256n7, 260n6, 260n8, 262n18, 263n25, 264n28, 267n16; relationship with black South Africans, 6, 8, 9–11, 12, 13–15, 17–19, 21, 29, 32–33, 38, 39, 40, 44–45, 46, 49, 52, 54, 56, 58, 59–62, 67, 68, 71, 75, 78, 84, 86, 90, 105, 118, 119, 120, 123–26, 135–36, 140–48, 151, 153–55, 156–57, 161, 163, 167, 170, 174–77, 181–82, 183, 186, 204–5, 215, 236n6, 237n11, 240n32, 241n38, 241n39, 242n47, 247n13, 248n21, 256n10, 262n16, 262n19, 262n21, 267n19; relationship with Coloured South Africans, 10, 13, 27, 29, 40, 44, 73, 74, 75, 82–83, 86, 89–90, 99, 102, 105, 108, 109, 111, 142, 240n30, 240n31, 255n4; relationship with India, 10, 25, 28, 39, 41–42, 43, 51, 53, 60–61, 68, 71, 90, 97, 103, 108, 112, 121, 122, 128, 130–32, 133–36, 161, 163–65, 167, 173, 176, 208–9, 219, 235n1, 263n24, 264n33, 269n9; relationship with land, 2, 9, 11, 13, 18, 31, 60, 77, 82, 97, 104, 105, 116, 122–24, 127, 132–33, 145, 157, 209, 212, 261n11, 261n13; relationship with white South Africans, 9, 10, 11, 13, 16, 18, 19, 29, 31, 33, 37, 42–44, 48, 49, 50, 53, 54–56, 58, 59, 60–68, 71, 74–76, 77, 78–79, 82, 84, 85, 86, 87, 89, 90, 91, 98, 104–5, 106, 111, 120, 123, 124–26, 142, 144, 146, 154, 157, 164, 176, 177, 191, 196–97, 204, 207, 208, 215, 219, 220, 237n11, 241n39, 243n3, 248n21, 249n25, 253n22, 257n19, 263n27, 267n19; short story, 17–19, 23–27, 29, 34, 39, 42, 45–46, 72, 101, 143, 162, 168, 169–71, 173, 176, 185, 201, 242n5, 246n4, 258n23, 262n16; slavery, 9,

71, 89, 90, 120, 121, 221, 240n30, 254n29
Soraya (Empress of Iran), 104–5, 200, 257n19
Soweto, 13
space, 9, 10, 12, 25, 60, 76, 77, 80, 96, 107, 112, 121, 132, 137, 199, 236n3, 237n11, 242n48, 248n23. *See also* place
specificity, 2, 4, 6, 7, 17, 18, 19, 24, 26–28, 29, 31, 34, 39, 45–46, 56, 62, 71, 73, 104, 113, 131, 149, 154, 165
Spivak, Gayatri, 241–42n43, 246n7, 262n20
Srikanth, Rajini, 238n20
stability, 50, 150, 243n6
Staffrider, 24, 26, 29
Steger, Manfred, 240n32
Stein, Mark, 257n16
stereotype, 13, 53–56, 106, 125, 132, 142, 155, 157, 164, 204, 215, 228, 233
Stiebel, Lindy, and Liz Gunner, 237n15
Suzman, Helen, 244n9, 251n10
symbolism, 10, 12, 29, 30, 33, 35, 37, 41–43, 55, 71, 79–82, 84, 107, 109, 122, 136, 144, 158, 172, 190, 225, 249n25, 250n4, 252n13, 253n18, 265n7
Szeman, Imre, 250n2

Taylor, Timothy D., 247n8
Thiara, Ravi K., 240n32, 263n27
Third Prophecy, The (Essop), 21, 138, 149–59, 181, 182, 184, 188, 189, 190, 256n13, 267n17, 267n19
Thomas, Susie, 238n19
Tlali, Miriam, 252n13, 255n2
Tolstoy Farm, 65, 166, 249–50n28
Torabully, Khal, 6–8, 122, 236n9, 260n6
township, 41, 71, 74, 75, 78, 85, 213, 243n4, 253n22
trade, 9, 14, 71, 98, 104, 146, 158, 188, 266n9
transition (1990–1994), 18, 19, 40, 50, 68, 70–73, 76, 79, 86, 87, 91, 101, 139, 151, 156, 242n47, 250n3, 250n4, 251n7
tree/trees (imagery), 72, 77, 80–82, 85, 133, 253n18, 253n19
Truro, SS, 11, 13, 260n10
Truth and Reconciliation Commission (TRC), 92, 95, 115, 212–13, 215, 251n9

Turner, Tina, 40, 169–70
Tutu, Desmond, 249n5

Uganda, 140, 148, 262n21, 266n12
unbelonging, 21, 31, 46, 67, 75, 85, 97, 138, 139, 152–53, 155, 160, 267n15
United Kingdom (UK), 1, 2, 9, 49, 201, 256n8, 259n6
United States, 1, 2, 9, 49, 60, 162, 200, 242n44, 246n6, 256n8, 258n28, 259n6, 263n25, 269n8
utopia, 93, 143, 149, 265n6, 266n14

Vahed, Goolam, 264n34
Van Niekerk, Anne-Marie, 26, 29, 33, 239n23, 241n38, 244n14, 255n3
Vassanji, M. G., 201, 237n11, 237n12
Versi, Anver, 255n4
Vladislavic, Ivan, 141

Wedding, The (Coovadia), 20, 115–18, 128–37, 263n25, 264n28, 264n33
Weltman, Sharon, 245n18, 252n15
Westernization, 127, 186, 210, 239n26
What's Love Got to Do with It? (Padayachee), 18, 40–45, 169–70, 177, 245n27
whiteness, 2, 5, 8, 31, 33, 49, 56–57, 59–63, 66–67, 76, 79, 82, 84, 87, 91, 124–26, 239n25, 244n9, 247n13
Wicomb, Zoe, 23–26, 115, 141, 243n1, 244n8, 255n2
women, 29, 30, 32, 48, 55, 56, 59, 60, 62, 85, 89, 93–94, 96, 101, 104, 145, 164, 178, 195, 204, 206–7, 216, 227, 228–29, 241n36, 244n14, 245n25, 248n21, 255n2, 256n11, 258n19, 260n10, 261n12. *See also* gender
Woodward, Wendy, 79, 81, 253n18, 253n23, 253n26
Worcester, Kent, 16
Wright, Richard, 240n29
Writer's Network, 268n2

xenophobia, 144, 160

Young, Elaine, 250n4

Zambia, 255n4
Zulu, 4, 36, 42, 124–25, 142, 186, 211, 217, 242n46

www.ingramcontent.com/pod-product-compliance
Lightning Source LLC
Chambersburg PA
CBHW030108010526

44116CB00005B/147